Origami Tessellations

for Everyone

30+ Original Designs by Ilan Garibi

Hand-Drawn Diagrams by Franziska Schwarz

Origami Tessellations for Everyone

How to find me:

Internet Site: www.garibiorigami.com

E-mail: garibiilan@gmail.com

Facebook: Ilan Garibi

Instagram: garibiilan

Text Editor: Sherry Gerstein

Designer: Elina Gor

Cover image: verso view of Big and Small Cubes tessellation (page 67) from red elephant hide paper.

ISBN: 978-965-92700-0-2

To my wife, who shares my path in life

Acknowledgments

This book is a summary of the last ten years, since I took my first steps to become an origami artist. For 25 years I was a soldier, and this second career—becoming an artist, of all things—was a major surprise to me and to all who know me.

My major area of interest is tessellations, although I do have some modulars and figurative models in my portfolio. I adore the simple logic they follow, and the geometric aesthetic they convey.

I was delighted to learn that origami is not only about folding paper, but it is also about the people and communities. I met many people, and learned from each, a little or a lot. This journey had many turns, ups and downs, but all were around the same subject—origami.

This book would not be the same without the hand-drawn diagrams of **Franziska W. Schwarz**, an artist and an origamist. For more than three years—at in-person meetings (at origami conventions) and on Skype—she has labored to transform my rather plain diagrams into works of art. This is her book, just like it is mine!

Sherry Gerstein, my editor, raised this book to a professional level. With keen eyes and the full understanding of the common reader, she made sure this book will indeed fit everyone, beginners as well as practiced folders.

Elina Gor, my graphic designer, is a magician! With skillful hands and eyes, she beautified the book to a level beyond my expectations.

Many thanks to **Dasa Severova**, for walking me down the road of publishing with this book. Your tips and help have been invaluable!

My group of test folders—**Martin Rohrmann, Robin Scholz, Yara Yagi** and **Michał Kosmulski** (who also designed the only model in this book which is not mine)—showed me friendship and support, making this book a better one!

—Ilan Garibi

According to my mom, I started folding around the age of six during Christmas. If you come from Germany, the chances are quite high that the first thing you will ever fold is a Christmas star made of sheets of transparent colored paper. So paper folding at Christmas became a tradition for me. When I was 12, my mom and I were visiting a friend who had an astonishing paper object hanging from her chandelier. That very day I'd also learned my first Sonobe module and had already folded 52 of them! From that moment on, folding paper became an important part of my life. It appeals to my artistic side, but because of its strong affinity with mathematics, it appeals to my scientific side as well. To my great delight, my mother appreciates both aspects as well. She has been my biggest supporter and fan of all my achievements, either in arts or in science.

It was my mother who went with me to my first origami convention when I was in my twenties. I had just started my masters of science in nutrition and my time would have been much better employed by studying molecular formulas. But this origami convention was like stepping into another universe. Meeting all those amazing people and making new friends opened up a whole different world to me. I started attending other European conventions, and that is when I met Ilan Garibi. We met up again at an origami convention in Italy, and we became fast friends. Once he saw that I could draw origami diagrams, it was as if he'd found the missing piece to a puzzle he'd been working on. It is a little odd to think that those drawings were the start of an amazing collaboration, what you now hold in your hands as a finished book. I hope you enjoy it, this product of a passion that initially started at the age of six, was nurtured by a loving mom and supported by many incredible friends since then.

—Franziska Schwarz

Contents

Chapter 6—The Complex Family 128

Chapter 7—The Pineapple Family 148

Introduction

Methods for manipulating a fabric surface into a repetitive pattern have been known for centuries. Ruffles, pleats, and smocking are all well-established techniques in fashion, but it takes a considerable amount of costly materials (like the fabric), not to mention the know-how and experience to do it well. Luckily, you can manipulate paper (a much less expensive material!) in a similar way—and all you need is your fingers.

This may be the reason for the increasing interest and popularity of this origami genre in the international community.

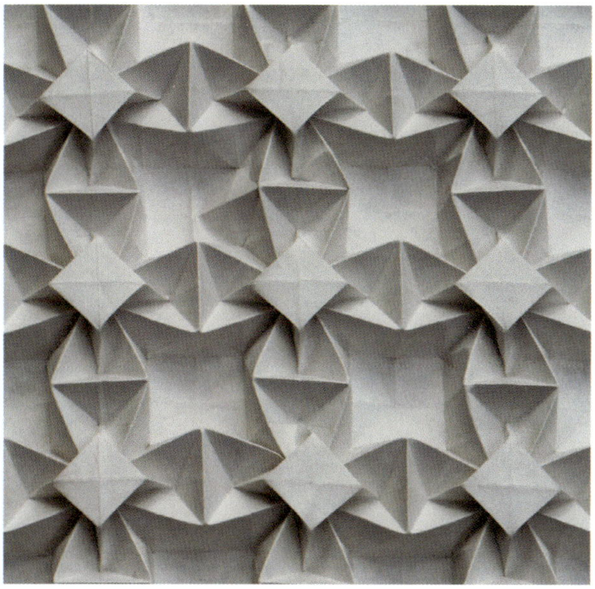

Templar Garden tessellation—the molecules expands identically in all directions.

What is an Origami Tessellation?

That's a good question.

Tessellation is a mosaic. In other words, it is a covering of an infinite geometric plane with repetitive geometric shapes, without gaps or overlaps. In origami, it is the name we give geometric origami folded with a single sheet of paper. There are many categories and subcategories—corrugations, curved tessellations, self-similarity folds, to name a few.

The core property of all tessellations is that of a mosaic, the repetitive pattern made by folding a single sheet of paper. A fold (or a group of folds) is repeated again and again, and in all directions. In this book, this grouping is called a **molecule**.

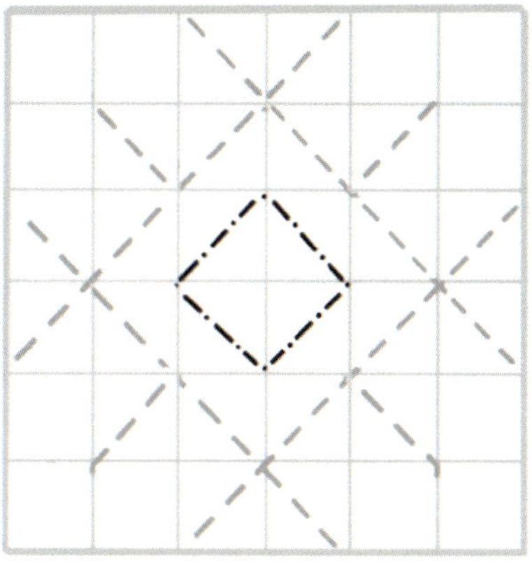

Templar Garden molecule crease pattern.

Some tessellations are based on a square grid (above) while others use a grid made of equilateral triangles that form hexagons.

A molecule can be identical on all four sides, like the Templar Garden molecule, or have a different pattern on the top and bottom than what's on the left and right sides, as shown below.

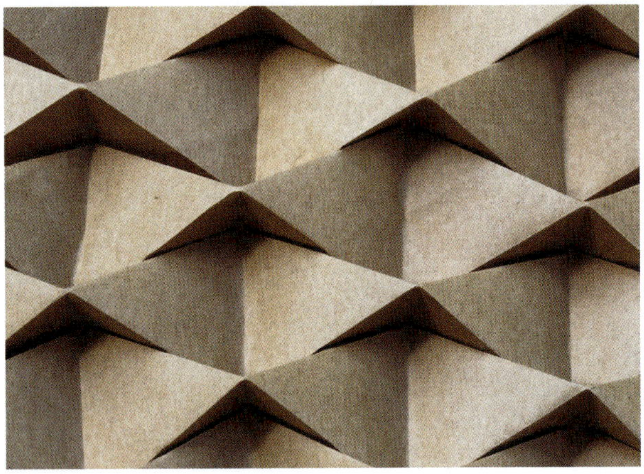

Diamonds corrugation.

Types of Tessellations

A **standard tessellation** is a mosaic, a surface covered without gaps or overlaps in the pattern. It can be flat or have dimensional features; it can be based on a square or a hexagon (AKA triangle) grid.

While the pattern itself doesn't overlap, the paper may have several overlapping layers. The surface of the final model will always have an odd number of layers (one, three, five or even more) throughout. This is because whenever the paper is first folded this way, it must be folded the other way, too, to allow continuity. This variation in the number of layers can be shown to great effect when you backlight your model. One layer is somewhat transparent; additional layers are progressively more opaque. For that reason, one tessellation can give you three distinct impressions: the first side, the other side, and either side when backlit.

Corrugation is a surface that has been formed into ridges, wrinkles, or furrows.

This type of tessellation has no overlapping layers. The entire surface of the paper is visible to the eye, and the pattern is usually in the form of waves.

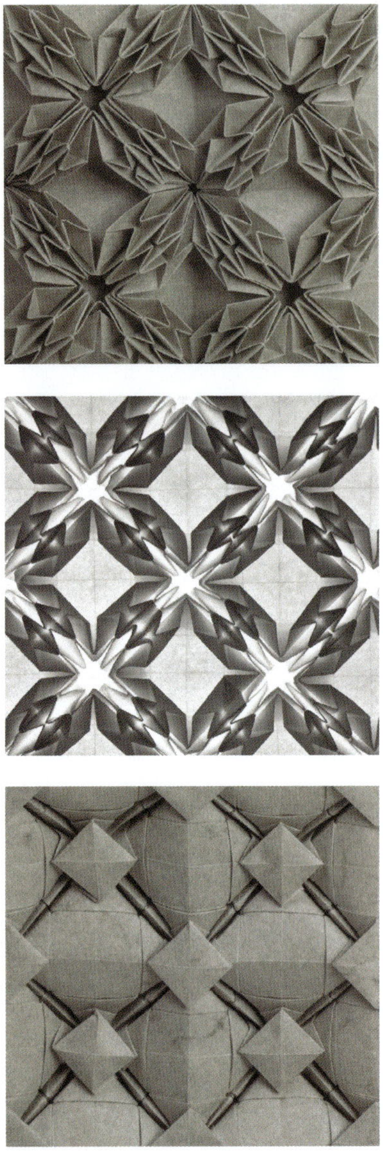

Pineapple tessellation: Recto (top), recto with backlighting (center) and verso (bottom).

Self-similarity tessellations are unique. The idea with self-similarity tessellations is to repeat the same fold, but on a progressively smaller scale. One such model is shown on the next page. The hydrangeas created by Shuzo Fujimoto are classic examples of this type of tessellation.

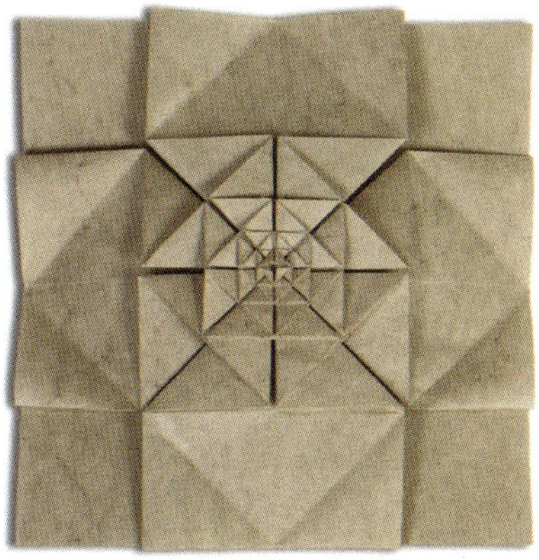

Notice how the squares alternate their orientation while each layer gets smaller. The center is tiny!

There are also **hybrids** of categories. The most common combination of categories is a tessellation of a self-similarity molecule. In the example below, a repeating pattern is made of four self-similarity models.

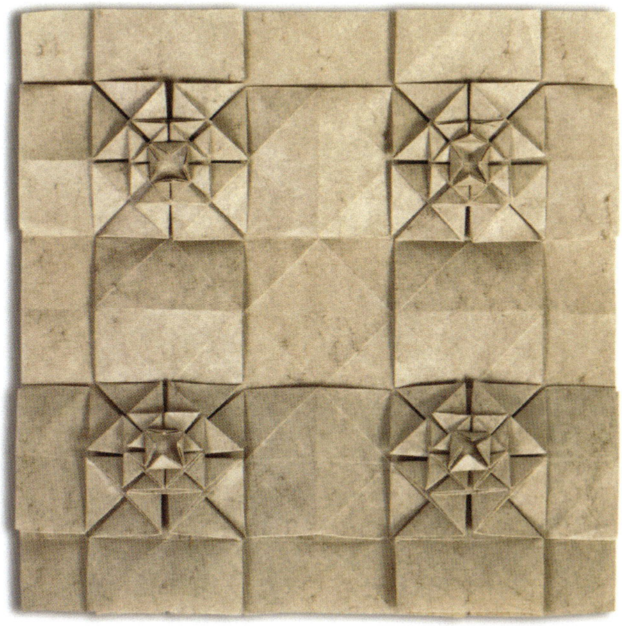

Four molecules of the previous model make an interesting pattern.

Why Does It Work?

A tessellation is built from a repetitive pattern. This pattern, the basic building block, is called a molecule, as mentioned earlier.

The molecule must have two main properties. This concept is easier to understand if we first think of a tessellation that repeats the same way in all directions.

A. Each molecule must be fully rotationally symmetric, which means it looks the same if rotated by 90° or 180°; it should be a design that has the same pattern of folds on all of its (four) sides.

B. The edge of the single molecule is the edge of the original sheet of paper it was folded from. A design that keeps all the molecule edges on the original edges of the paper also satisfied this rule.

With these two simple rules in mind, it is easy to see that two identical molecules can be positioned, one next to the other, and their edges will match. In other words, if those two molecules are unfolded and spread flat, it would be possible to tape them together and collapse them as one sheet. This is the equivalent of folding the two molecules from a 1:2 rectangle.

Here is an example, using the molecules for my Red Flower tessellation.

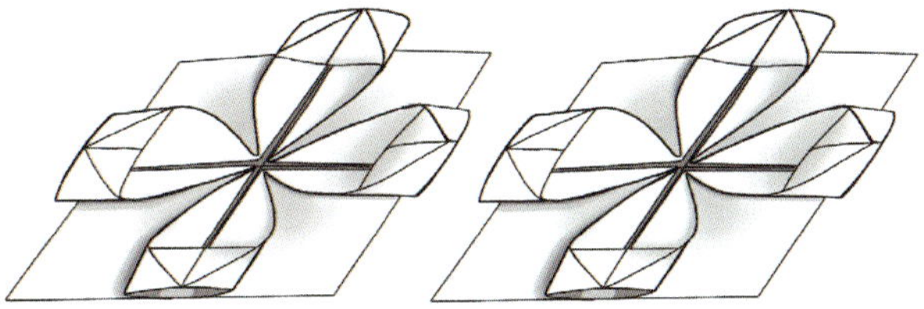

Two molecules, side by side.

If you unfold the common edges (the ones next to each other), tape them together, and then collapse both of them, you get a 1 × 2 molecule tessellation.

Of course, if you can tape together the two, why not simply start with two connected squares—in other words, use a rectangle of 1:2 proportions?

You could execute all folds and collapse the entire rectangle.

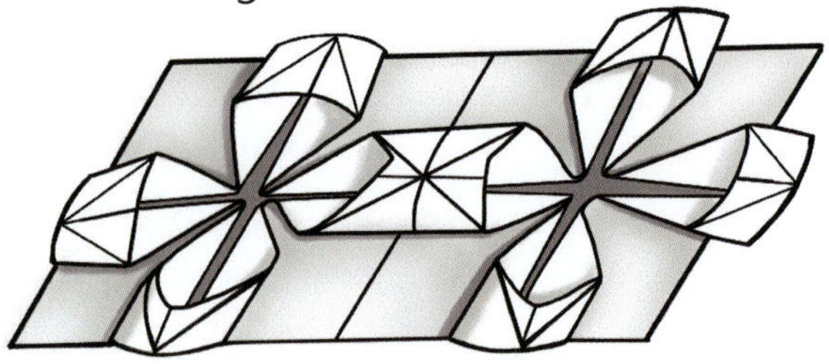

Two molecules form a rectangle.

Mirroring or Shifting

As we just saw above, if a molecule edge is fully symmetrical, you can add the next one just by shifting the molecule to the side.

But not all the molecules can be shifted so easily. Look at these basic square-twist molecules:

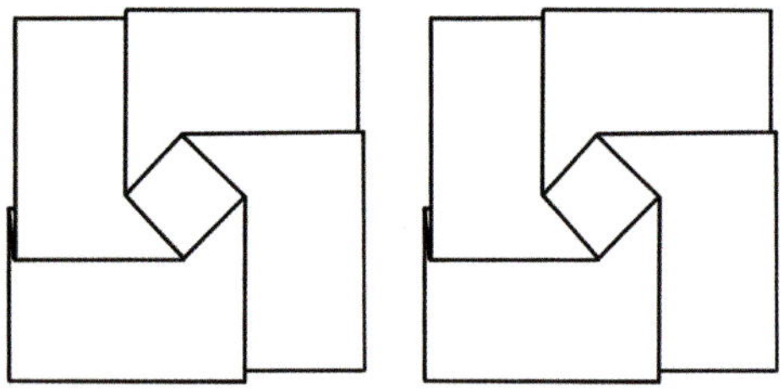

One molecule has been shifted to the right of the other.

Positioning these molecules side by side won't work, since the mountain folds on the common edge do not match up. The molecules are similar, but the edges do not align.

The folds on the shared edge will align if you mirror the molecule:

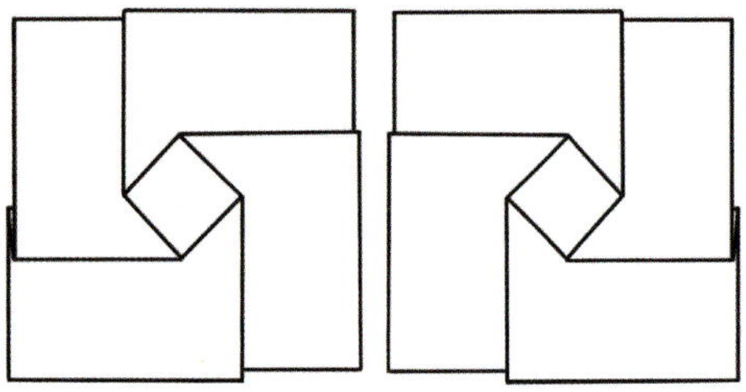

Two molecules, mirrored.

Now the mountain folds match up with each other, and it would be possible to fold it from a single rectangle.

These are simple rules, it's true, but they work with just about all classic tessellations.

How to Make a Tessellation: the Three Basic Steps

Step 1—Make a grid.

The grid serves two purposes: it provides reference points for all the precreases and it almost always plays a role in the molecule structure.

Step 2—Add all precreases.

This step includes all the creases beside the grid that are needed to enable a collapse. Most of them are made before you start to collapse. Some, quite rarely, will be added during or after the collapse. Putting in the precreases is usually the longest part.

Some tessellation doesn't need any precreases and are build as we go using the grid lines as references.

Step 3—Collapse.

The process of executing the folds to form a three-dimensional state is the most challenging and satisfying step. However, the phase in which part of the paper is still flat while another part is already folded may create a tension that isn't always easy to handle. Just saying.

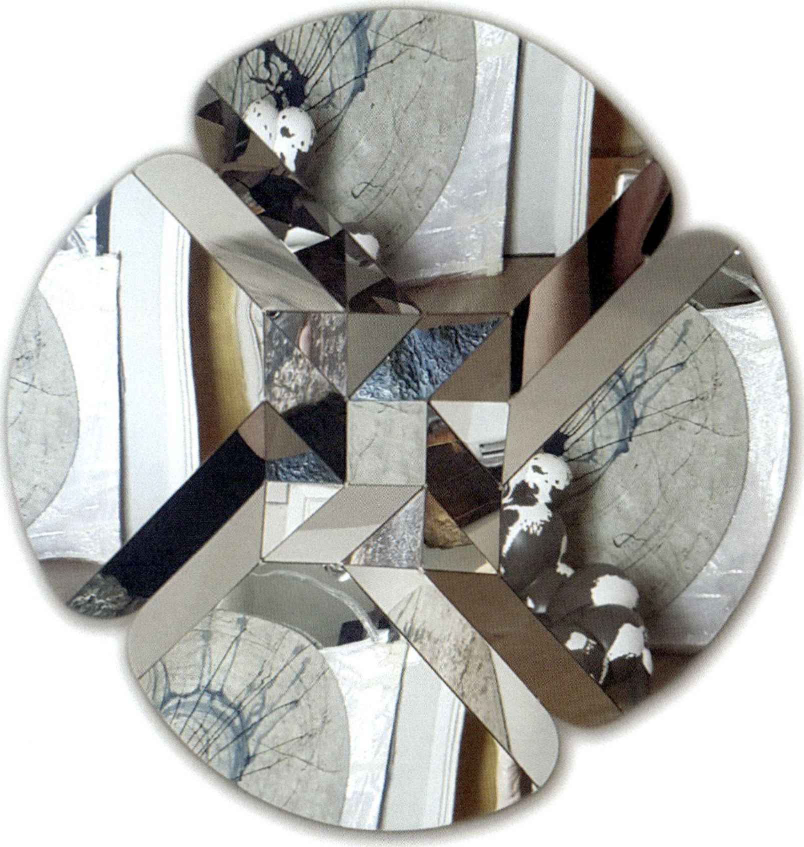

A single molecule of NSNS (page 138) made from mirror-finish stainless steel.

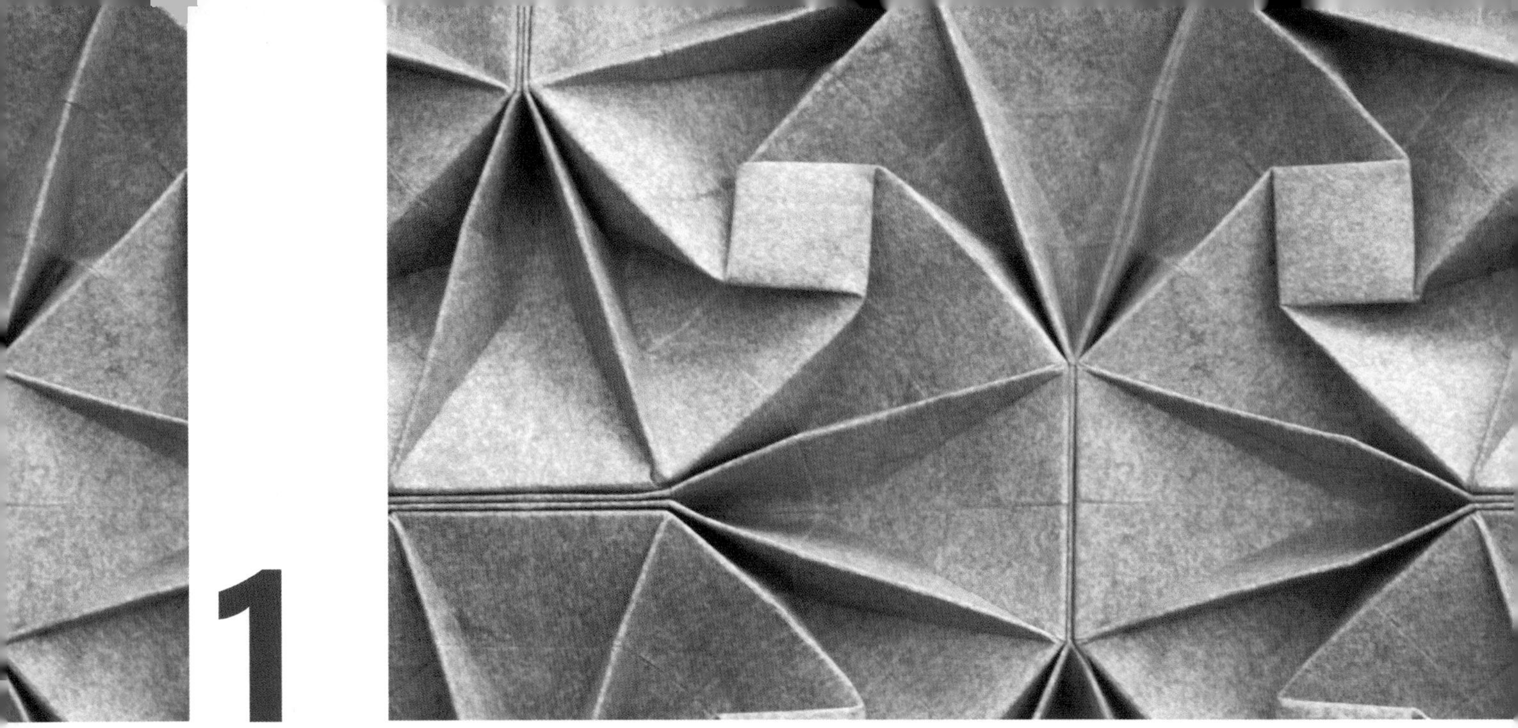

1 How to Use This Book

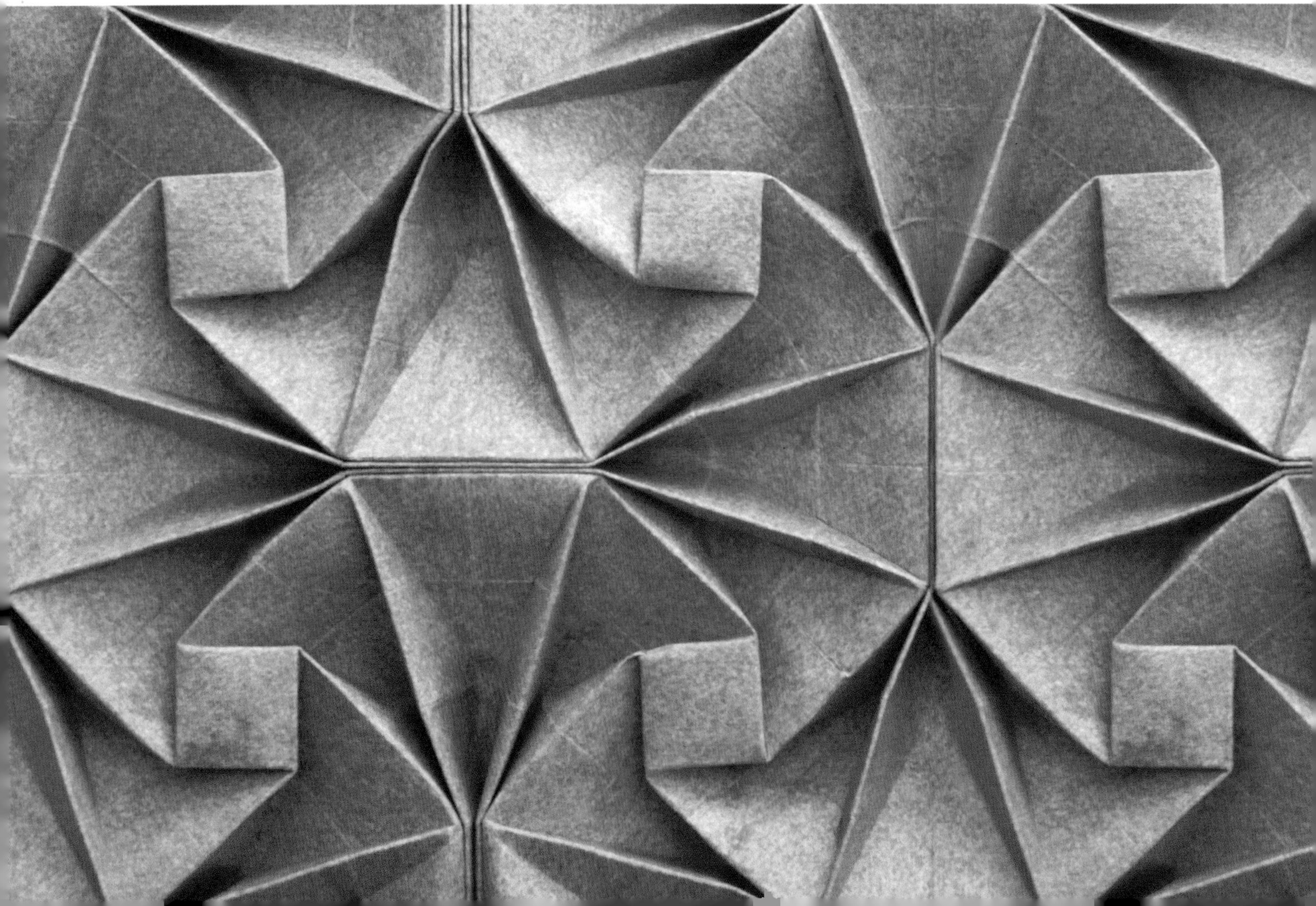

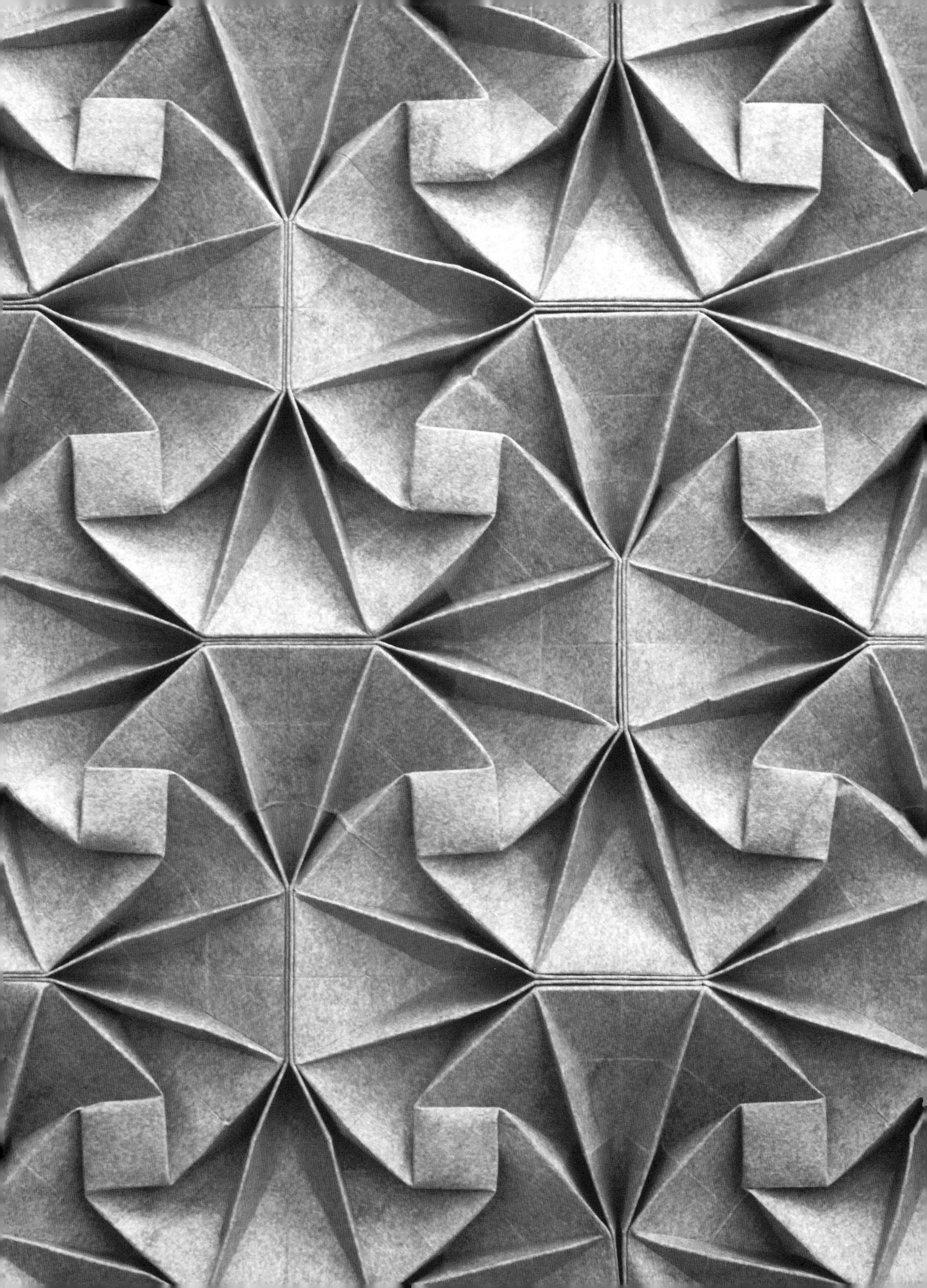

1 1 The Structure of the Book

This book is divided into families of tessellations. Each family is based on a certain principle, which is presented in the first (easiest) model.

From there I explore some variations on that principle. Every variation is presented in three (or more) stages.

The first stage is always the simplest—*the single molecule*. Learning how to form the single unit will help the folder understand the logic of the molecule and how it collapses.

To keep the diagrams easy to understand, I may not clutter things up by showing all the crease lines that align with the grid. However, they will still be used during the collapse and shown on the complete *crease pattern* (CP) later on.

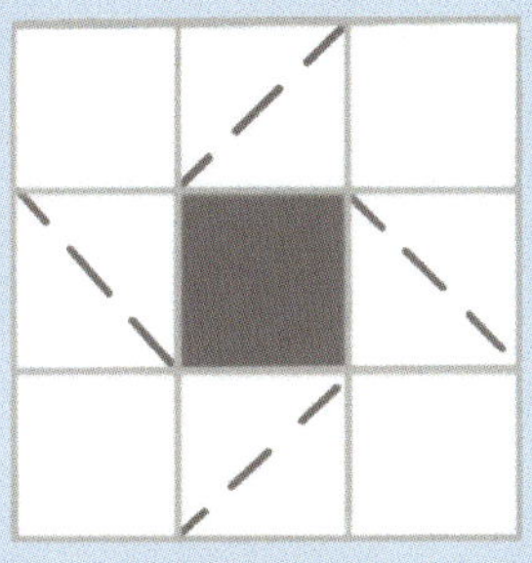

Single molecule, precreases only and no added edges.

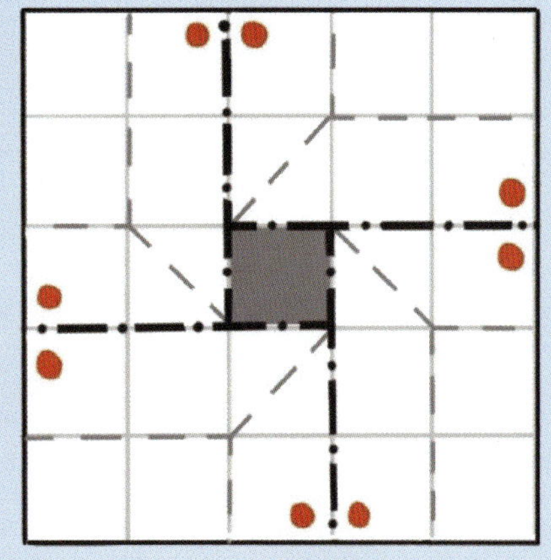

The complete CP (with edges).

While folding a tessellation, it is usually easier to handle it if there's a little extra paper around the edge of the project. A border one square wide goes around the molecule, providing something to hold onto or a place to pinch the sides of the molecules. This extra space is presented on the step-by-step instructions of the single molecule as well as on the larger projects, if needed.

Here I also present how much the molecule shrinks in comparison to the original size of the paper. For example, a shrinkage rate of 5:3 means that the starting size of a molecule was 5 by 5 squares, while the size of the collapsed molecule is 3 by 3 squares.

Next is a *2 by 2–molecule project.* A CP is presented with all precreases needed, as well as a 3D isometric projection of the final project.

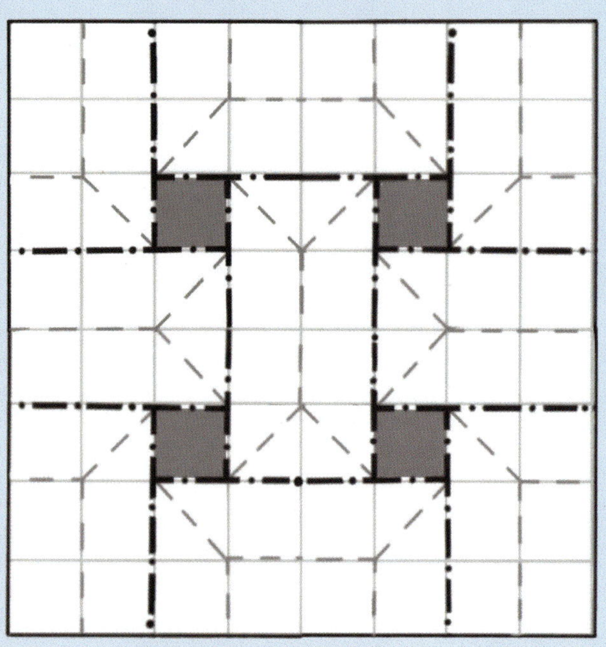

A crease pattern for a 2 by 2 project.

I always include some general tips and advice at this stage, but each model has its own tricks and I present these as well.

At this stage, try not to be sidelined by the beautiful 4 by 4 project that comes next! Practice the 2 by 2 projects and get your skills down first.

Next is the *4 by 4 project*, complete with step-by-step instructions, a full CP, and my recommended shortcuts and special techniques I've developed over the years to make the process as efficient as possible. Images at the beginning of the model's instructions present the 4 by 4 project from both sides, and can help you to understand the mechanics of the collapse.

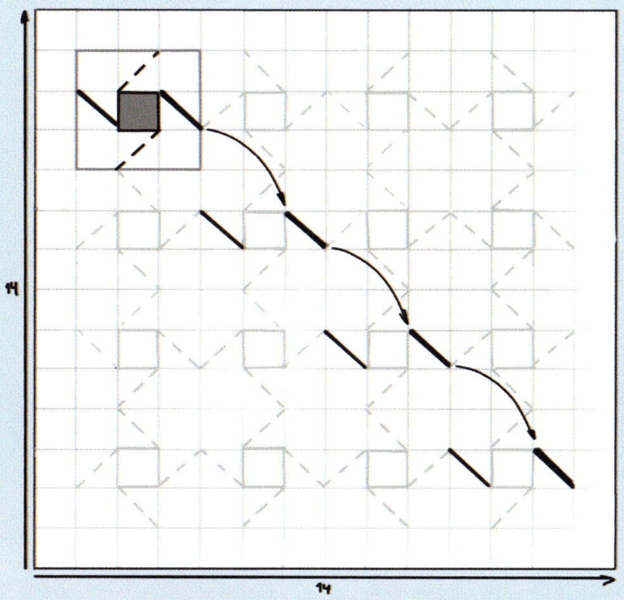

This crease pattern shows the placement of many molecules and my recommendation for folding shortcuts.

For many tessellations, you do not need to precrease molecule by molecule. There are shortcuts you can take to shorten the workload. Folding molecule by molecule requires too many rotations and movements of the big sheet. It is highly inefficient. Instead, I show you how to align folds from adjacent molecules so they can all be executed quickly, one after the other.

By using these techniques, some of the tessellations may need only a single rotation of the paper! Generally, you fold all the top-left to bottom-right diagonals first, then rotate the paper 90°, and complete all the missing diagonals.

Another important feature of the 4 by 4 CP is the *grid size*. The vertical axis represents the total number of rows, while the horizontal axis is divided into columns with a numerical sequence. For example, the Pineapple tessellation has a grid sequence expressed like this: 1 + 4 x 6 + 1. This tells you that you need a grid 26 squares tall and 26 squares wide, or simply a grid of 26. Proceeding from left to right, there is the extra square, then 4 molecules that are 6 squares wide, followed by another extra square, or a total of 26 squares.

This formula is the way to figure the grid size for any project. A project of 8 by 8 molecules (the molecules measuring 6 squares wide as above) will need a grid of 50 = 1 + 8 x 6 +1 squares.

Here I also present the final size (in squares) of the resulting model.

Last, *Above and Beyond* shows the potential of the molecule, either by showing a large scale model or a special use for the design, like a pendant or wall tiles.

1 2 How to Read the Diagrams

Unlike traditional origami diagrams with arrows and fold-as-you-go instructions, the diagrams here show the slow transformation of a flat sheet of paper into an object with dimensionality. But there are still some symbols that you must learn in order to make the right folds and execute the collapse properly.

Symbols

In some models, I use the traditional symbol system:

A *valley fold* is marked with a dashed line. In traditional diagrams, an arrow will accompany it. The paper is always folded forward from the tail of the arrow to its head.

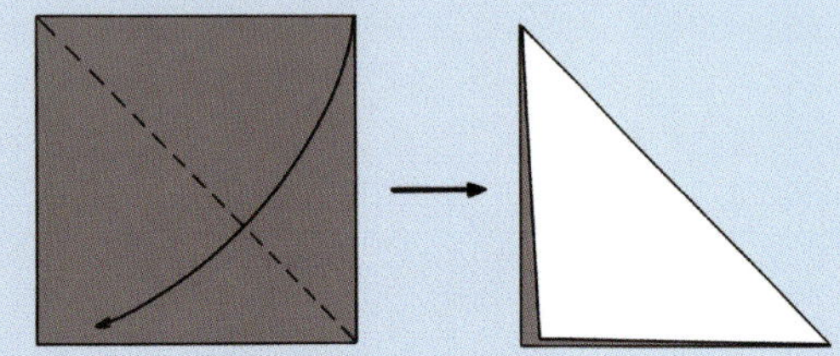

If you are using a sheet that has one side colored and the other white, this process reveals the white side.

I also use *arrows* to indicate the workflow of my recommended shortcuts. In this figure the bold lines indicate where to put the valley folds and the arrows indicate where to skip to next on the same diagonal.

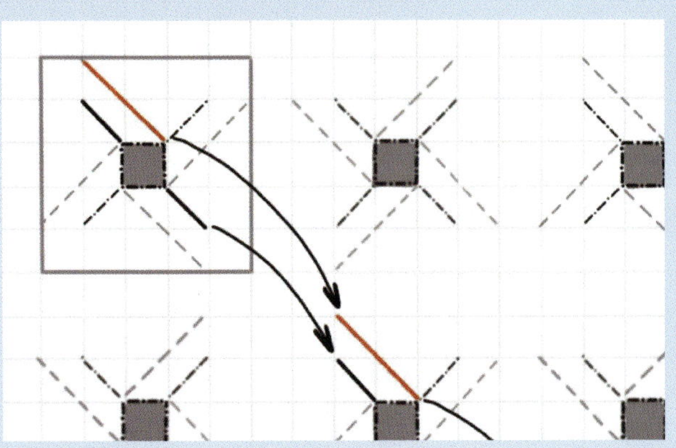

The bottom arrow tells you to skip diagonally across three squares to find the next valley to fold. This is true of all the valleys on the CP.

A *mountain fold* is marked with a broken dashed line. In a traditional diagram, a hollow arrow head will accompany it, indicating that you should fold behind.

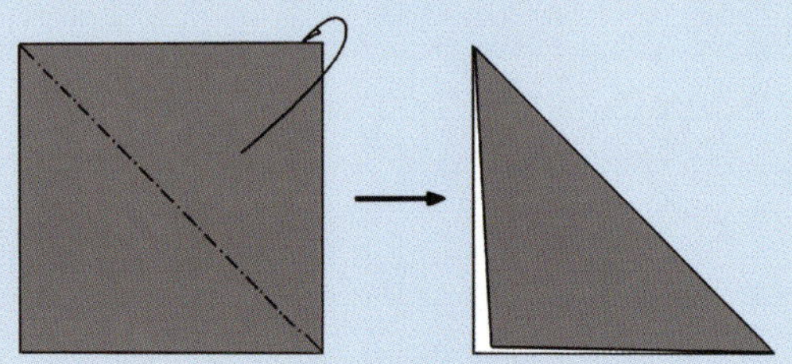

Fold and unfold is shown using a double arrow, back and forth from the starting point. Note that after the paper is unfolded, a thin crease line appears. The grid creases are always shown with these thin lines.

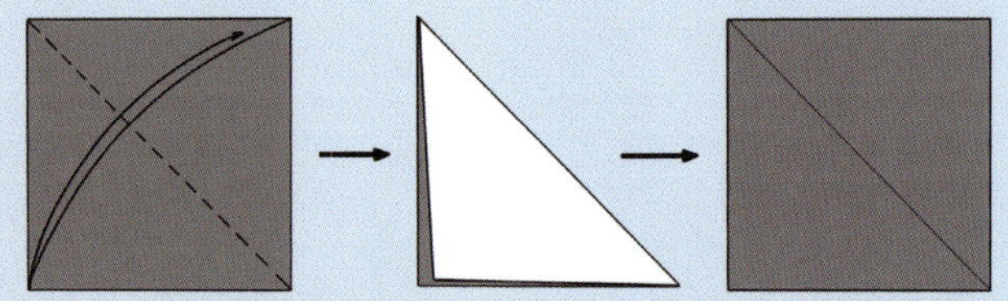

The repeat arrow—an arrow with lines crossing the arrow shaft—means that you should repeat the last command given on the marked area. Repeat as many times as you have lines crossing the arrow shaft.

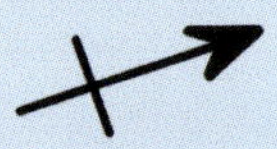

Turn over—a spiraled arrow tells you to flip the paper over to the other side.

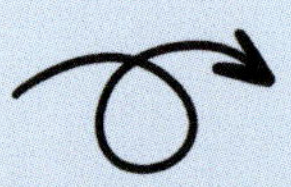

Areas of interest are shown with white circles around them. Red dots are used to show where to *pinch or hold* the paper.

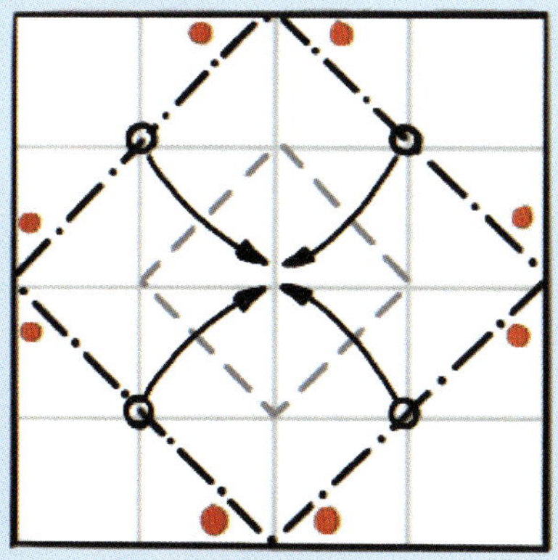

Pleated edges—a zigzag line below the model shows how the edges of the paper are folded. This helps you understand how the edges of the molecule are formed.

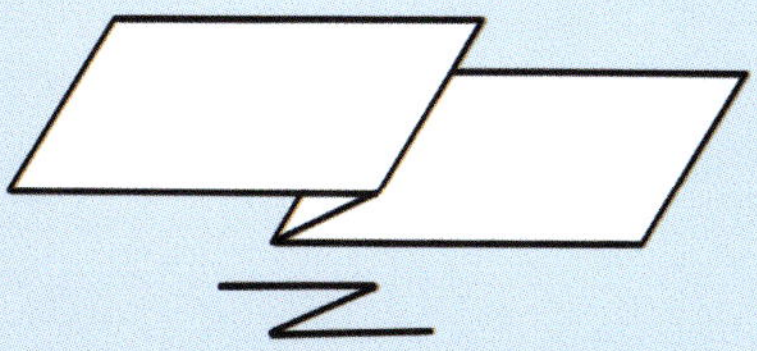

Inside Reverse Fold—a fold line is reversed to switch its orientation. The command is presented by a wide white arrow. Here the upper part of the mountain crease is reversed to be a valley by collapsing inward (hence the name).

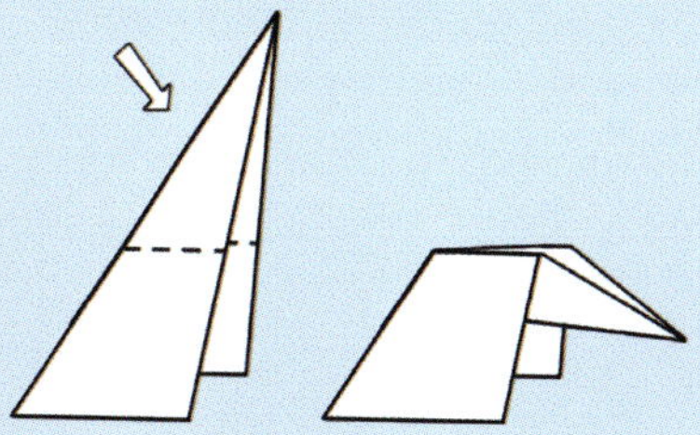

1 3 How to Read a Crease Pattern (CP)

A CP holds a lot of information: the size of the grid, the structure of the molecule, the number of the molecules included in the project—all of this can be found in one handy diagram. Valley and mountain fold lines show where to mark the precreases, and the orientation of the folds when you are ready to execute the collapse.

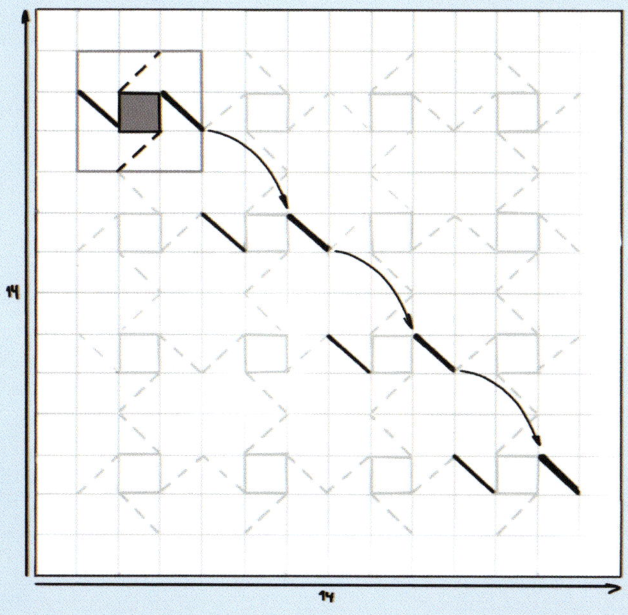

As I mentioned earlier, in many tessellations, there are ways to make the precreasing process much more efficient than molecule by molecule. The idea is to combine creases that are on the same diagonal or straight line in order to minimize the number of times you move or rotate the paper.

These shortcuts are presented in a workflow or pattern that points out which single-square diagonals to fold and which to skip while your hand is moving along the imaginary line that connects them. I can't stress enough that you must fold one square at a time or your accuracy will be compromised. The lines to be folded are bolded and arrows show which ones to skip.

Deciding on the Paper Size

As you will notice, I don't provide a paper size in the diagrams; I leave that for the folder to decide.

All you really need to decide on is the size of the molecule, and from there you can determine the grid size (see later on).

A grid made of two cm (¾") square is a good size for beginners. A one cm (⅜") grid square is more of a challenge. Try your hand at any 2 by 2 project folding molecule of various sizes before you determine which suits you best.

Deciding on the Grid Size

All my 2 by 2 projects CPs show the breakdown of the grid width on the horizontal axis.

Most of the tessellations in this book call for a border around the molecules. This border is usually an extra row and column on all sides. This border has two important uses—it is easier to fold the edge molecule with something to hold onto or clip together, and it brings a nice frame to the finished model.

To determine the grid size, you have to calculate the sum of this equation: the width of borders plus (the width of a molecule x the number of molecules). For example, in the figure shown on page 21, there are four molecules and each is three squares wide. Therefore, the total number of squares needed for the molecules alone is 3 x 4, or 12. If we add a row to the left and right, two extra squares need to be counted, for a width of 14 squares. This can be expressed as 1 + 4 x 3 +1 = 14.

1 4 How to Make a Grid

Tessellations are usually made from grids. A grid can be made from squares or from equilateral triangles that form hexagons (which is why these grids are usually referred to as hexagon grids). There are other shapes that can be tessellated to cover a surface, such as a rectangle, or a rhombus, but they are rarely used for origami tessellations. Each unit (square, triangle, etc.) is called a tile.

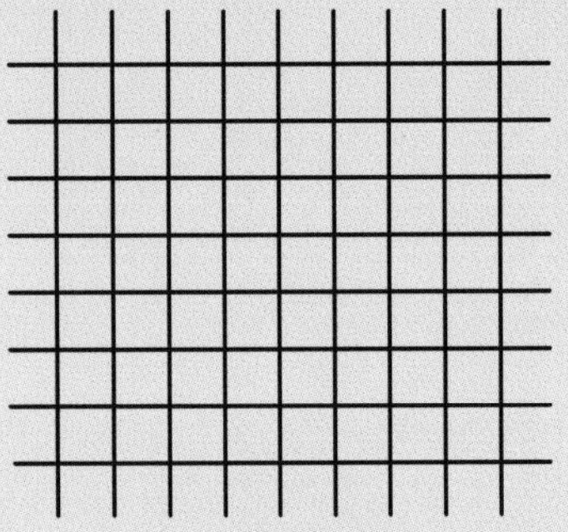

Square grid

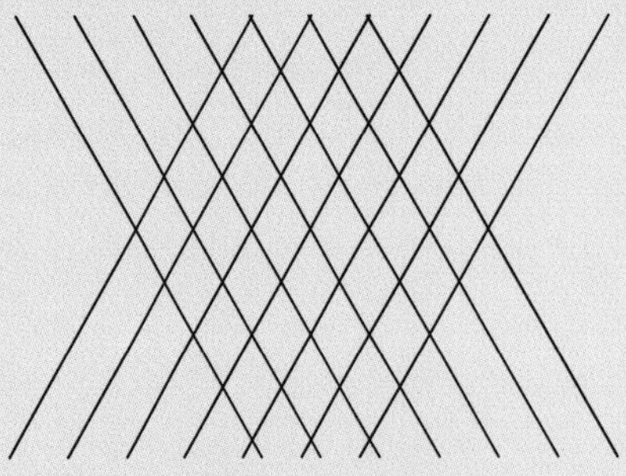

Diamond grid

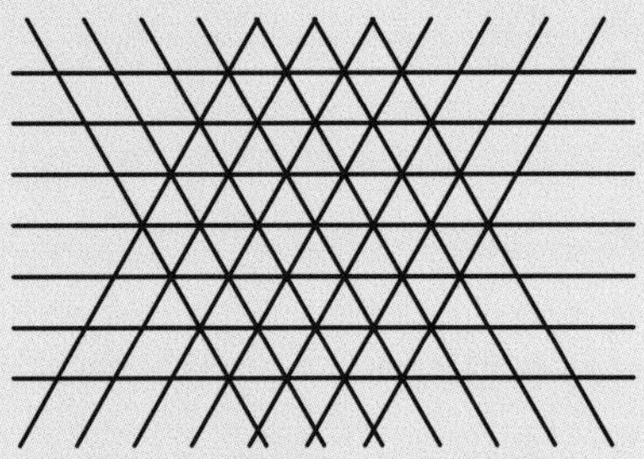

Triangle/Hexagon grid

Grid size is determined by the number of rows and columns. For a square grid, two numbers are given: 16 by 16, or for short, grid 16. For a hexagon grid, three numbers are given, one for each pair of parallel edges.

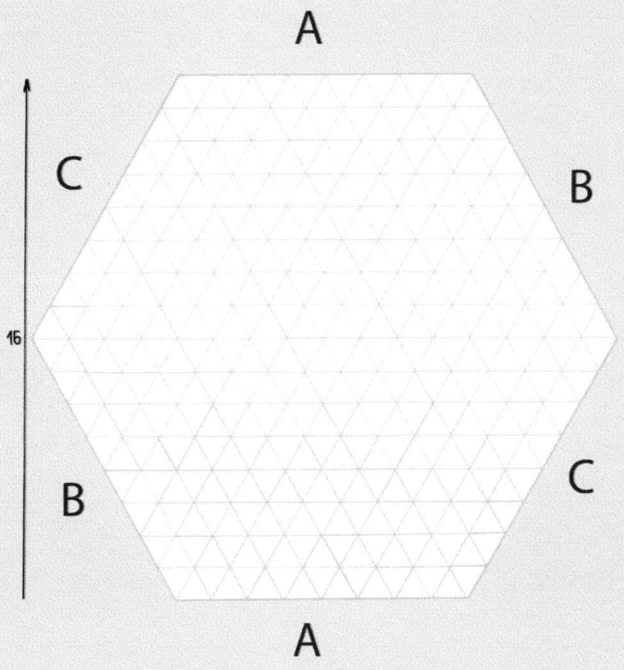

This CP shows 16 rows (15 divisions) between every pair of edges; AA, BB and CC, so the grid size would be 16 x 16 x 16.

Folding a Grid

Making a grid may seem like a fairly simple undertaking, but the truth is, it requires quite a lot of skill and mastery.

To get a 2 by 2 grid, you need one horizontal crease and one perpendicular to it. That's easy enough to do—just divide a square sheet by folding it in half in both directions.

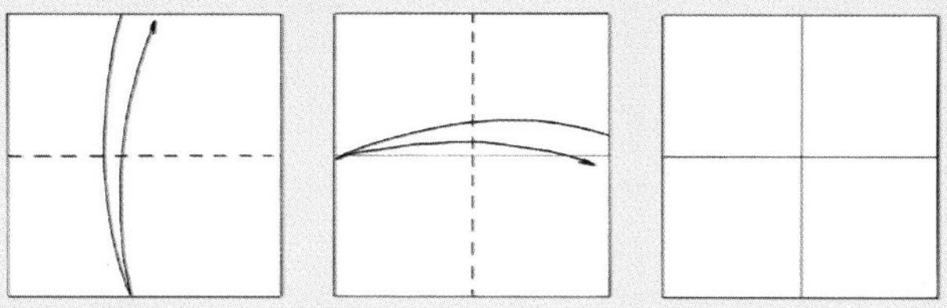

The process of folding 2 by 2 grid.

To get a 4 by 4 grid, divide all halves in half again. This is still easy; this is also known as a cupboard fold (done twice—horizontally and vertically).

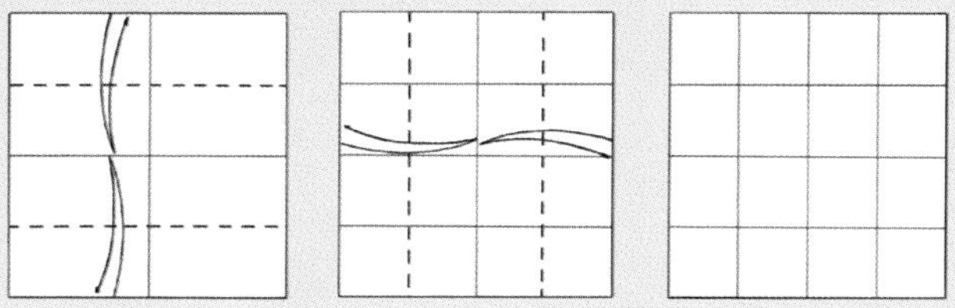

Now try an 8 by 8 grid. Getting the first 1/8 line is easy; you just fold the edge to the 1/4 line. But how do you get the 3/8 line?

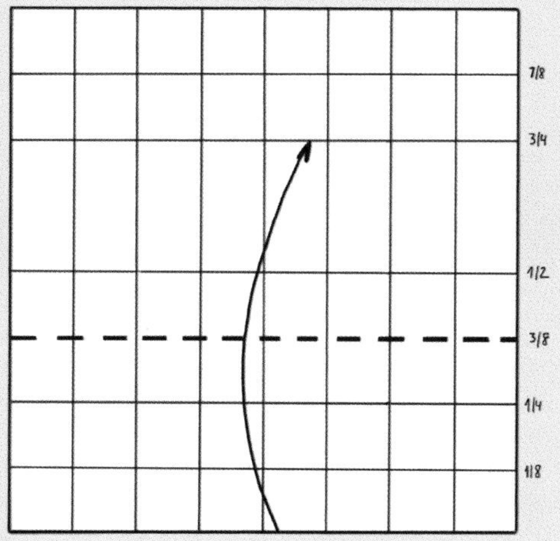

One solution: fold the edge to the 3/4 line, which divides this length to 3/8. This works well enough for an 8 by 8 grid, but it gets worse the more tiles a grid has. That's because every crease shrinks the paper a bit—you lose a tiny bit of paper to the crease. For instance, when you fold the edge to the 46/64 line to get the 23/64 line, the distance of the 46th line is not 46/64 of the paper, but teeny bit shorter than that.

The photo on the next page shows how much of a difference this can make when you have a lot of creases. A full sheet of paper after folding a 128 by 128 grid is clearly shorter and narrower than the unfolded paper beneath it, and yet both sheets are aligned with each other at the bottom left corner.

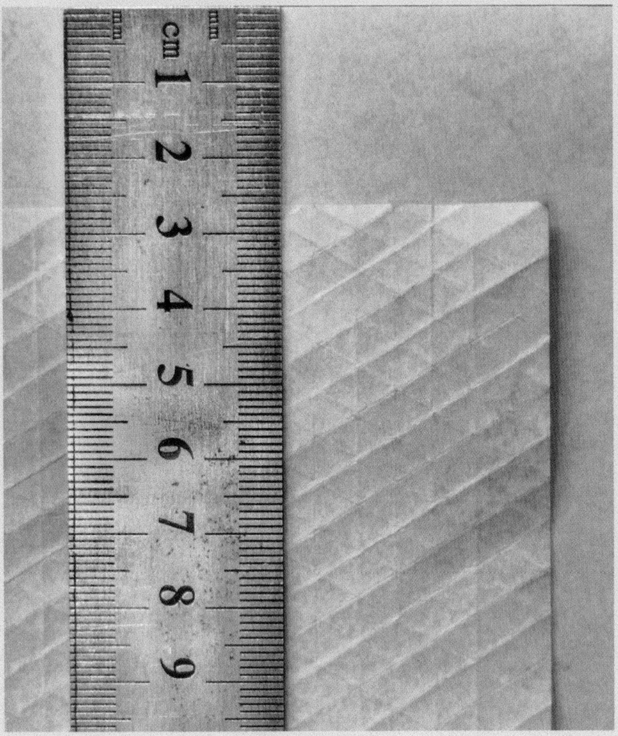

The corner of a grid 128 sheet on top of an unfolded sheet.

It may seem negligible, shrinkage of just 2.6%, but it does have a major impact. Suddenly, squares are no longer squares, and diagonal creases do not bisect the corners anymore.

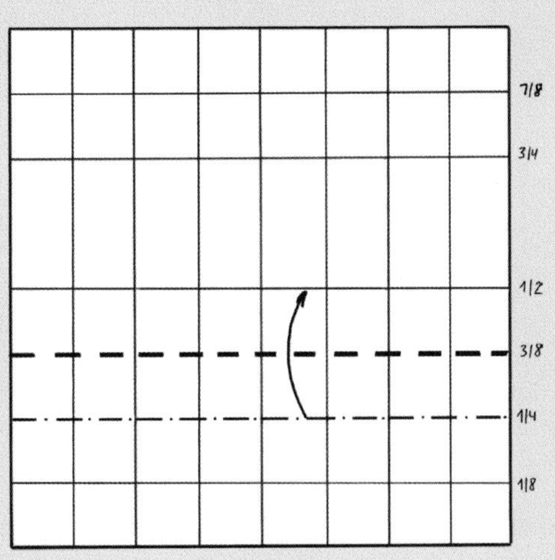

The diagram here shows a better way. In order to get the 3/8 crease, pinch the 1/4 line and fold the edge to the 1/2 line. To get the 23/64 line, pinch the 22nd line to the nearest crease.

There are different methods to fold a grid, but this is my favorite!

How to get odd grid sizes

You may need a grid of 14 by 14, 46 by 46, etc. Since the presented method is good for 16, 32 and 64 divisions, we need to find a way to make grids that are not based on multiples of two.

If your grid size is a little under the power of two numbers—for example, a grid of 30—make a grid of 32 and cut off the extra squares. Or you can just have a wider border around your final model.

For the rest, use a ruler to mark the nearest power of two number. If you need a grid of 34, and you use 1 cm for the square size, mark 2 cm from the edge, which divides the paper into 2 squares plus 32 squares. Fold the 32 divisions first, and add the last one to divide the 2 cm gap when finished.

Tips

- I always make my creases bidirectional. It is double the effort, but it is often very helpful in the collapse phase. At the end of folding the grid, make sure all your creases have the same orientation (mountains or valleys).
- Rotate the paper after every division. Since it is quite difficult to make a perpendicular crease against 64 mountain fold lines, do not crease 64 horizontal creases and then rotate the paper to complete the perpendicular ones. Instead, divide a side in half and rotate. Divide the new side into quarters and rotate. Back to the first side, divide it into 8ths and rotate. Divide into 16ths and rotate, and so on.
- The same logic applies to the hexagon grid.

1 5 How to Fold a Hexagon and Hexagon Grid

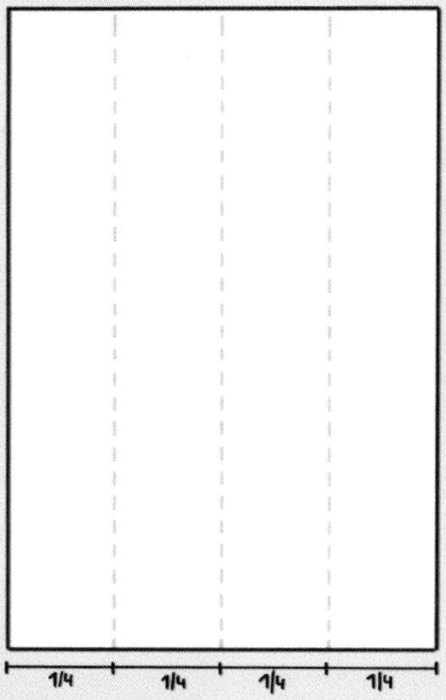

Start with a sheet of printer paper in portrait orientation. Letter size or A4 will both work fine. Divide the sheet into four columns.

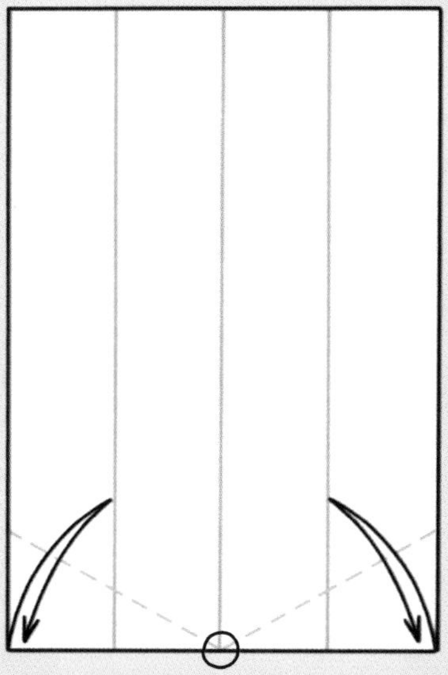

Fold and unfold the bottom corners to their nearest fold lines. Make sure the new crease starts where the center fold line meets the bottom edge.

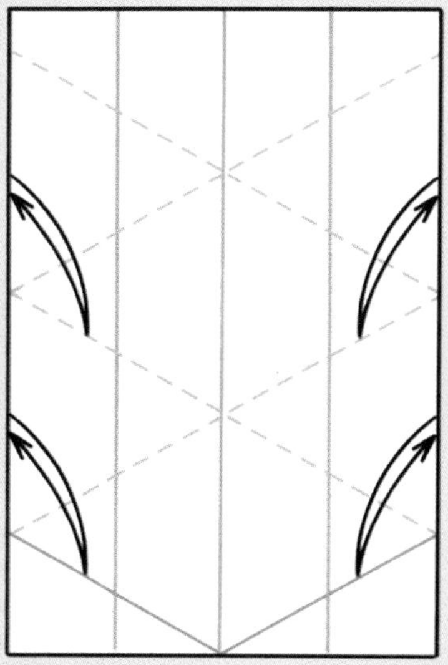

Fold the edges of the paper to the creases you just made. Now you can see the hexagon forming. Fold the edges to the new creases you just created as well. This completes the top edges of the hexagon.

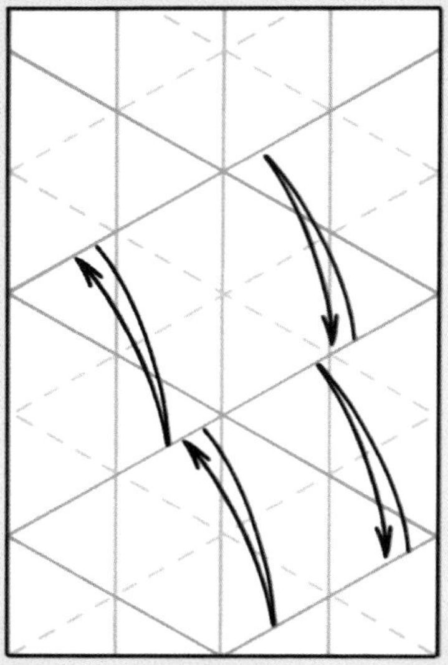

Add creases between every two fold lines to make more tiles.

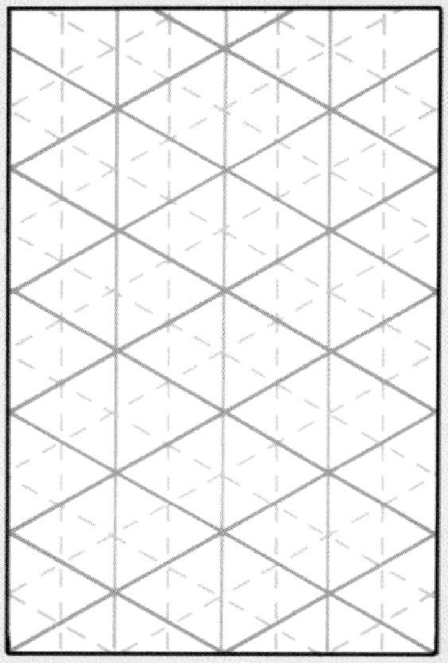

Repeat.

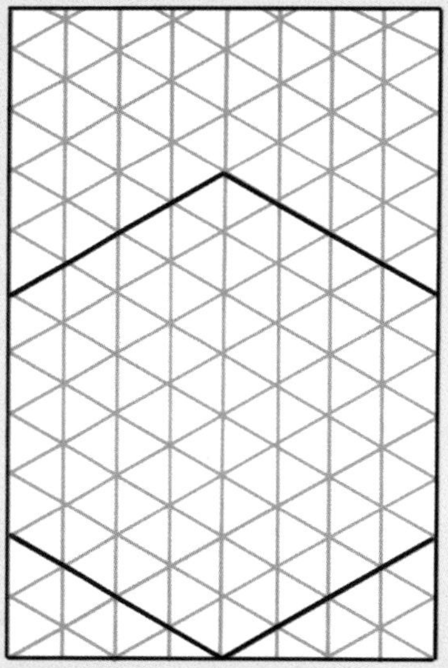

The marked hexagon is divided into a grid of 8 x 8 x 8 (meaning there are 8 rows between every pair of edges).

1 6 How to Precrease

Unlike traditional origami, tessellations are mostly based on precreases that you complete before you start to fold. Some have a step-by-step way to get there, but for most, you will have to prepare all the folds in advance and then collapse the model.

For most tessellations, this is the most time-consuming phase. The most basic molecule in this book needs four creases; usually there are many more.

Luckily, there are shortcuts for this process. Many creases will align and can be folded in one stroke.

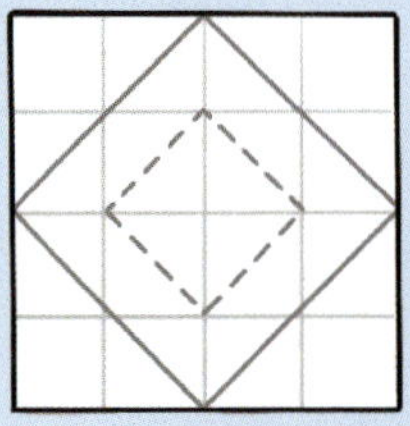

To the right is the single molecule of the Red Flower tessellation. Below is the CP of a 3 by 3–molecule project. Notice that molecules 1, 2 and 3 in the CP below all contribute to one straight line, AD (shown in red): the top-left fold line of molecule 2 (AB); the bottom-right line of molecule 1 (BC); and again the top-left fold line of molecule 3 (CD). So folding line AD in a row gives you a major shortcut.

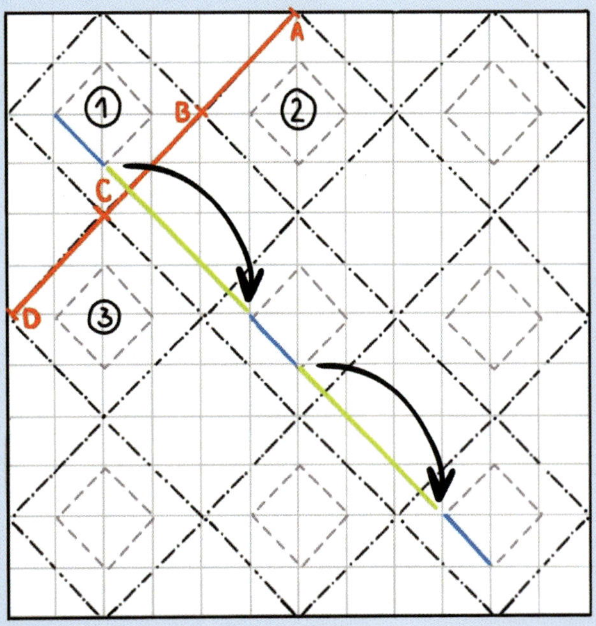

Finding a shortcut is a bit harder for the inner squares that do not form a connected diagonal. Here we move to another method: counting. All three blue lines are aligned, so if we start with the blue line of molecule 1, we count three squares (marked in green) to skip to get to the next square with a diagonal to fold (shown in blue again). So this is the pattern of work: crease one (diagonal), count/skip three (diagonals), and crease one, etc. The black arrows indicate the skipped diagonals.

IMPORTANT: Long diagonal creases need to be folded one square at a time. I can't stress this enough. That means you should crease from corner to corner across one square before moving on to the next part of the diagonal. This is tedious, it is true, but the increased accuracy is worth it!

For example, to fold line AB you can locate the lower right corner at the grid-cross (in the big red circle) as a general guide only, but when you mark the fold, refer to each single square as one—fold from the corner of it to the opposite one, and move to the next square (in the small red circles).

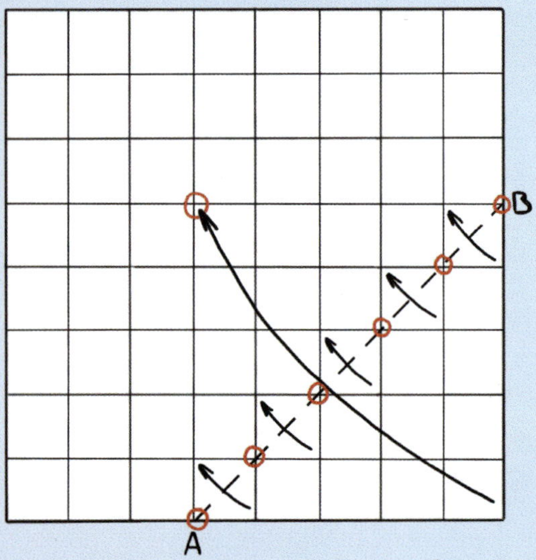

Tips

- Make only mountain folds (valley them second to make them bidirectional). If you are asked to make a valley, turn the paper over and fold a mountain. Why? For short point-to-point creases, mountains are much easier—and more accurate—to fold than valleys.
- Once you start working on larger projects, you'll find that you will occasionally make mistakes like miscounting, jumping over the wrong fold line, etc. Don't feel bad. It's pretty much a cosmic law that you will experience this. To avoid the problem, mark the center of each of the molecules with a pencil or bit of Blu Tack (or some other reusable adhesive putty—you can find different varieties at hardware or office supply stores).
- Remember not to make a precrease in the first and last row or column! If you are folding this area, you misstepped somewhere.
- If you follow my advice and make all the grid lines bidirectional (both valley and mountain), you will see there is one side of the paper where the creases are more evident. You can use this side to mark your precreases where it is easier to see the grid.

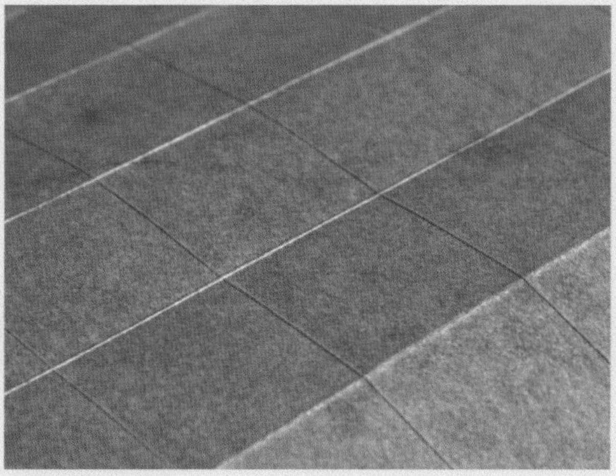
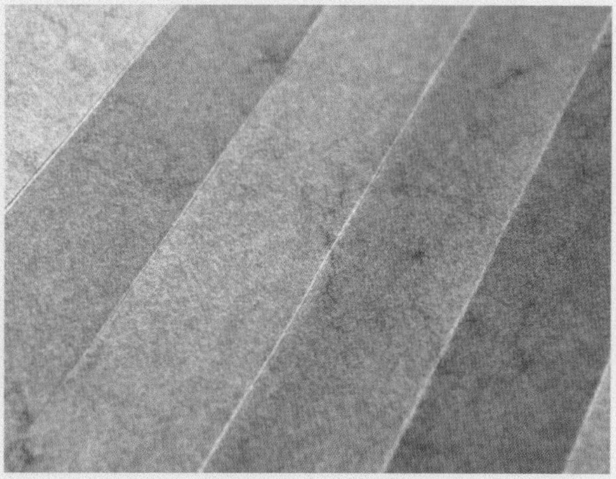

Ridges left by folding are evident on the left ("top" side), while they are hardly seen on the right ("bottom" side).

1 7 How to Collapse

"I can't do it! I just can't do it! Oh, maybe I can. (Deep breath) *Oh, yes... I can!"* I can hear you now.

Yep, the collapse is the stage that really tests your sanity. You hear the phrase "It can't be done!" over and over in your mind again, while the cat jumps whenever a cry of frustration comes out of your mouth. But trust me—it can be done. Look at the final image of the model in the book to believe! If I can do it, so can you!

Keep in mind that collapsing a model made from a square grid is different from a hexagon grid.

With a square grid, you start at the upper left corner and complete one molecule. Then add another one to the right, working one molecule at a time to complete a row.

The first row is simple. The first molecule on the second row starts easily enough, but the second molecule is surrounded on two sides with folded molecules and the other two sides are flat paper. This is where the difficulties lie. If you can manage to fold that second molecule, you can do the rest!

With some tessellations, it is good to partially collapse all molecules in a row before collapsing each completely, one by one. This saves a bit of work by unfolding creases that will be in your way for the next row.

For a hexagon tessellation, I recommend that you start from the center, making one molecule that the others are clustered around.

Then you make a ring around the center with six molecules. The last one (and sometimes even the fifth one) may give you some trouble, as it coincides with the first one and involves unfolding some pleats made earlier to allow you to work on the paper. When opening the paper, you need to be careful not to unfold the adjoining molecules too much, but some unfolding will be necessary to complete that final molecule. If this proves too difficult, try to fold the fifth and sixth together instead! The folding continues in this fashion, building rings around the center.

Tips

- Take heart! Do not give up! The folder is stronger than the paper.
- Use clips (see the next section) to hold folds and edges in place, if needed.
- There is literally always another side with an origami tessellation. Many times it is easier to work the collapse from both sides of the model. The structure might be more visible to you from the other side and so even easier to handle. Give it a try.
- When folding a tessellation, sometimes you work out that there is a special rhythm or pattern of work that makes things easier. Write it down the moment you realize that sequence. It will help you tremendously the next time you try to fold it. For example, for the Cubes tessellation, while finishing a row during the collapse, there are mountain folds that go all the way to the bottom of the sheet. The pattern is that two mountains are joined together, and the next pair is two squares away. When you collapse, look for those pairs.

1 8 The Right Tools for the Job

Clips

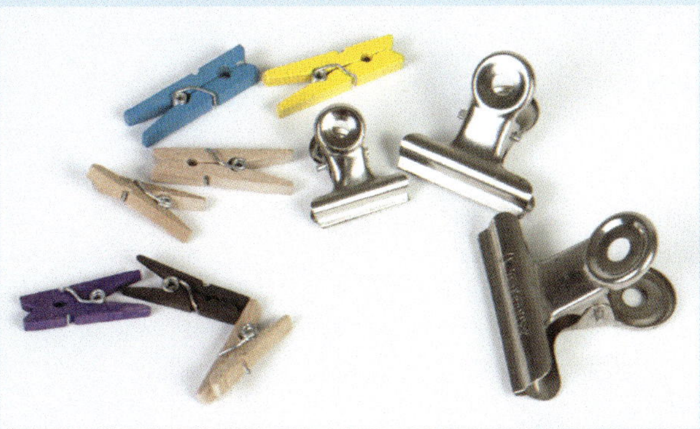

Metal and wooden clips.

Clips, either metal or wood, are a must! The more, the better. The wood ones keep your paper unmarked, but they are usually not as strong as the metal ones. Just be careful, because some of the metal ones are too strong and leave their marks on the paper. Metal binder clips can be found at an office supply store. Tiny clothespins can be found at craft stores in the scrapbooking section.

Bone Folder

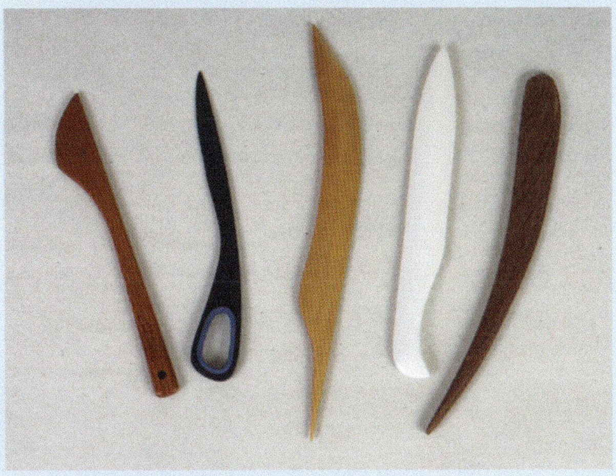

Various types of bone folders.

A bone folder (probably really made from bone at one time) can be used to press the paper into nice, sharp creases. There are many types—wood, metal or plastic—and they help to ease the fatigue in your hands from folding a lot. My favorite is the middle one, in the photo below left, bought from Origami-Shop (www.origami-shop.com). It is made of a very sturdy wood, easy to hold, and the pointed tip is very helpful in tight spots. Various types of bone folders can be found at craft and/or art supply stores.

Reusable Adhesive Putty

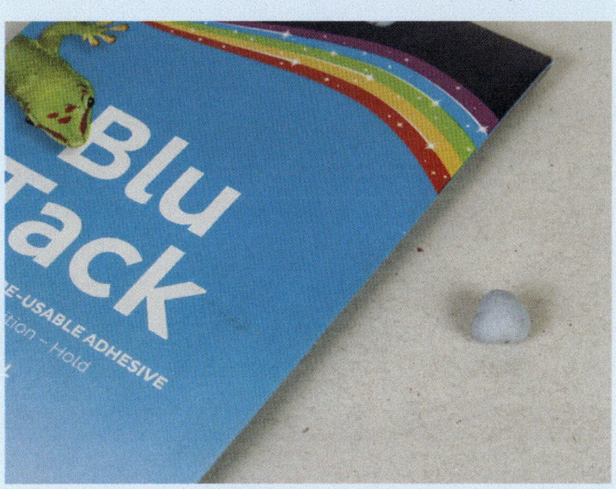

Blu Tack can be used to mark tiles.

I use this to help me keep track of where I am during the long precreasing process. I like to use tiny bits to mark the centers of molecules or help me block off the border rows and columns. You could always use light pencil marks, but the putty is easier to see. It can easily be removed without any residue, and will help you stay oriented throughout.

Scoring Tools

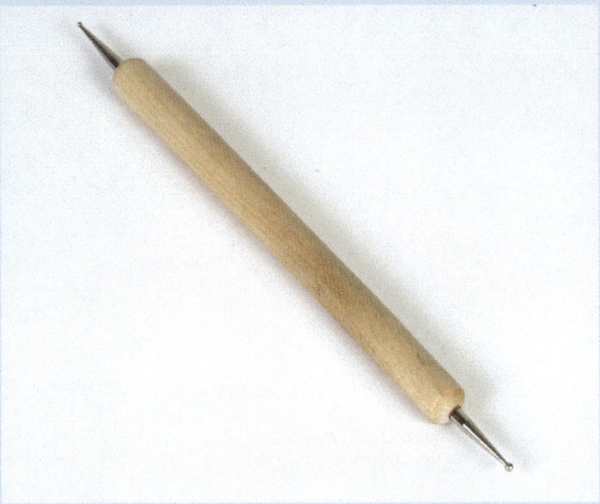

Scoring is a procedure that weakens the paper where you want a fold to be. You use tools to depress lines in the paper and this provides a folding guide for later. You can buy a scoring tool at a craft store, but it is just as easy to use a pen for that (just be sure that the cartridge is empty of ink first!). Use a ruler or some other kind of straight edge to score against to help you keep your work straight. You can also use a machine called a plotter to help you score very complicated patterns. The masters even use laser plotters! For our purposes, though, a hand tool will be all you need. This book contains only one tessellation that requires hand scoring (Rounded Cubes, page 51).

Cotton Swabs

Cotton swabs are helpful to puff and stretch paper molecules that include a pocket, or a rounded face, without tearing it. Any swab with a soft tip works well.

19 Papers I Love

Elephant hide is probably the best paper for tessellations. It has a great "memory": creases stay sharp and the paper tends to keep its new location after the crease was made (in other words, it doesn't come unfolded so easily). It also reverses well.

Its weight is 110 grams per square meter (GSM), which is the standard way to measure the weight of a paper type (you will even find it on the package next time you buy a ream of printer paper). Normal printer paper is around 90 GSM, while simple kami—the most popular kind of paper used for traditional origami, is around 50 GSM.

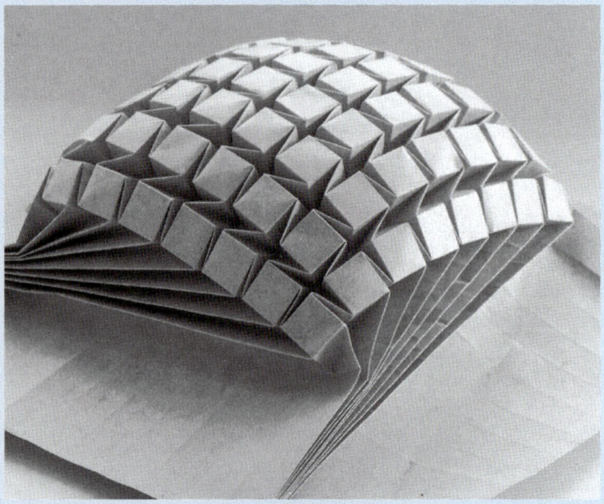

But back to elephant hide: the thickness is 0.1 mm, which makes it highly durable and hard to tear. Nowadays there are only seven colors in a pale palette. The light shades are translucent enough to allow the light through and show the beauty of the layers.

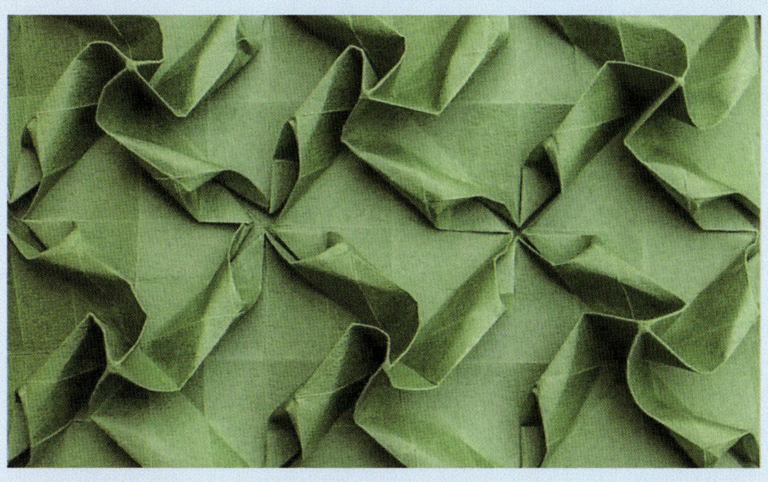

Tant is thinner paper (80 GSM), but still solid enough to hold the creases well. Its best property is that it comes in 100 colors. It is not as translucent as elephant hide.

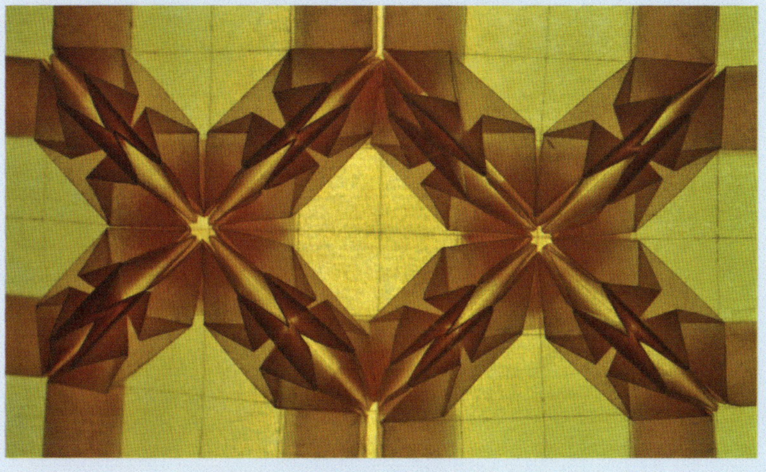

Glassine is the thinnest paper I like to use at 40 GSM. It is best for small projects. It is easy to tear and very hard to reverse. The memory, though, is almost perfect. Its best feature that it allows light through beautifully and creates a great play of light and shadow.

1 10 Understanding the Way Variations Are Made

Once I get a molecule down, I like to try to find variations. The Cubes molecule (see page 36) is a great example. I created a whole series of interesting models just by looking for the variations.

Finding a variation can be done in two ways: you can play with the folds and physically experiment, or you can explore the possibilities directly on the CP.

First, try changing the order of the paper layers. Many tessellations are constructed of paper layers and when you change the order of those layers, you will find new models. Change the direction of the fold, or switch from a square grid to a hexagon grid, but use the same overall folding procedure. Or try repeating procedures on a smaller scale.

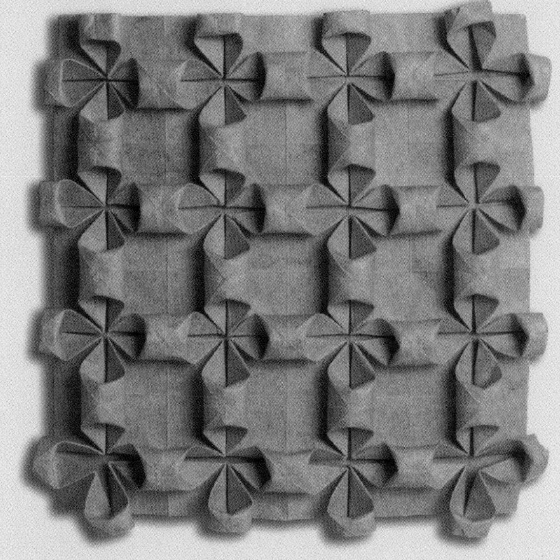

Red Flower tessellation.

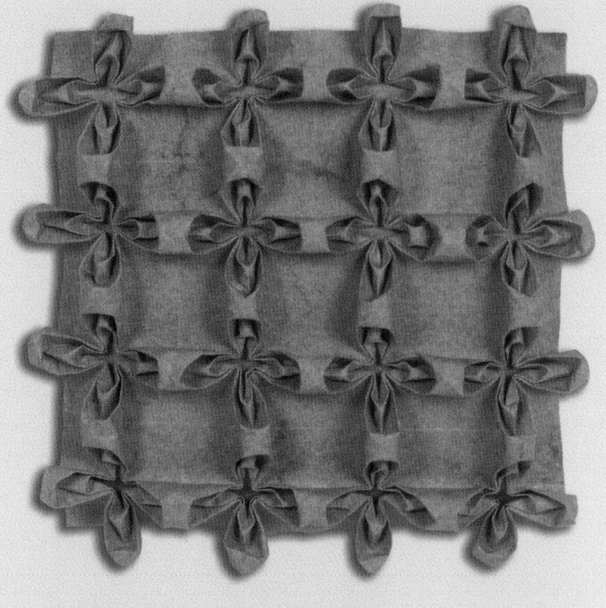

Double Red Flower tessellation repeats the procedure on a smaller scale.

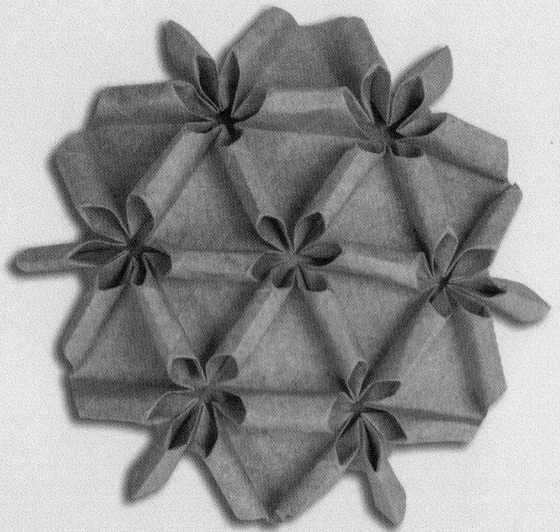

Hexa Flower tessellation uses the same procedure on a hexagon grid.

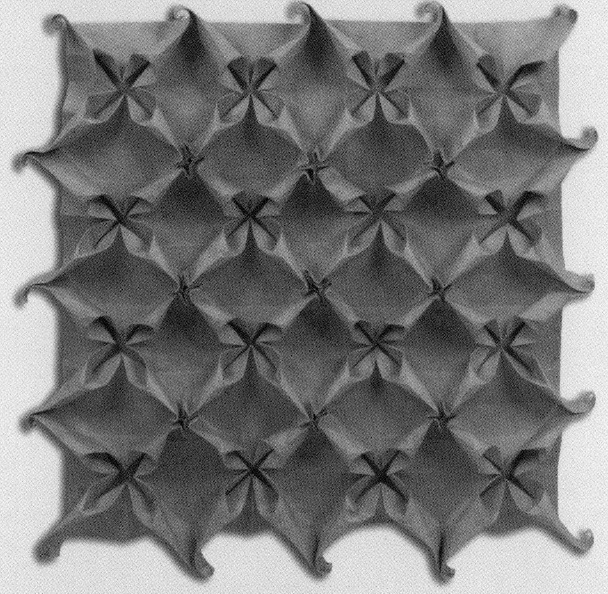

Green Flower tessellation is similar to the Red Flower tessellation, but the molecules are rotated 45°.

To use a diagram as the basis for variations, start by studying any tessellation CP. A simple way to do this is to print out a CP and actually cut out the molecules. As long as you maintain the rules of the molecules, you are bound to make tessellations out of your efforts. Take a look at the Cubes CP on the next page; notice how the molecules are connected (two crease lines make a V shape). Now see what happens if you cut out one molecule and paste it one or two rows to the left, adding a space between the molecules. I call this process *spacing*.

Using a two-row spacing is exactly how I developed the Wave tessellation from Cubes.

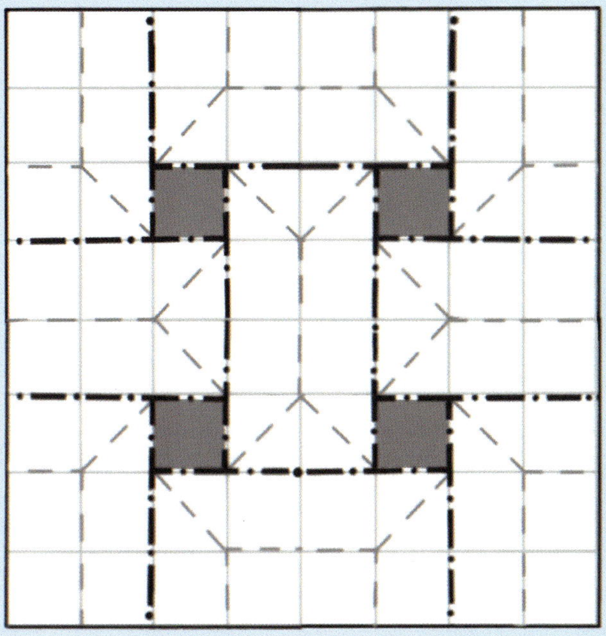

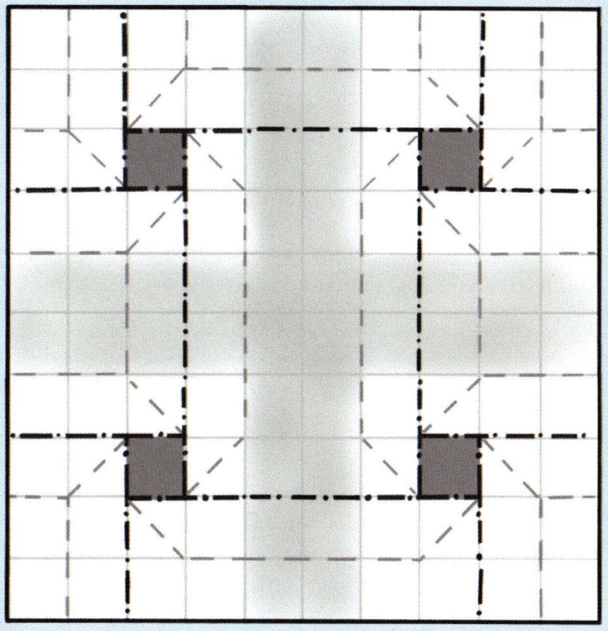

***Comparison between Cubes (left) and Waves (right)*.**

Another simple method is to change the length of the crease lines. What will happen if a diagonal crease crosses two squares instead of one? The result is very different, and it is actually hard to fold. But if you add a one row and one column around each new molecule—voilá, you get Bricks!

You can also try playing with angles. In Cubes, all diagonal folds are 45°, going from corner to corner of a square. But if the diagonal is of a rectangle, at a ratio of 1:2, the angles of the folds change and it results in a lovely corrugation. I named it Quadilic.

Another variation is altering the line's nature. Instead making them straight, they can be curved. Rounded Cubes is a great example of this.

You can change other parameters as well: the size of the inner square and its shape (rectangle instead of a square). What others can you think of?

1 11 The Process of Original Creation

The process of creating has always been an indescribable experience for me. This is the part that cannot be boiled down into lines of code. But understanding the logic and rules of tessellating will help you develop your own process. And that comes with practice.

So here is my advice: Start simple. Dare to play around. Dare to doodle with paper; grid it, mold it, and then try again. And again. Don't be afraid to make mistakes. Ask yourself what will happen if you try something new or different. Once you allow yourself the freedom to experiment, the creative process will get easier, and your own designs will most definitely follow!

2
The Cube Family

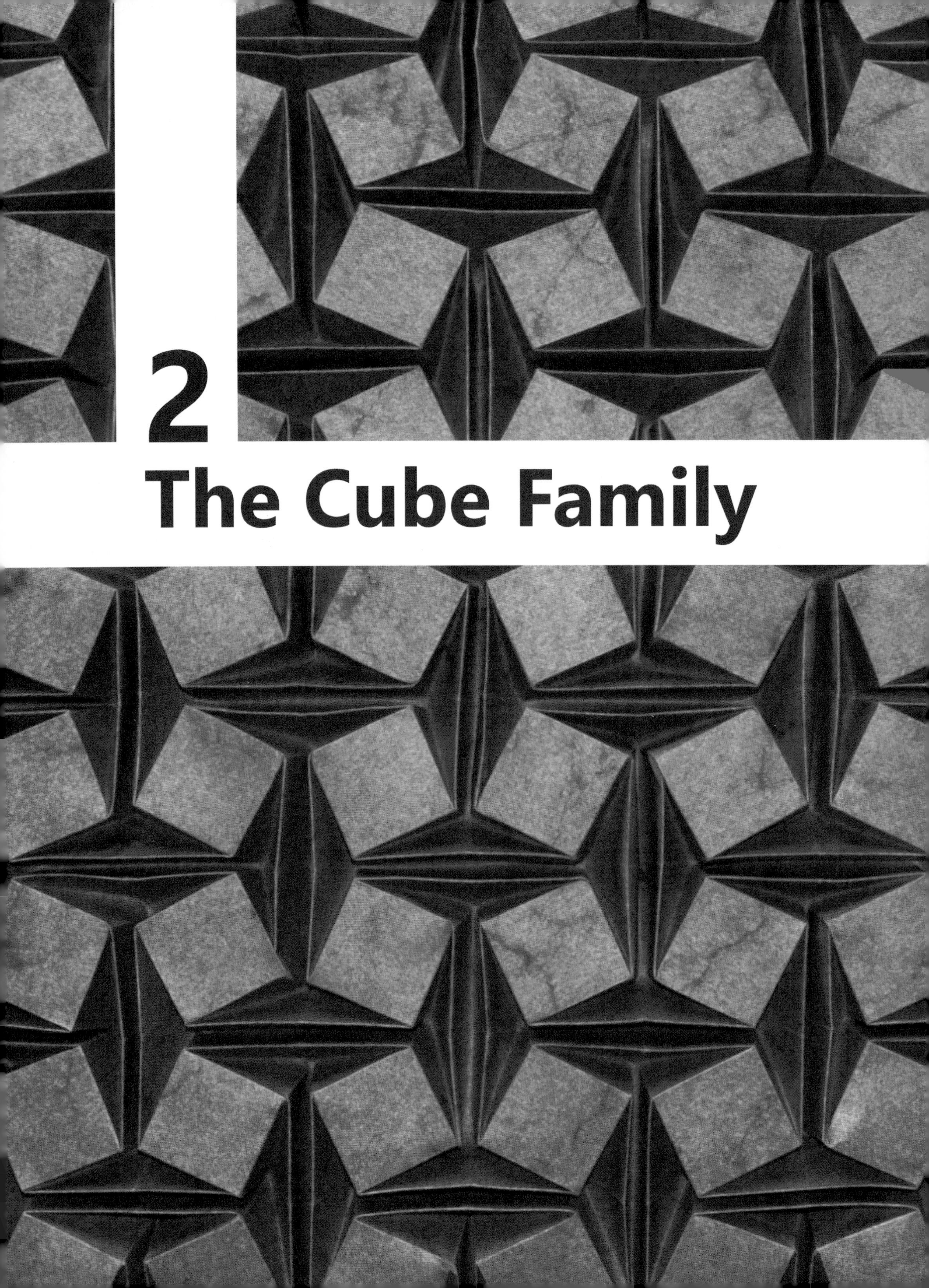

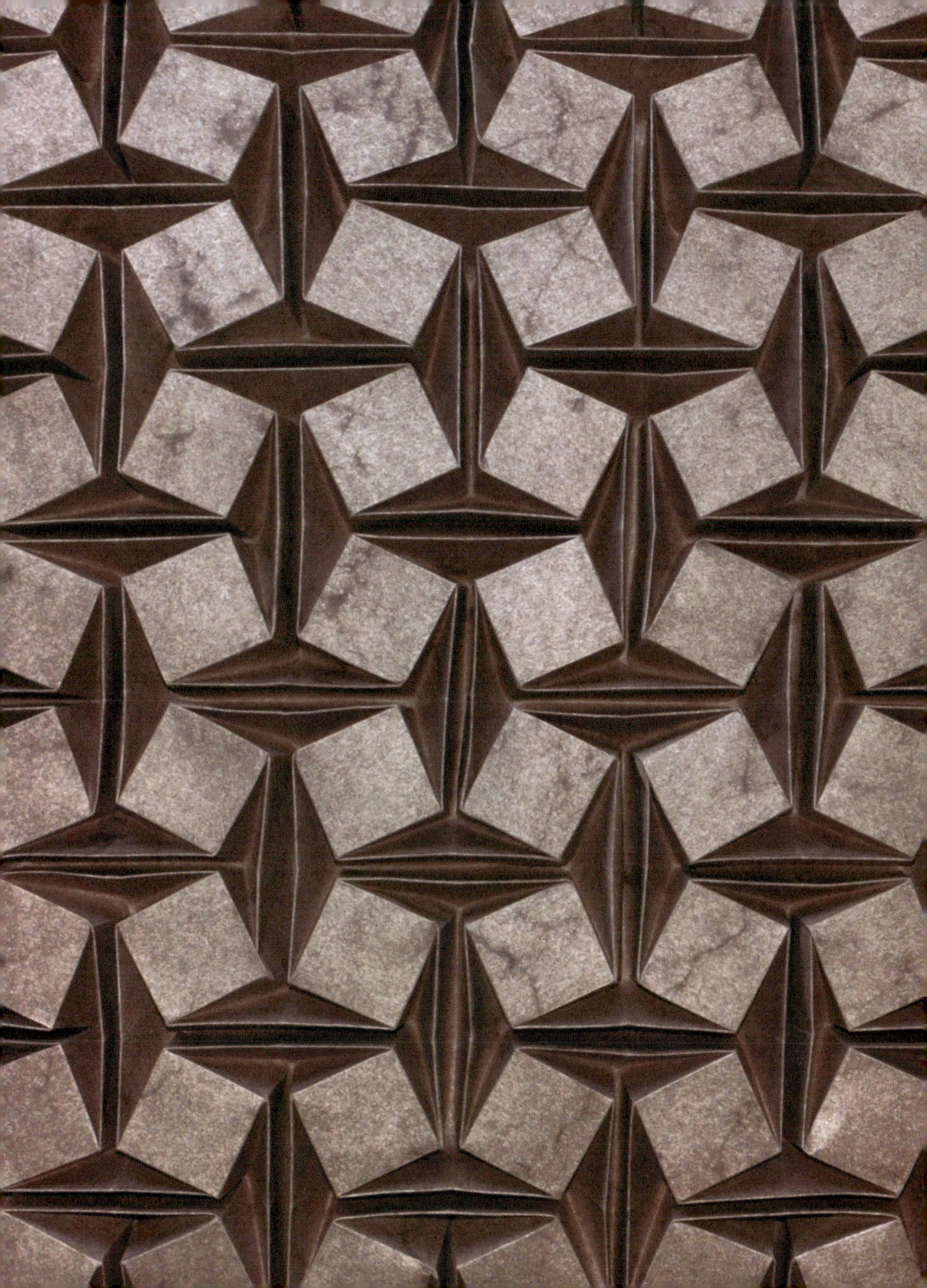

Introduction

The Cube tessellation family is based on a 3D molecule with a simple structure. It uses a grid of 3 by 3 squares with only four additional creases.

From this simple starting point, there are many ways to make new variations. You can change the number of spaces between the molecules, expand various properties of the molecule, using either shifting or mirroring for tessellation, or you can change the size or length of crease lines, etc.

Combinations of those options are possible as well, increasing the diversity of models.

In all cases, the collapse is done by rotating the middle square. It's like a twist fold that creates volume.

2 1 Cubes

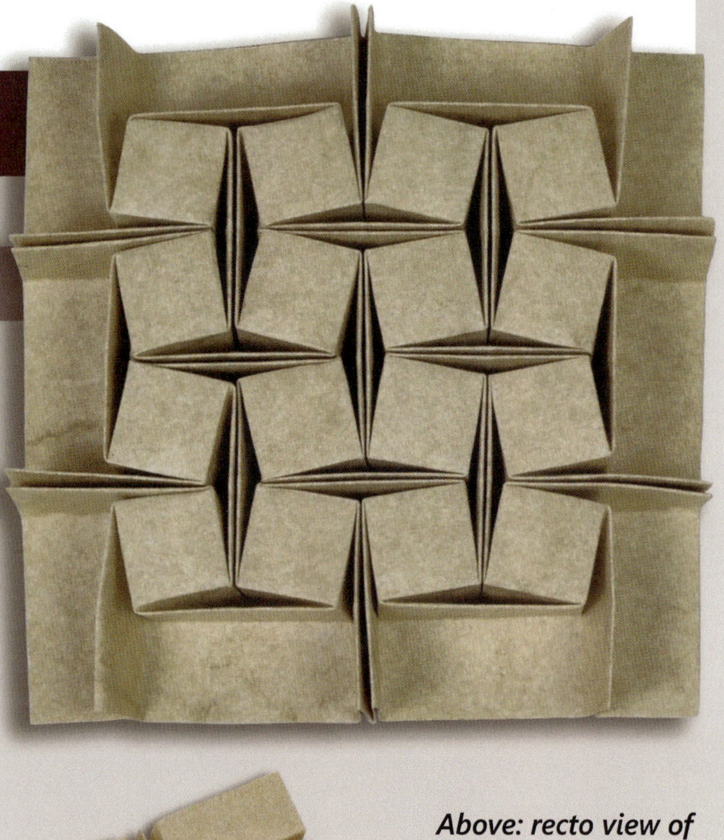

The Single Molecule

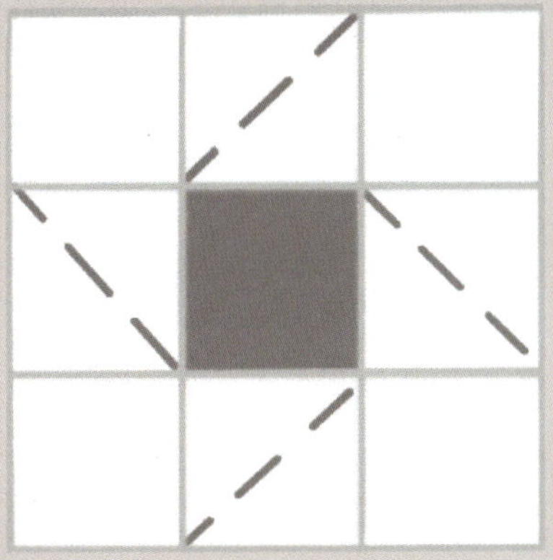

The simplest molecule in this family is a cube made of a 3 by 3 grid.

While the cube is formed, the central square (in gray) is rotated by 90°.

Molecules are tessellated by mirroring, which means that every two adjacent molecules are mirror images of each other.

The shrinkage ratio is 3:1.

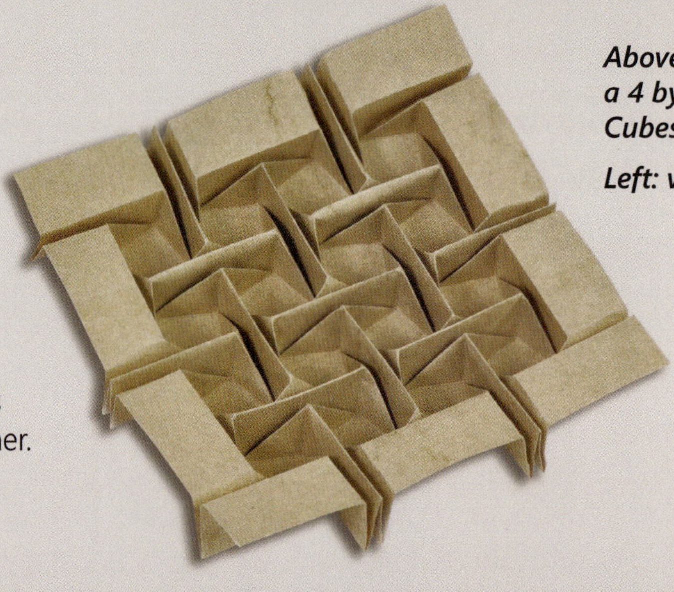

Above: recto view of a 4 by 4–molecules Cubes tessellation.

Left: verso view.

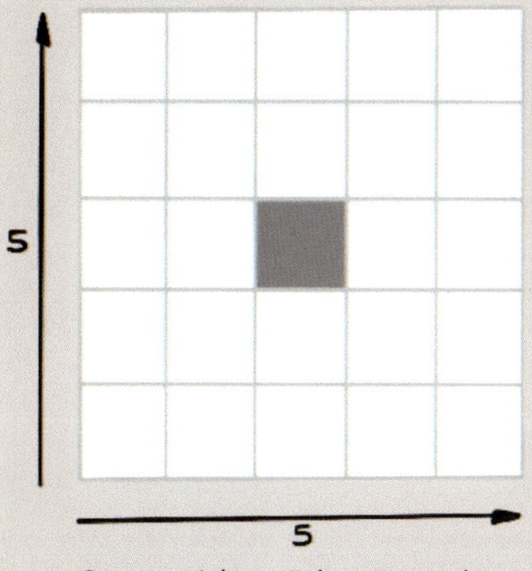

Start with a 5 by 5 grid, mountain side up. Mark the central square.

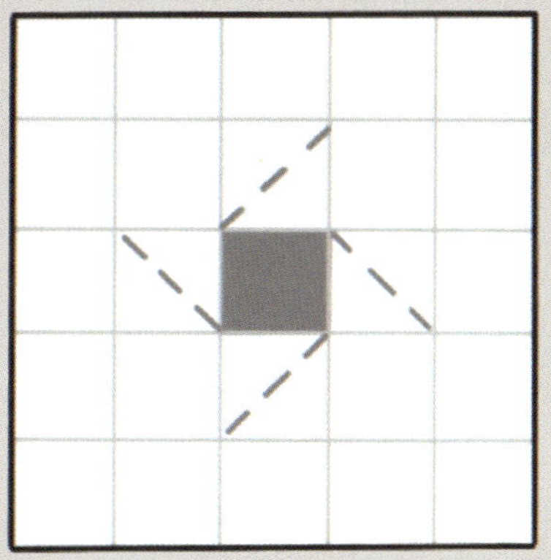

Valley fold the four diagonals.

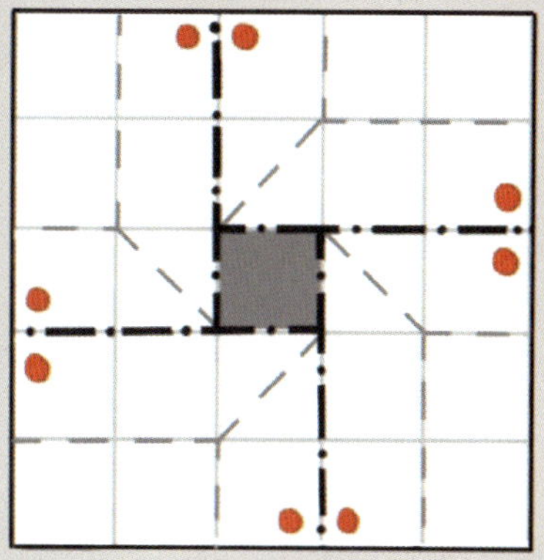

Put in remaining creases as shown. Pinch at the dots to collapse, forming mountain folds that extend from the central square to the edges.

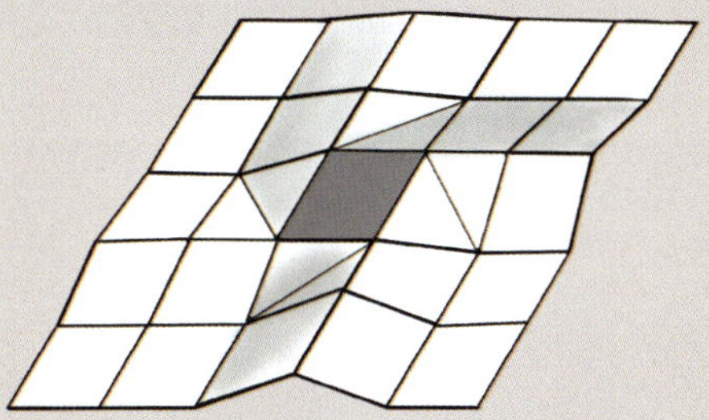

Pinch the mountain folds. The central square should be raised.

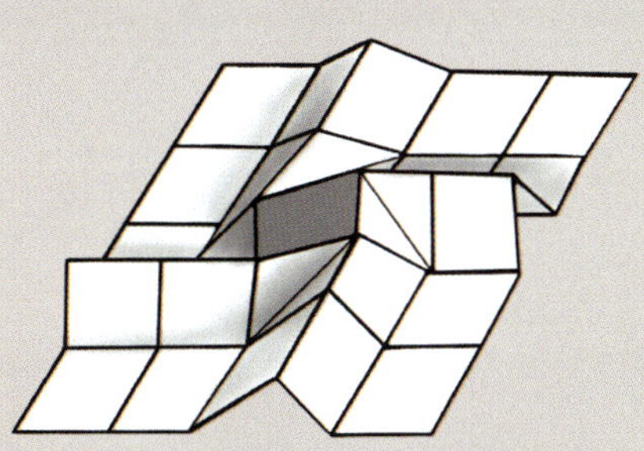

In process. The central square rotates counterclockwise, pushing it up.

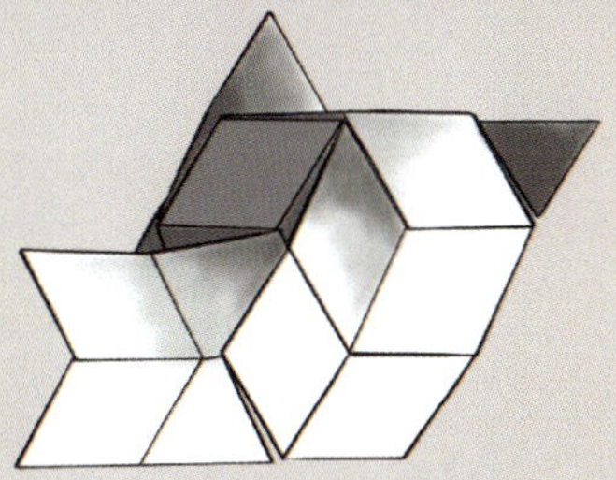

Fully collapsed, the height of the middle square is one square. It was rotated by 90°.

2 by 2 Molecules

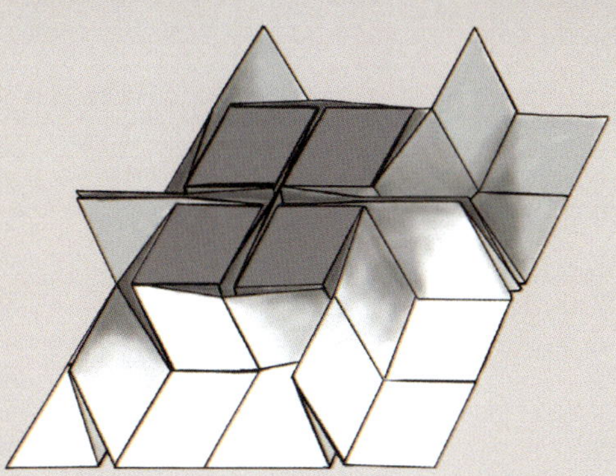

Use a grid of 8 by 8. Add all precreases.

First collapse only the top left molecule, and take all the mountain folds to the edges.

Collapse the top right molecule.

While collapsing the next row of molecules, rotate both into place at the same time.

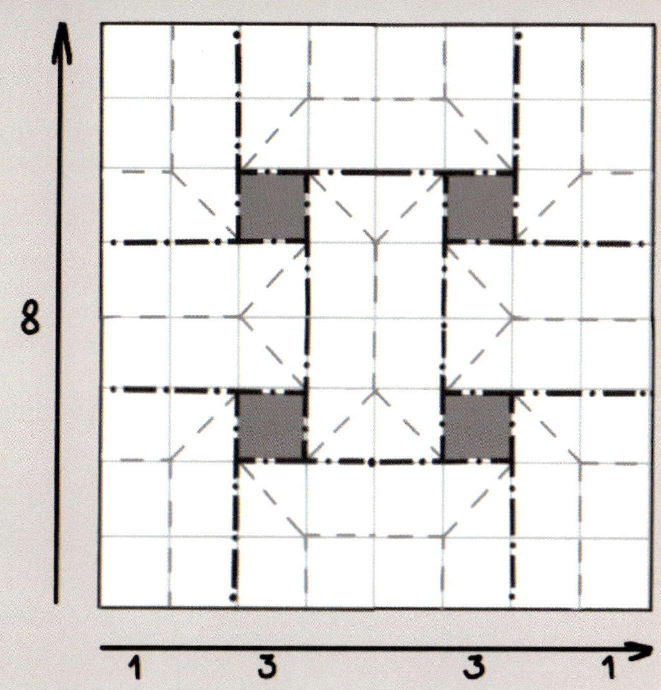

4 by 4 Molecules

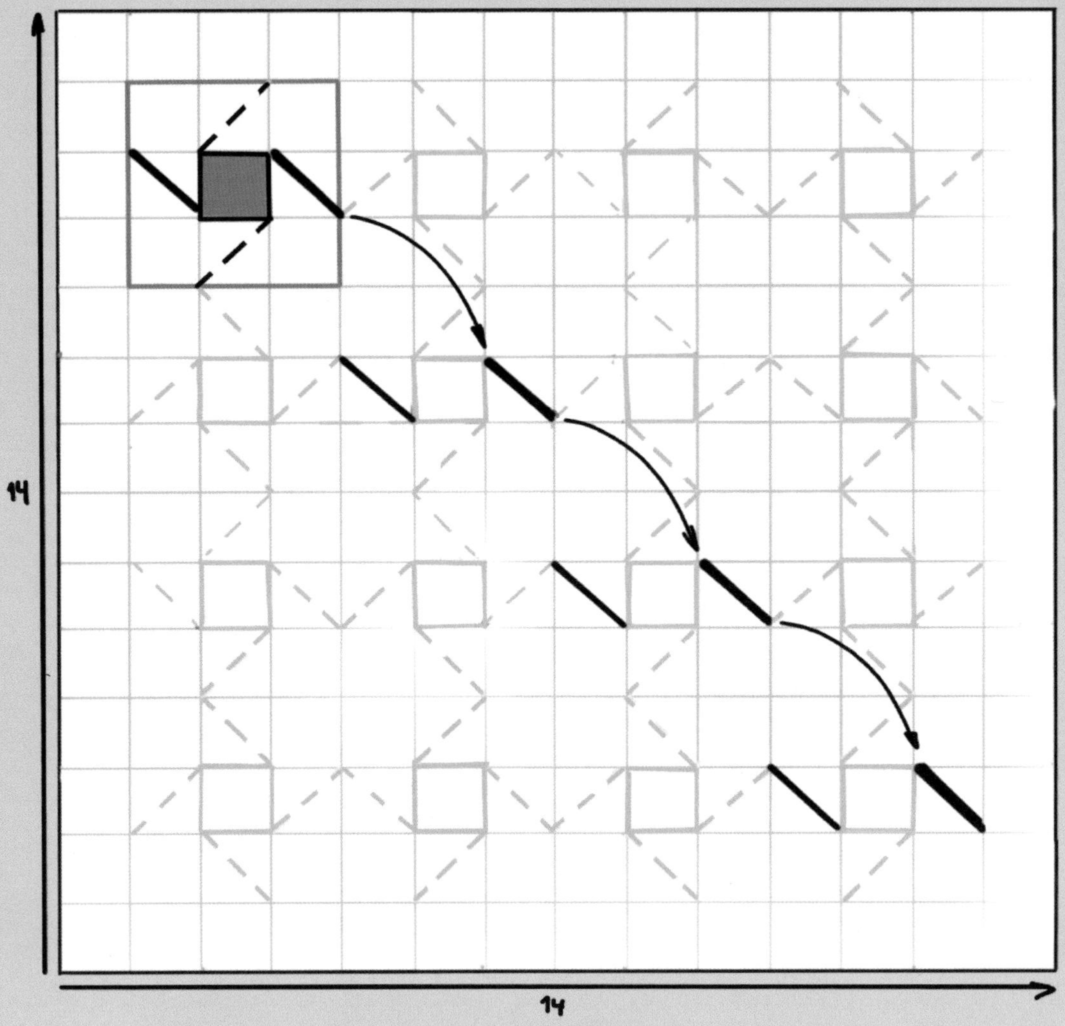

For a 4 by 4–molecule project, start with a 14 by 14 grid: 1 + 4 x 3 + 1 = 14.

The final result will be six squares wide.

Make all the precreases marked above. Note the pattern of the precreases. If you start with the top left molecule, it is easier and faster if you continue making all the creases that are on the same diagonal line.

Fold the first diagonal to bisect a square, then skip two squares to fold the next diagonal in line (see arrows). You can repeat this action on the parallel diagonals opposite as you come back from the bottom right molecule.

When finished with the first set of diagonals, complete the creases of the top left molecule. Move on to the next molecule, and follow the "fold one, skip two" shortcut again.

Repeat the process, until all the precreases are made.

Follow the collapse process outlined in the 2 by 2 project. Start at the top corner and collapse row by row.

Use clips to hold the folded edges in place as you proceed with the collapse.

Above and Beyond—Rings and Pendant

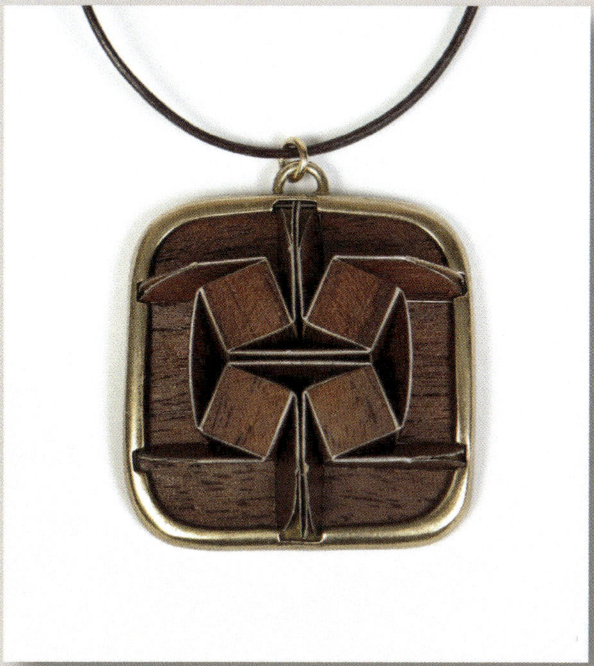

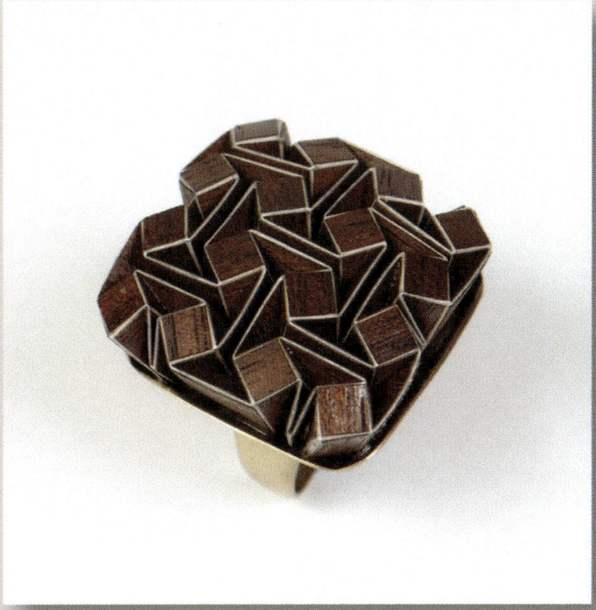

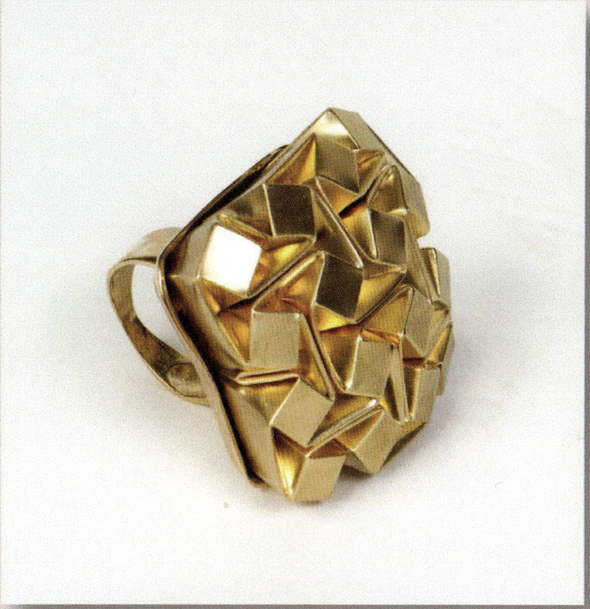

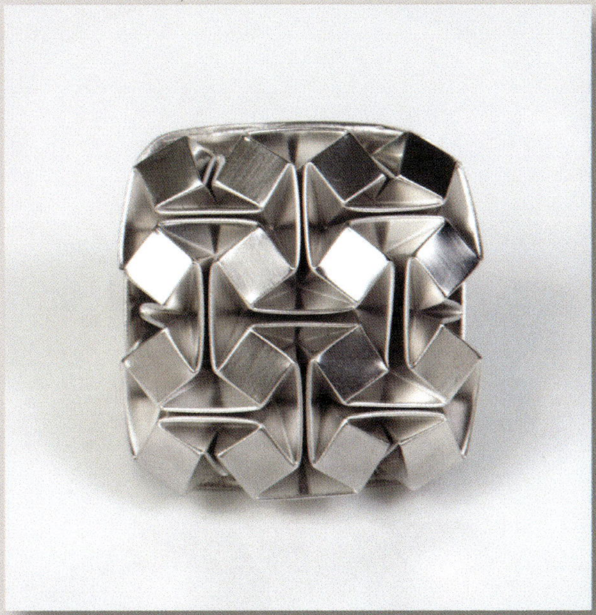

Variations on the Cubes tessellation turn sheets of brass and wood into a shimmering collection of jewelry, all hand folded.

22 Waves

Right: Verso view of an 8 by 8 molecule Waves tessellation.

Below center: recto view of a 4 by 4–molecule project.

Verso view is shown at bottom.

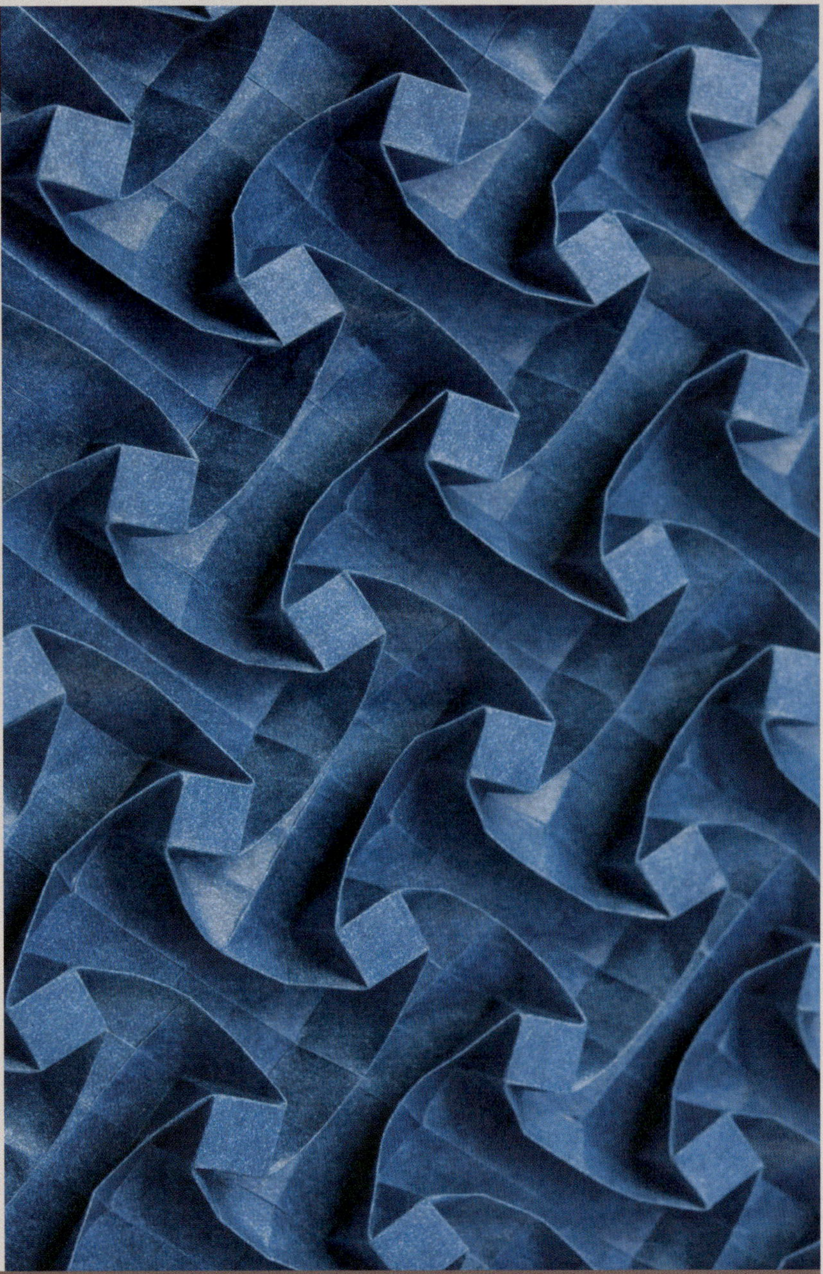

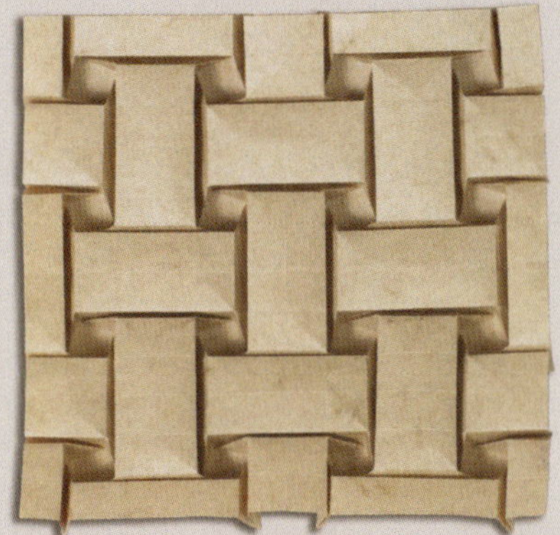

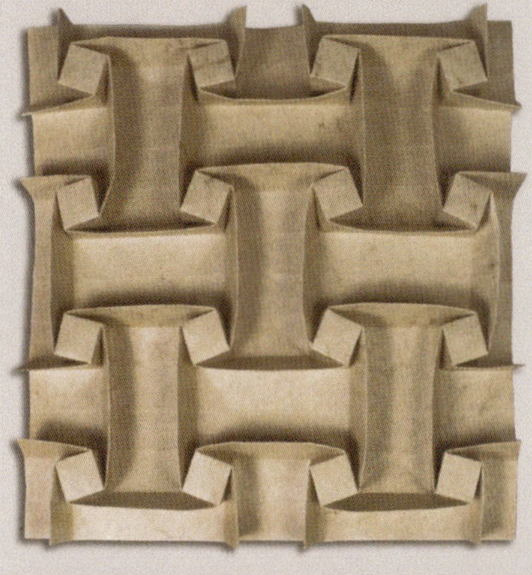

The Single Molecule

The Waves tessellation uses the same molecule as Cubes, but with two extra rows and columns, so you need a 5 by 5 grid.

Adding a single row around the molecule, as we do here, creates a gap that totally changes the look of the model.

It is tessellated by mirroring, just like Cubes. But it is easier to collapse than Cubes, since you have a gap between every two molecules.

The shrinkage ratio is 5:3.

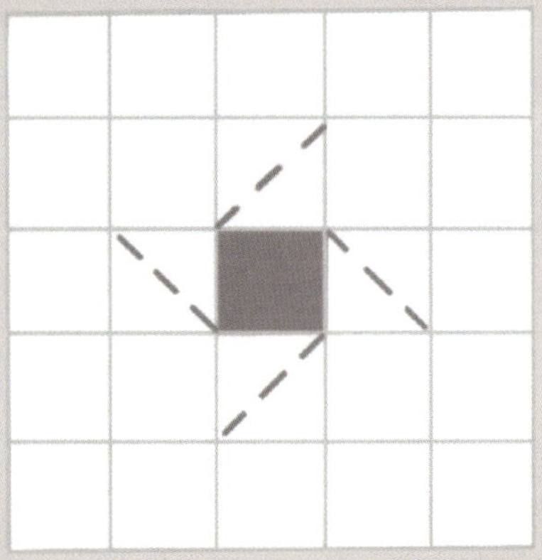

2 by 2 Molecules

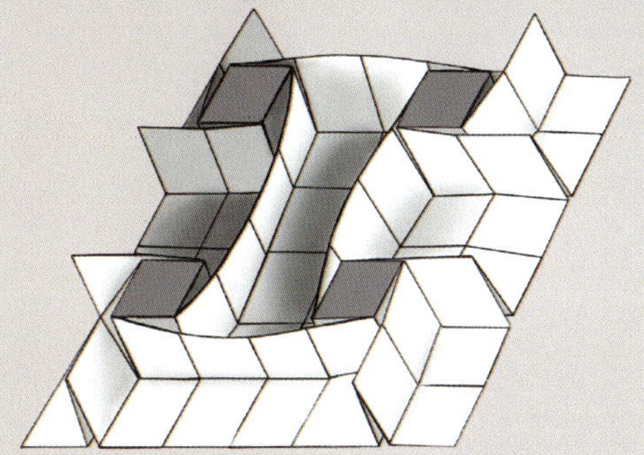

Start with a 10 by 10 grid.

Mark the four central squares, and add all the precreases around them.

Collapse exactly like the Cubes tessellation (see page 37).

The extra row we have around the molecule creates the needed gaps on the outer rim of the model, so there is no need to add spaces to make the collapse easier.

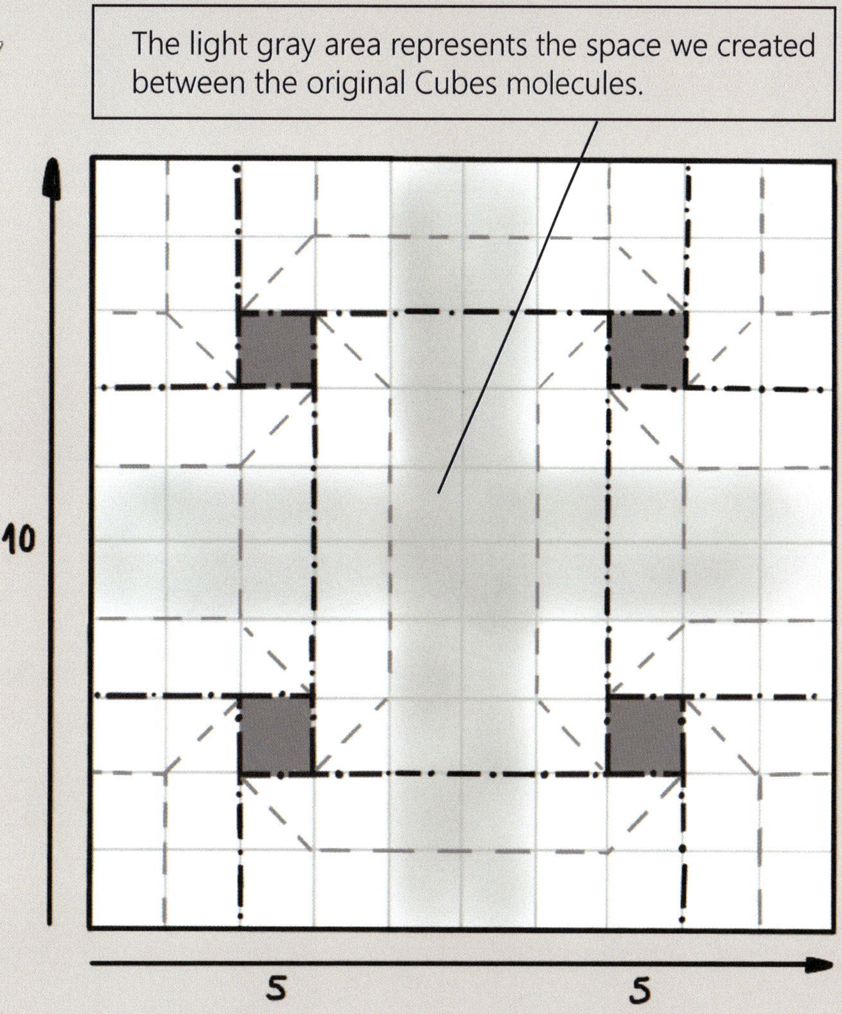

Above and Beyond—An 8 by 8 Project (detail)

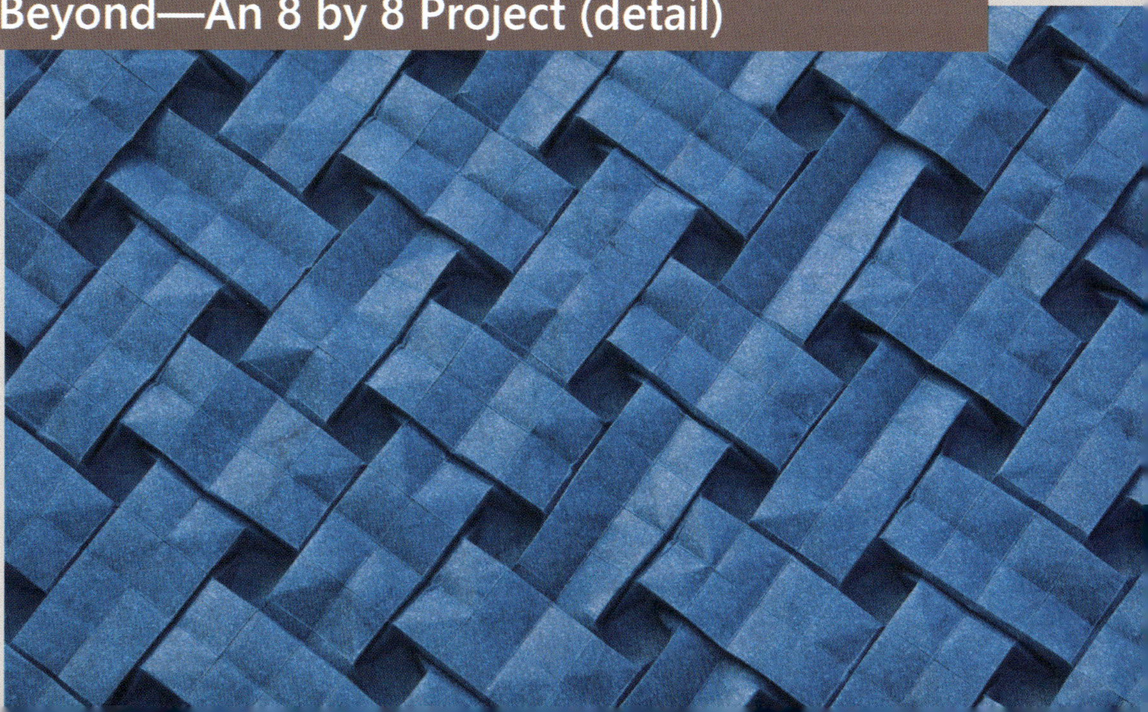

Recto view of a 40 by 40 grid project with 8 by 8 molecules. It creates the appearance of a woven lattice from a single sheet of paper.

4 by 4 Molecules

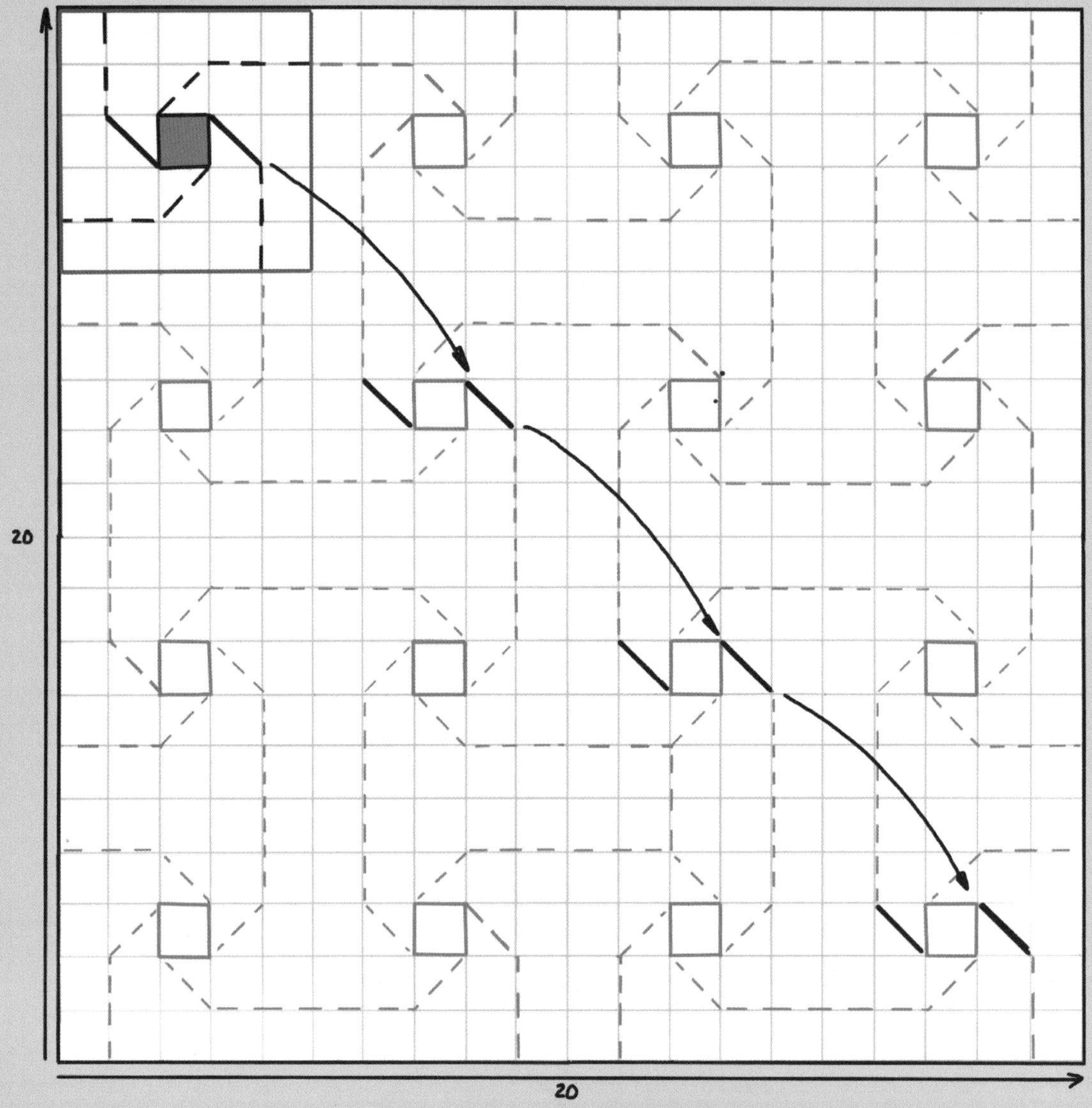

For a 4 by 4–molecule project, start with a 20 by 20 grid: 4 x 5 = 20. There is no need for an extra row or column.

The final result will be 12 squares wide.

Make all the precreases marked above. Use the same Cubes shortcut and fold all creases on the same diagonal at once.

Fold the first square diagonal and then skip four squares to fold the next diagonal in line. Since every diagonal has a parallel fold on the other side of the central square, you can repeat this action as you come back from the bottom right molecule.

When finished with the first row of diagonals, complete the creases of the top left molecule. Move on to the next molecule to the right, and follow the "fold one, skip four" shortcut again.

Repeat the process, until all the precreases are made.

Start at the top corner and collapse the first row.

While collapsing the next row of molecules, rotate both into place at the same time.

2 3 Bricks

The Single Molecule

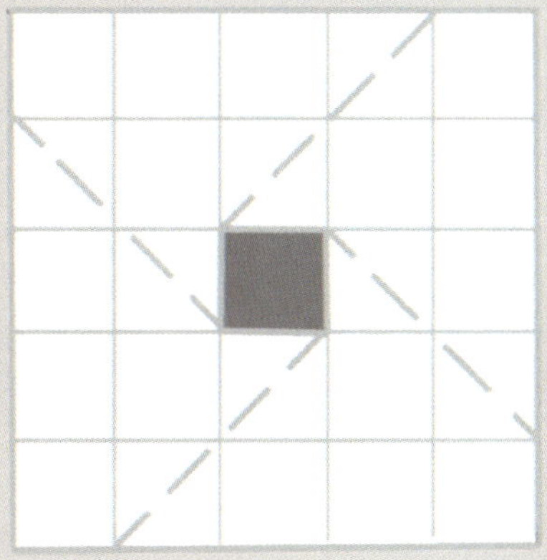

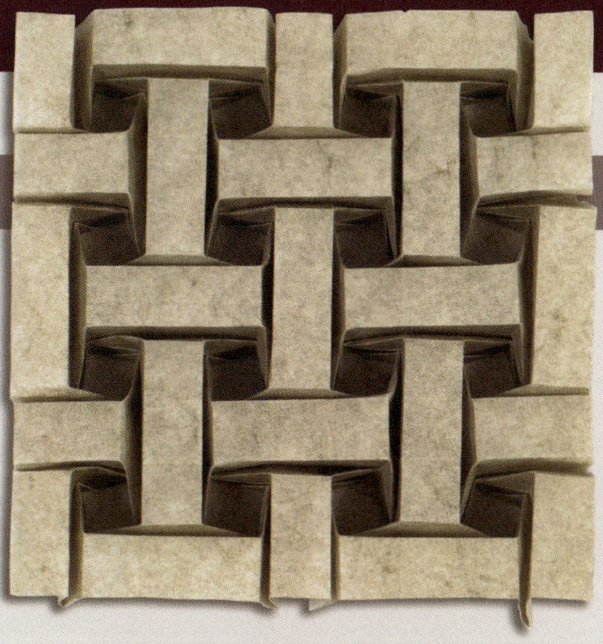

The Bricks variation is similar to Waves (page 40). It starts with the same grid size as Waves, but every diagonal goes through two squares, not one. This creates a doubled rotation, in effect.

The central square rises to a height of two squares and it completes a 180° rotation.

The shrinkage ratio is 5:1.

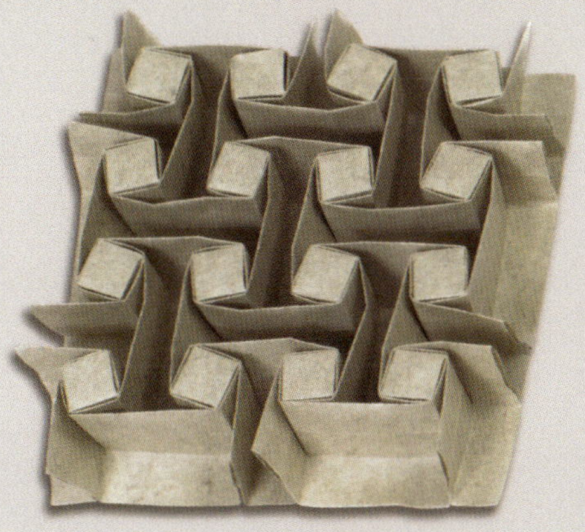

Above: recto view of a 4 by 4–molecule Bricks tessellation.

Verso view is to the left.

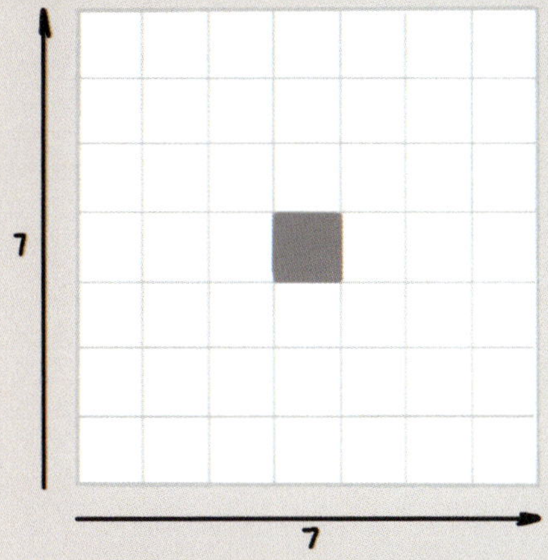

Start with a 7 by 7 grid (to allow an extra row around, for a better grip), the mountain side up. Mark the central square.

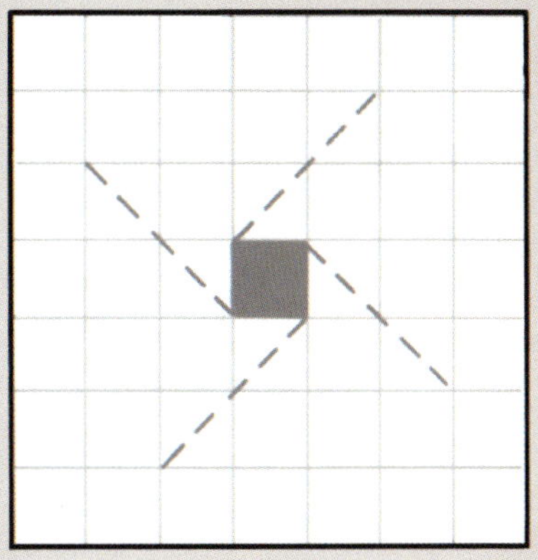

Valley fold the four diagonals.

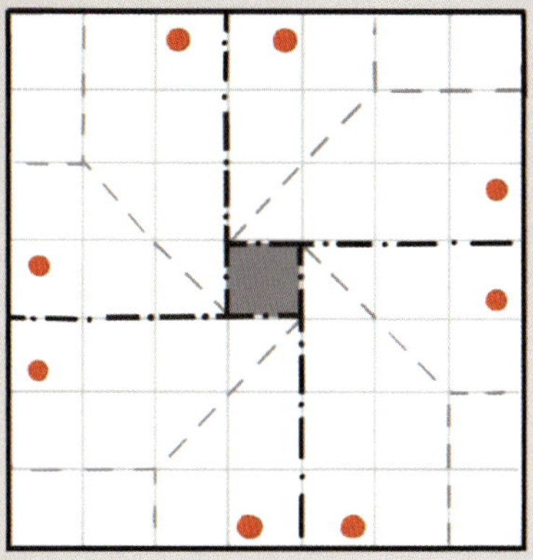

All the needed creases are shown.

Start the collapse with the mountain folds extending out of the middle square.

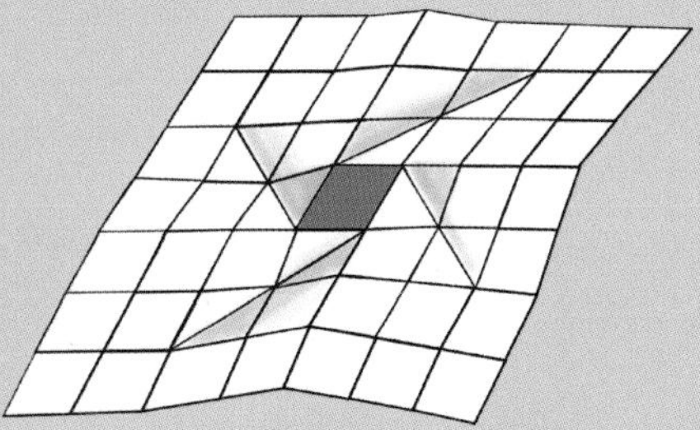

Pinch the mountain folds. The central square should be raised.

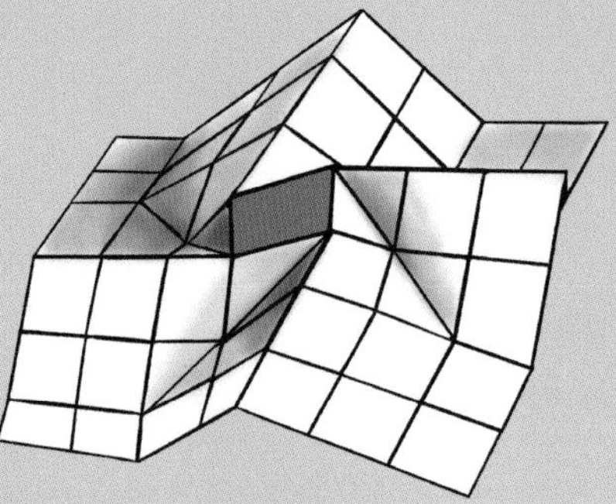

In process. The central square continues to rise and rotate counterclockwise.

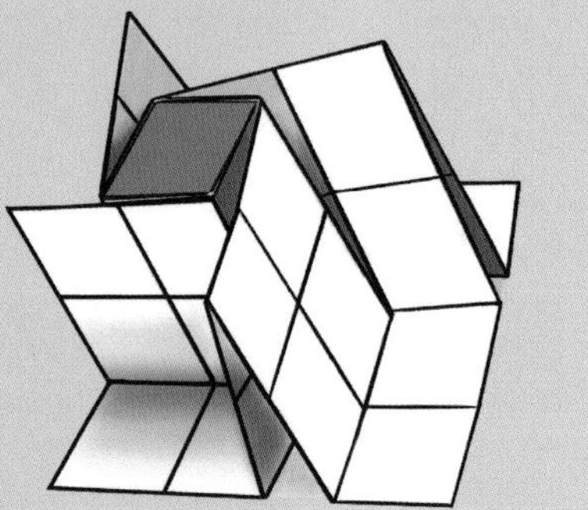

Fully collapsed, the height of the middle square is two squares, and it is rotated by 180°.

2 by 2 Molecules

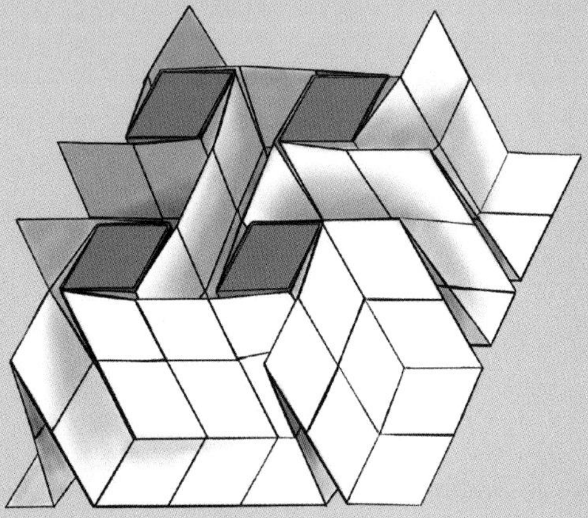

Start with a 13 by 13 grid.

For this tessellation we use spacing and mirroring.

Mark the four central squares and add all the precreases around them.

Collapse: start at the top left and complete the row with the right molecule.

Complete the second row of molecules simultaneously.

While collapsing, make sure every molecule rotates 180°.

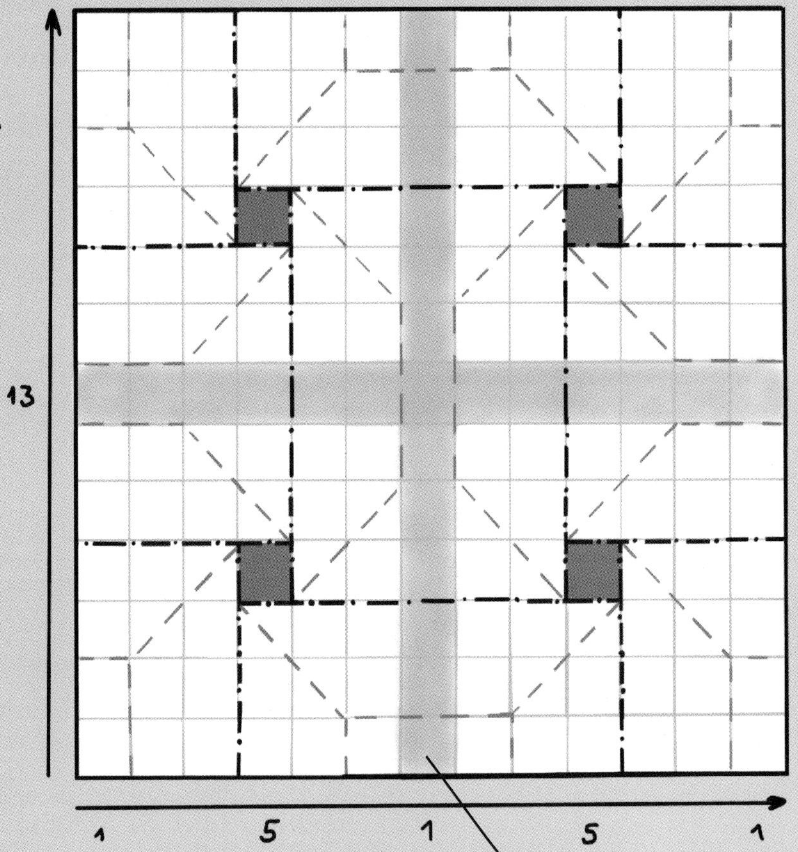

The light gray area represents the space we created between the original Bricks molecules.

4 by 4 Molecules

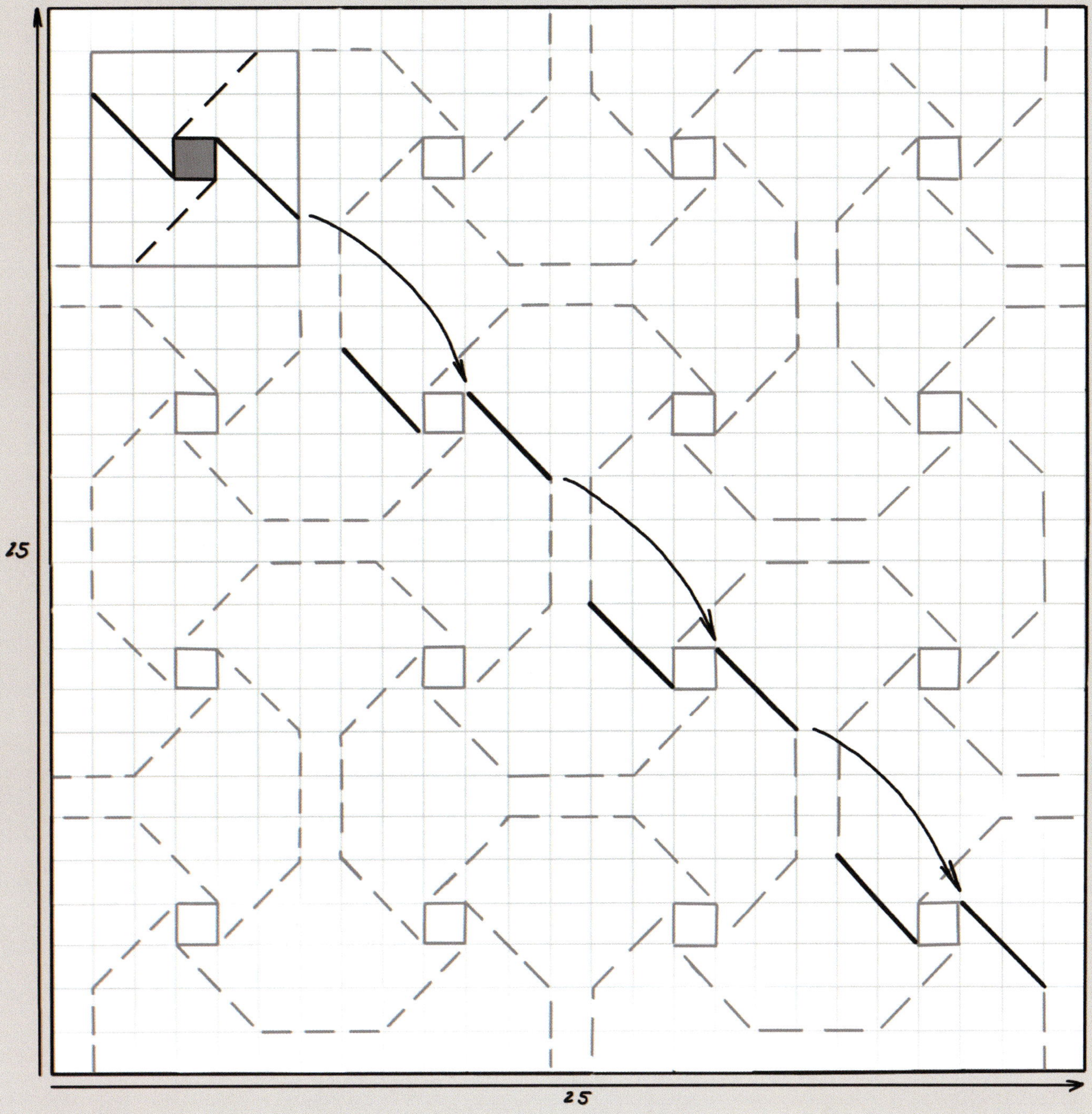

Start with a 25 by 25 grid: You will need five squares each for four molecules plus a square between each molecule and at the edges. The formula is: (5 x 4) + (5 x 1) = 25.

The final result will be nine squares wide.

There is a pattern to putting in the precreases—fold two square diagonals; skip four; repeat.

If you find the collapse too hard to do, try collapsing as if the diagonals are one square length only. Then finish collapsing every molecule into its final position.

Above and Beyond—A 10 by 10 Project (detail)

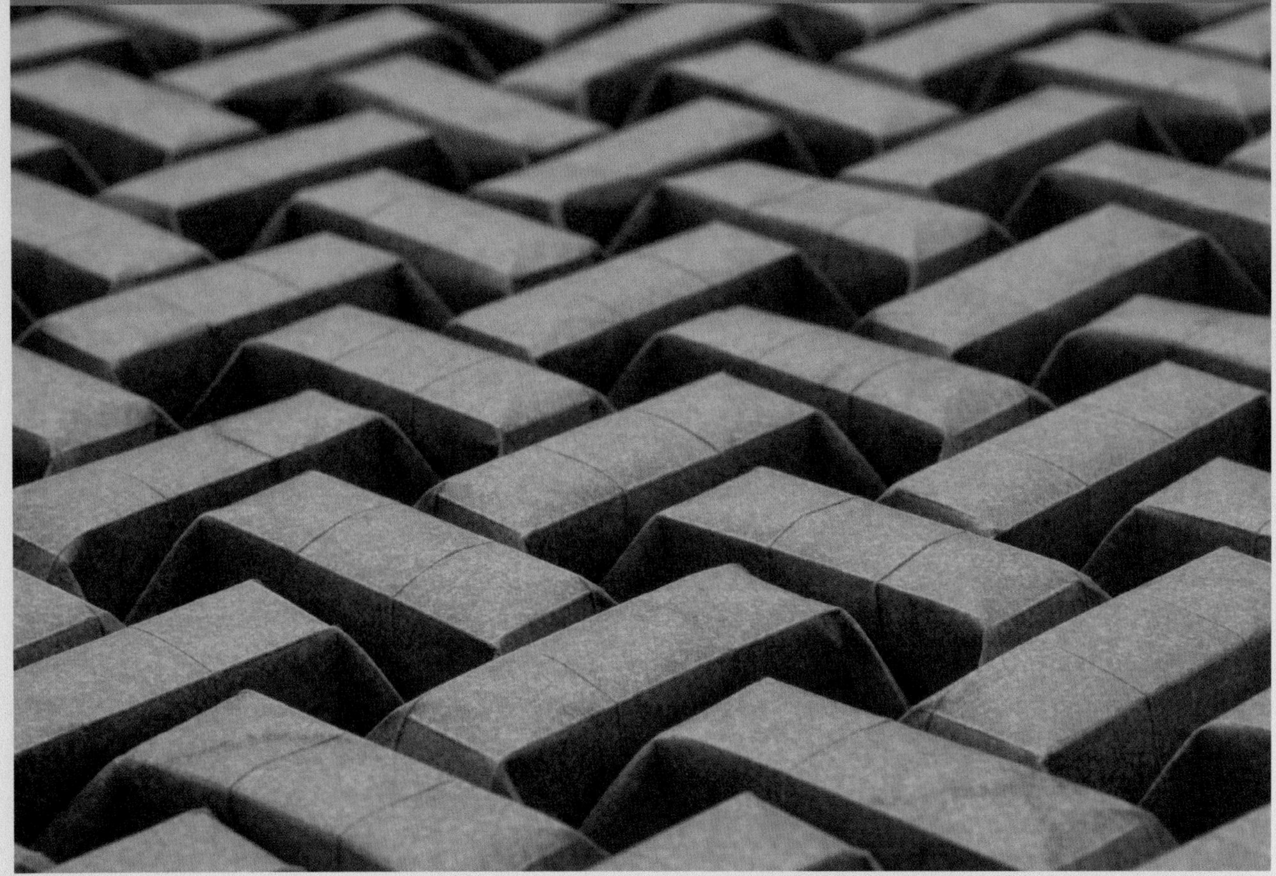

This project, folded from gray elephant hide, shows exactly why this tessellation is called "Bricks". The other side of the same model is below.

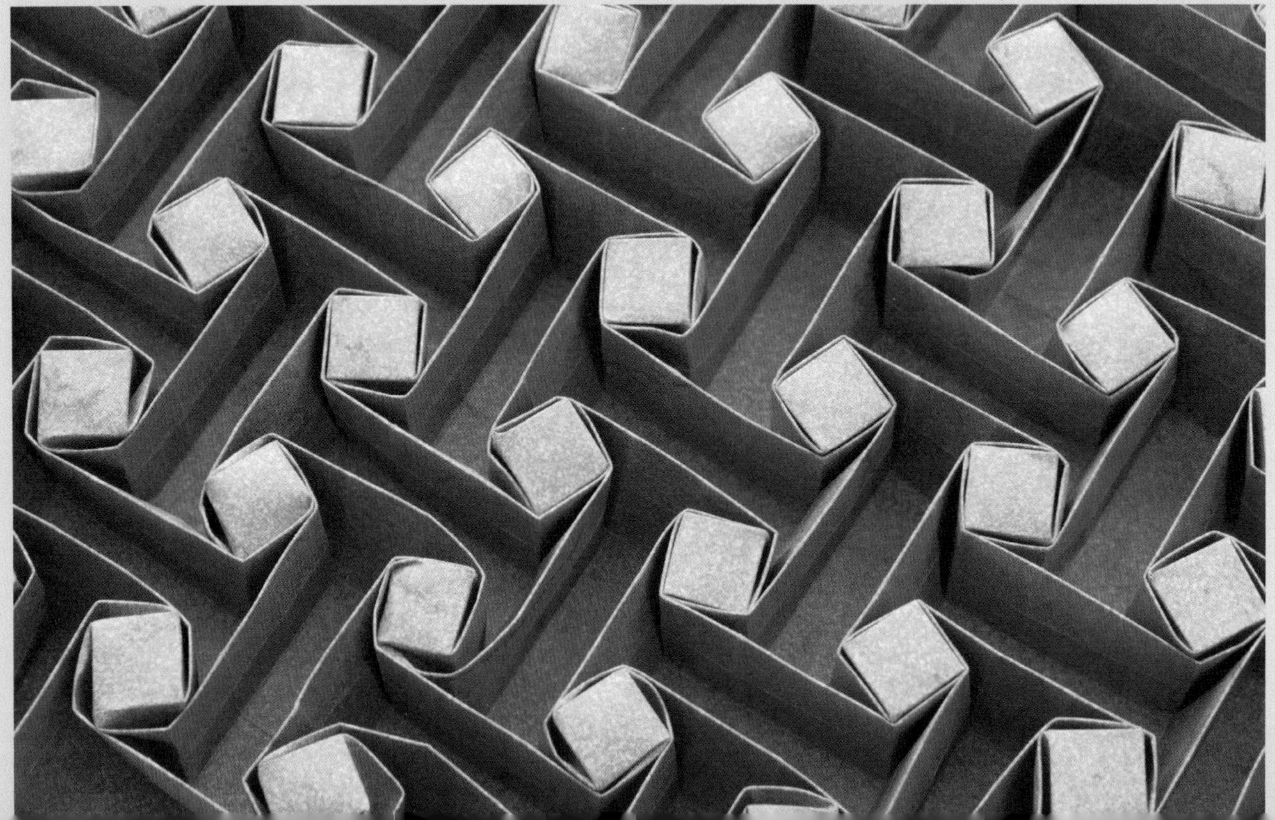

2 4 Quadilic

The Single Molecule

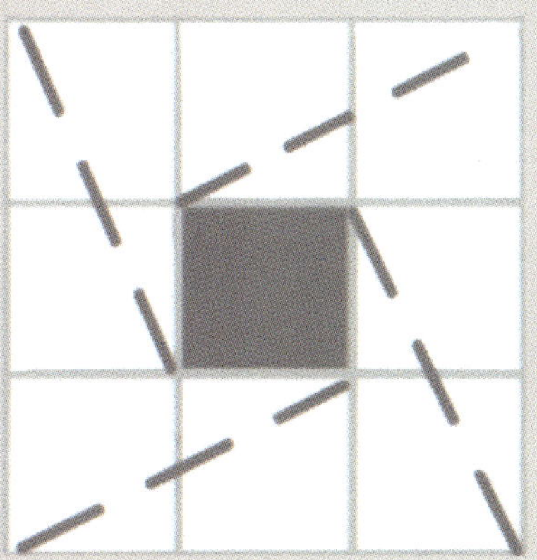

Changing the angle of the diagonal creates a third variation on the Cubes tessellation.

These precreases are diagonals that bisect a rectangle made out of two squares.

The shrinkage ratio is 3:2.

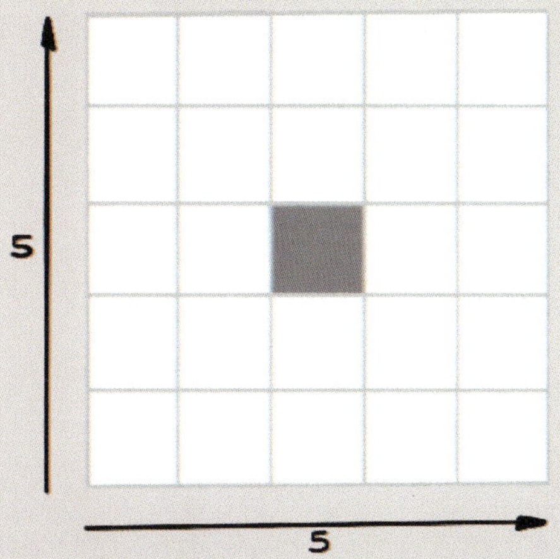

Start with a grid of 5 by 5. Mark the central square.

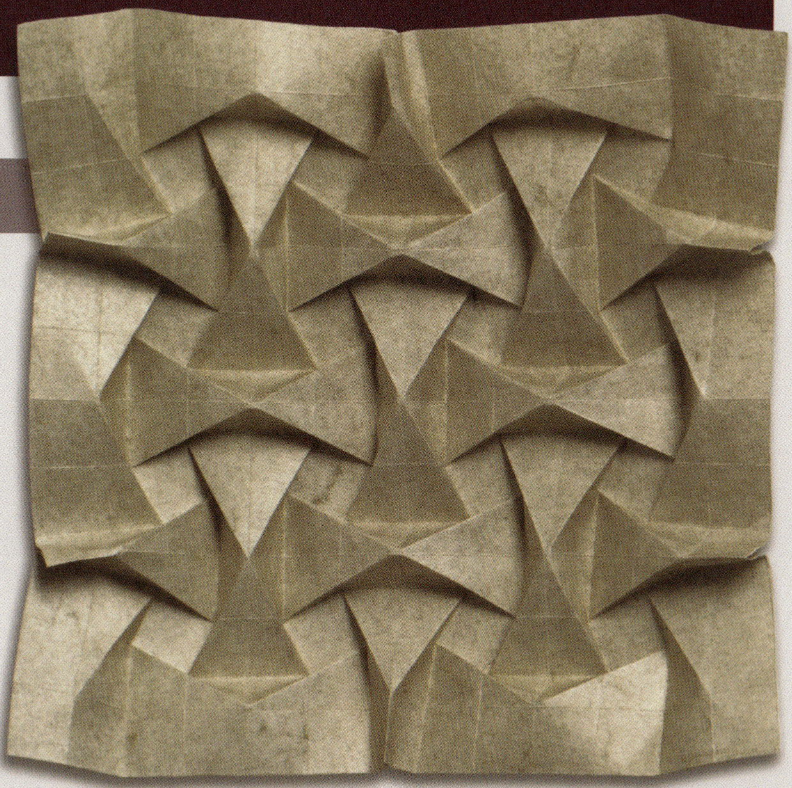

Top: recto view of a 4 by 4–molecule Quadilic tessellation. Verso view is below.

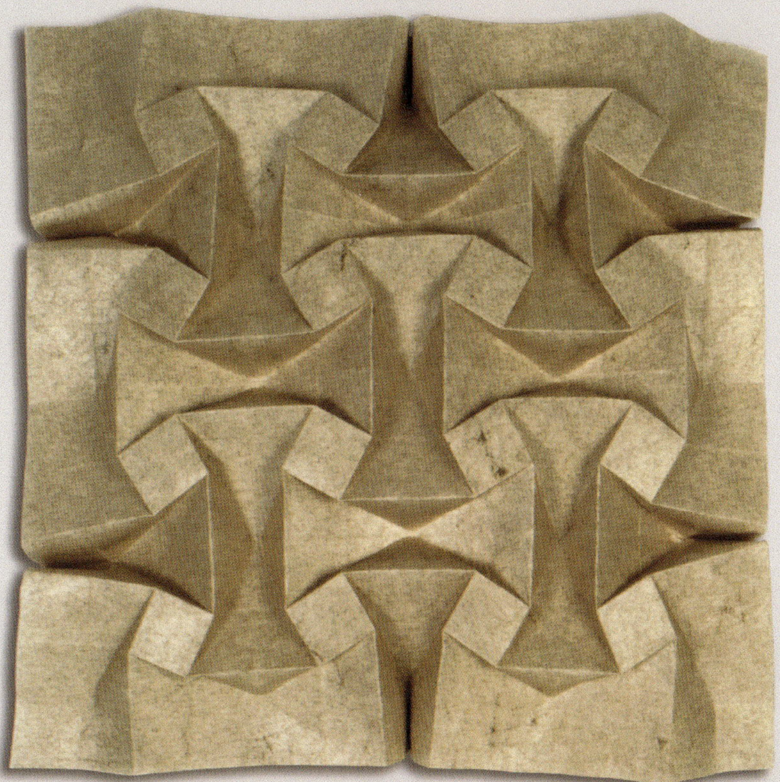

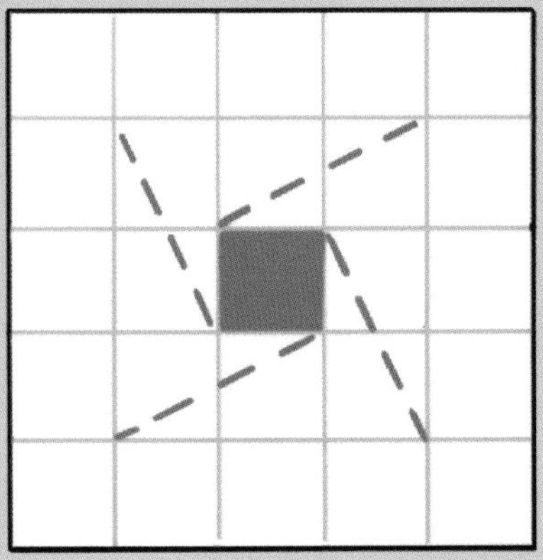

Valley fold the four diagonals. Note how they extend from one corner of a 1:2 rectangle to the opposite corner.

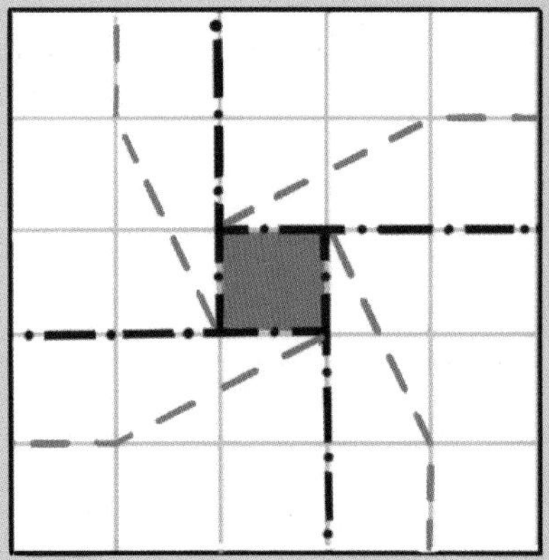

Add precreases as shown.

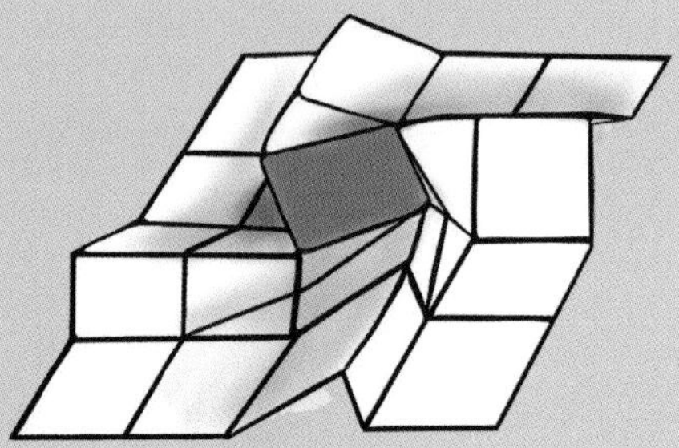

The collapse is more challenging with this variation because the creases easily unfold.

2 by 2 Molecules

Make an 8 by 8 grid.

Mark the central squares and add all precreases as marked.

The collapse is done as usual, but it's more difficult to keep the folds in place. Do not hesitate to use clips to hold the edges.

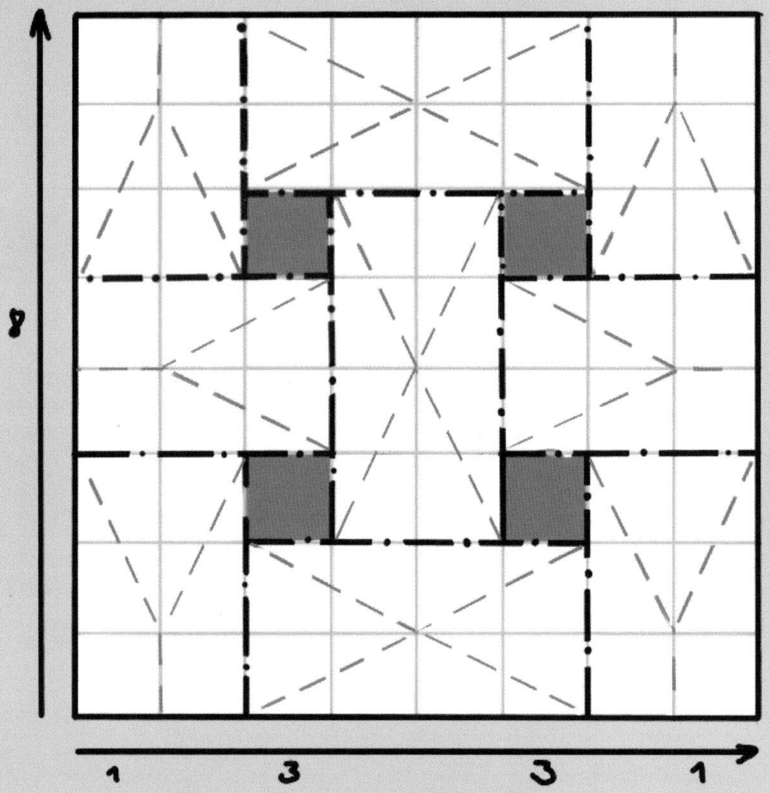

4 by 4 Molecules

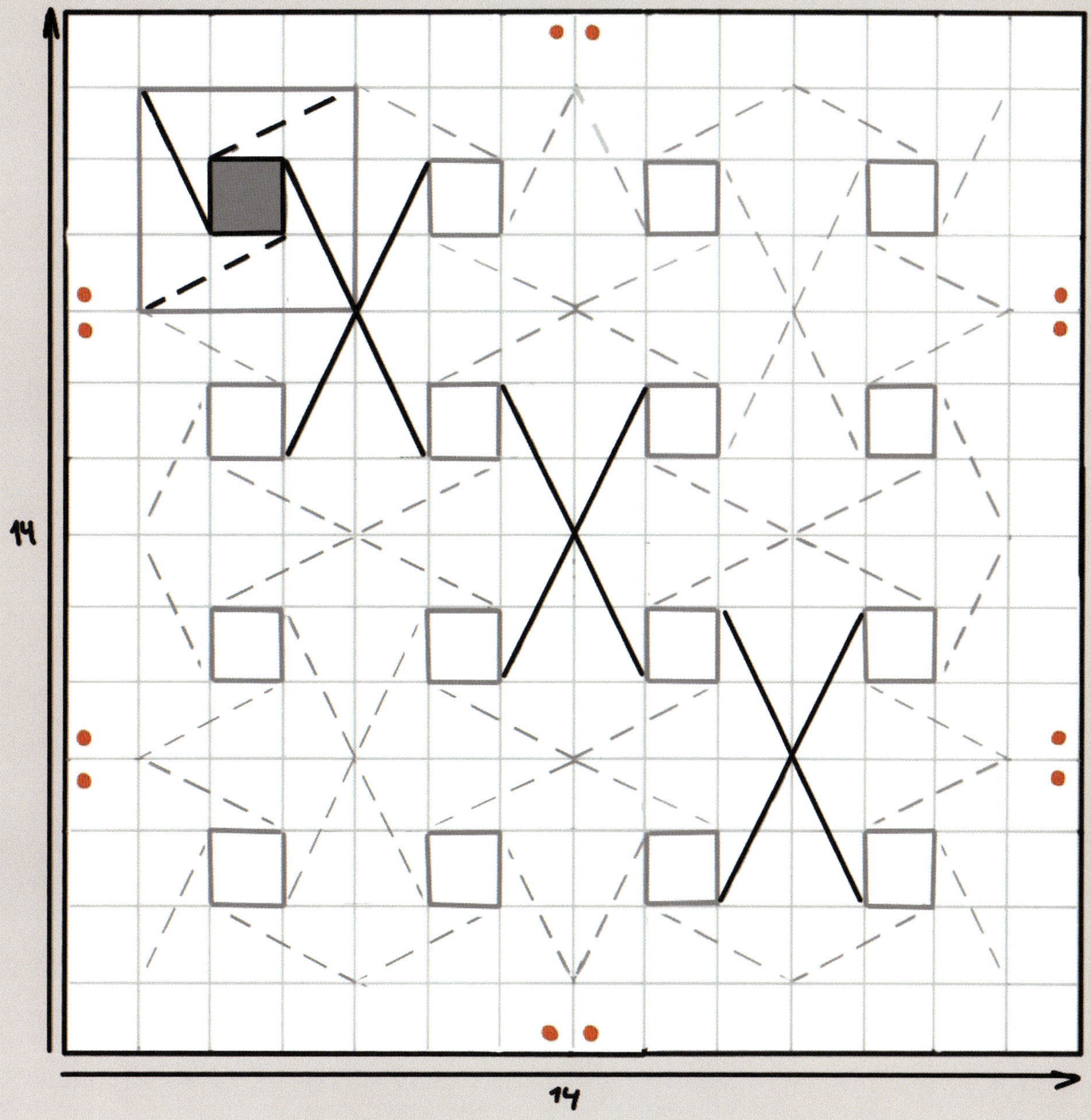

Use a 14 by 14 grid:

1 + 4 x 3 + 1 = 14

The final result will be around 10 squares wide.

There is no real shortcut to putting in the precreases, but you can make the narrow Xs in between the marked squares first. Note they alternate in orientation; one X stands up vertically while one next to it lies horizontally.

Again, the collapse unfolds easily, so use clips to hold the edges together at the dots. This will help train the molecules into their folded positions.

Above and Beyond—Cement Wall Tiles

What makes Quadilic unique is its relative flatness. In a way, it is a corrugation. The complete surface of the paper is visible and there are no overlapping layers or vertical faces.

Its flatness makes Quadilic a really interesting shape for a tile, like the one designed for Kaza Concrete.

Images courtesy of Kaza Concrete.

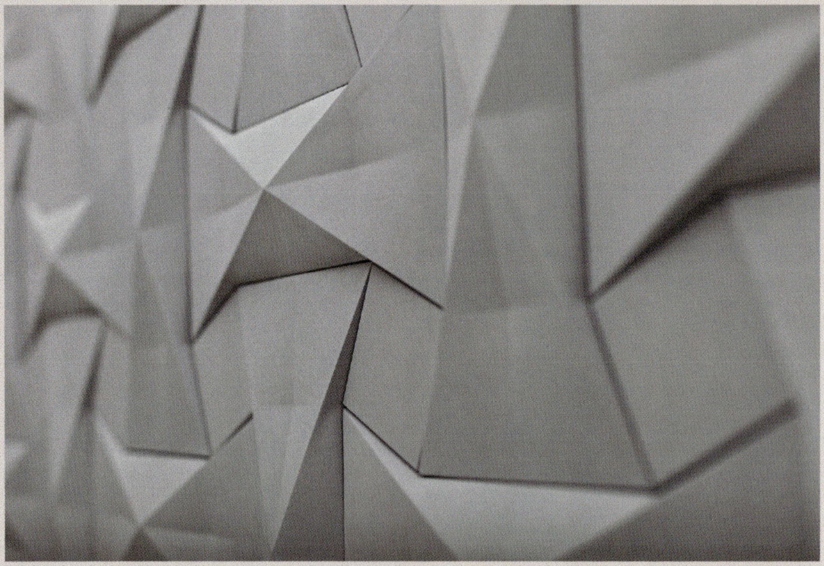

A detailed view of the concrete tiles.

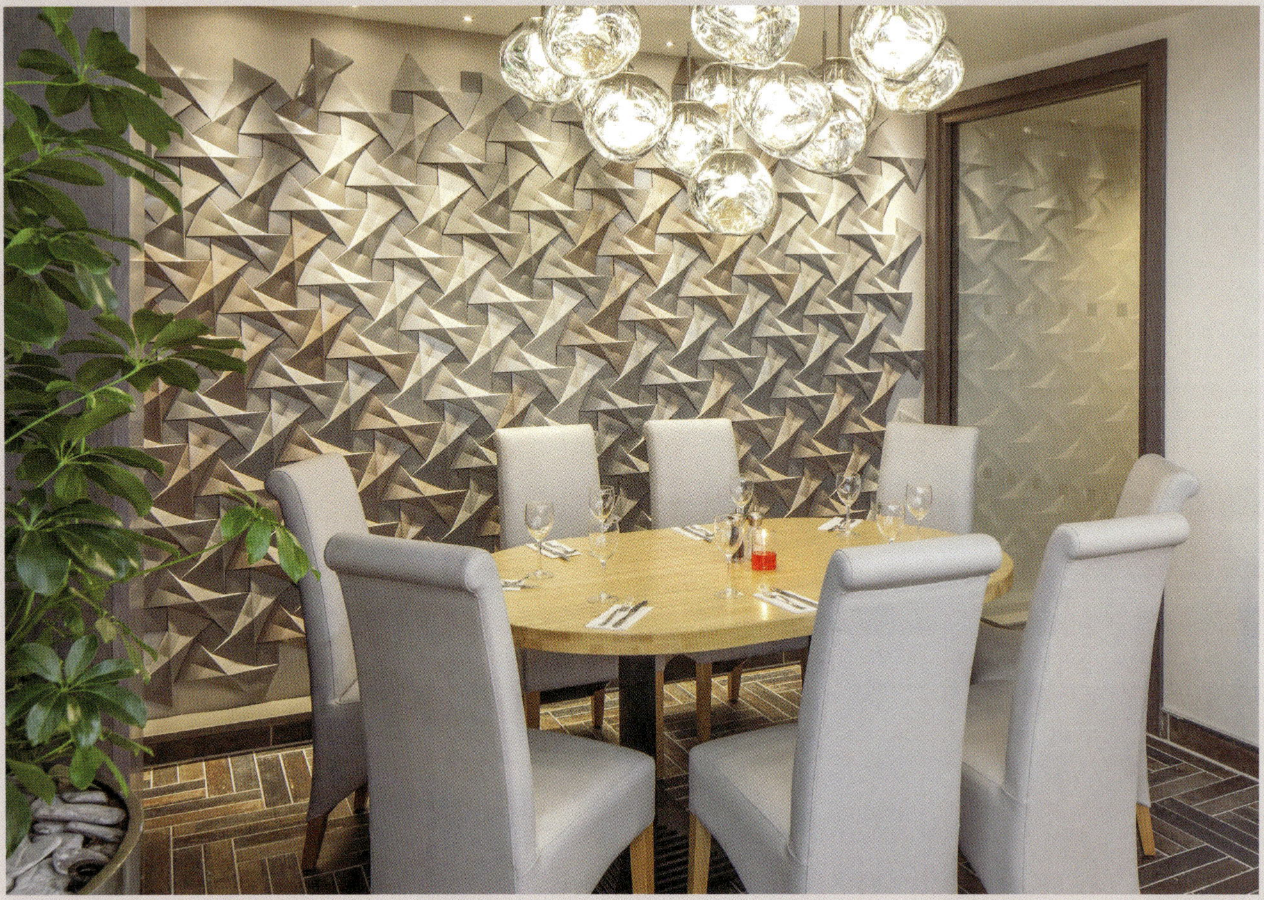

A restaurant decorated with Quadilic tiles.

2 5 Rounded Cubes

The Single Molecule

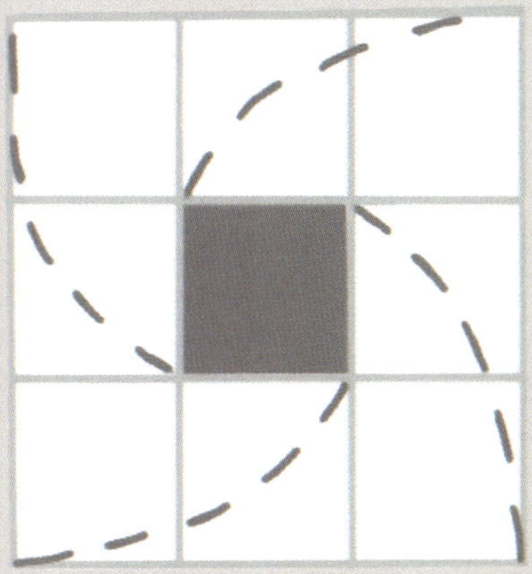

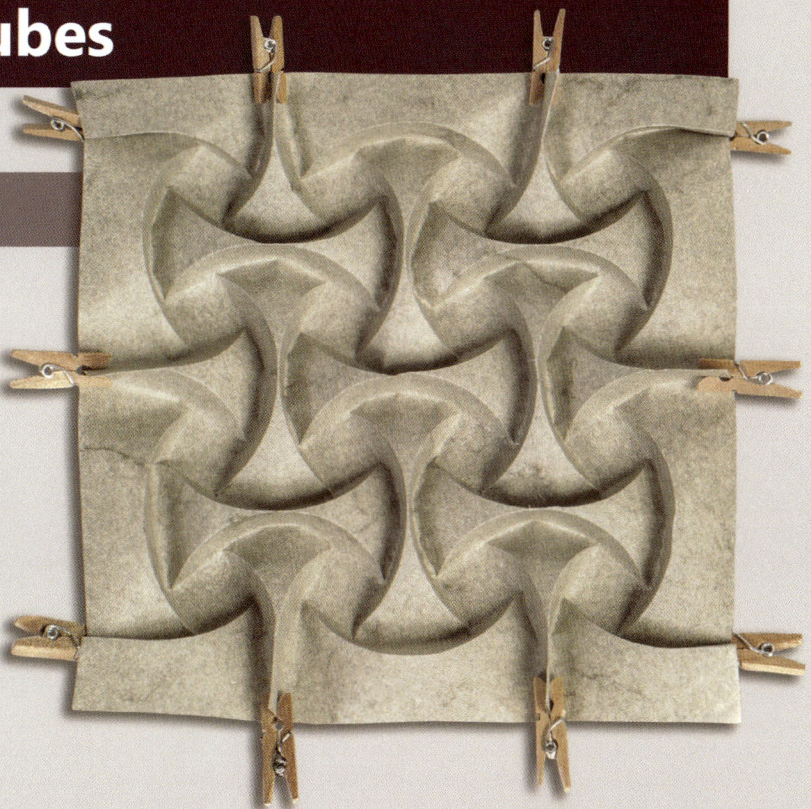

Above: recto view of a 4 by 4–molecule Rounded Cubes tessellation.

Verso view is below.

The Quadilic tessellation is the inspiration for this curved-crease model.

Instead of straight diagonals, there are curved creases connecting the opposing corners.

The easiest way to make these curves is to score the paper with a ballpoint pen with an empty cartridge, using a curved edge (from a glass or a CD) as a template.

The shrinkage ratio is about 3:2.

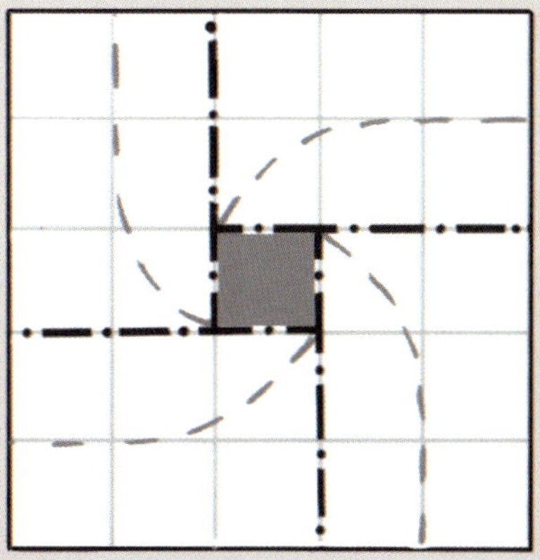

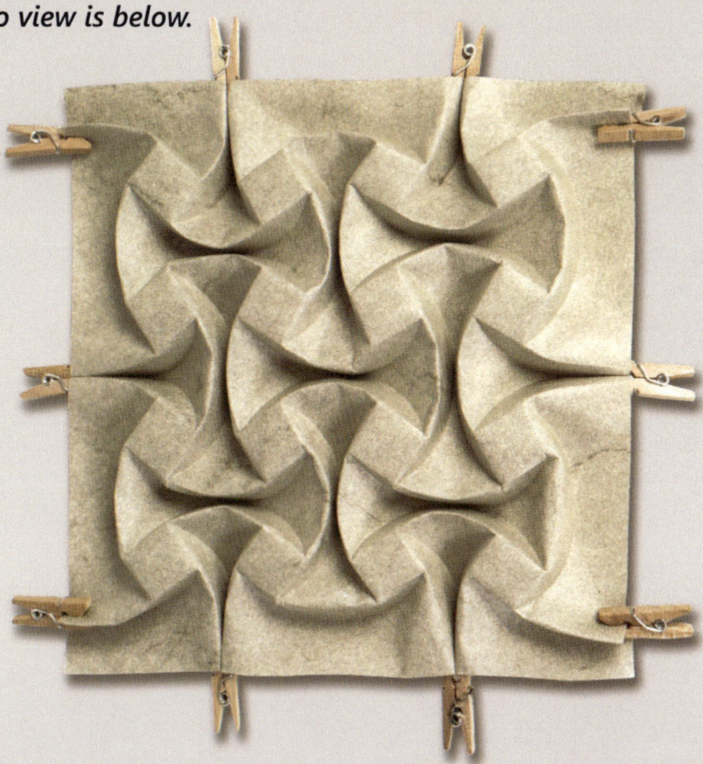

Use the process on pages 47–49 (single Quadilic molecule) to fold this molecule.

2 by 2 Molecules

Use a grid of 8 by 8.

Mark all the creases with a pen on one side of the paper using a curved template.

Form all creases before you start the collapse.

Use the Quadilic collapse process (see page 48).

Since it's more difficult to keep the folds in place, do not hesitate to use clips to hold the edges together.

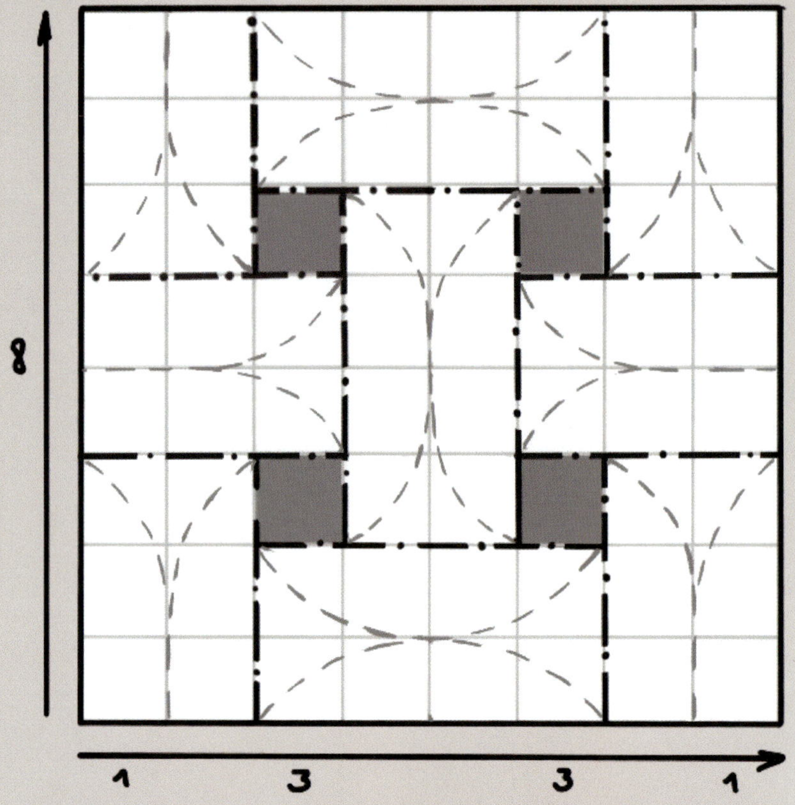

Above and Beyond—Metal Pendant

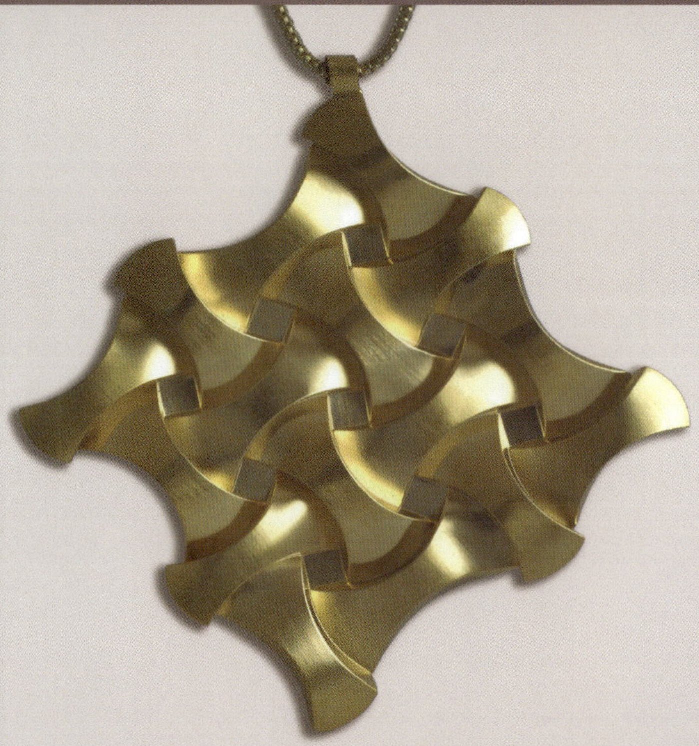

Curvy lines bring a unique aesthetic to this 3 by 3 molecule pendant made from a sheet of brass, especially when the finish is matte. Unlike the paper version, the curves do not meet in the center. Instead, they form a gap that refines the model.

4 by 4 Molecules

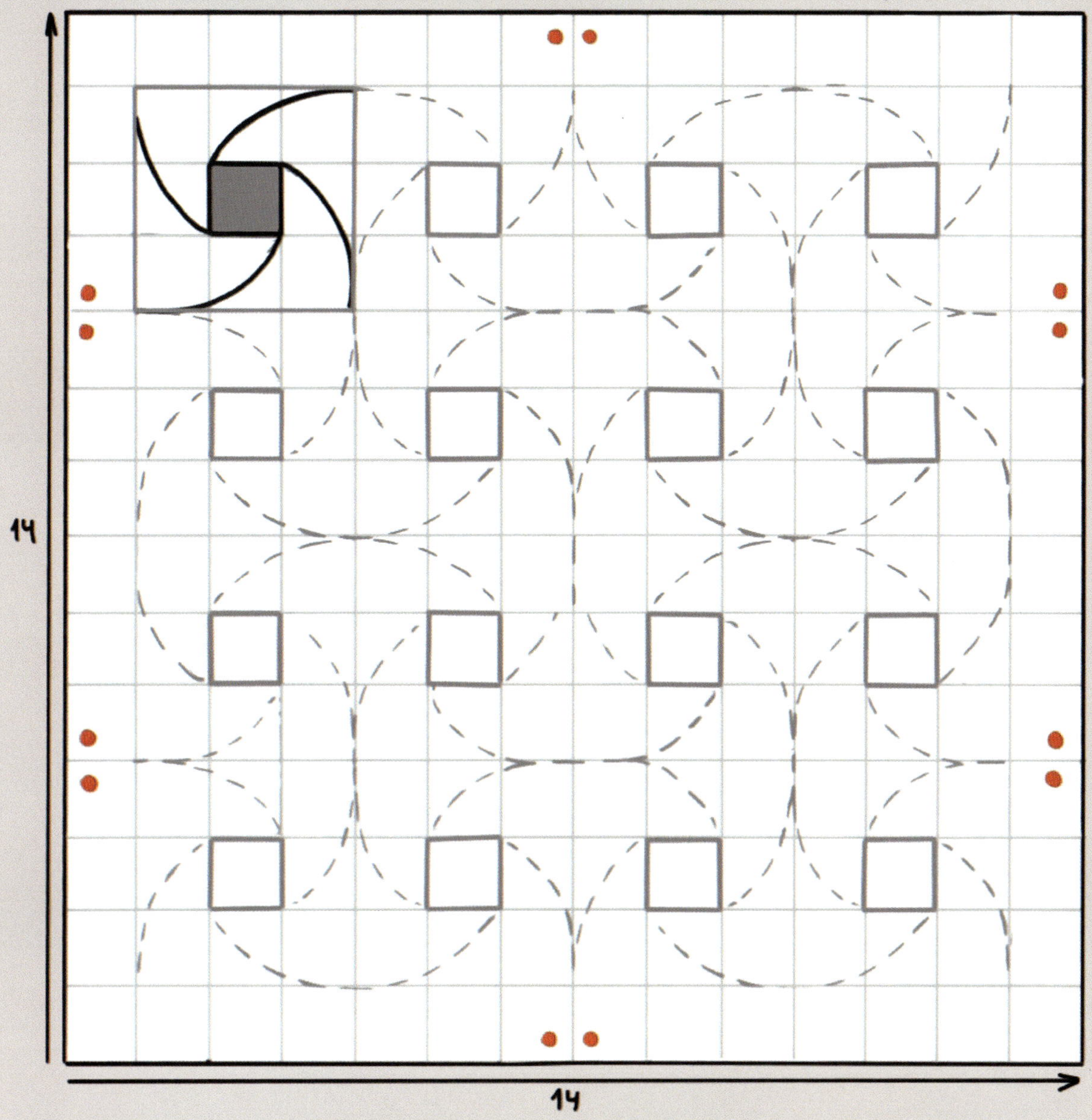

Use a 14 by 14 grid for this project:
1 + 4 x 3 + 1 = 14

The final result will be around 10 squares wide.

Like the Quadilic tessellations, there are no shortcuts or specific order for folding.

Form all the creases before you start the collapse.

Start with the outer molecules; pinch the dots together and hold them with clips. Then push the inner molecules into the collapsed position.

2 6 Water Bomb

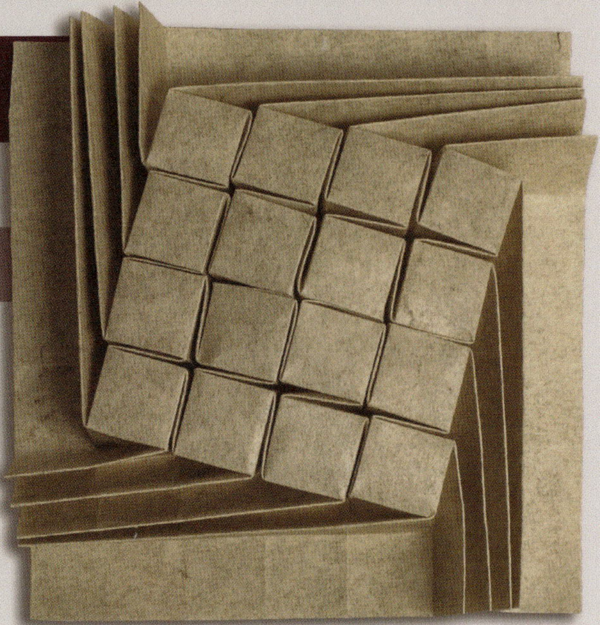

The Single Molecule

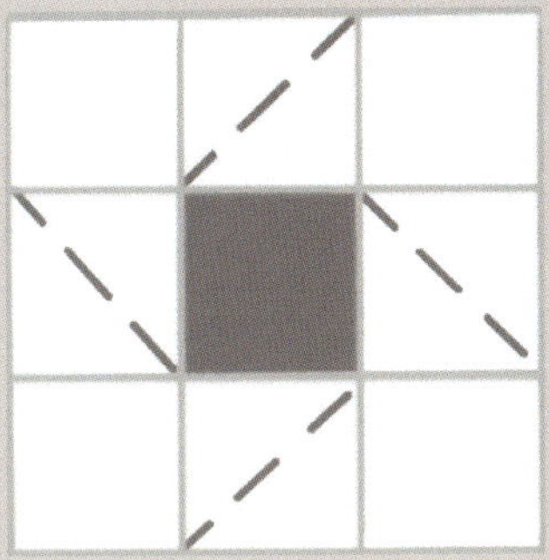

The molecule is identical to the Cubes tessellation molecule. The difference is in the way the molecules are grouped together.

This model was designed by Ron Resch.

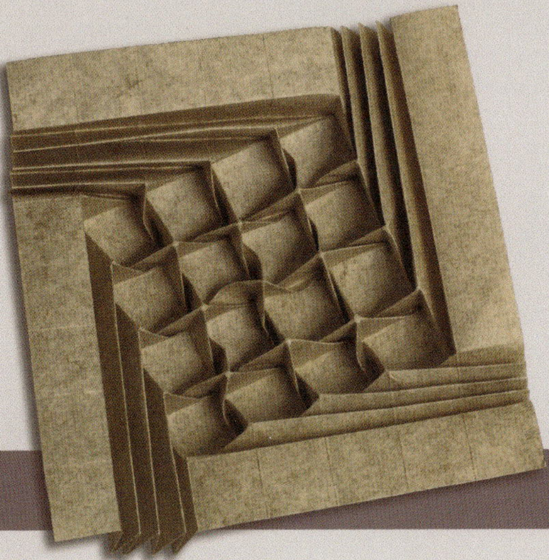

Above: recto view of a 4 by 4–molecule Water Bomb tessellation.

Verso view is to the left.

2 by 2 Molecules

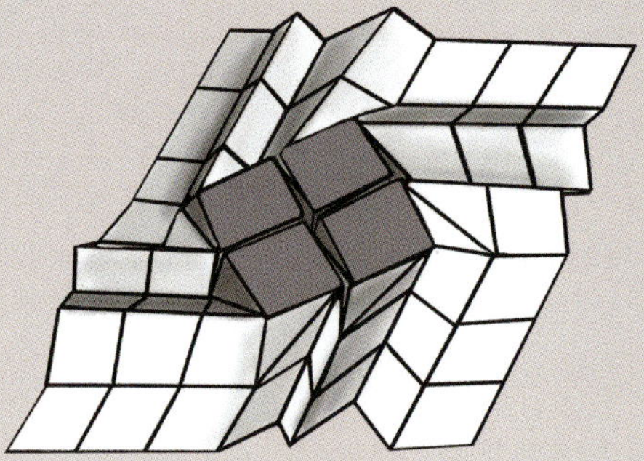

Use a grid of 8 by 8.

Here the molecules are not mirrored. Instead, the central square of the next molecule is shifted in a Chess Knight move.

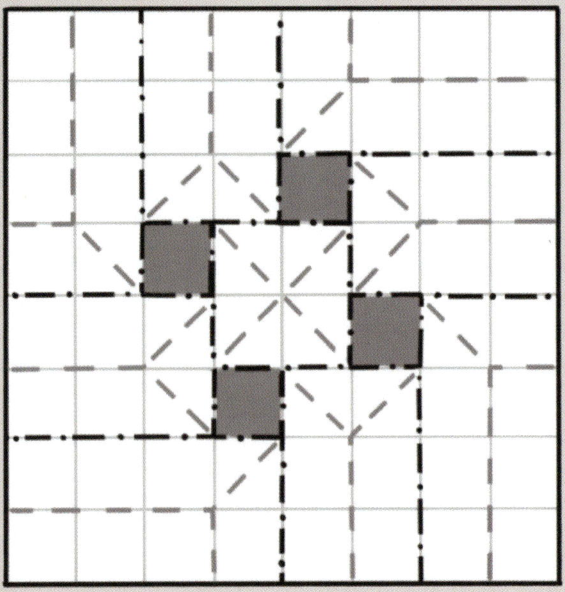

This grouping of the four molecules creates a water bomb base in the center of them all, formed by four diagonals joined together.

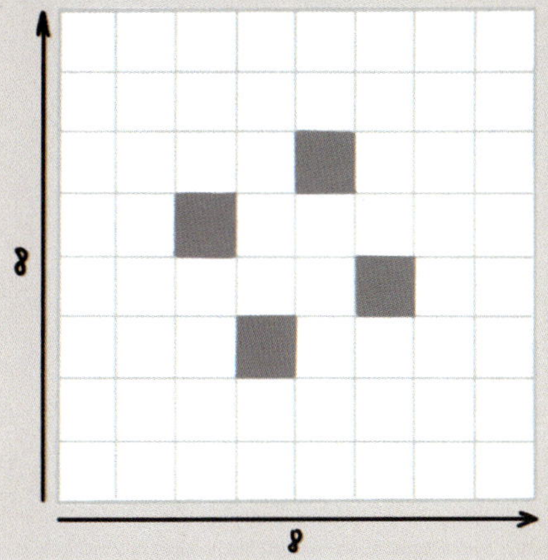

Start with an 8 by 8 grid and mark off the central squares

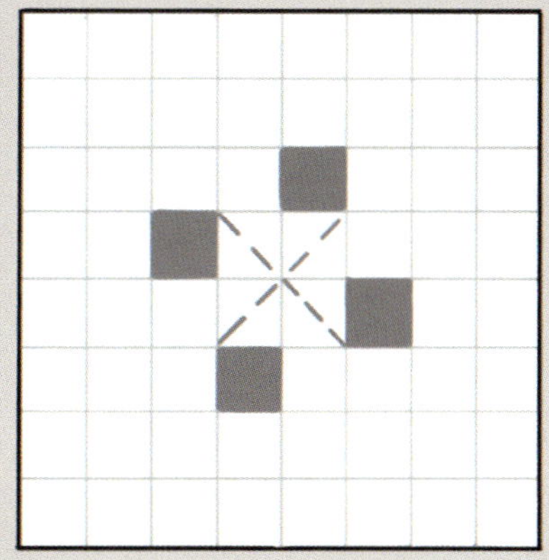

Crease the X between the four squares.

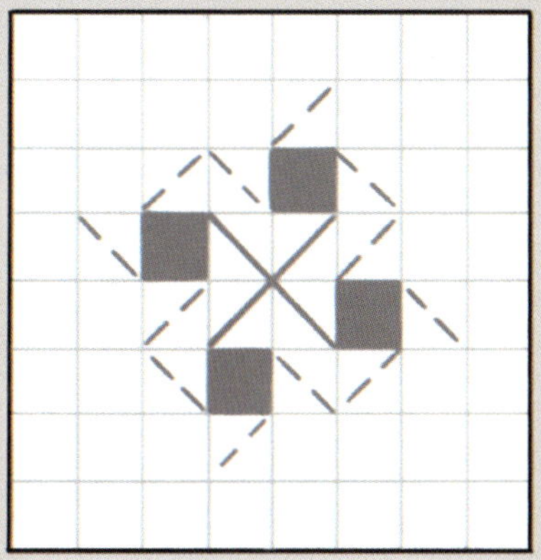

Surround each square with the other three valleys needed.

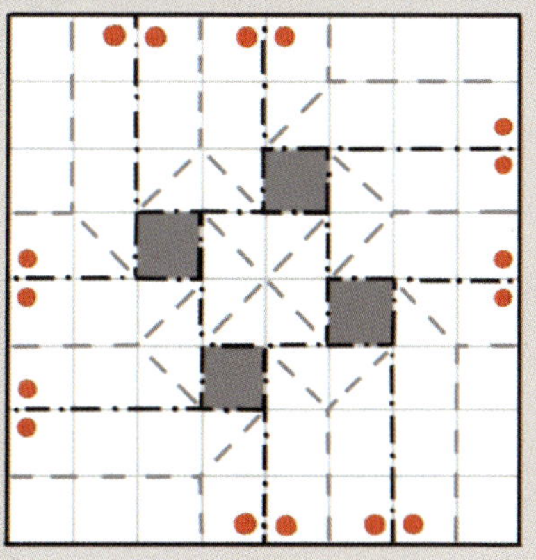

Add the remaining creases as shown.

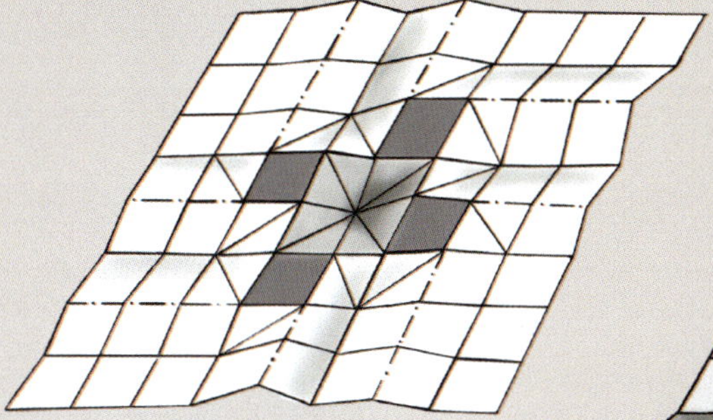

Note the twin mountain folds extending out to the edges. Begin the collapse there. Form all the mountain lines from the squares to the edges in pairs.

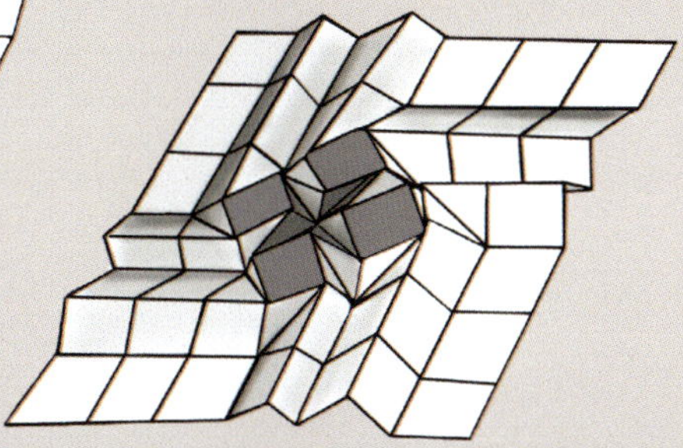

In process. Note the water bomb base is forming in the center.

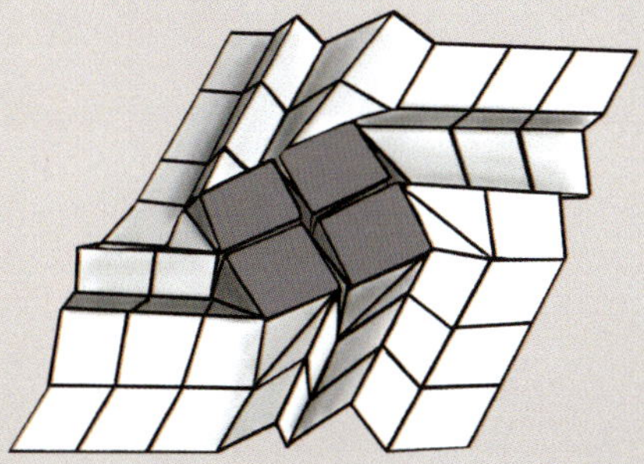

Close up the water bomb base in the center to complete the move.

Understanding the Structure

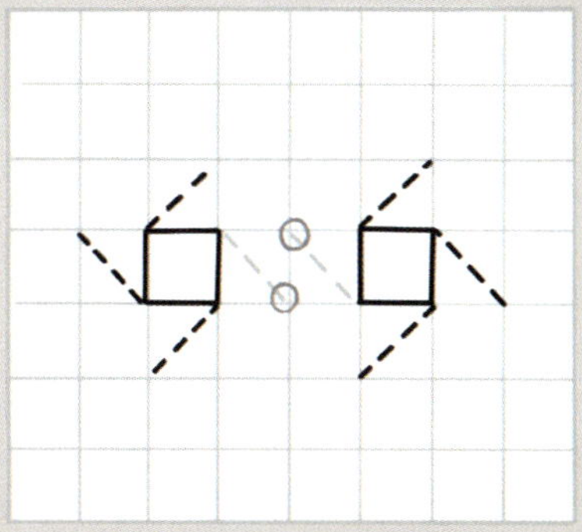

These diagrams show why shifting a molecule to the right is not enough;
a conflict is created where valleys (in gray) don't meet.

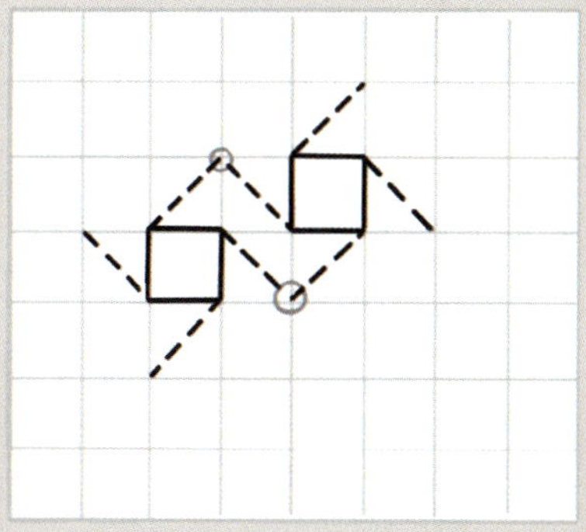

Taking the right molecule one square to the left and one up fixes this problem (now the valleys meet).

4 by 4 Molecules

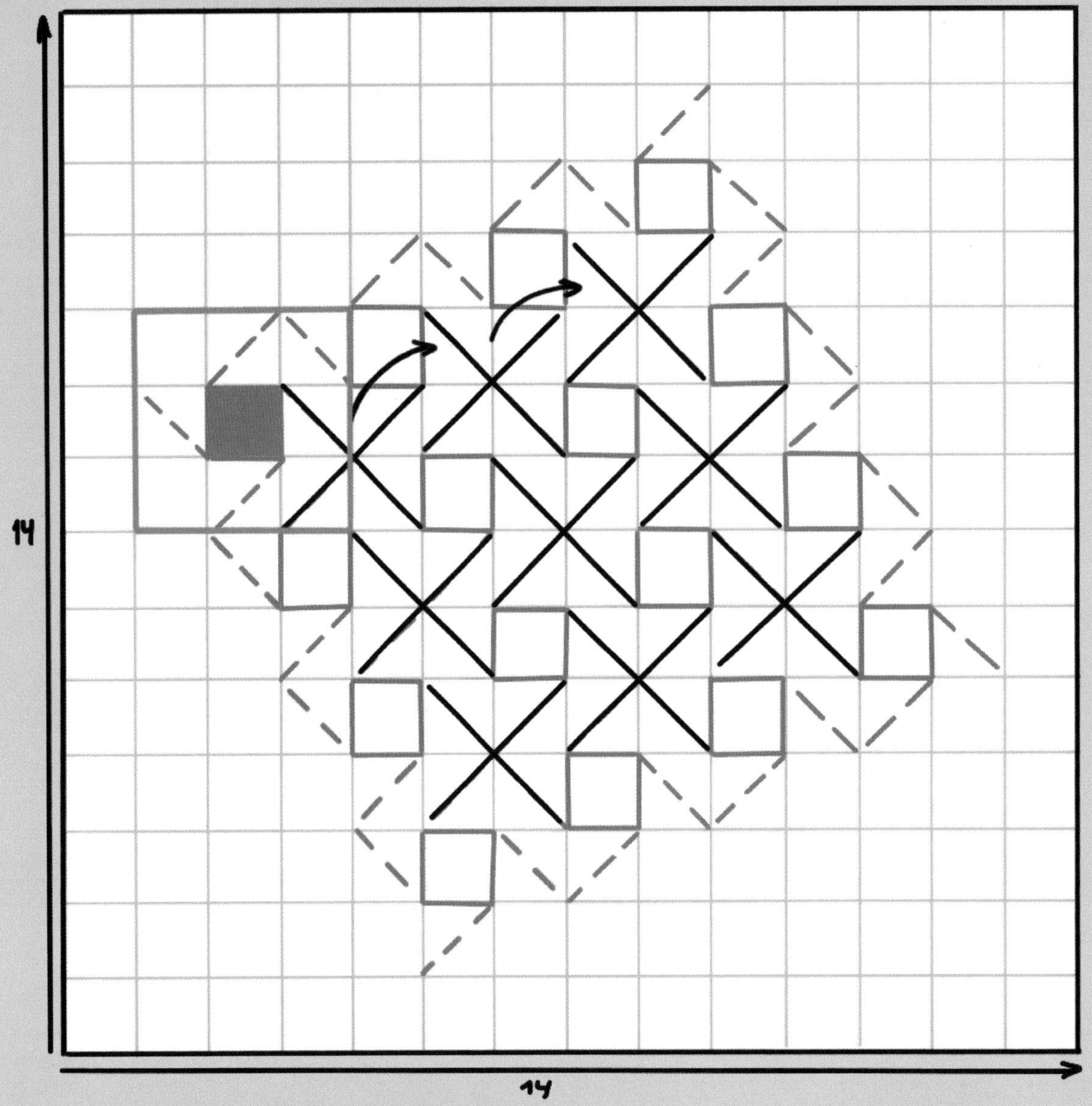

Start with a 14 by 14 grid. The fact that the molecules are shifted (and not mirrored as with the Cubes tessellation), doesn't change the way to calculate the final sheet size. The grid used is exactly the same size as for a 4 by 4-Cubes project.

If you mark a diagonal line from the left-most molecule to the right-most one, you can see why—every molecule needs a 3 by 3 space, and there are four molecules on this line.

The final result will be six squares wide.

There is no particular best order for the precreases, since none is aligned with any other, but it is easier if you put in all the Xs first.

The collapse is done around the water bombs (the Xs). Make the first one on the outer rim and continue along the edge (following the arrows).

Complete the model by following this process on the next rows of Xs.

Above and Beyond—Sheep

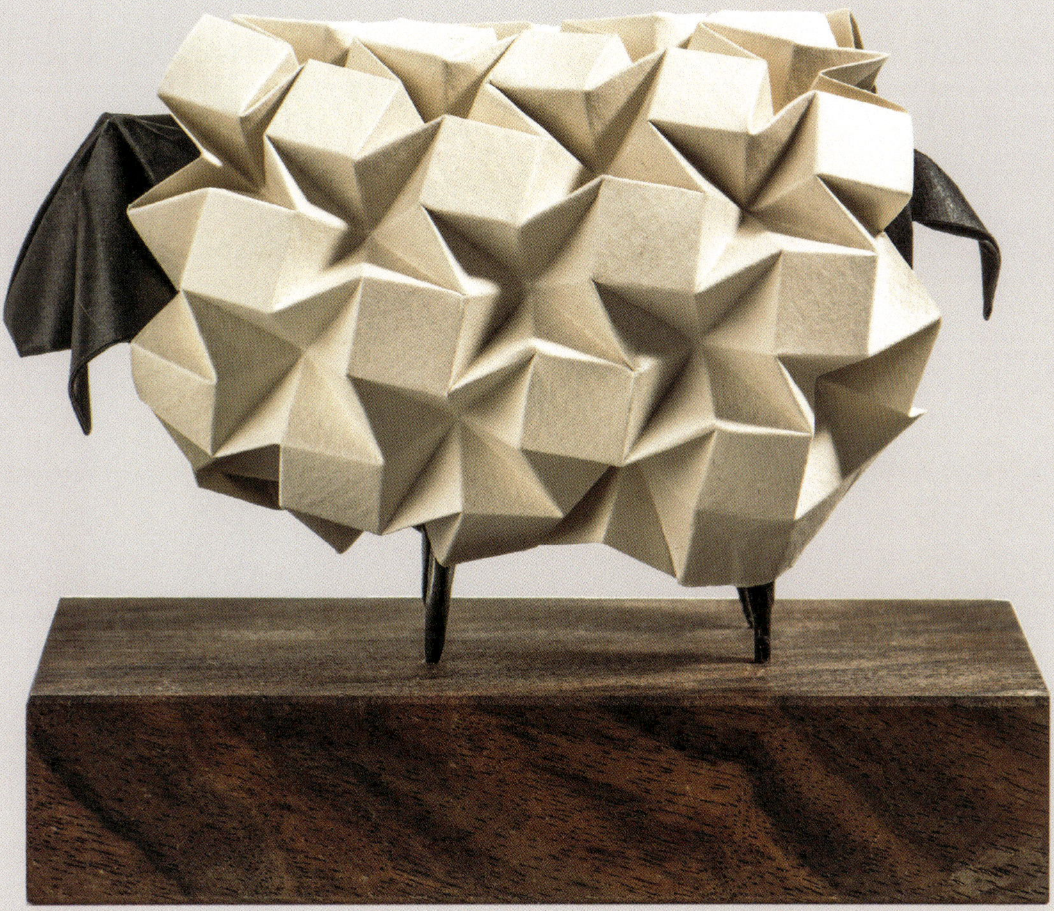

This model by Beth Johnson uses a Water Bomb tessellation to form the body of a sheep. Image courtesy of Beth Johnson.

27 Gradient

The Single Molecule

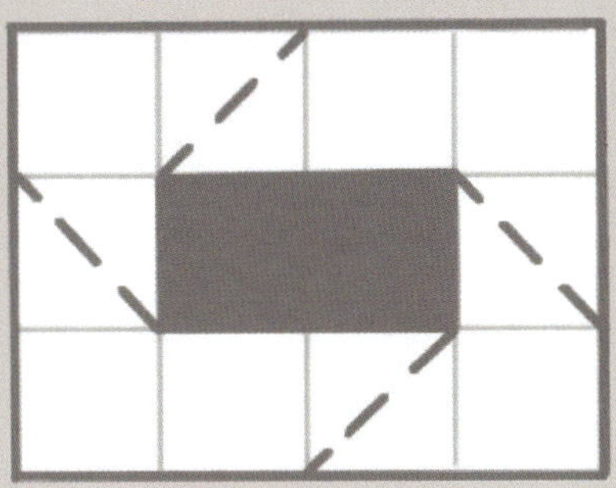

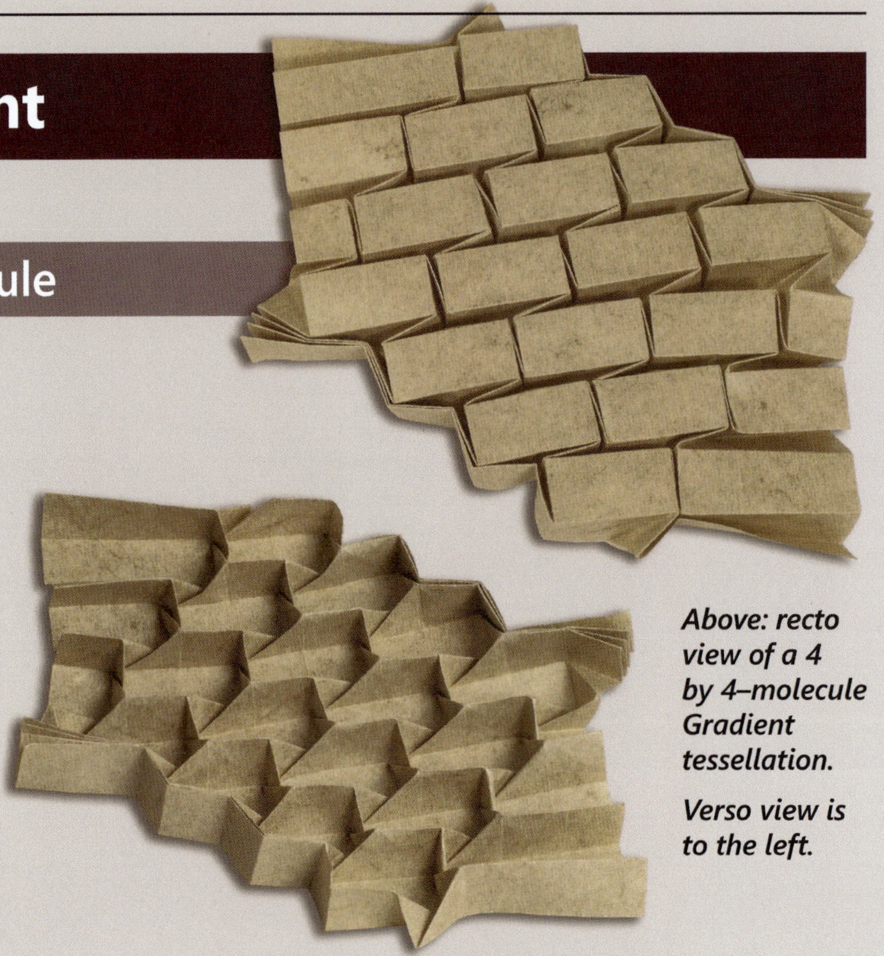

Above: recto view of a 4 by 4–molecule Gradient tessellation.

Verso view is to the left.

This Cubes variation uses a center rectangle instead of a square. But nothing else has changed in the molecule.

The shrinkage ratio is 3:1 vertically and 2:1 horizontally.

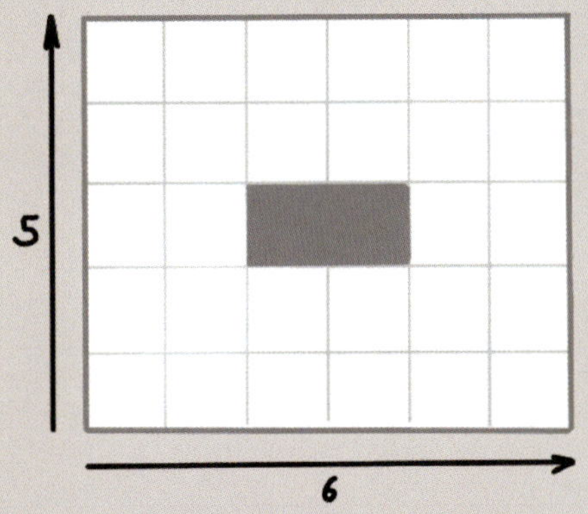

Use a 5 by 6 grid. Mark the central rectangle of 1:2.

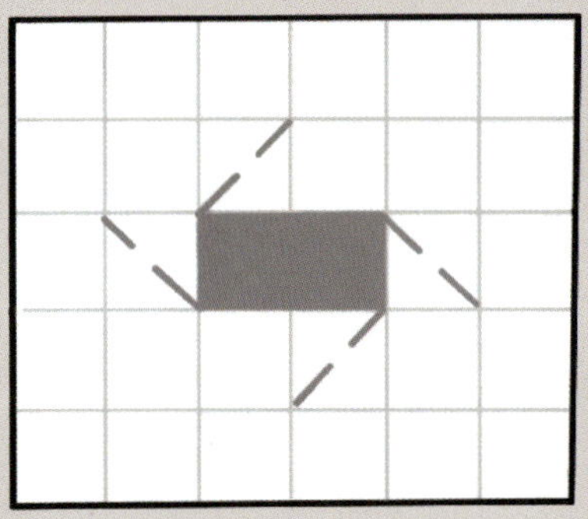

Valley fold the four diagonals around the rectangle.

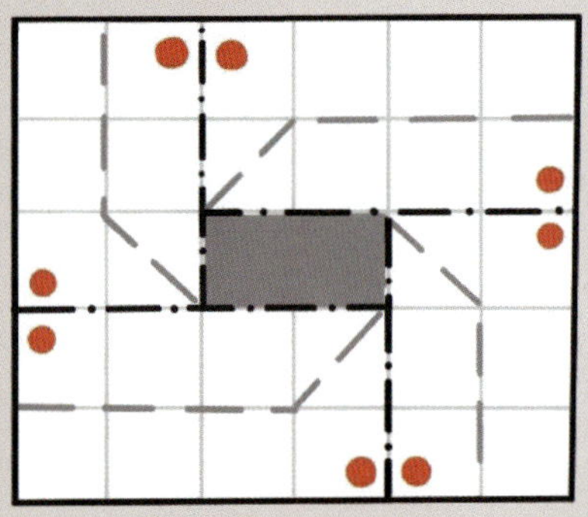

All the needed creases are shown.

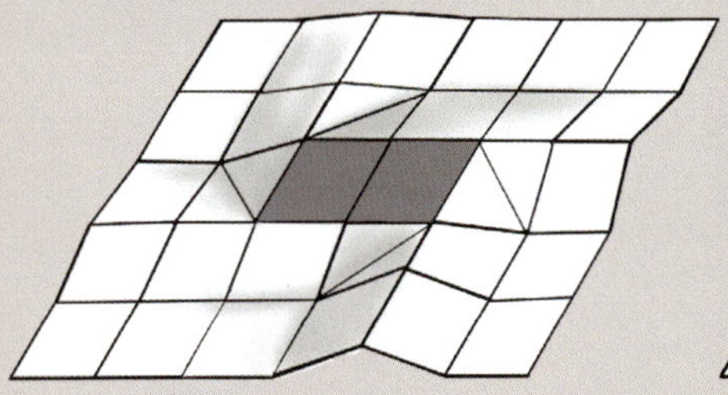

Start the collapse by pinching the mountains.

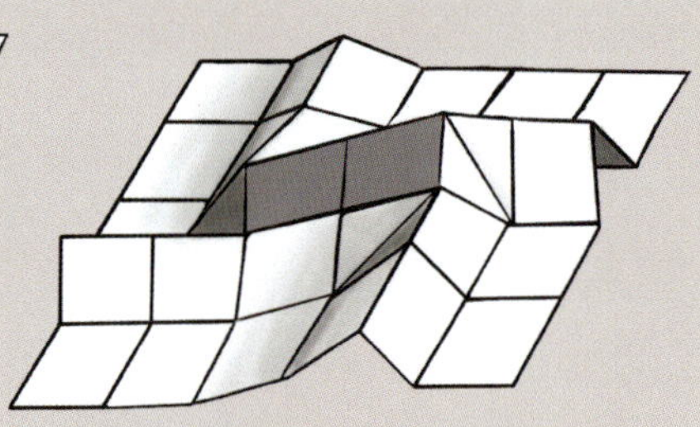

In process.

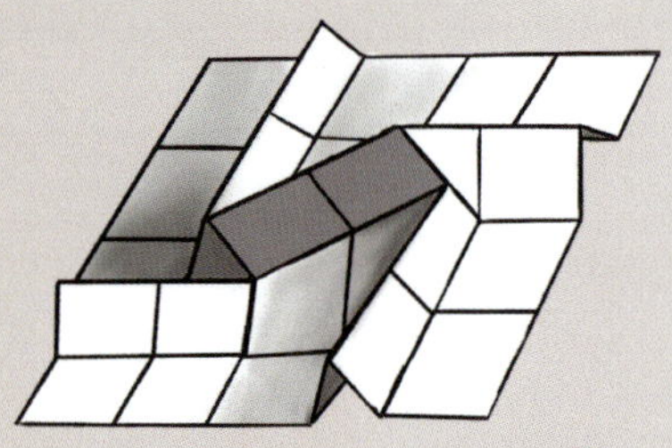

Fully collapsed, the central rectangle is rotated by 45°.

2 by 2 Molecules

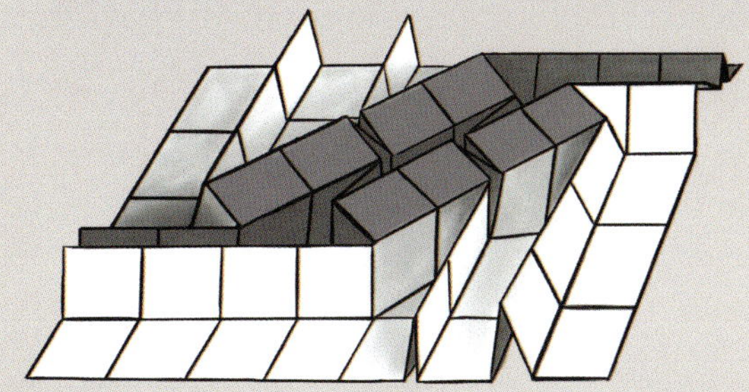

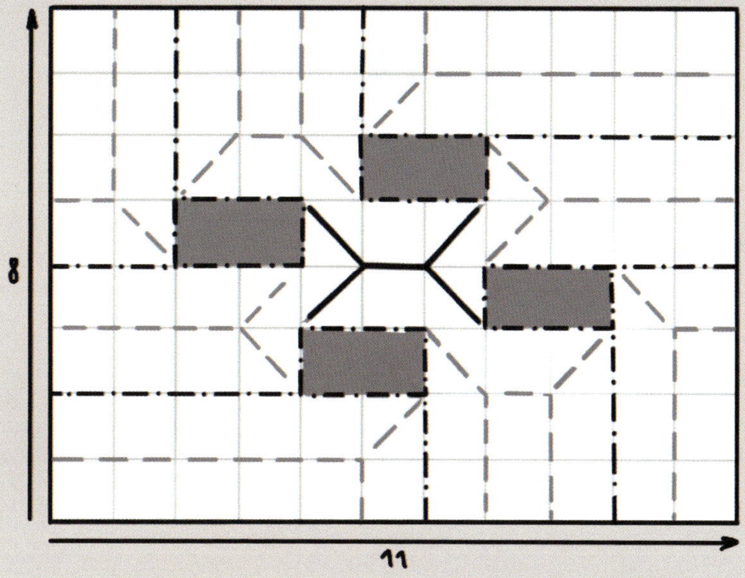

Use a 8 by 11 grid.

Collapse the mountain folds that go to the edges first, and then add the stretched water bomb base in the middle.

Every central rectangle is now rotated by 22.5°. Since the long mountains are forced to go by the grid lines, this model cannot lie flat, unless you add more molecules to cover the grid.

Understanding the Structure

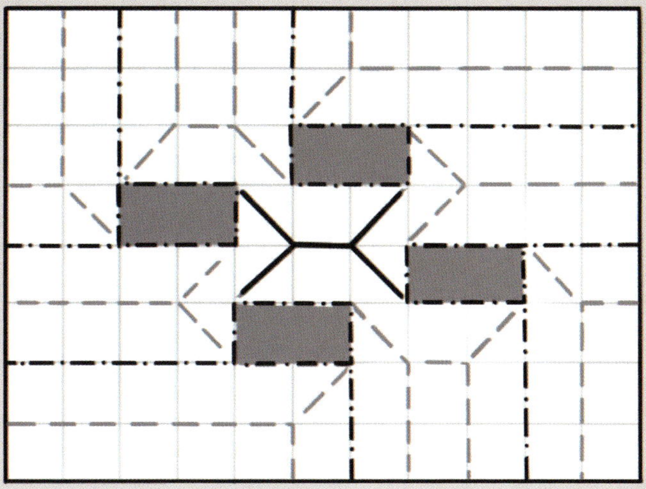

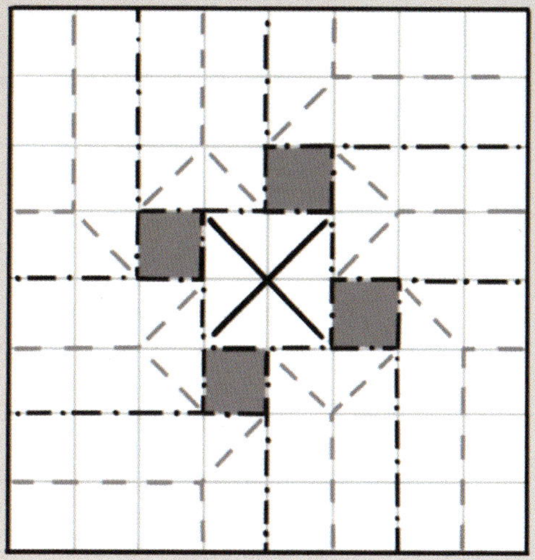

When you compare the Gradient molecule (above) with the Water Bomb molecule (right), you can see there is a shift in the CP. With Gradient, every central square has increased in size, while the diagonal creases have moved further from the center to stay on the corners of the new rectangle.

Unlike shifting a full column (or row) of molecules, the shift on the larger rectangular molecule is smaller, resulting in a gradient.

4 by 4 Molecules

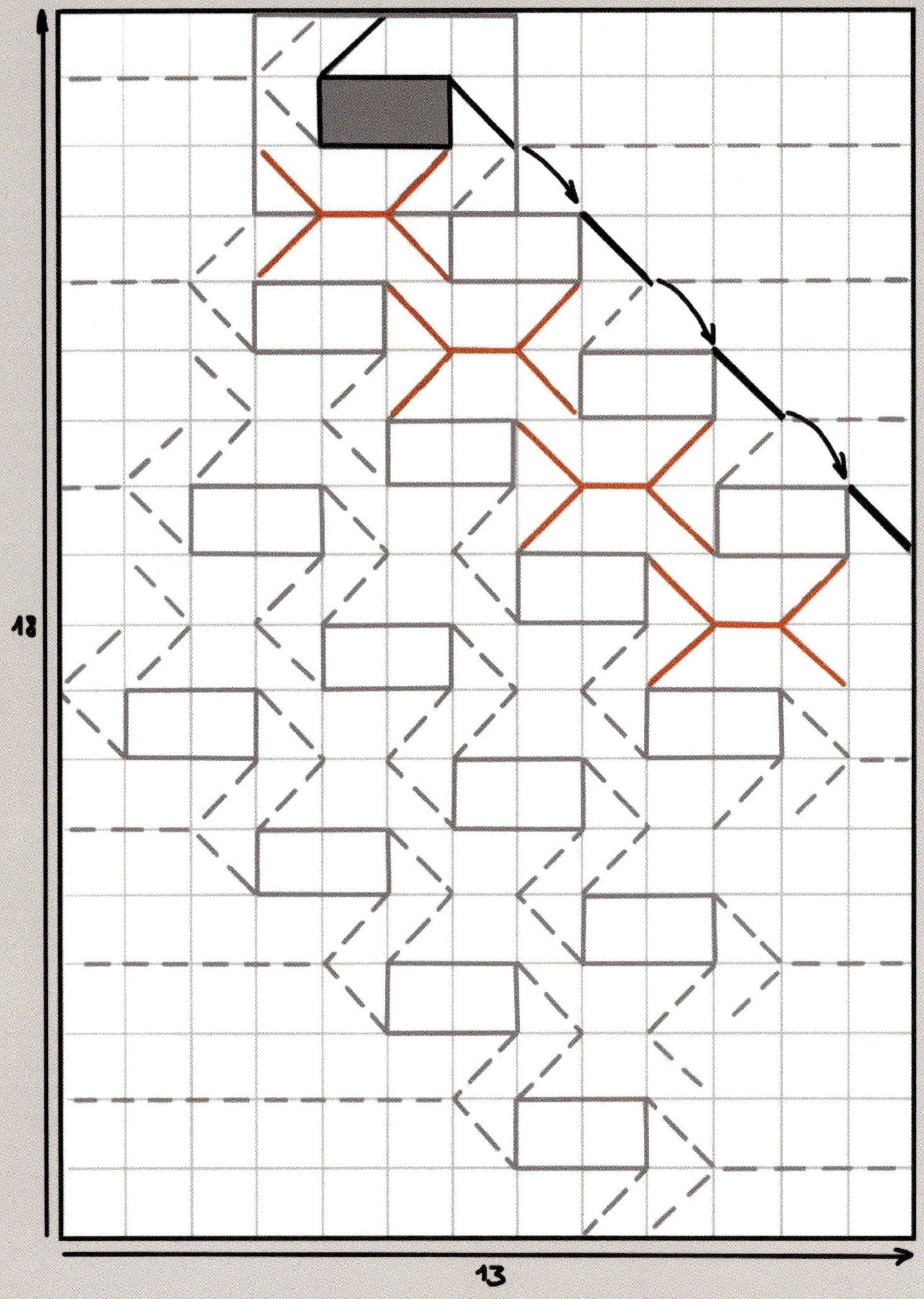

Use an 18 by 13 grid.

For the height, count six complete molecules, so the formula is 6 x 3 = 18.

Width wise, every molecule overlaps the next by a square:

4 x 4 – 3 x 1 = 13.

The final result will be eight squares wide by seven squares high.

There is a shortcut for folding the short side diagonals—fold the diagonal of the first molecule, skip a square and repeat. Add all the other creases when this is done.

Start the collapse by forming the extended water bomb base on the top (marked in orange). While doing that, make sure the 1:2 rectangles are always kept straight and level, rising above the extended water bomb bases.

Continue to add water bomb bases as you go down and to the right.

Above and Beyond—A 10 by 10 Project

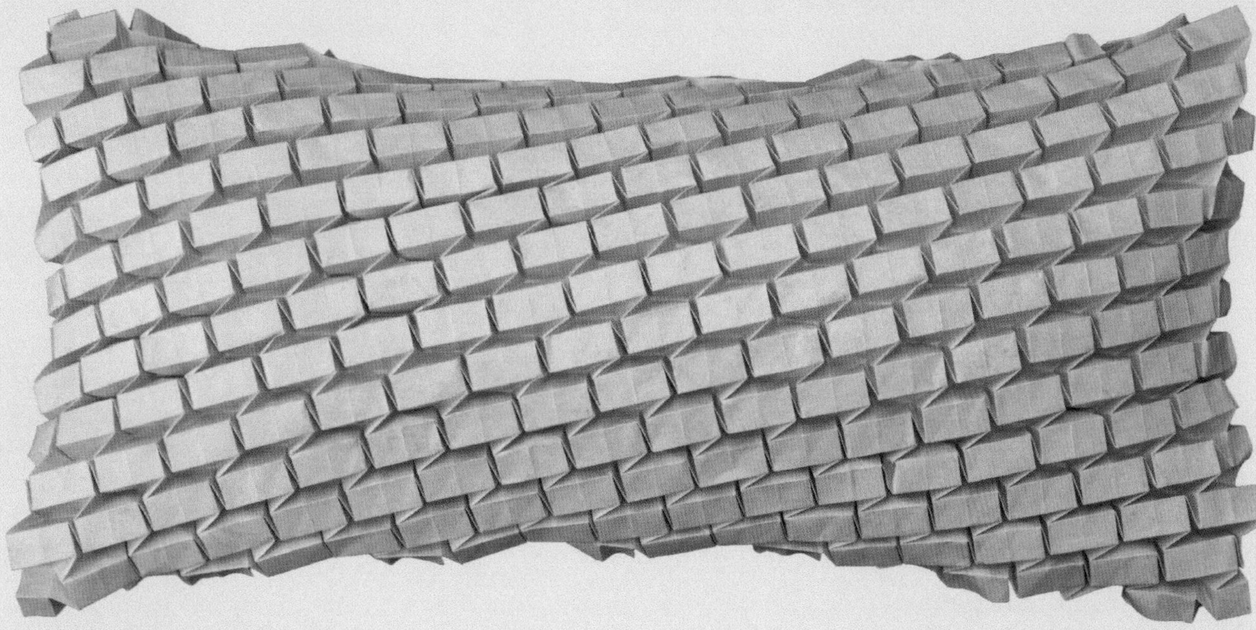

This picture of a finished 10 by 10–molecule project, folded on white elephant hide, shows why I call this tessellation "Gradient." Below is the verso view.

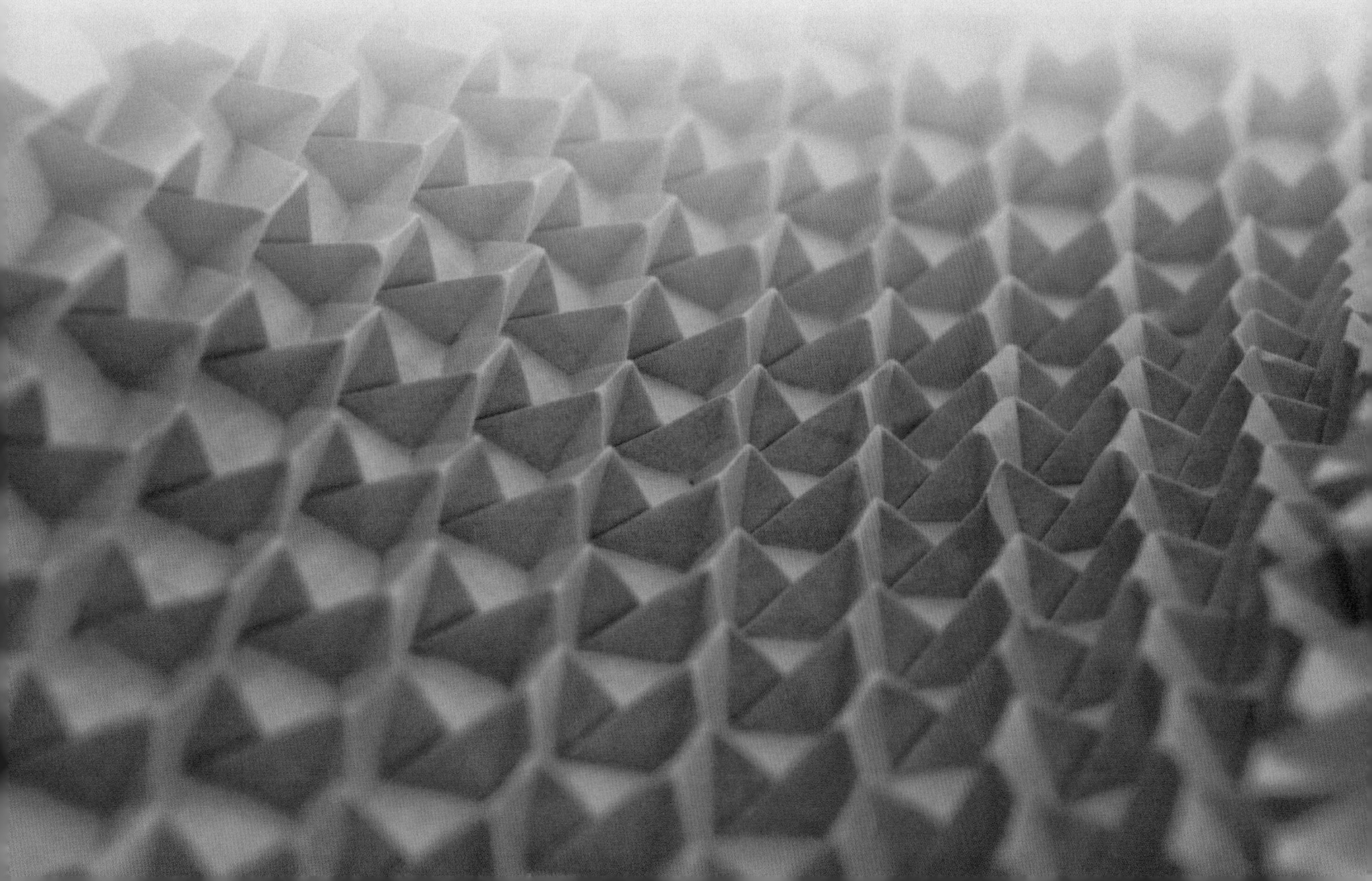

2 8 Rotated Bricks

The Single Molecule

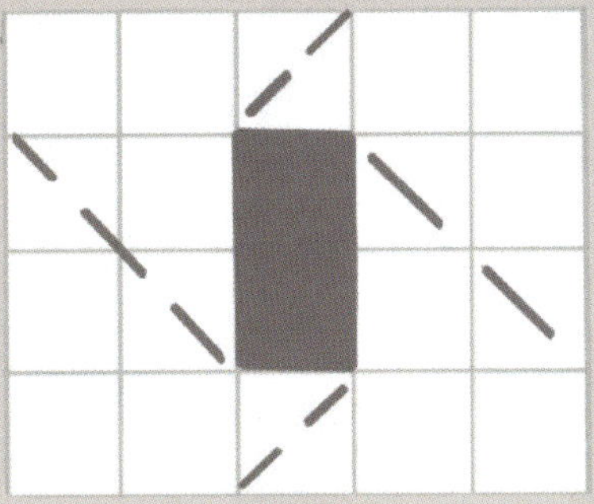

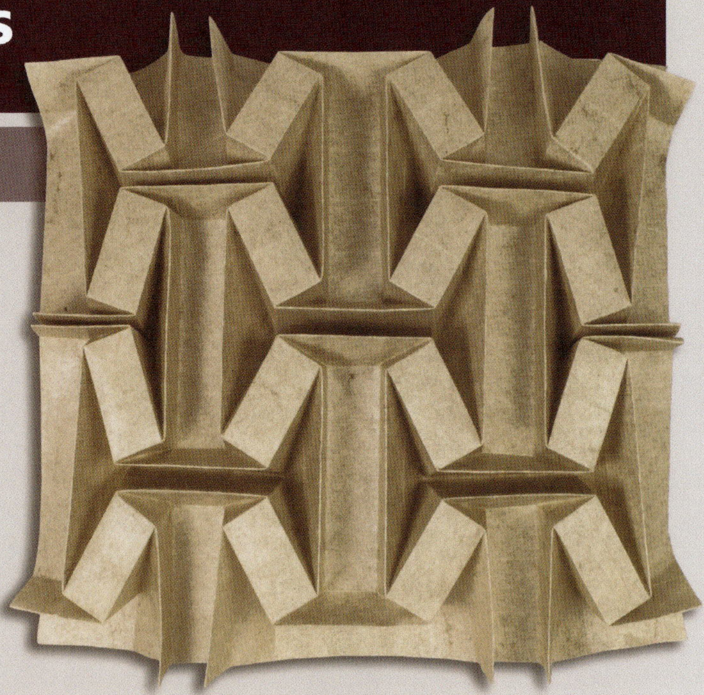

While the structure of Gradient doesn't allow a full 90° rotation, using the longer diagonals makes it possible to rotate further.

Yet the fact that two diagonals are double the length increases their height to two squares, while the short diagonals are one square high only. This creates a conflict, which can be resolved with a sink fold (shown in 2 by 2 CP next page).

Shrinkage ratio is 5:1 horizontally and 2:1 vertically.

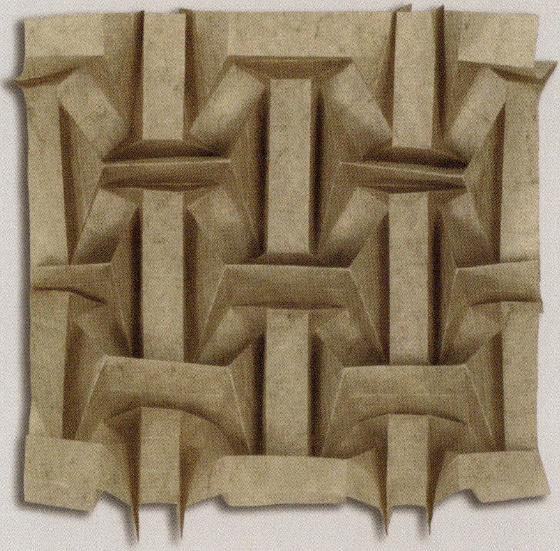

Above: recto view of a 4 by 4–molecule Rotated Bricks tessellation.

Verso view is to the left.

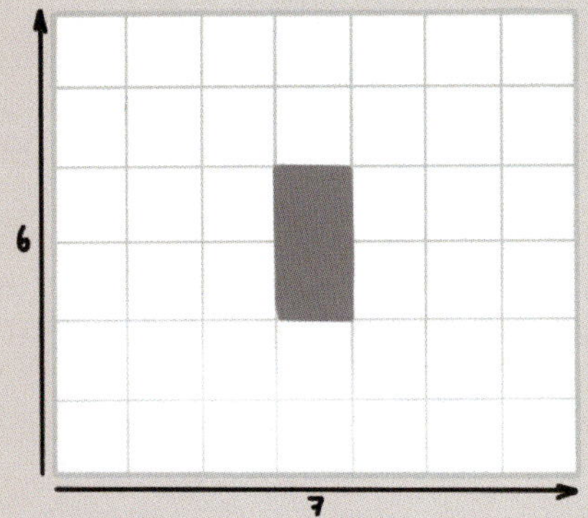

Start with a grid of 6 by 7. Mark the central rectangle.

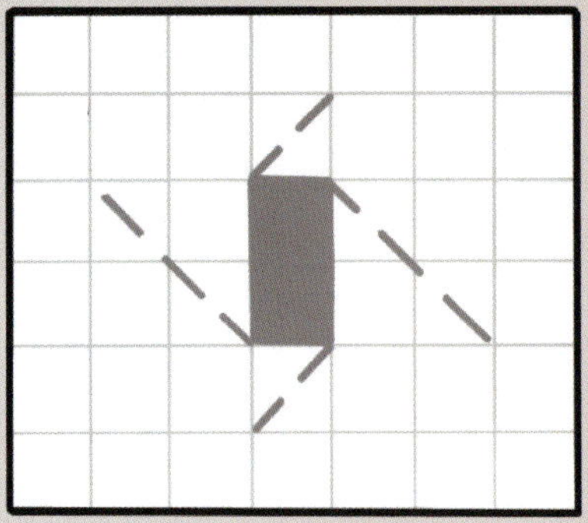

Add the precreases: two short diagonals and two long ones (double the length).

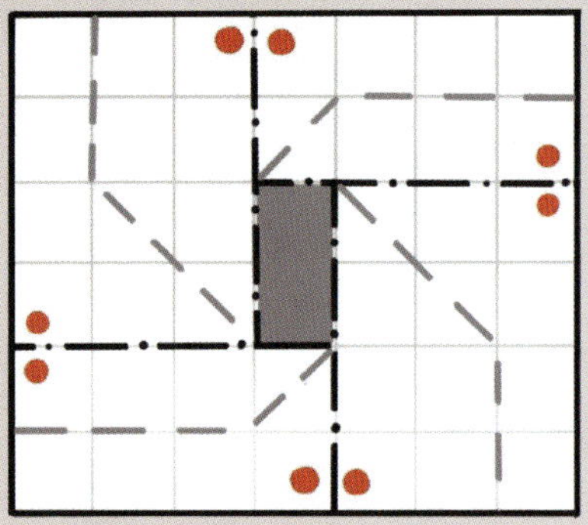

Add remaining creases as shown.

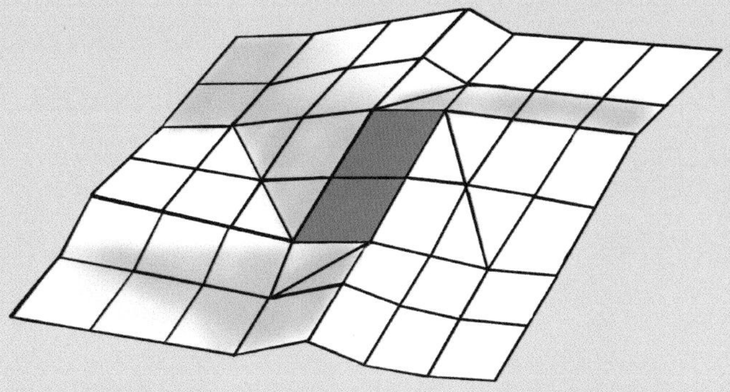

Pinch the mountains to start the collapse.

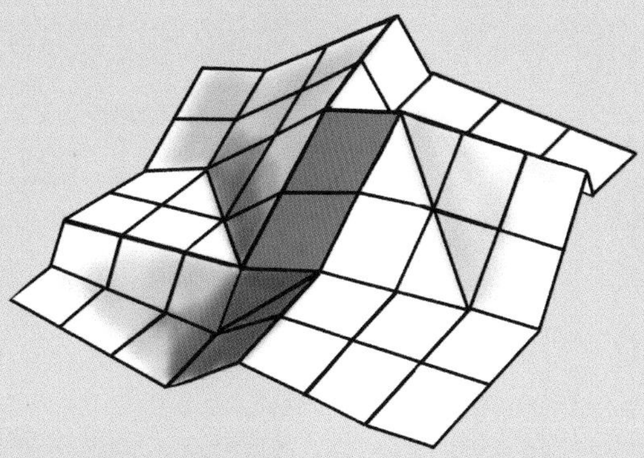

In process.

As the collapse progresses, you can see that the layers around the long sides are two squares high, but only one square high at the short sides.

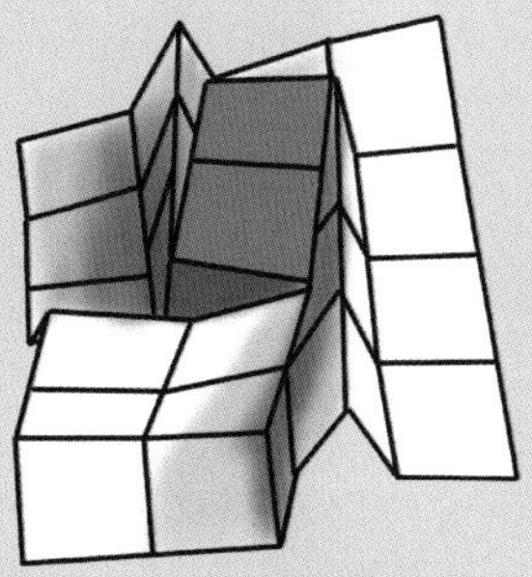

Fully collapsed.

The central rectangle was rotated by 90°.

2 by 2 Molecules

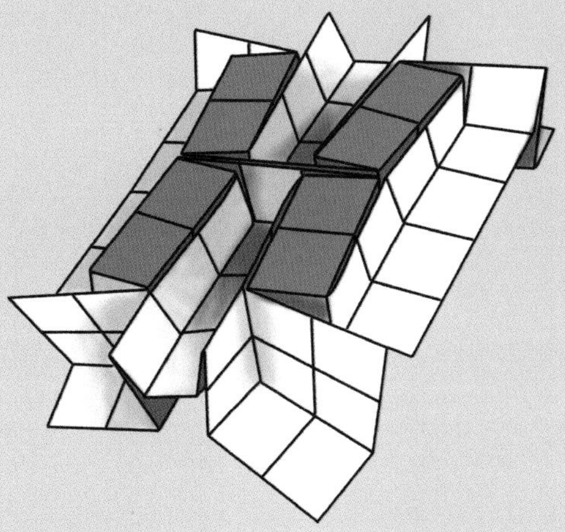

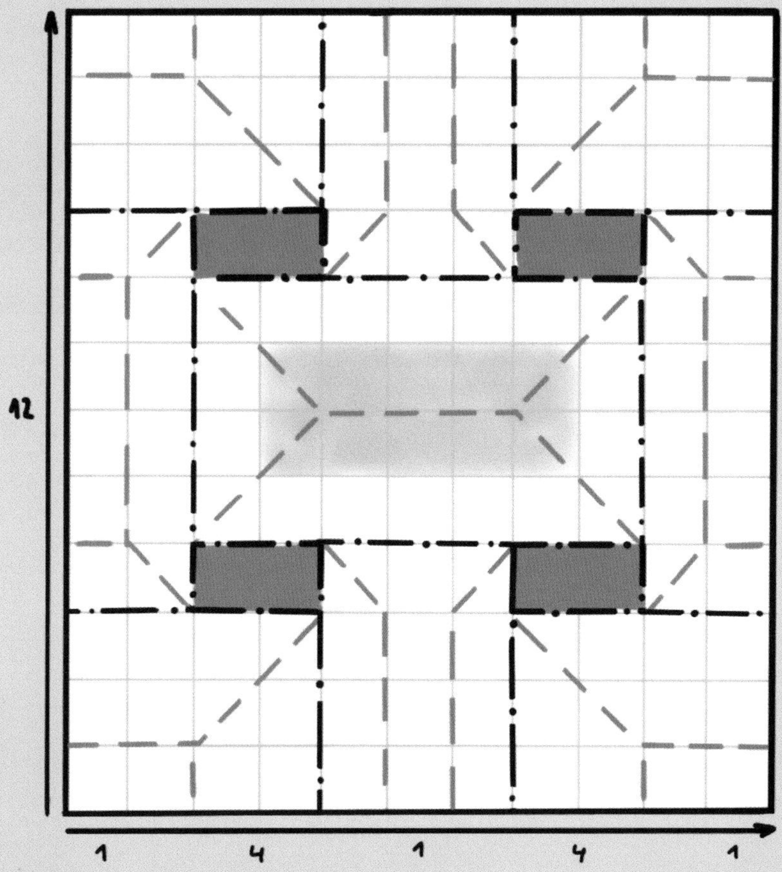

Use a grid of 12 by 11.

Here molecules are mirrored and a vertical line of space was added.

Add all precreases and start to collapse from the top left corner.

Note that the marked area (in gray) has the height of two squares. You can adjust that by making an open sink fold (mentioned before) at the end of the collapse.

4 by 4 Molecules

Single Spacing

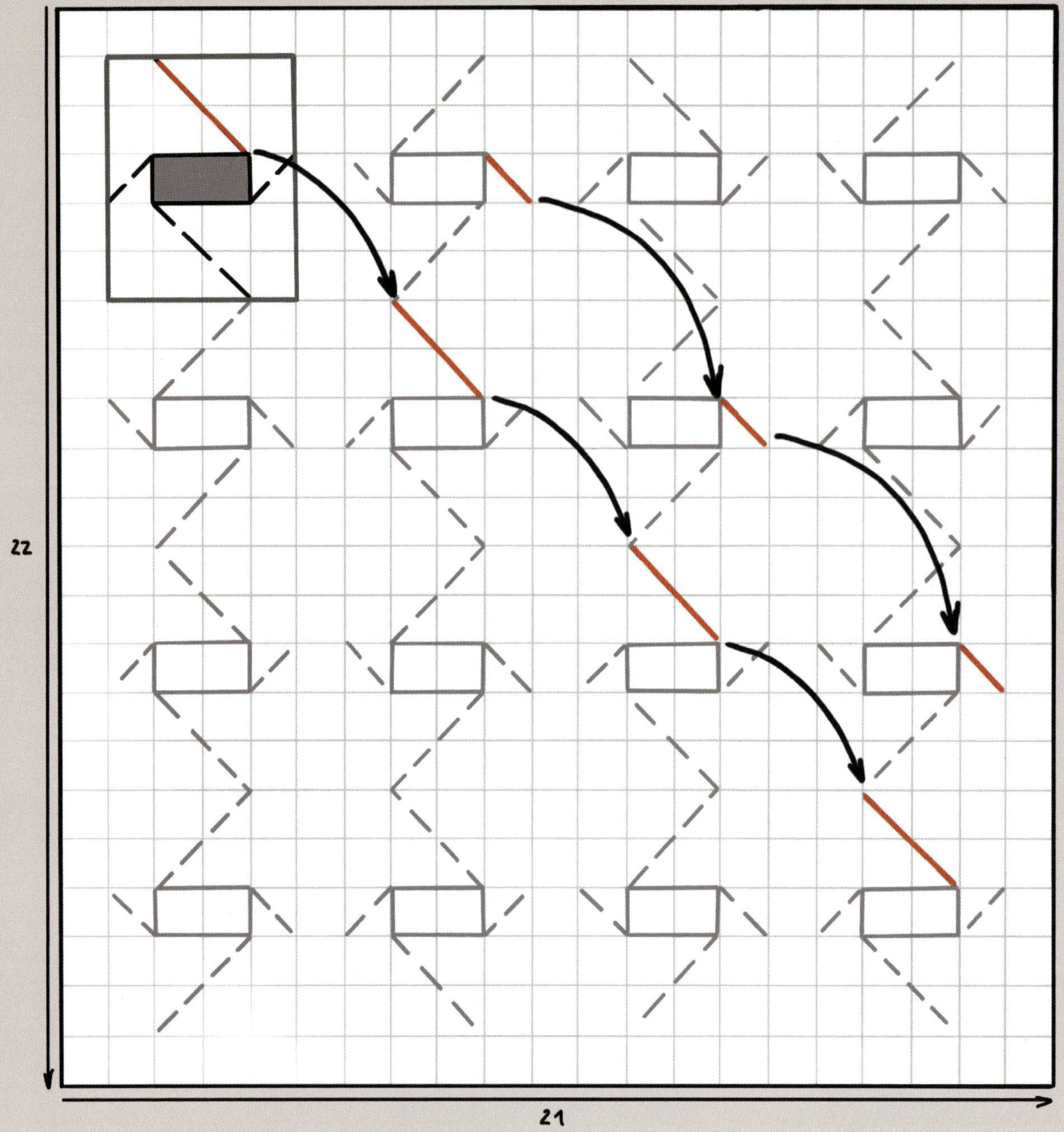

Make a 22 by 21 grid.
The formula for the height is 1 + 4 x 5 + 1 = 22. For the width it is 4 x 4 + 5 x 1 = 21. The final result will be 10 squares height and 9 squares wide.

Luckily, the added spacing creates two shortcuts.

For the long diagonals it is fold two, skip three.

For the short diagonals it is fold one, skip four.

Start the collapse in upper left corner and proceed from left to right, row by row.

This version has vertical columns one space wide between the molecules (following the 4 by 4–molecule project image).

If you want to sink the central area to close up that space, do it after you finish the collapse.

4 by 4 Molecules

No Spacing

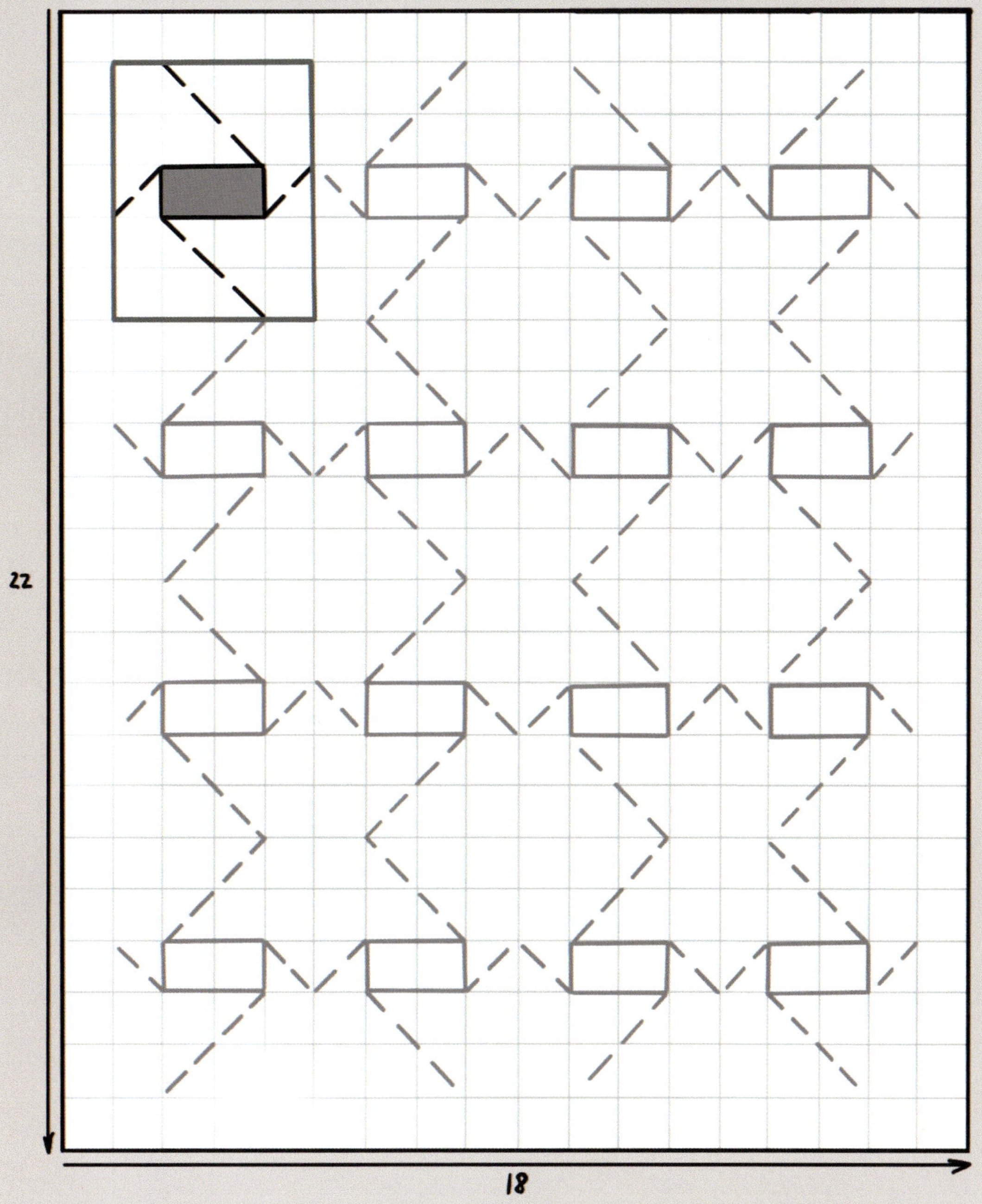

Here is the diagram of the same model, but without the vertical spacing.

Make a grid 22 by 18 grid.

The formula for the height is 1 + 4 x 5 + 1 = 22.

For the width it is 1 + 4 x 4 + 1 = 18. The final result is 10 squares high and 6 squares wide.

You can see here that the lack of the spacing eliminates the shortcuts!

Start the collapse in the upper left corner and proceed from left to right.

Above and Beyond—An 8 by 8 Project (detail)

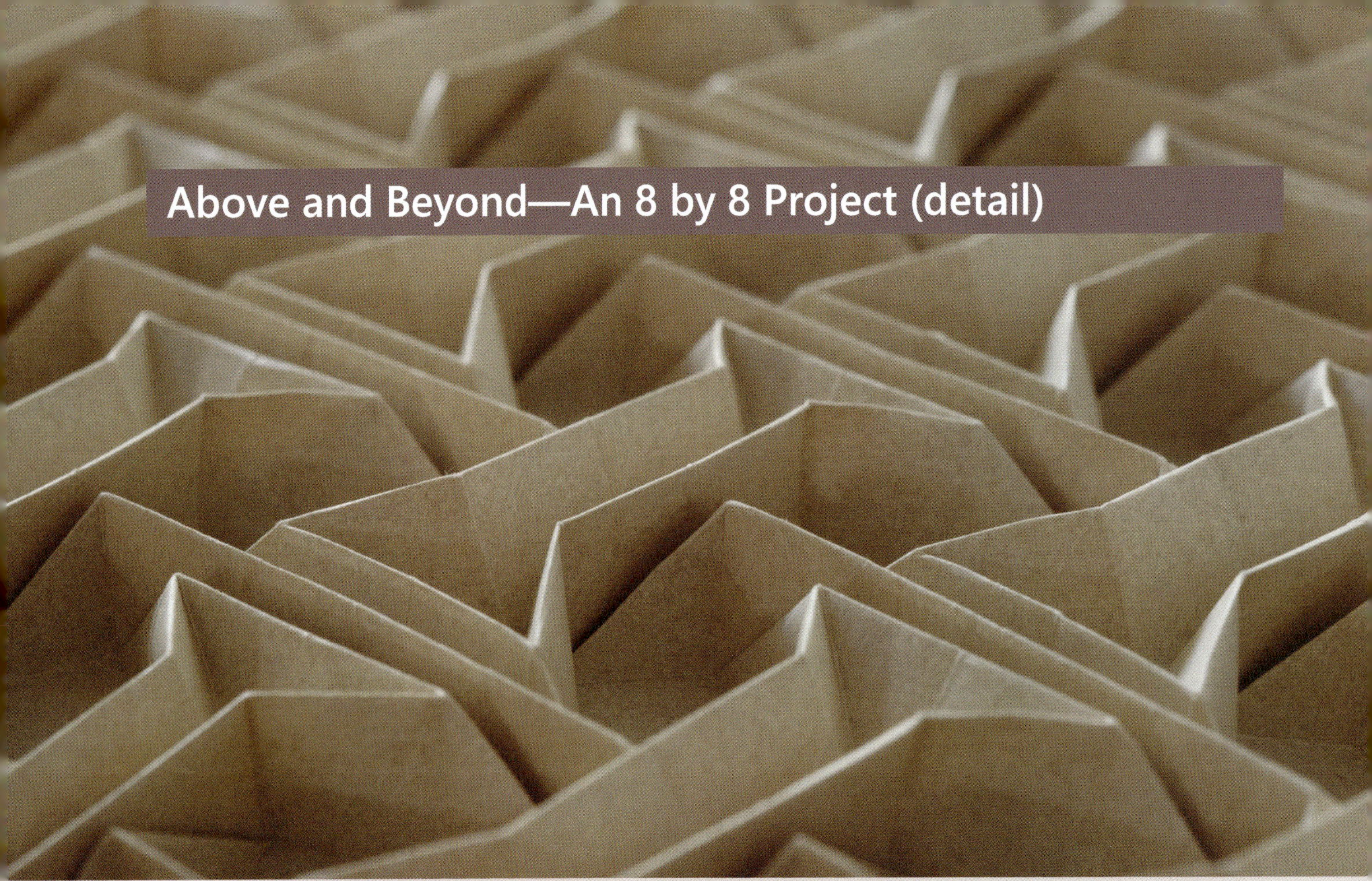

Both sides of a Rotated Bricks project folded from white elephant hide. The molecules do not have any spacing in between.

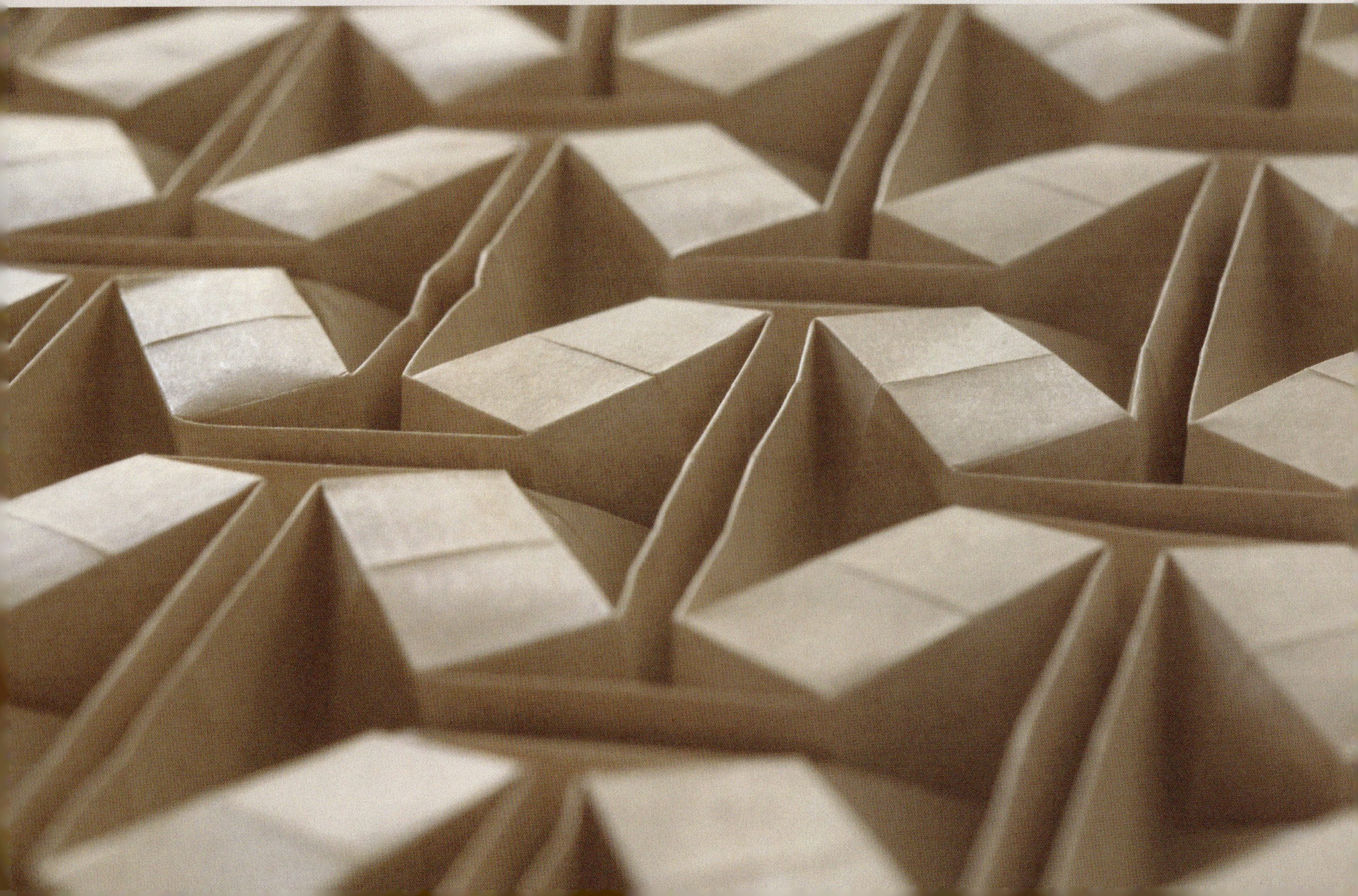

29 Big and Small Cubes

The Single Molecule

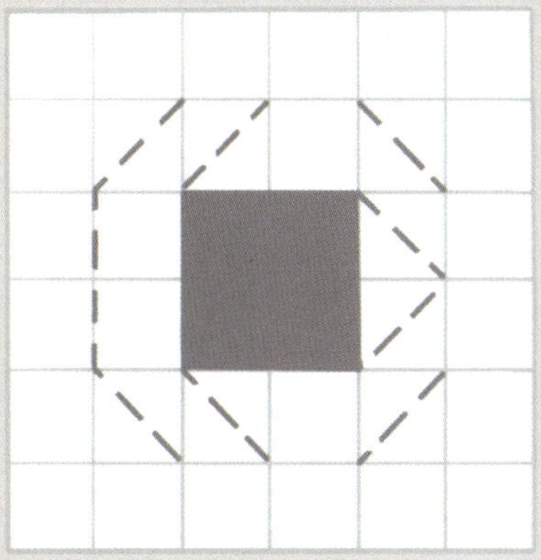

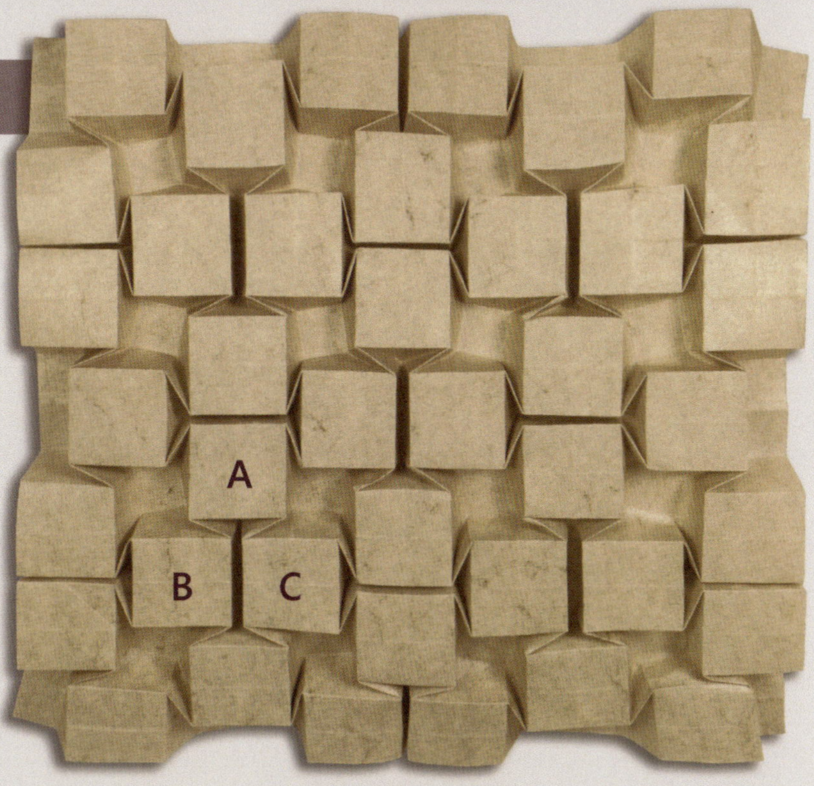

This is a unique molecule, as the creases around the central square are not rotationally symmetric.

The central square is 2 by 2.

Every two molecules are either a mirror image of the other or rotated. Molecules B and C are mirrored while A and B are rotated.

Shrinkage ratio is 2:1.

Above: recto view of a 4 by 4–molecule Big and Small Cubes tessellation; showing the big cubes.

Verso view is below, showing the small cubes raised.

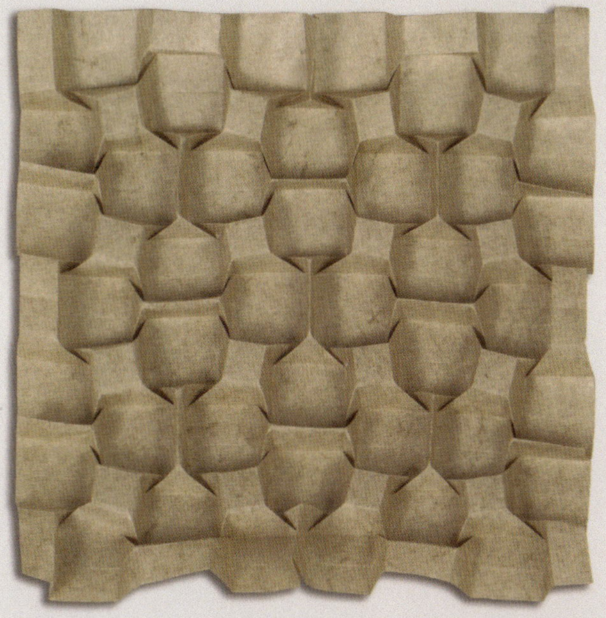

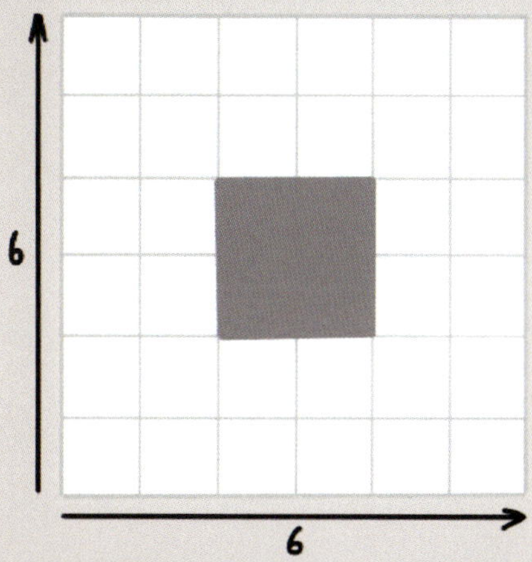

Start with a 6 by 6 grid.

Mark a 2 by 2 square in the center.

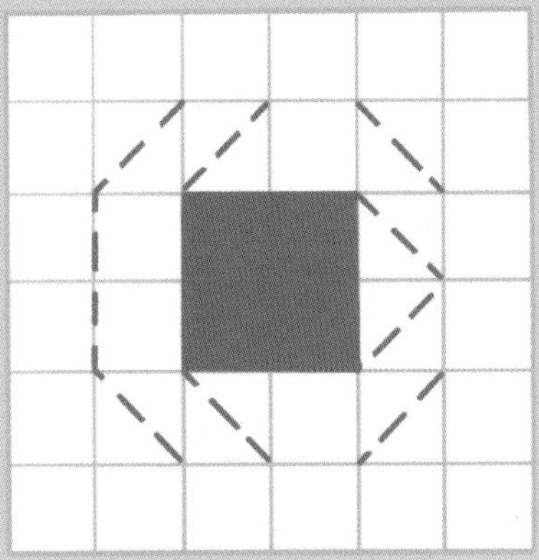

Add all the precreases as shown.

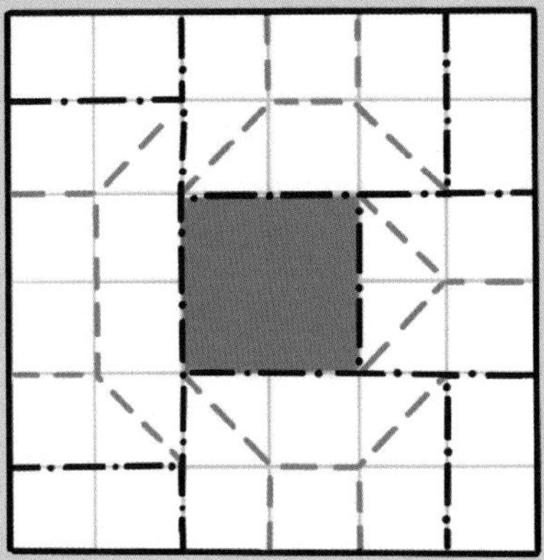

All the needed creases are shown.

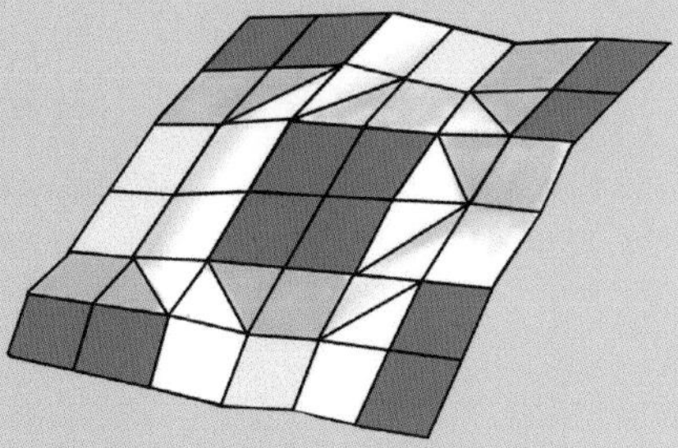

Collapse so all dark gray parts are on the same elevated level.

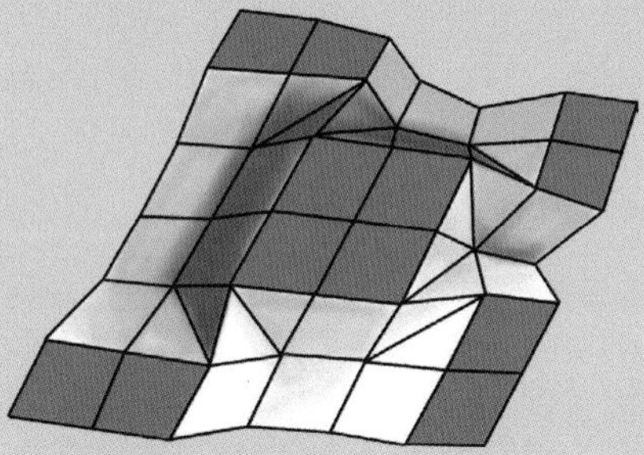

In process.

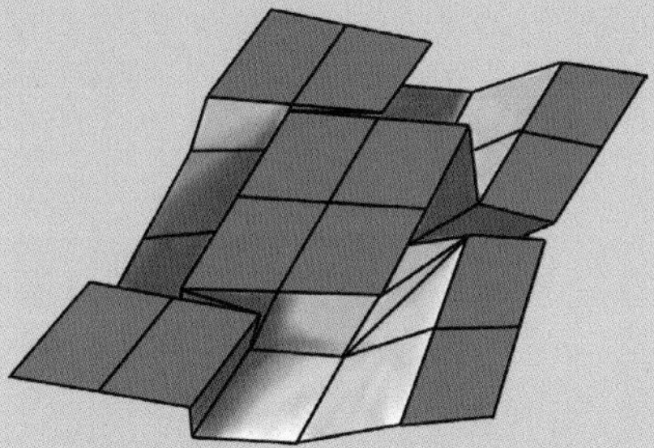

Fully collapsed.

2 by 2 Molecules

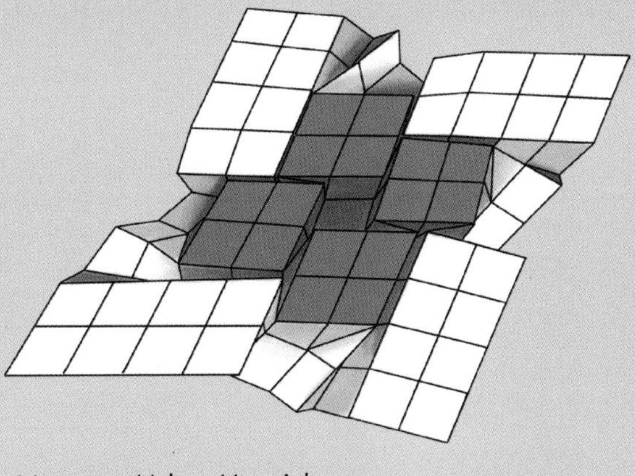

Use an 11 by 11 grid.

Precrease as indicated.

Collapse in rotation. Note which area is elevated and use the central square as your reference.

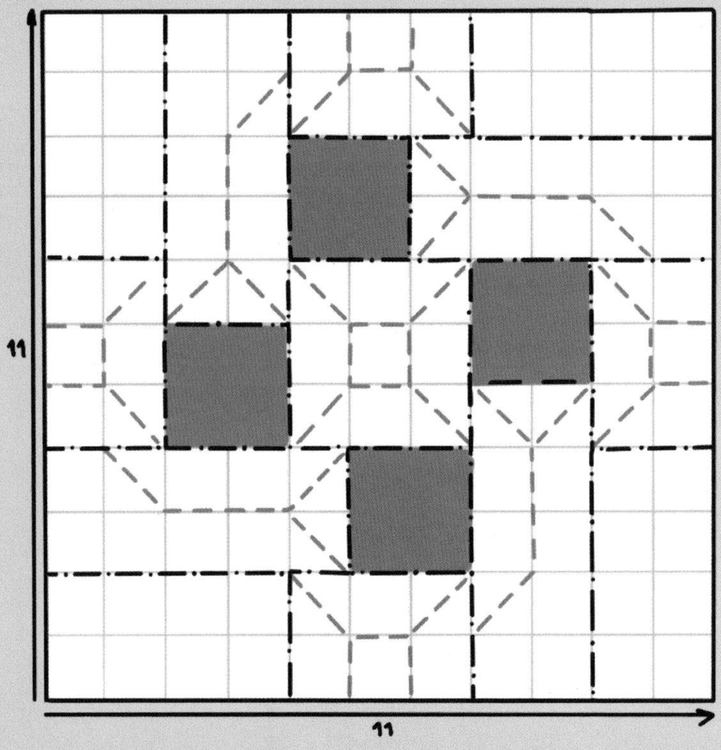

4 by 4 Molecules

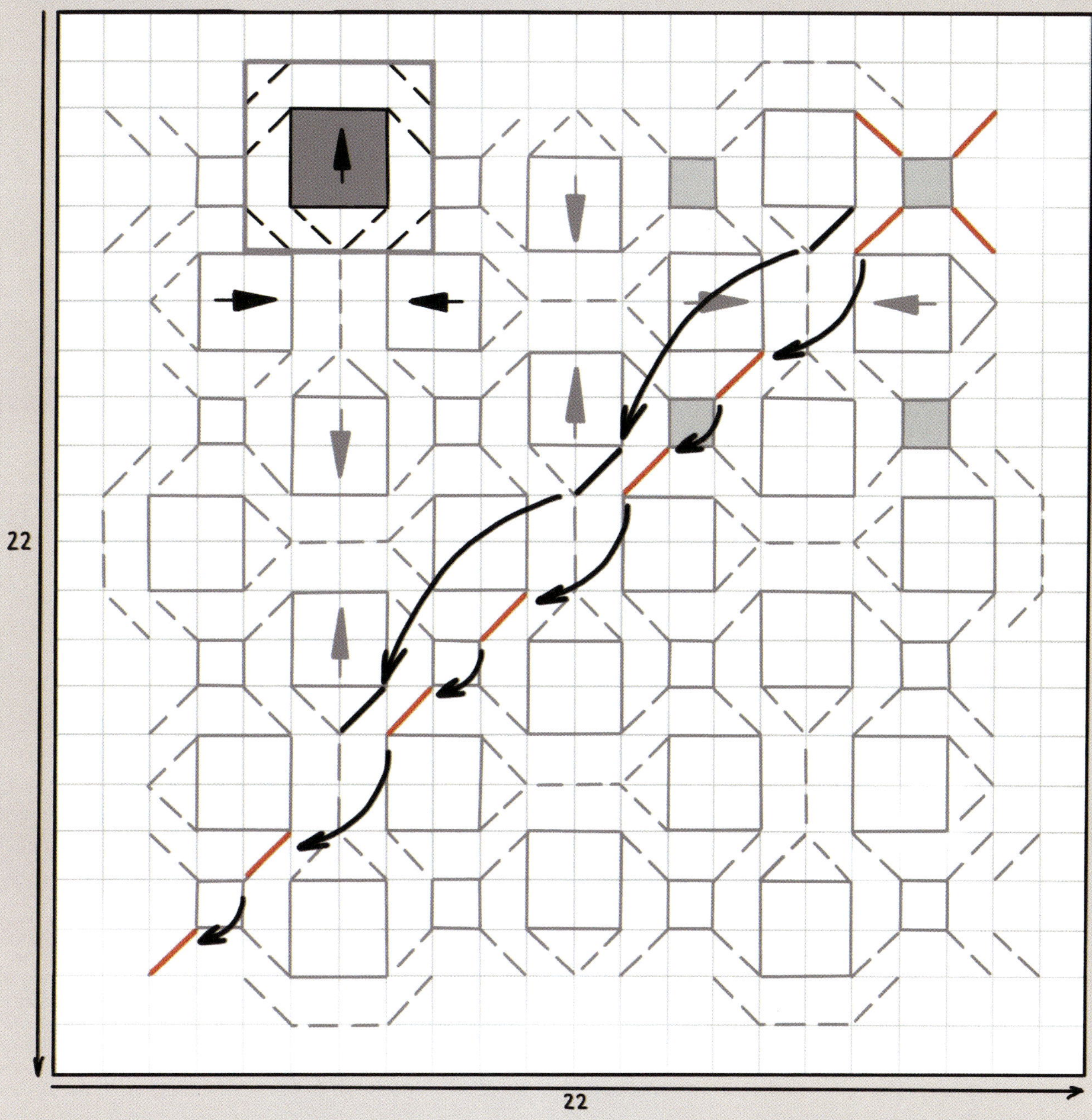

Use a 22 by 22 grid. There is no easy formula for the calculation. It is better to diagram the CP and count out the squares.

The final result will be 14 squares wide.

Precrease as indicated. Start by marking the *small* squares (marked by light gray).

Surround them with short diagonals, following the fold one, skip one, fold one, skip two pattern (marked by orange lines).

For the rest of the diagonals, use fold one, skip four pattern (marked by bold black lines).

Collapse the outer molecules first, and work your way inward.

Note which area is elevated, and use the central square as your reference.

During the collapse, look for the adjacent squares (marked with two arrows pointing to each other) to help understand the process.

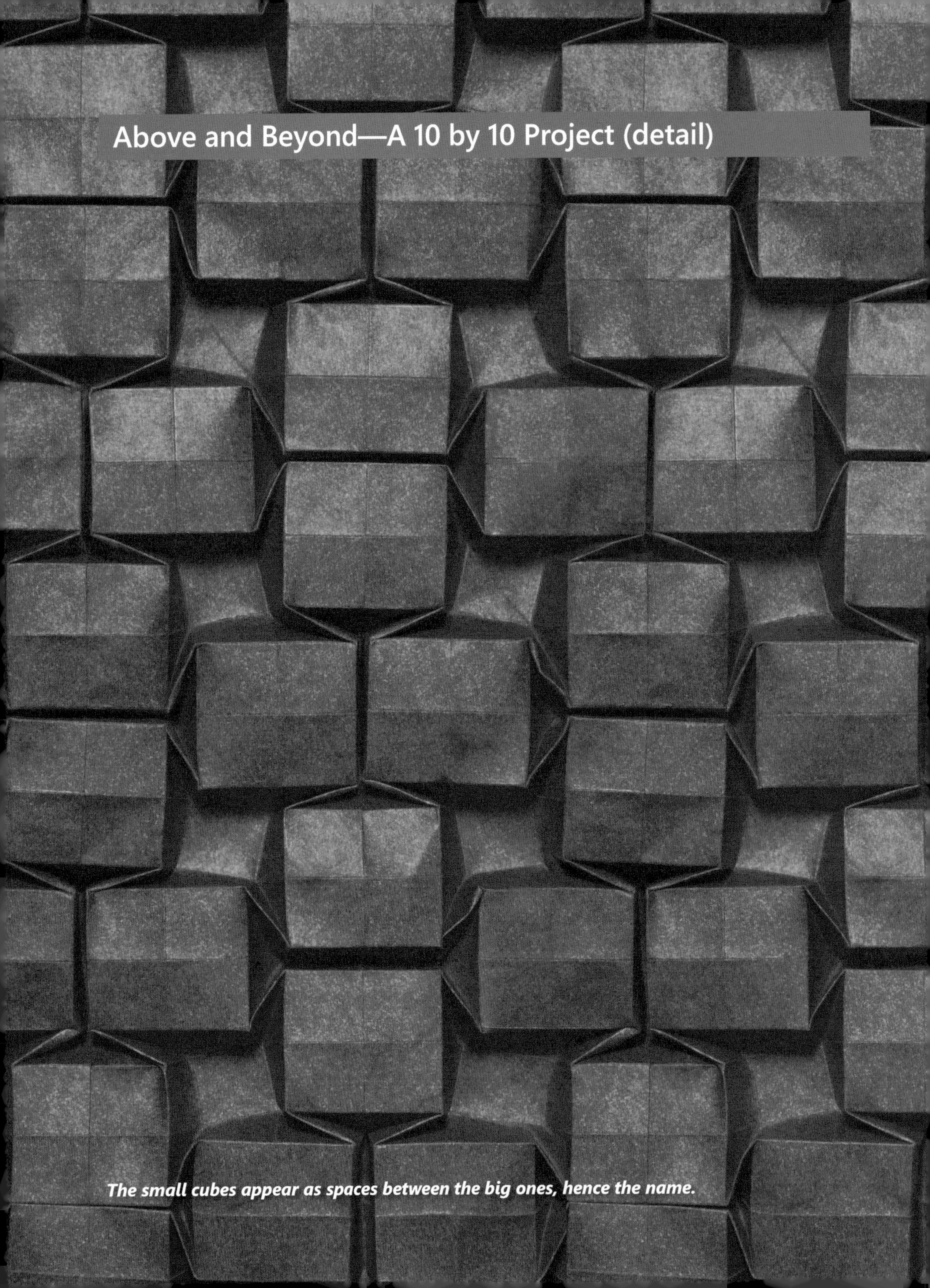
Above and Beyond—A 10 by 10 Project (detail)

The small cubes appear as spaces between the big ones, hence the name.

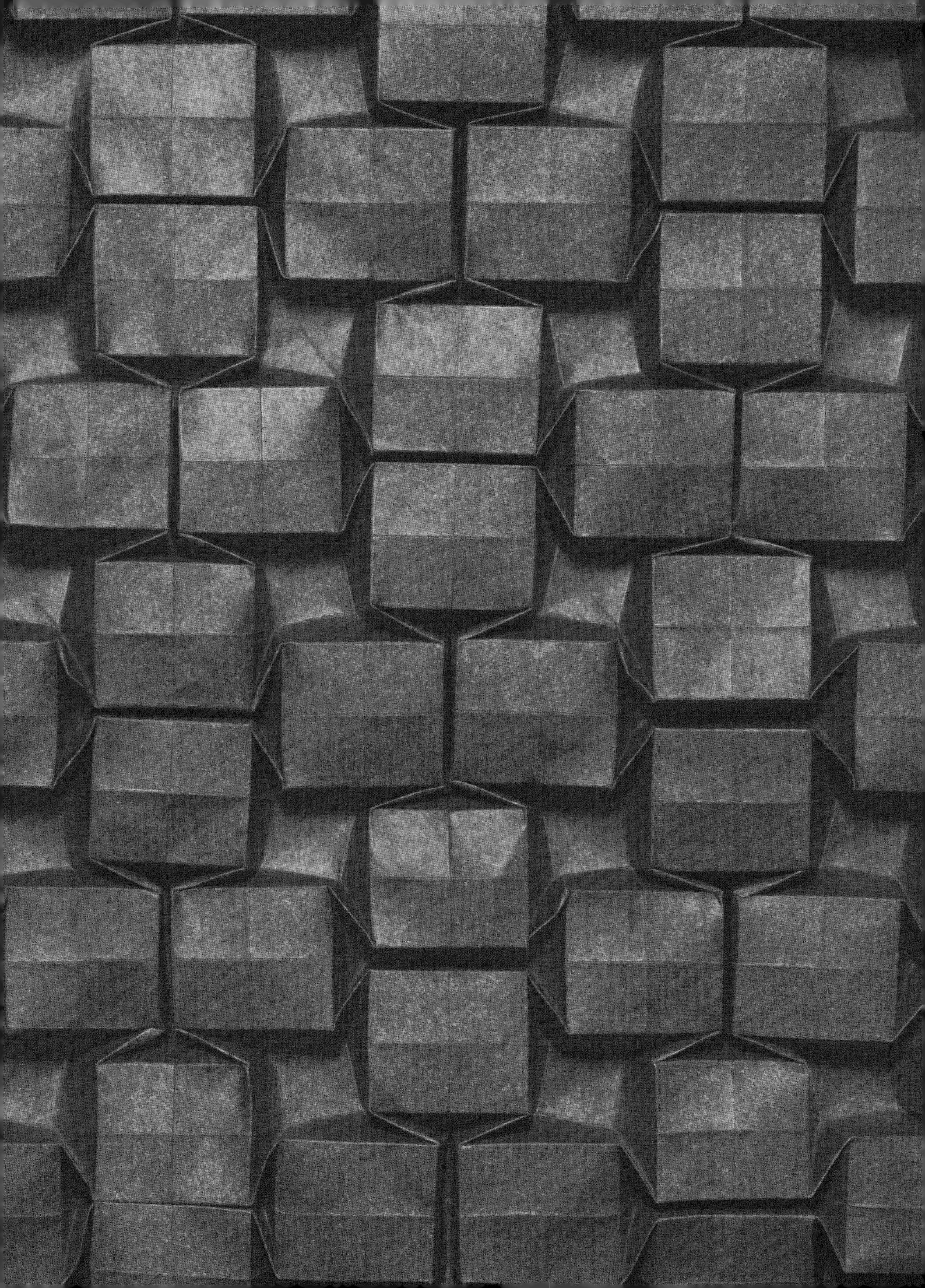

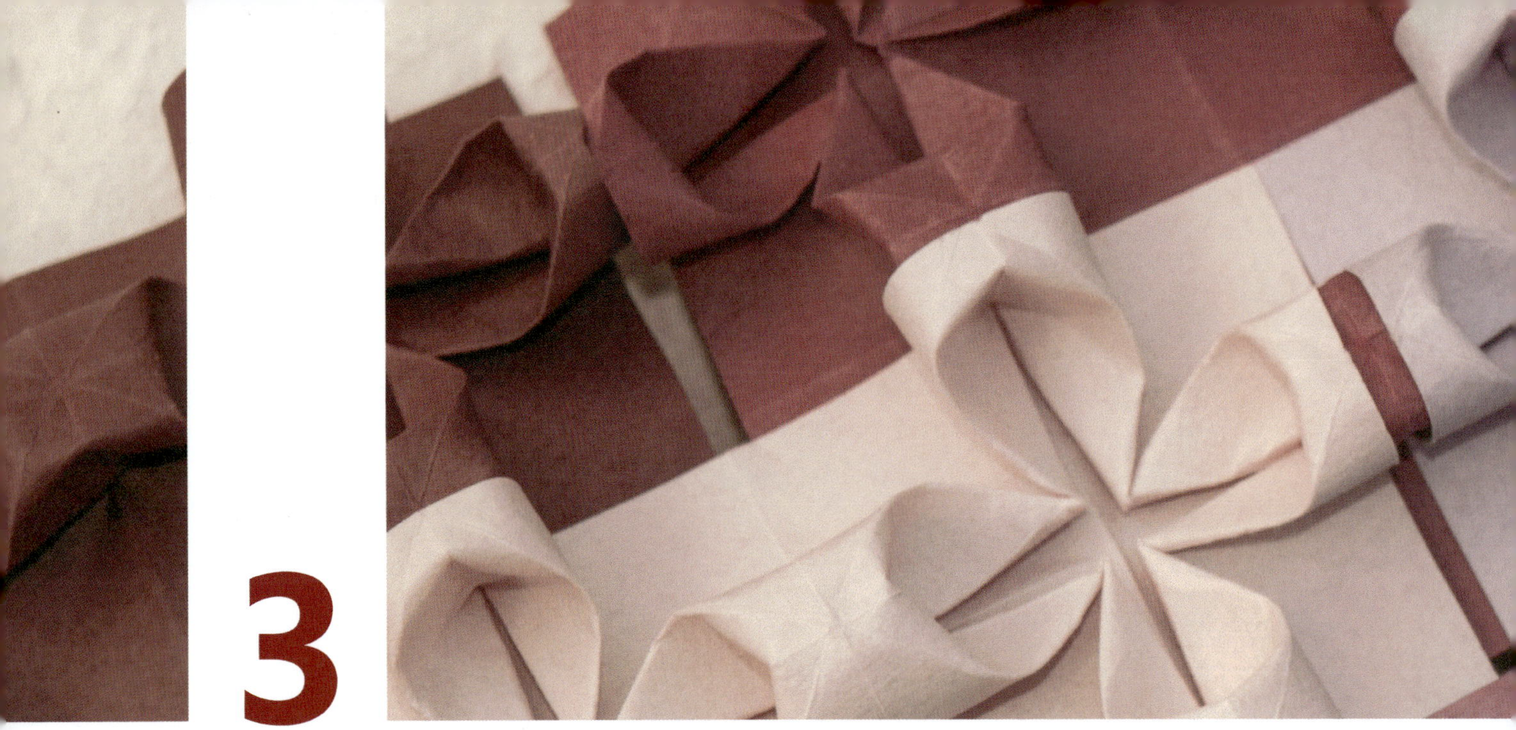

3
The Red Flower Family

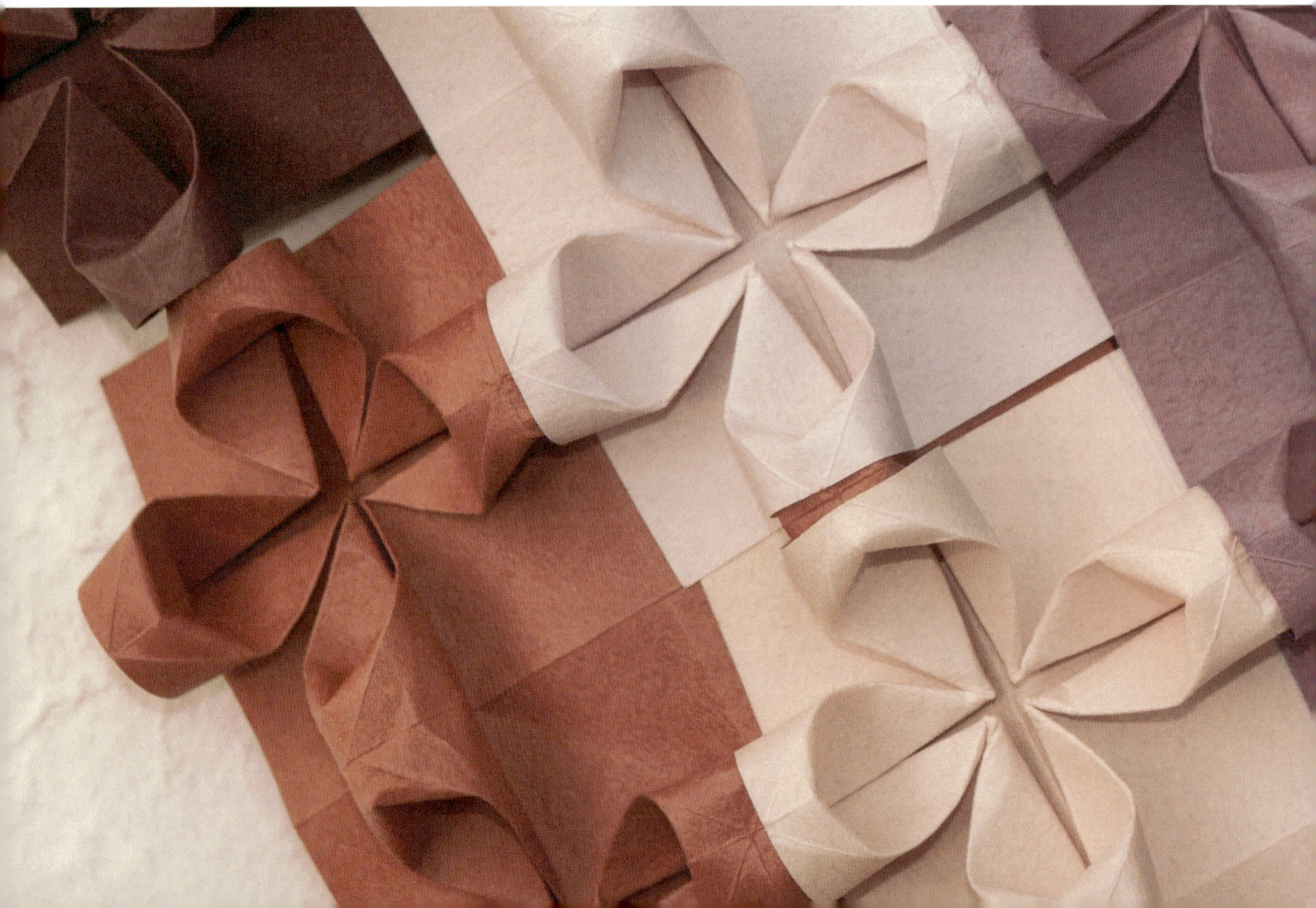

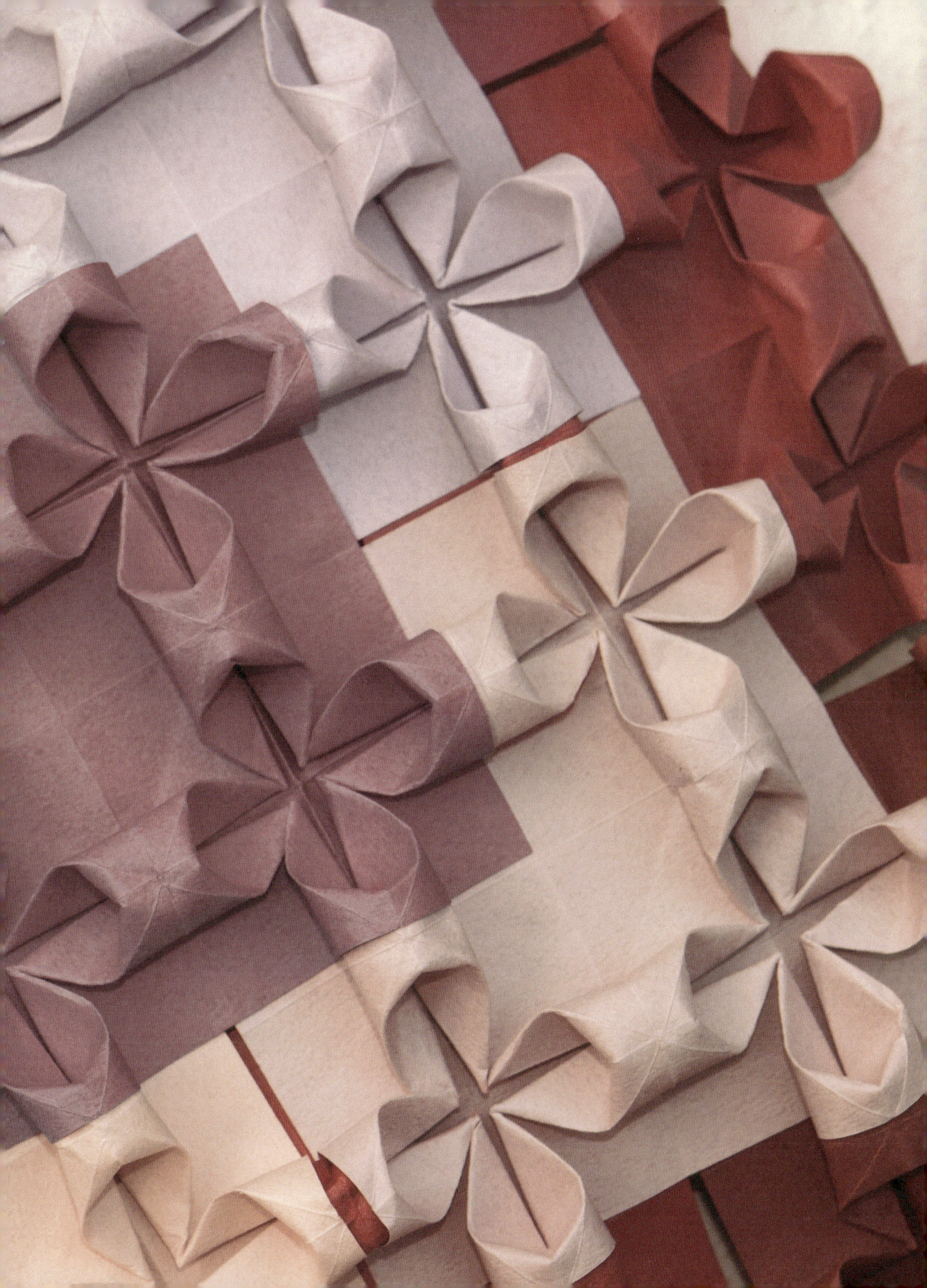

Introduction

The Red Flower family is based on a 4 by 4 grid with a tilted square that connects all the midpoints of the edges. The one step to join all those points in the center of the grid is the essence of the process, and this chapter revolves around it. The name came from the model's flower-like look and the paper I used while discovering it—a red tant.

Variations are based on duplicating the process to get an inner flower, rotating the CP on the grid, and using the same steps on a hexagon grid.

I am not the first to find this model, but I believe the variations are unprecedented.

3 1 Red Flower

Right: recto view of a 4 by 4–molecule Red Flower tessellation.

Verso view is below.

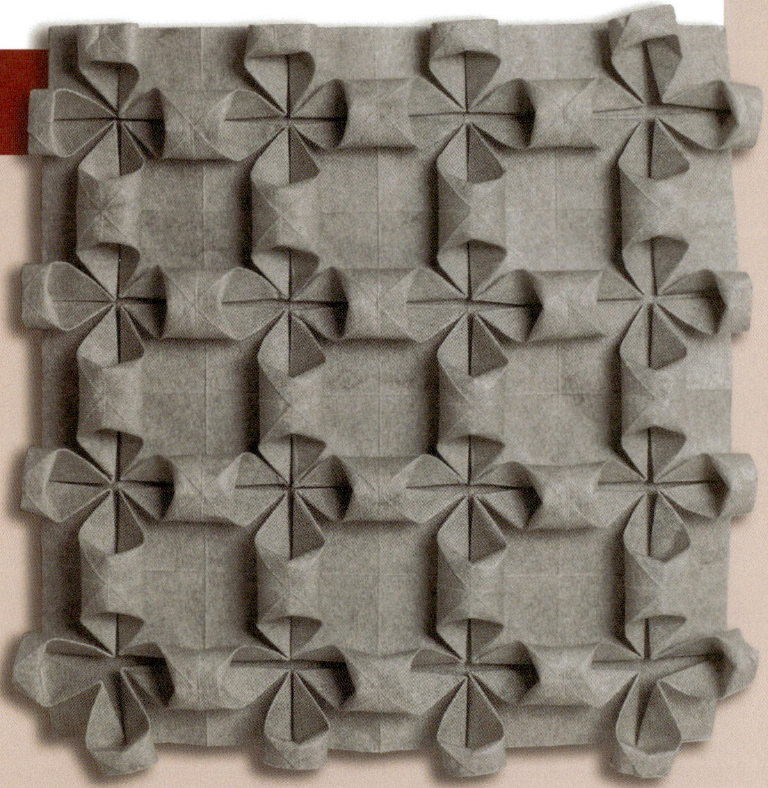

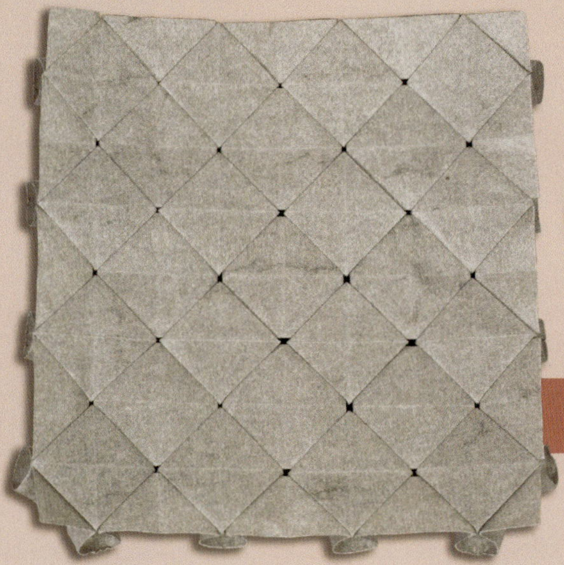

The Single Molecule

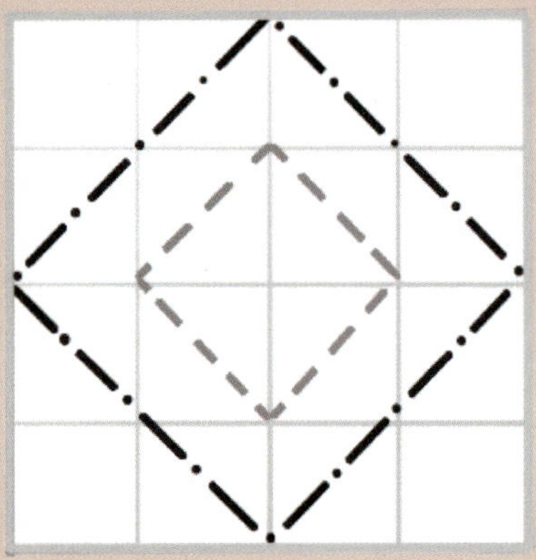

On a 4 by 4 grid, eight crease lines create a square within a square. Since every molecule is symmetrical, you only need to shift the molecule to tessellate it.

Be warned: this model blooms only on the last step!

The shrinkage ratio is 2:1.

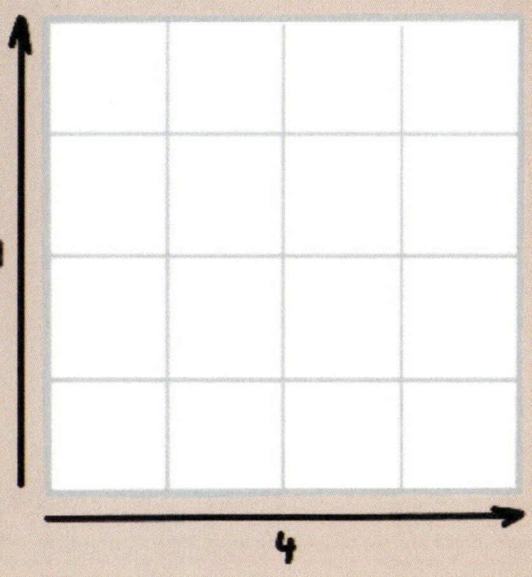

For this model, there is no need for an extra row or column around the molecules.

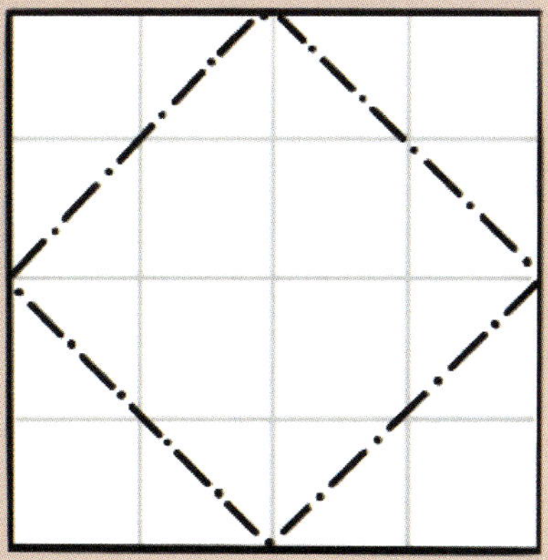

Mountain fold a tilted square connecting all the midpoints.

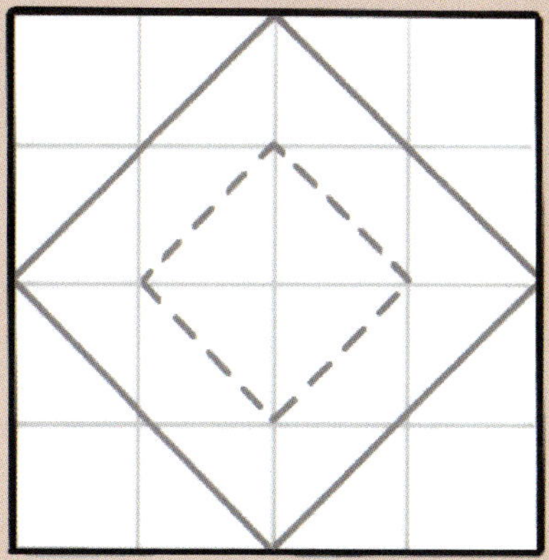

Add a smaller inner square with valleys. It is easier to fold these by pinching the mountain lines and aligning them with the center point to mark the valley folds.

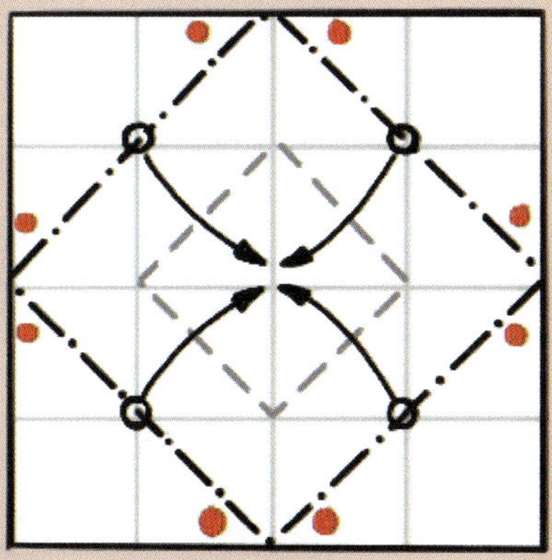

Collapse by pinching all the corners of the tilted square (marked with red dots), while gathering all the midpoints at the grid center.

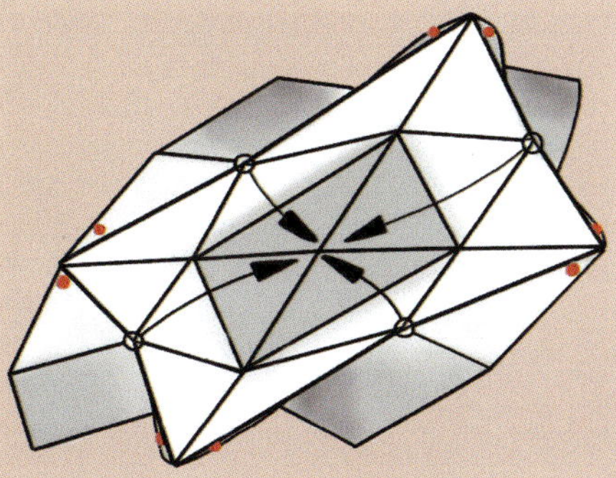

In process.

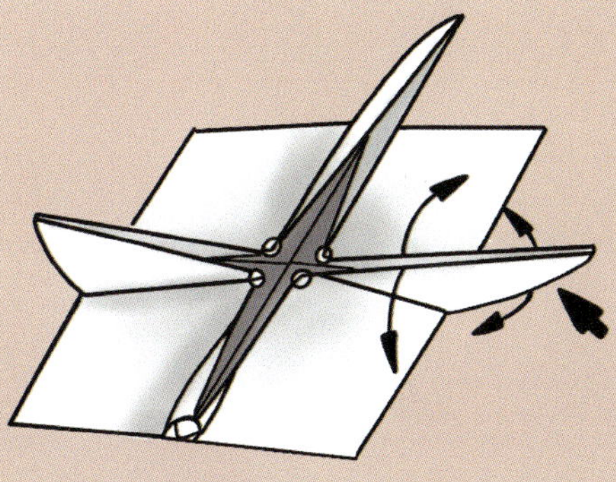

Fully collapsed.

Shape a petal by spreading the “lips” of the standing triangle.

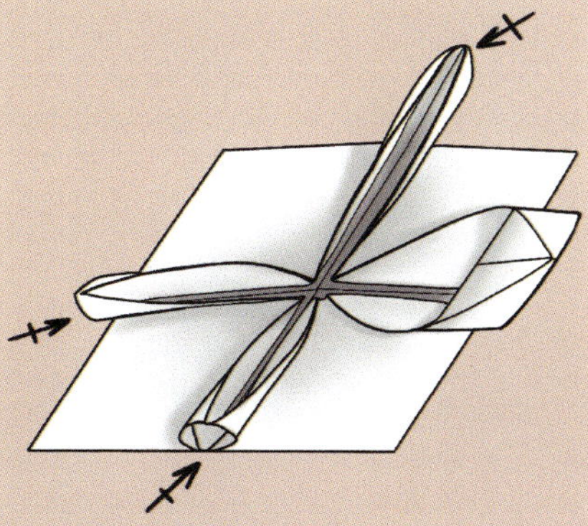

Repeat all over.

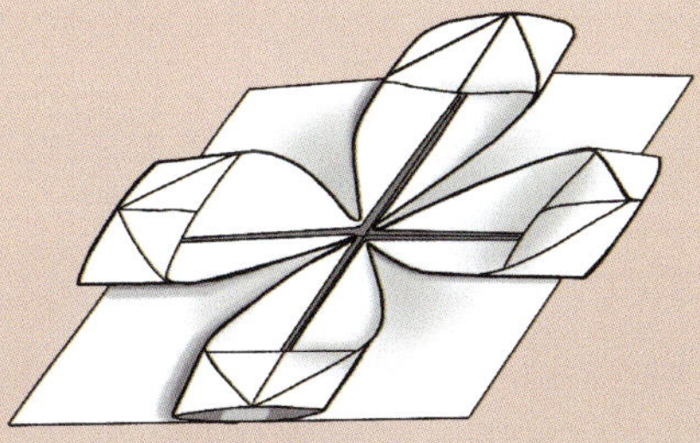

The finished molecule.

2 by 2 Molecules

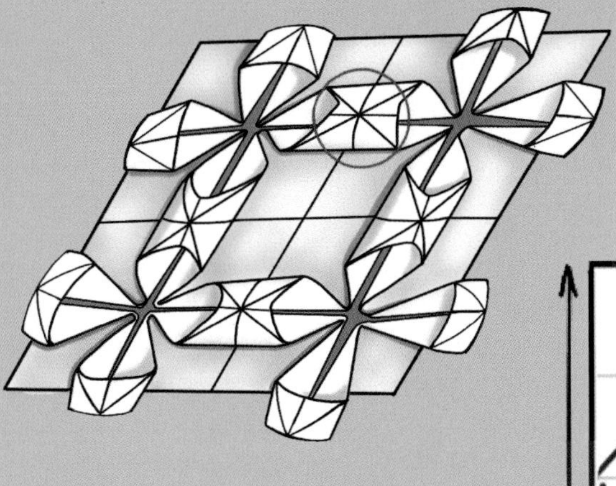

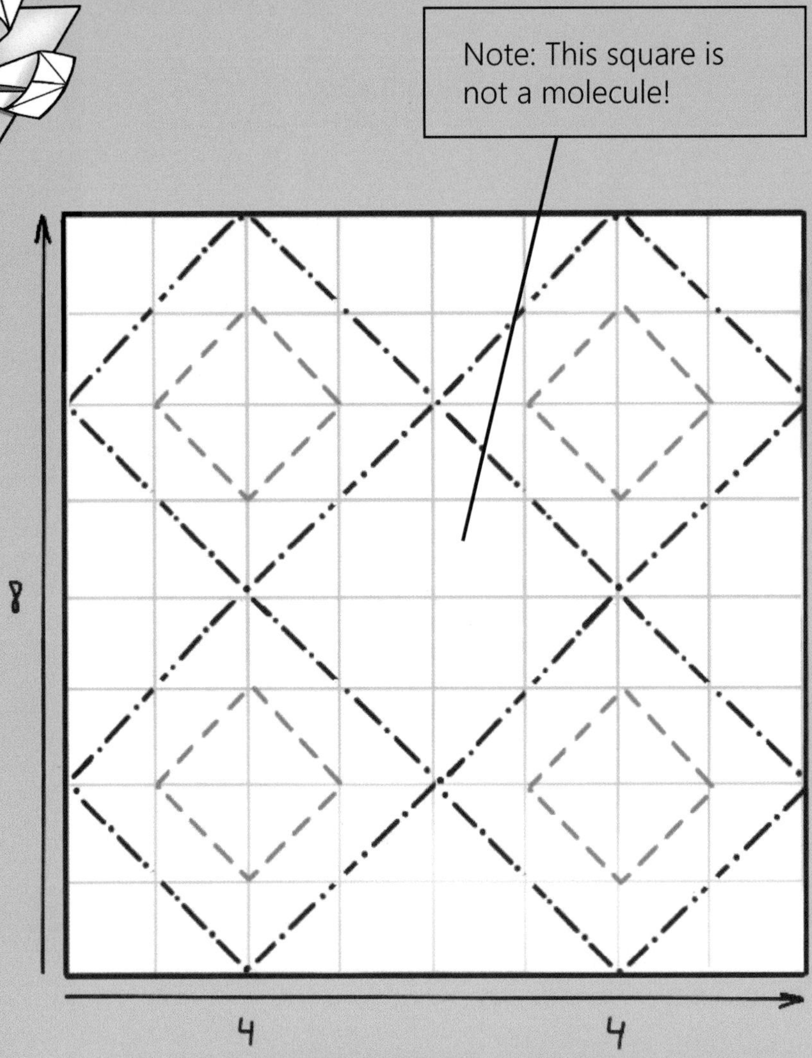

Use a grid of 8 by 8. Add all precreases.

Note that the mountain fold lines of the outer squares align with each other and can be creased with one stroke.

Be sure to keep the center square free of folds. It is not a molecule.

Collapse the top left molecule first and then add the right one. Try to collapse the bottom two together.

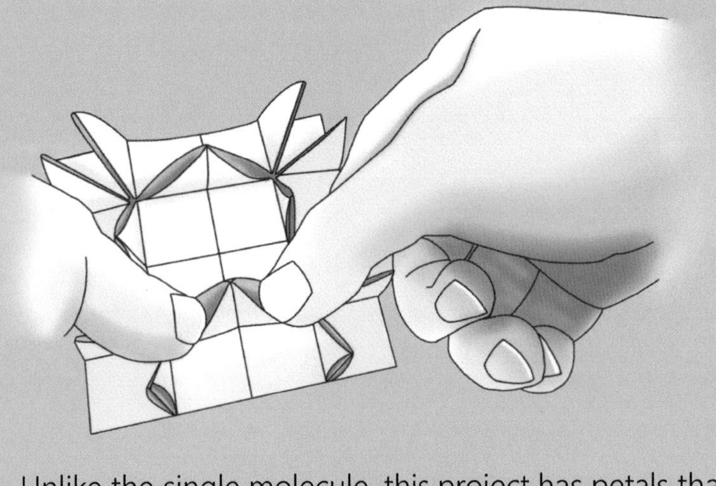

Unlike the single molecule, this project has petals that are not on the edge of the paper (marked in red, top left drawing). To puff them, use both thumbs, inserting them into the pockets and spreading out the lips, causing the point to spread to the sides.

4 by 4 Molecules

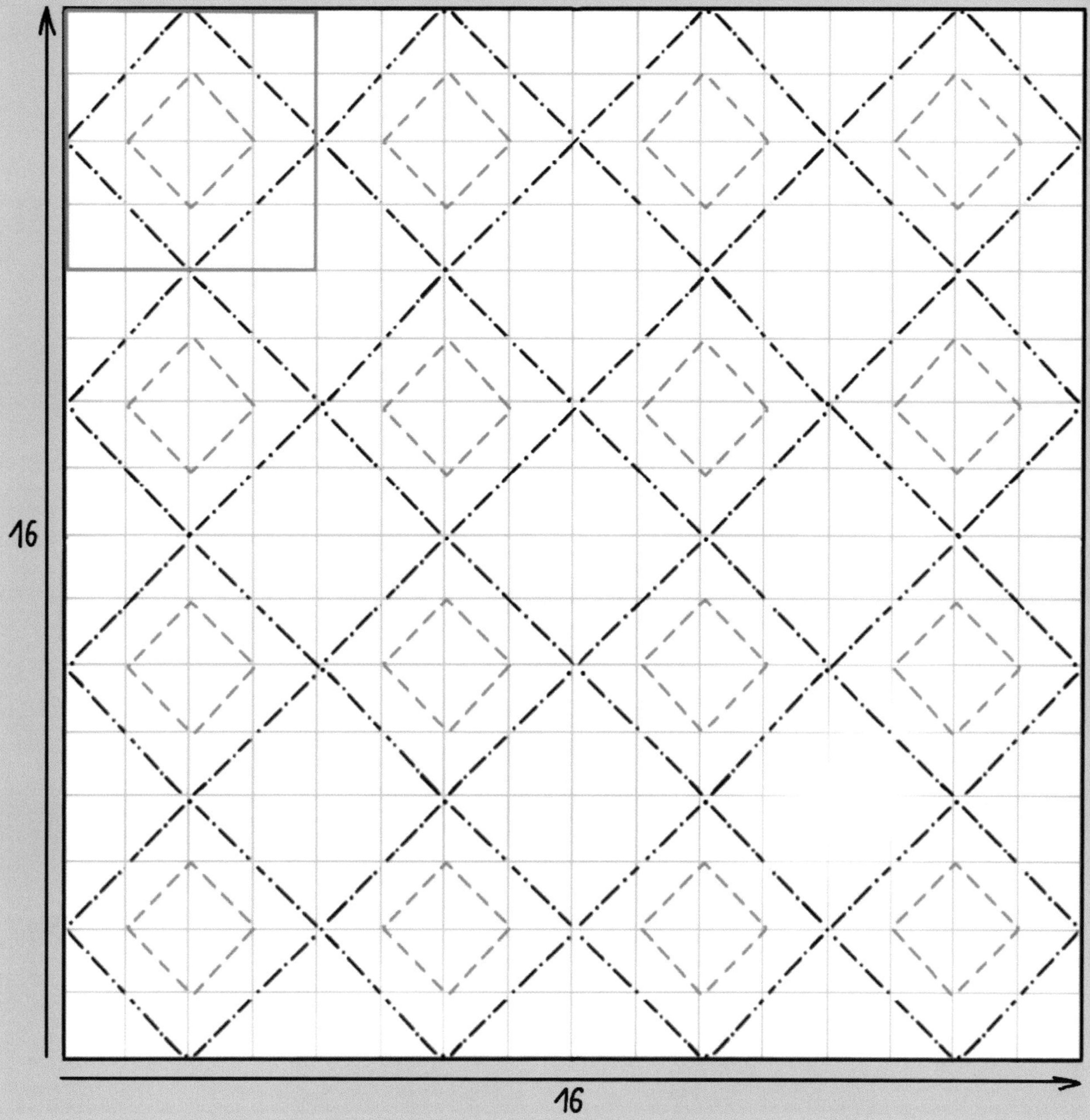

For a 4 by 4–molecule project, start with a 16 by 16 grid: 4 x 4 = 16.

The final model will be eight squares wide.

Make all the precreases: fold all the mountain fold lines slanting in the same direction first, then fold all the creases slanting the other way. Now add all the valleys.

The collapse is done row by row, starting from the top left molecule. Extend the folds all the way to the edges of the paper and form the first molecule alone. To create the next molecule, make the mountain fold square first, and then sink the inner square.

Above and Beyond—A Floor Lamp

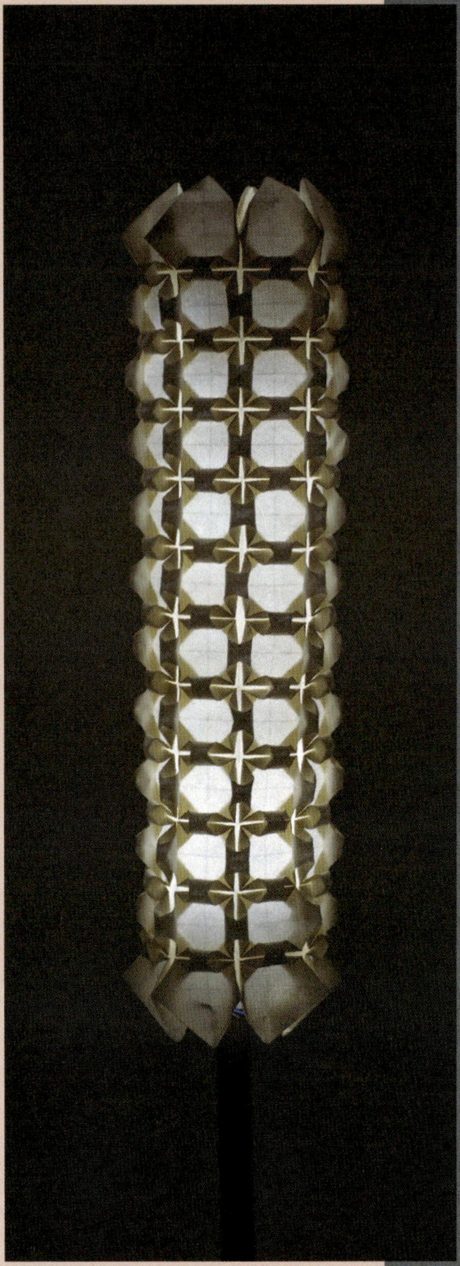

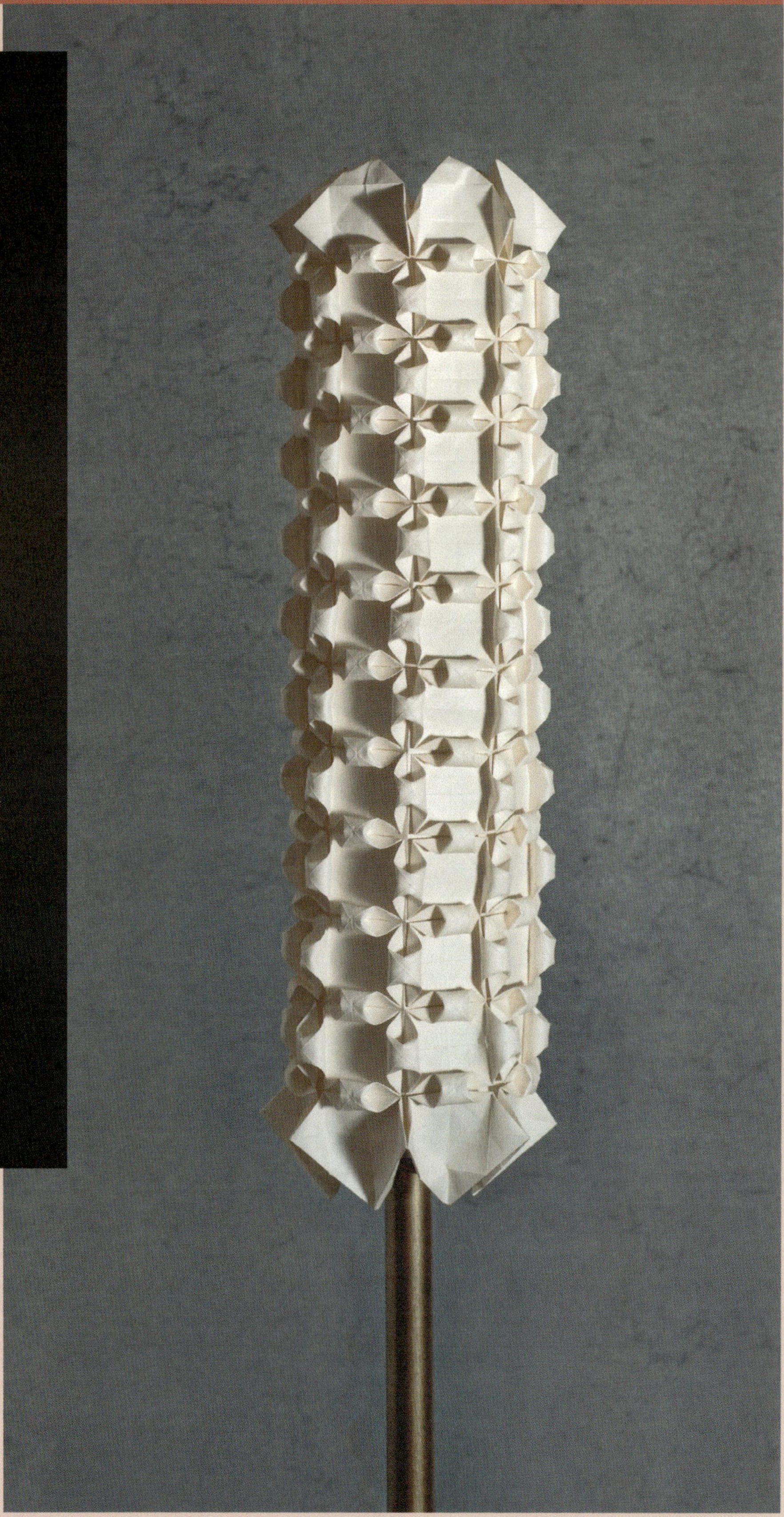

This lampshade is made from a sheet 8 molecules wide by 11 molecules high. To lock the sheet into a tube, the right column is aligned on top of the left column and they are collapsed together.

3 2 Double Red Flower

The Single Molecule

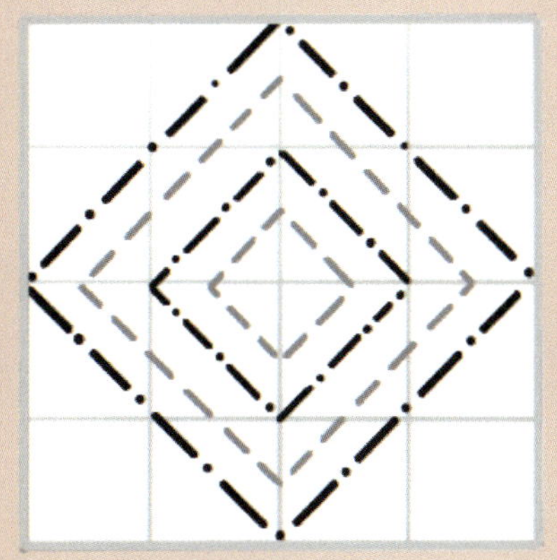

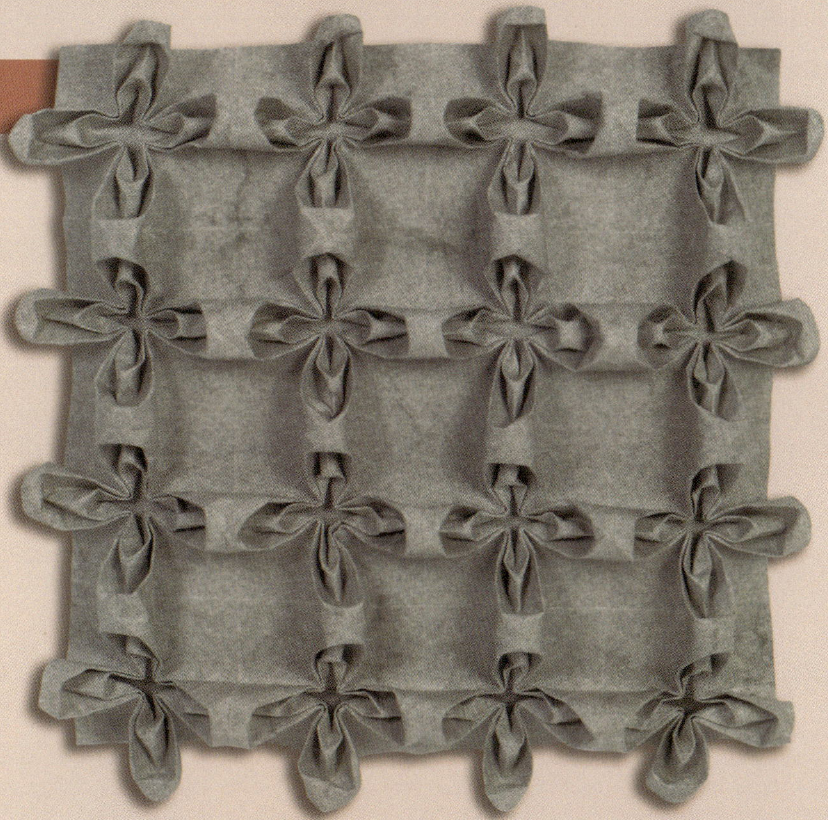

This molecule is the result of doubling the number of concentric squares from the Red Flower tessellation (page 74) to give more details to the petals. This is done by dividing the space between the tilted square to the center point by four, not two.

I highly recommend that you fold the Red Flower tessellation first for practice.

The shrinkage ratio is 2:1.

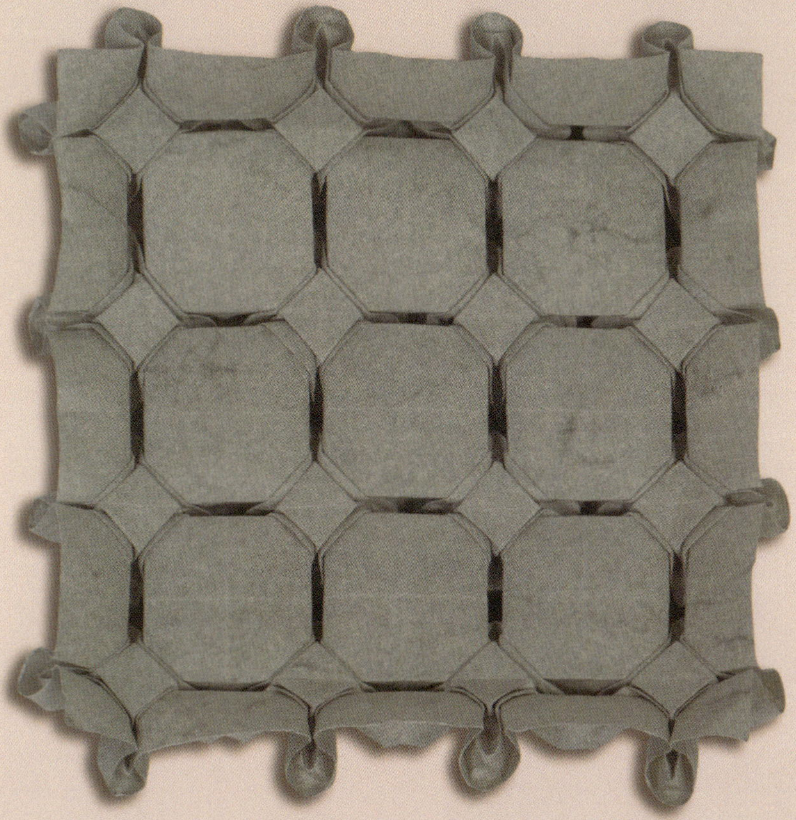

Above: recto view of a 4 by 4–molecule Double Red Flower tessellation.

Verso view is to the right.

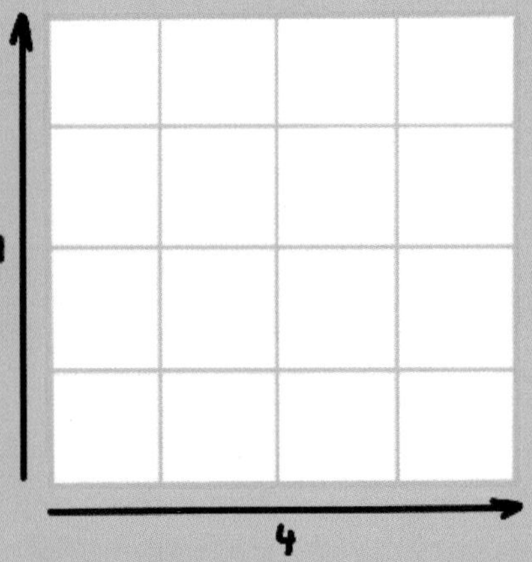

Start with a 4 by 4 grid. For this model there is no need for an extra row or column around the molecules.

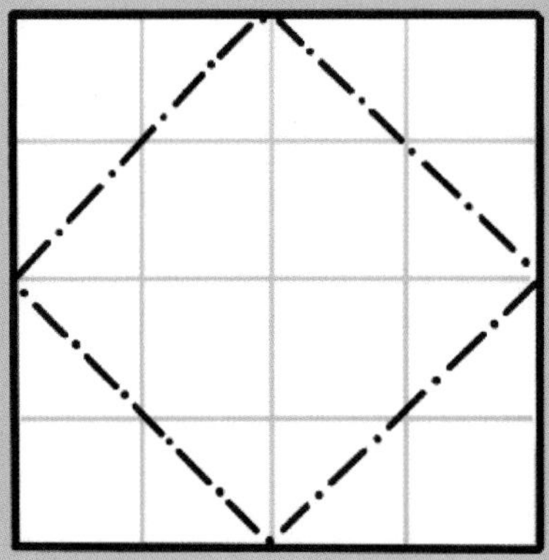

Mountain fold a tilted square, connecting all the midpoints of the grid.

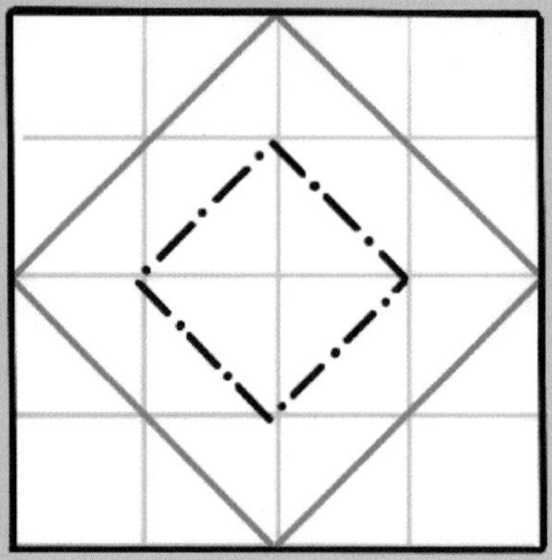

Add a smaller inner square, as mountains again.

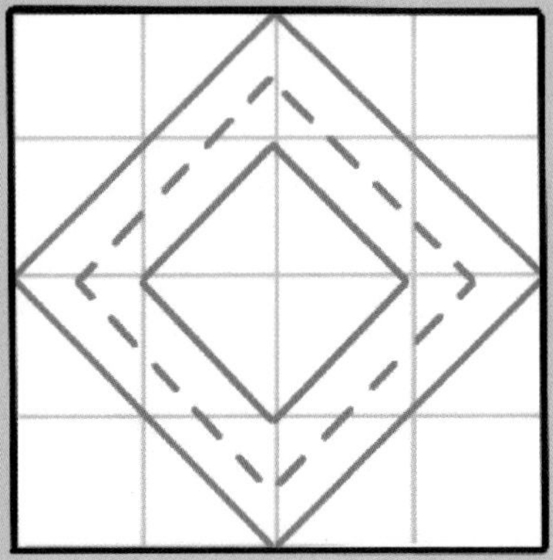

Now add the valleys. Pinch the outer mountain line and bring it to the inner one.

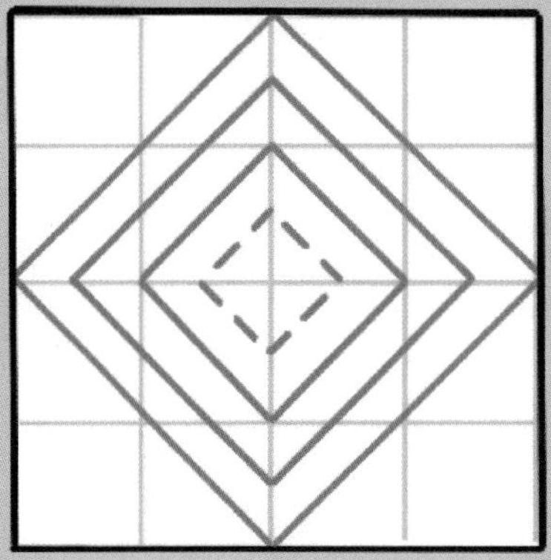

Now add the smallest square with valleys. Do it by pinching the inner mountain line and bringing it to the center.

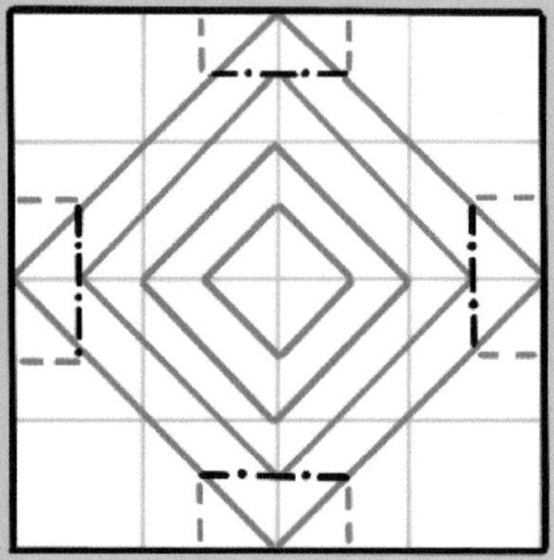

You can add these creases for an easier collapse (or you can skip this step). Note the orientation of the creases!

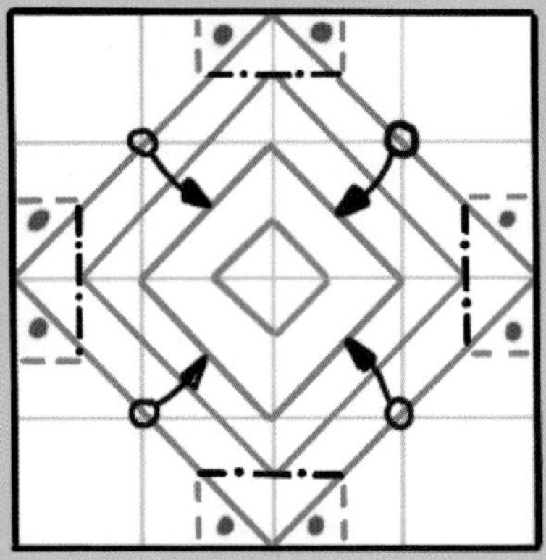

Start the collapse with the outer mountain and valley squares. Pinch the corners of the tilted square.

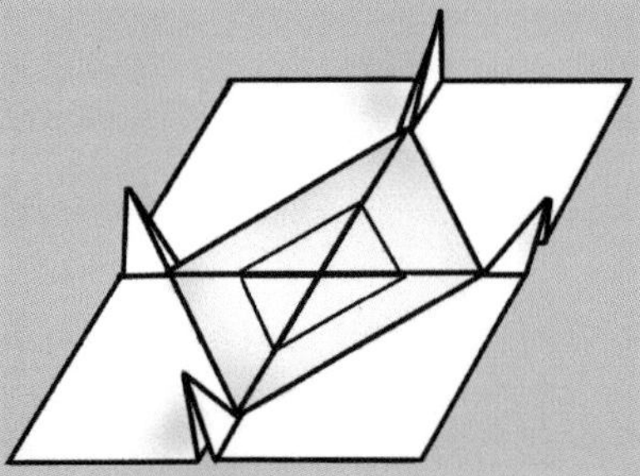

The result.

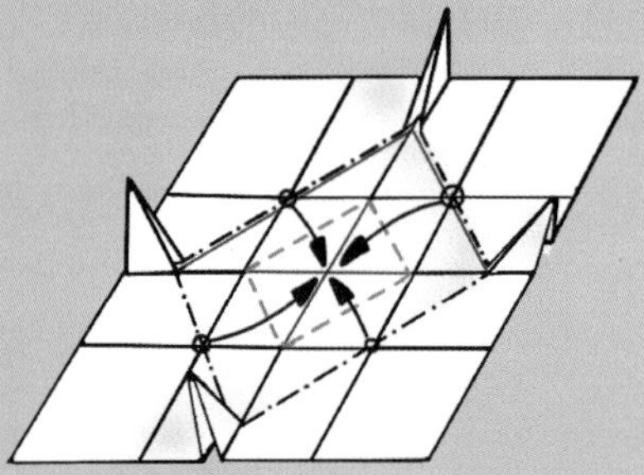

Now repeat the process on the inner squares.

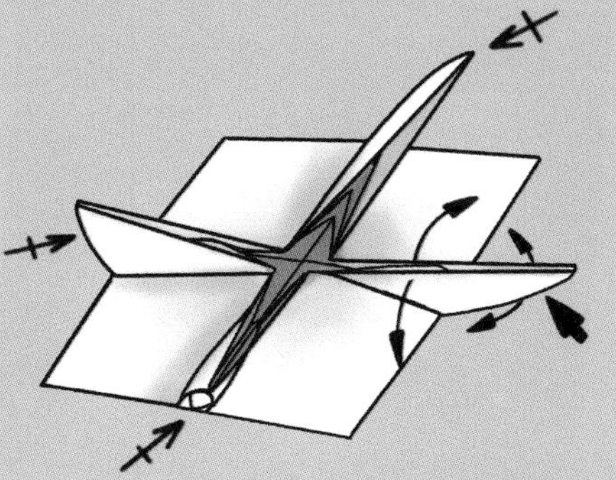

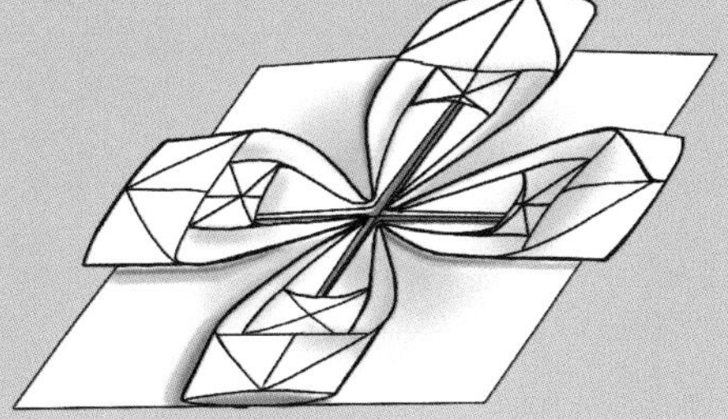

This results in double-layered triangles.

Spread each petal, starting with the inner parts, using your thumb. Once the inner part is spread, it is easier to spread the outer one, starting from the highest point.

The result.

You may need to use a cotton swab to puff and round the inner parts from beneath.

2 by 2 Molecules

Use a grid of 8 by 8. Add all precreases.

Note that the mountain lines of the bigger squares align with each other and can be creased with one stroke.

All the other squares must be made line by line; there is no shortcut for that.

Collapse the project in two stages. First, collapse the bigger squares all over; only then should you complete the collapse with the inner squares.

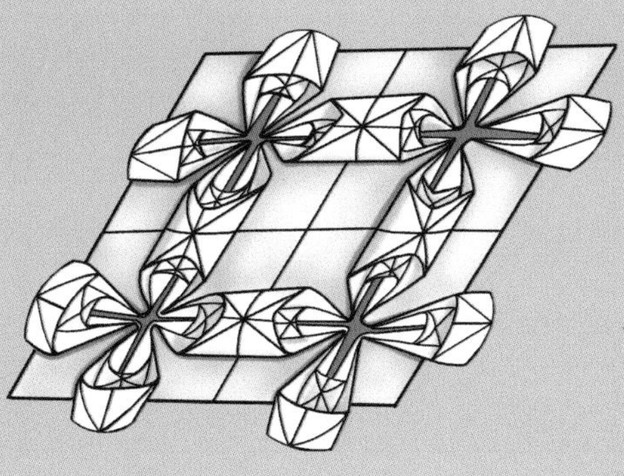

Always puff the inner petals first. Use a cotton swab to puff the petals from beneath.

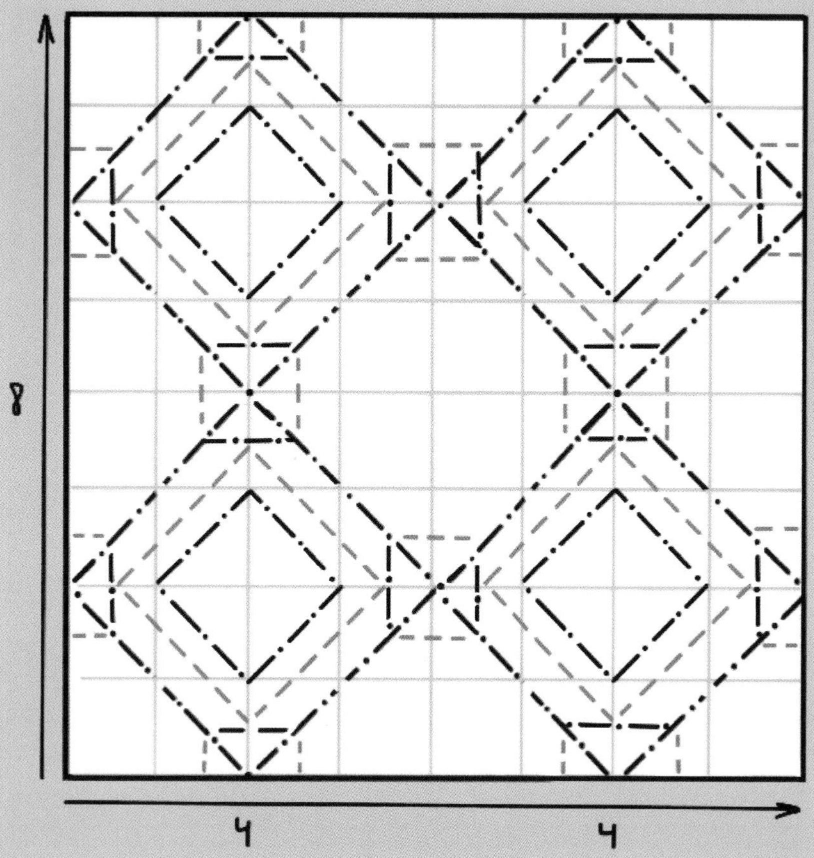

4 by 4 Molecules

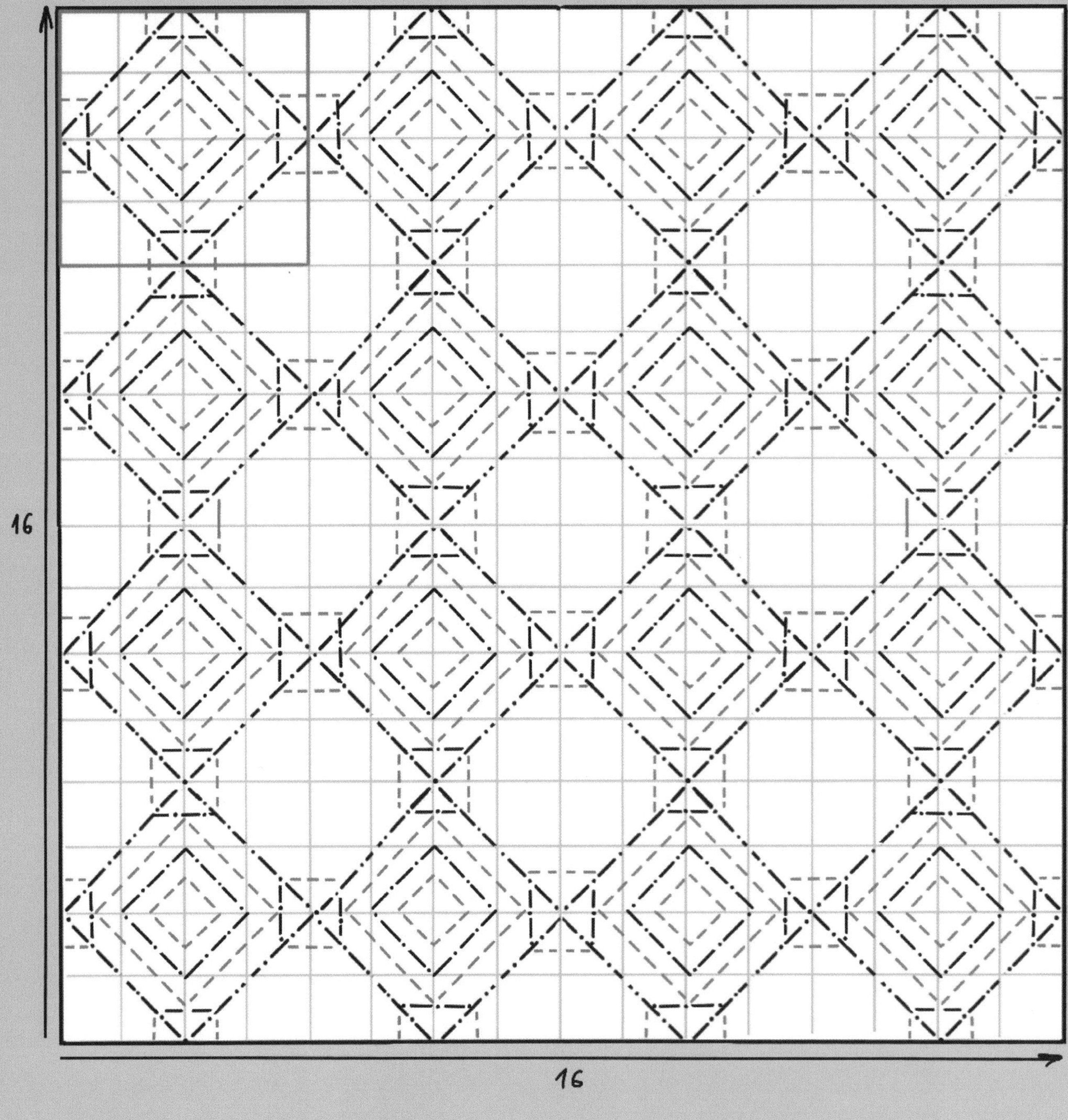

Use a grid of 16 by 16: 4 x 4 = 16.

The final model will be eight squares wide.

Add all precreases.

Follow the process presented in the 2 by 2 project, collapsing the bigger squares first and then the small ones.

3 3 Green Flower

The Single Molecule

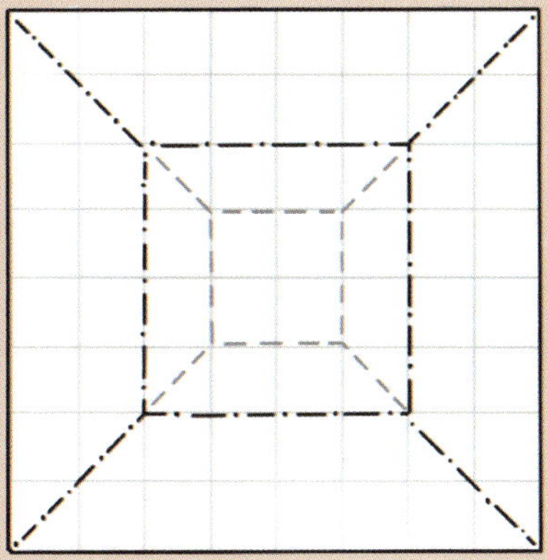

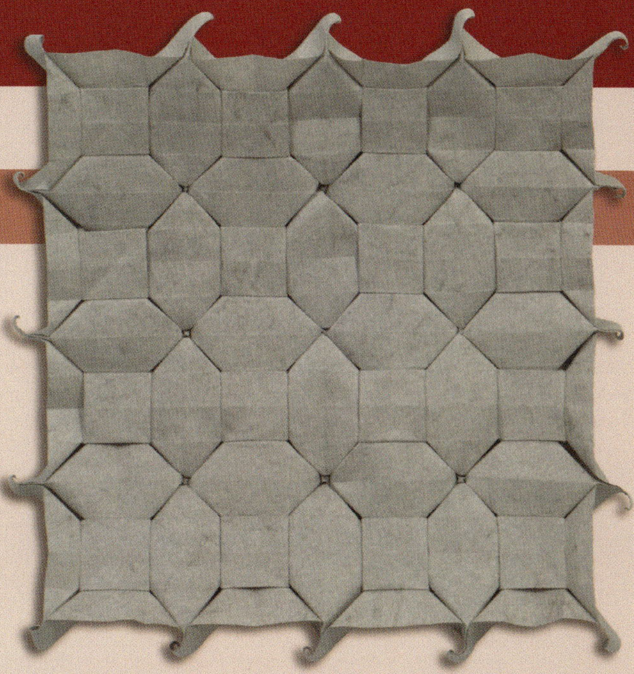

Top: recto view of a 4 by 4–molecule Green Flower tessellation. Verso view is below.

In this variation, the inner squares are not tilted. Instead, they are parallel with the molecule edges.

Bringing the midpoints of the outer square to the center is still part of the process.

The shrinkage ratio is 2:1.

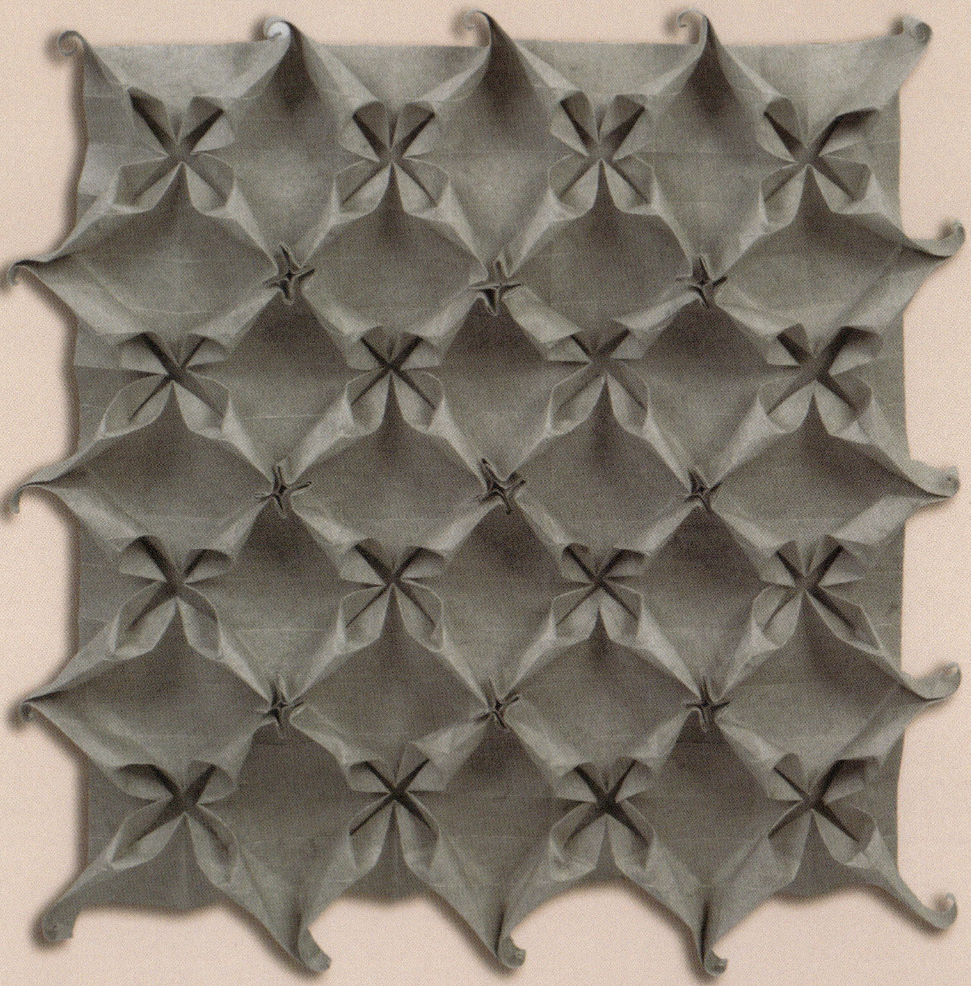

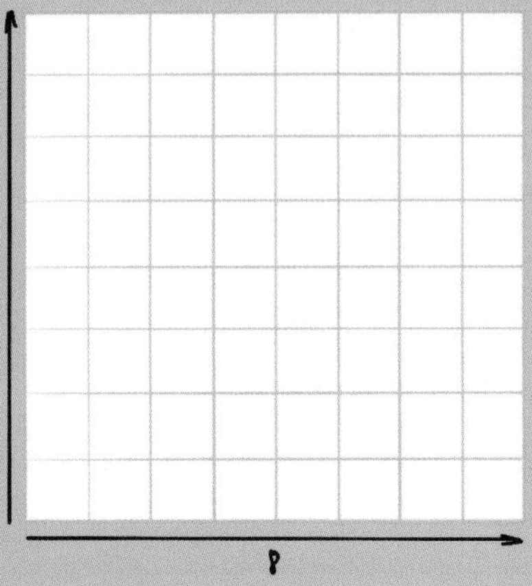

Start with an 8 by 8 grid. This molecule does not have an extra row or column.

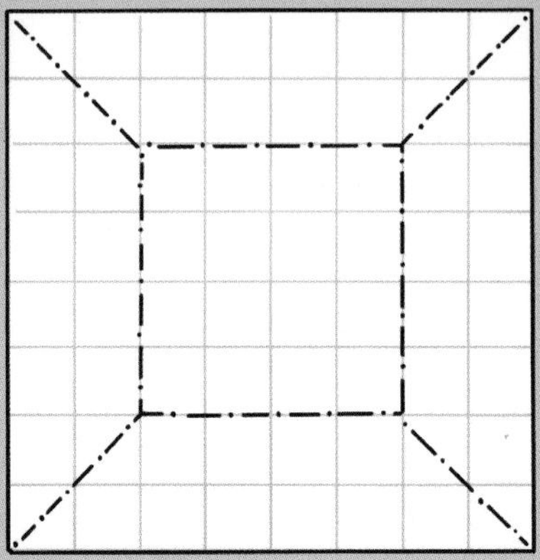

Mark a 4 by 4 square in the center with mountain creases. Add the diagonals as mountains, but do not fold them in the inner square.

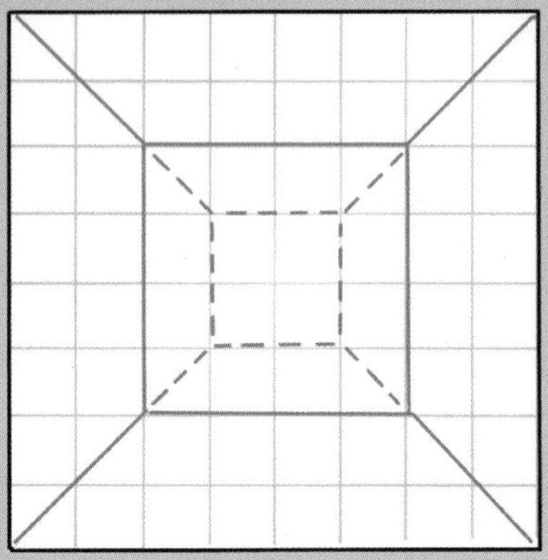

Add a 2 by 2 square in the center and mark the four short diagonals, all as valleys.

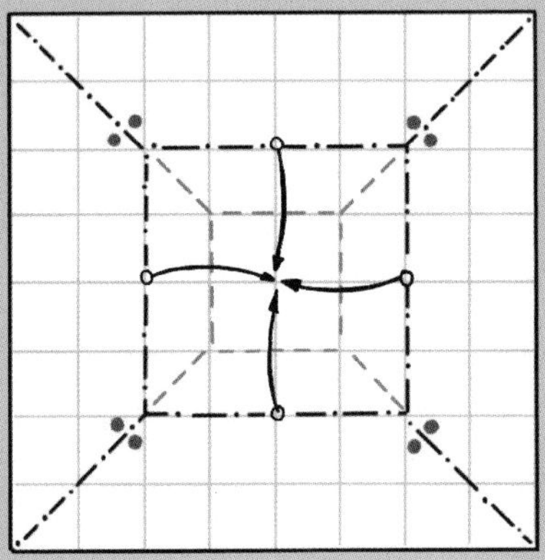

Start the collapse by bringing all the outer square midpoints to the center.

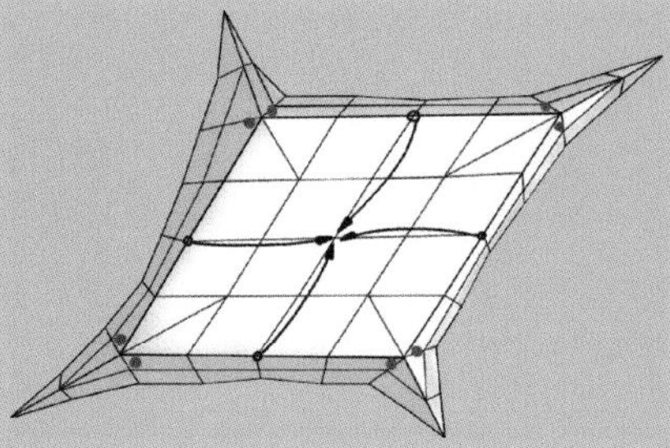

In process.

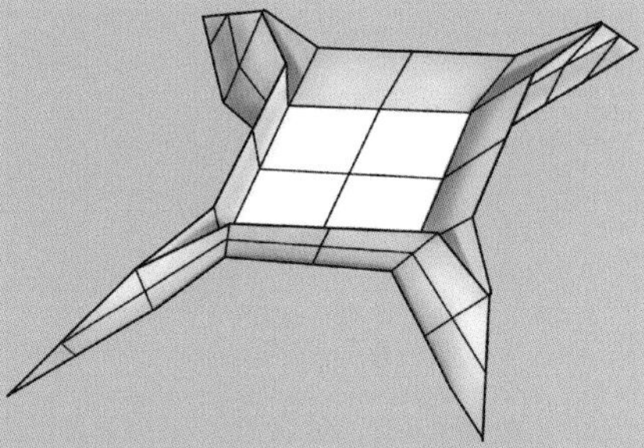

Almost there.

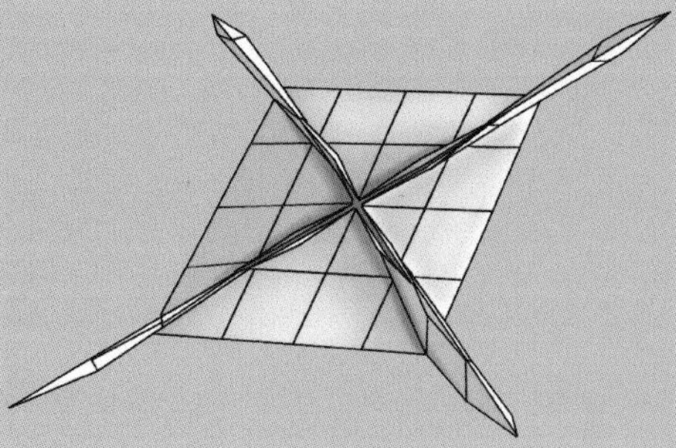

Fully collapsed.

Puff the petals by spreading the lips of the pockets open.

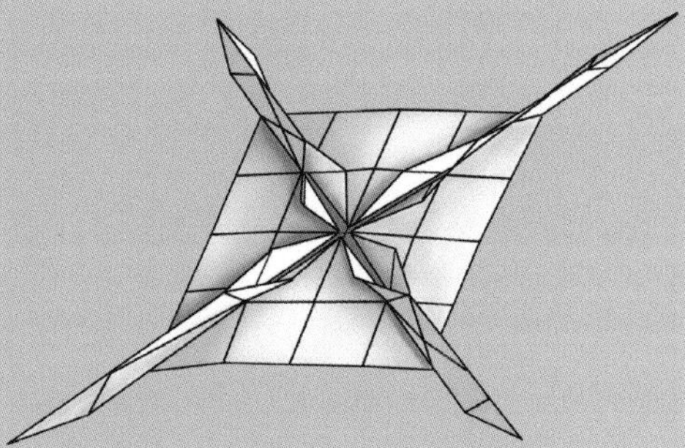

The complete molecule.

Note that the diagonals extend past the square base. This will require a special solution when we position two molecules next to each other.

2 by 2 Molecules

Use a grid of 16 by 16.

Add all precreases. Follow the diagonals, but skip the central 2 by 2 squares at the center of each molecule.

Start to collapse the top left molecule, and then complete a row.

There will be a lot of tension in the paper while collapsing. The corners of the four molecules coincide in the center of the model, and it is impossible to keep the paper flat. To solve that, twist this area, as is shown in the isometric view below.

Do not give up!

During the collapse, allow the molecules to remain open a little, to dial down the pressure.

Note the water bomb in the center. This is the result of the diagonals extending beyond the 4 by 4 inner square of the molecule. In order to stack them in, you have to twist this part. You can also sink this part in the shape of a water bomb base.

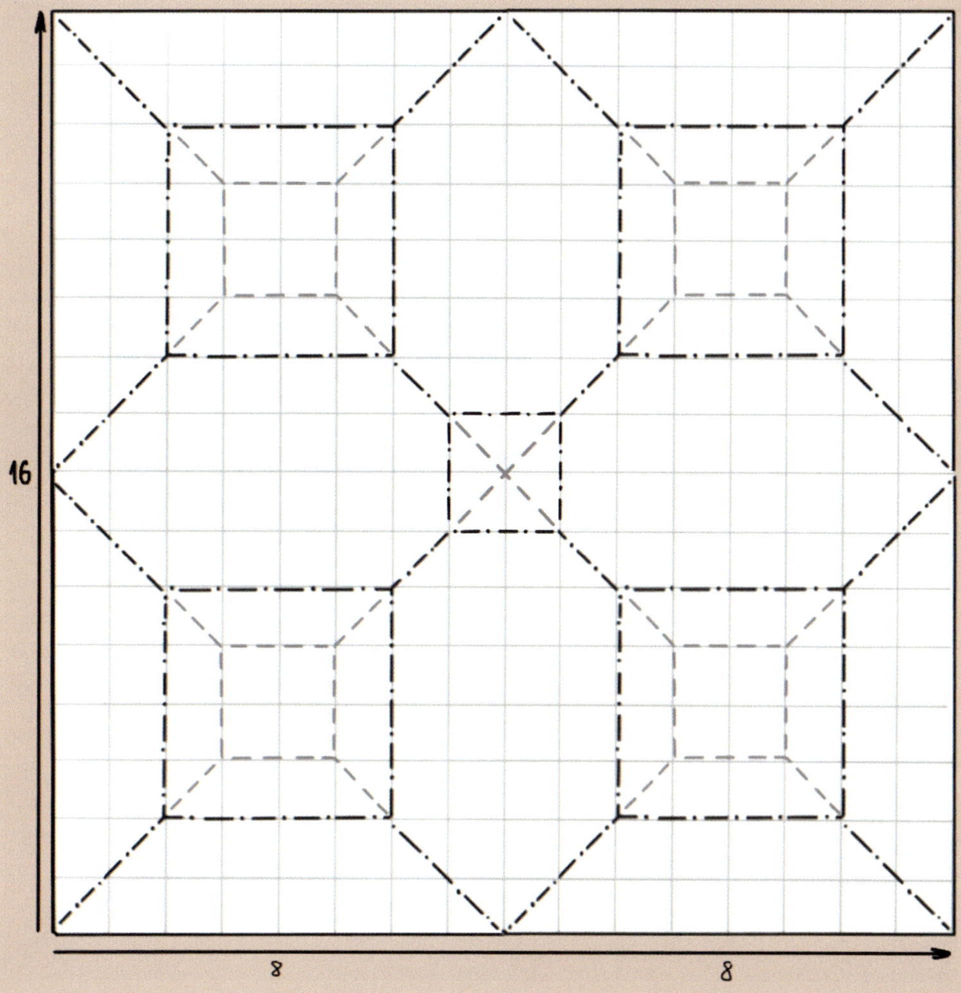

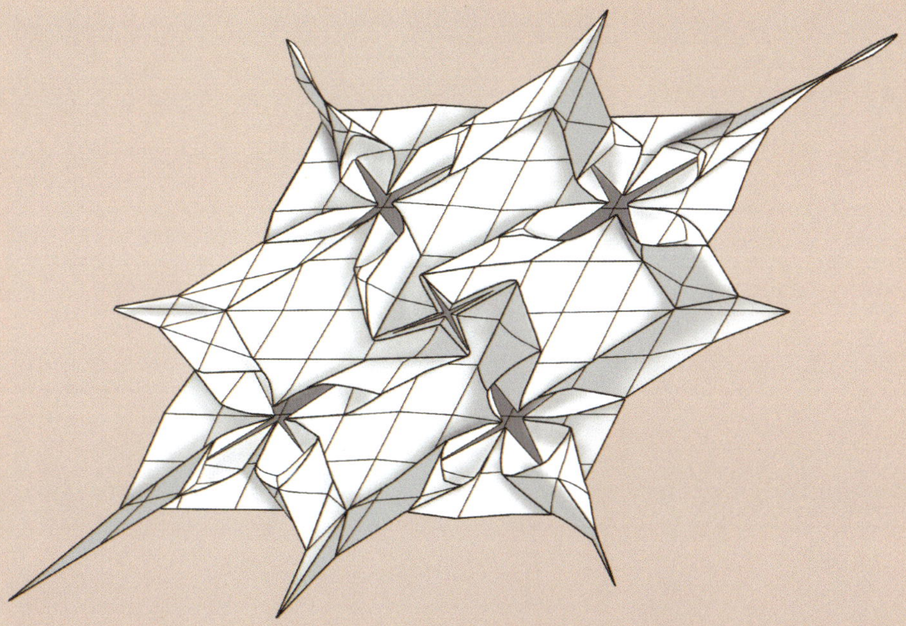

4 by 4 Molecules

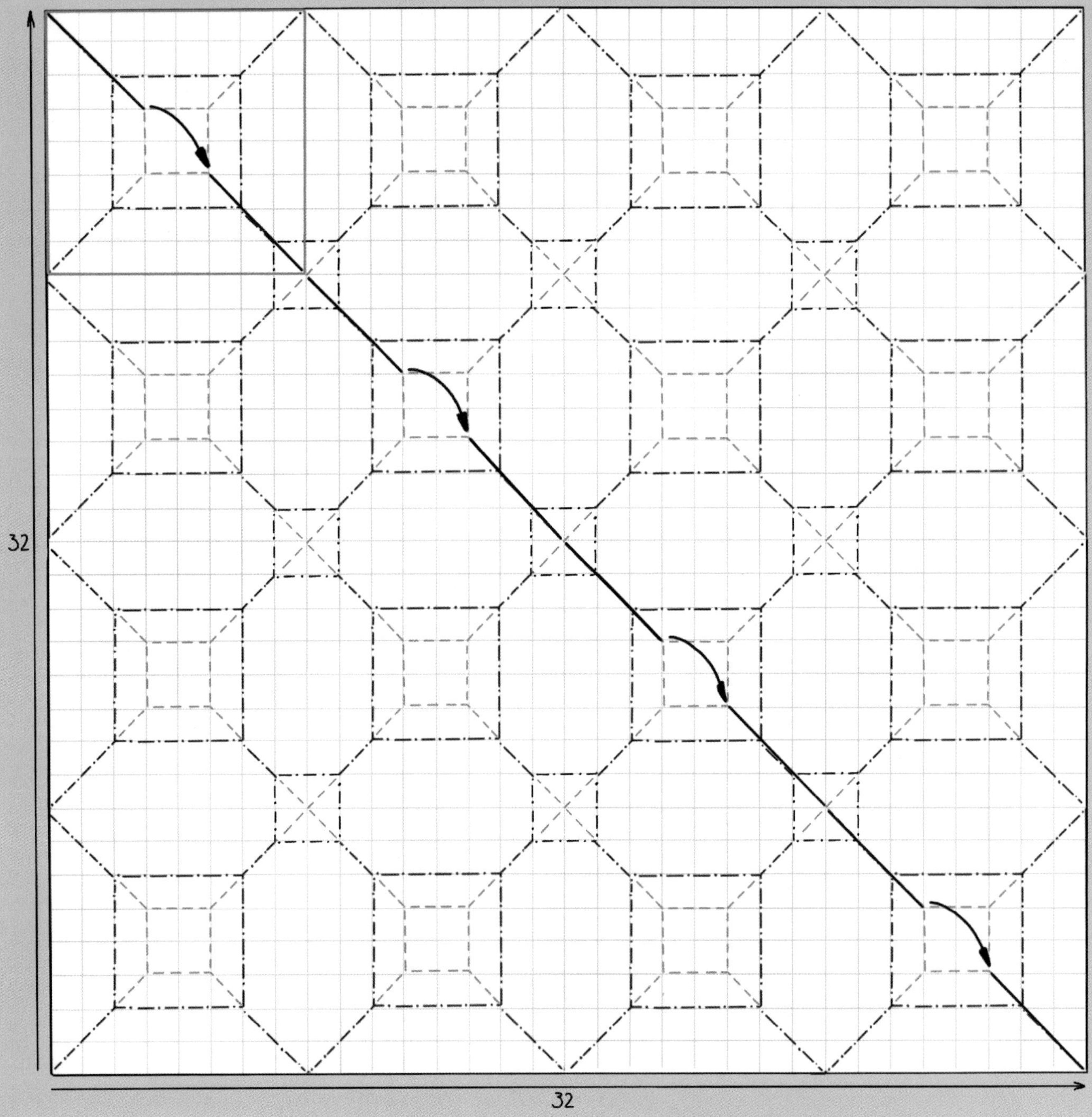

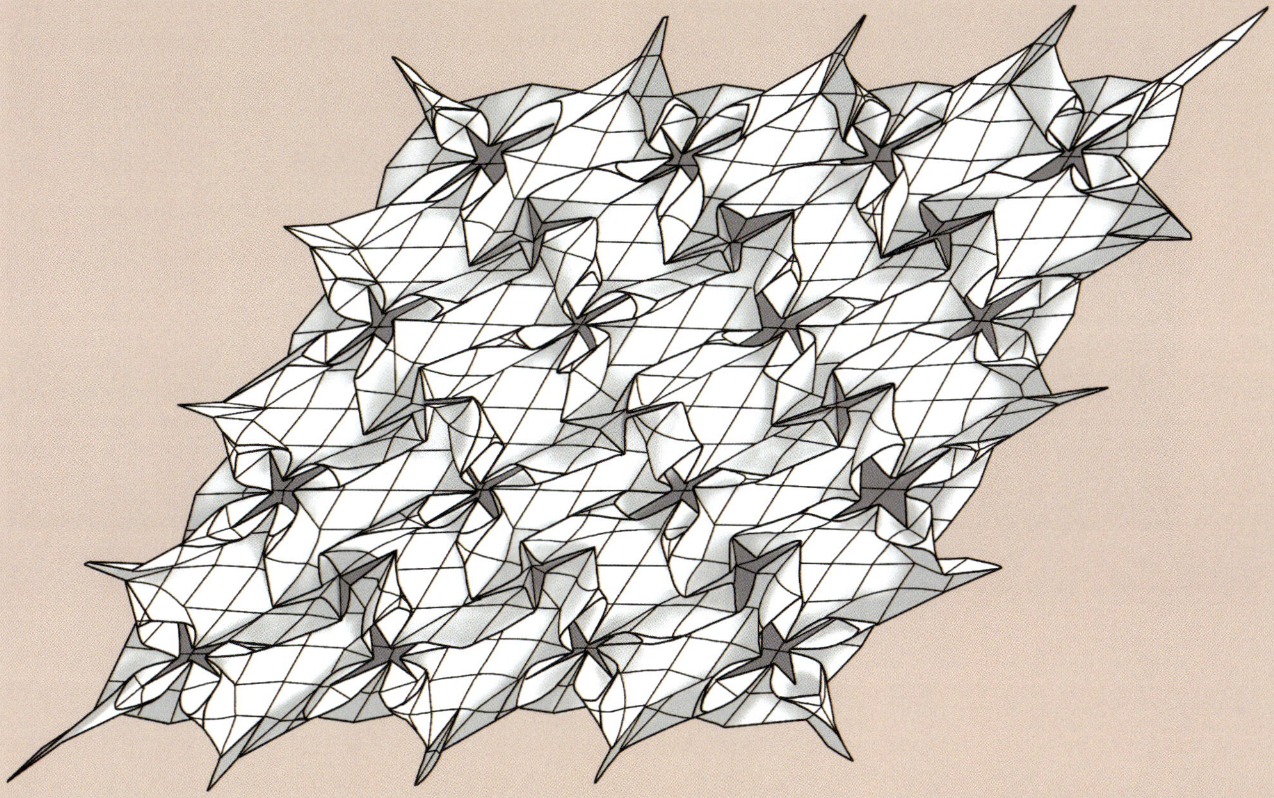

Use a grid of 32 by 32: 4 x 8 = 32.

The final result will be 16 squares wide.

Add all precreases, following the diagonals of every molecule, but skip the inner 2 by 2 squares.

Do remember to reverse the orientation of the inner parts of the diagonals from mountains to valleys!

Collapse row by row, following the 2 by 2 project process. In this project there is a lot of tension between all the molecule corners, so work carefully.

You can choose to sink all the water bombs or not.

To puff the inner parts of the flower, use the same technique presented in the Red Flower tessellation (page 76). The lips of the opening tend to lie to one side. To get the flower petals to align with the diagonals, you can pinch the extra paper, as shown below right.

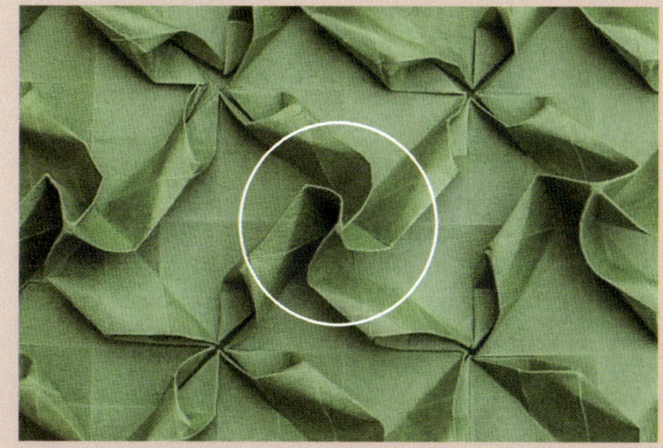

In the original version, the water bomb is left untouched.

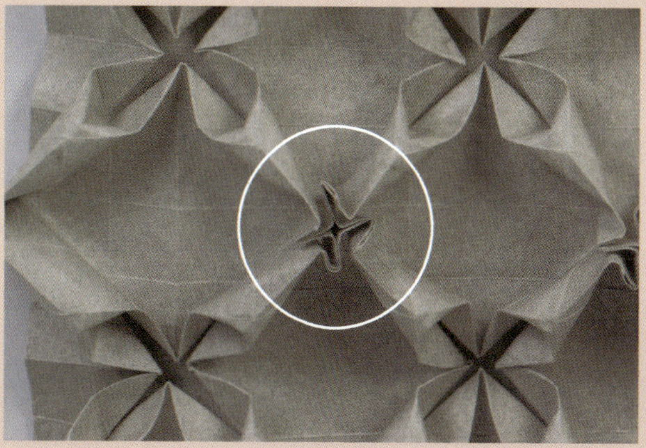

The extra paper is pinched shut for a cleaner look.

3 4 Bagan

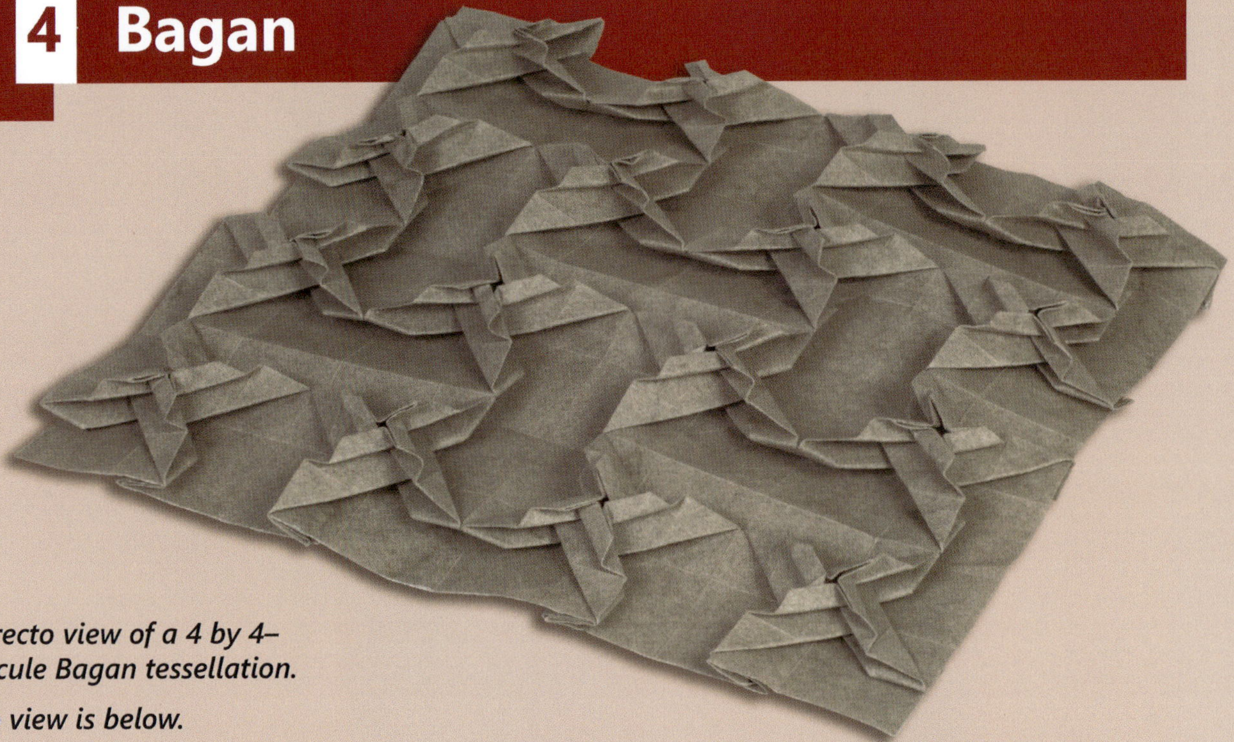

Top: recto view of a 4 by 4–molecule Bagan tessellation.

Verso view is below.

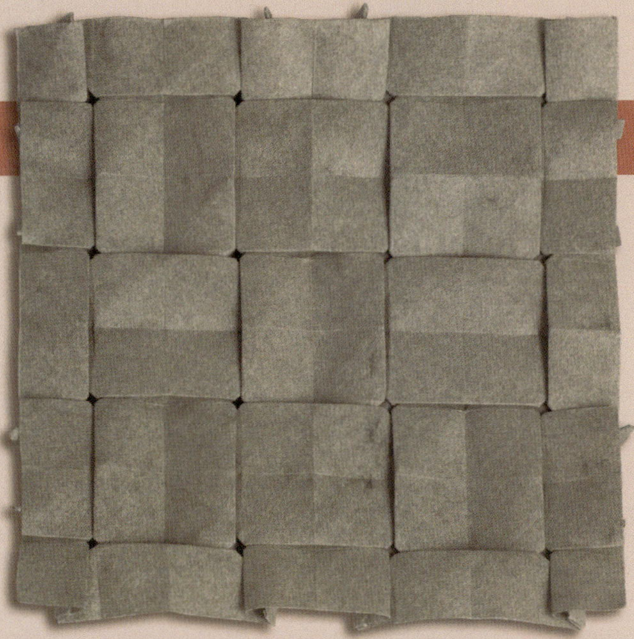

The Single Molecule

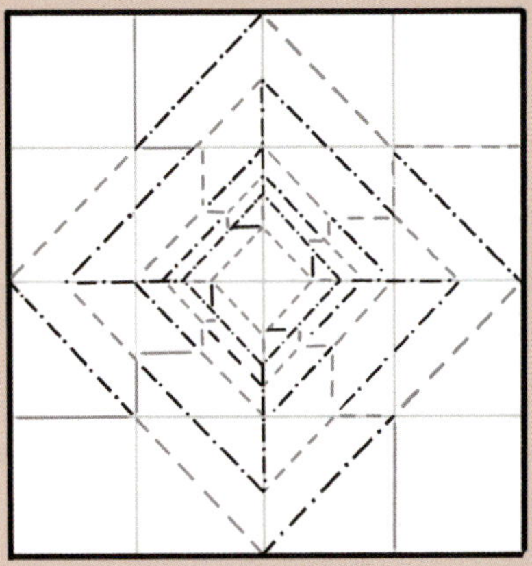

Out of the first step of the Red Flower tessellation (page 74) comes this multi-layered, pagoda-like construction.

Tessellating it reminded me of Bagan, a city in Myanmar with thousands of pagodas.

Compared to the Red Flower molecule, there are more fold lines. You can choose to fold them in advance or make them during the collapse process. The collapse is easier with them, but they make the precrease stage much longer.

The shrinkage ratio is 2:1.

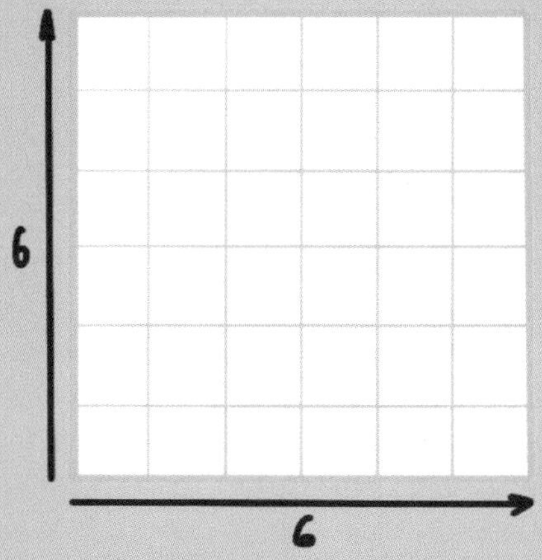

Start with a 6 by 6 grid. This includes an extra row and column that will help during the collapse.

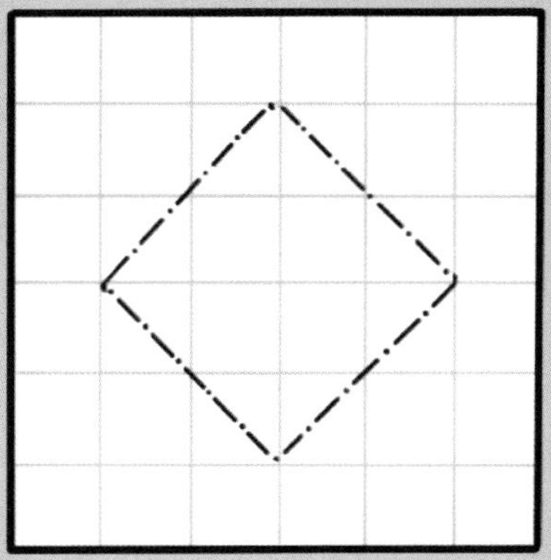

Add a tilted square with mountain folds.

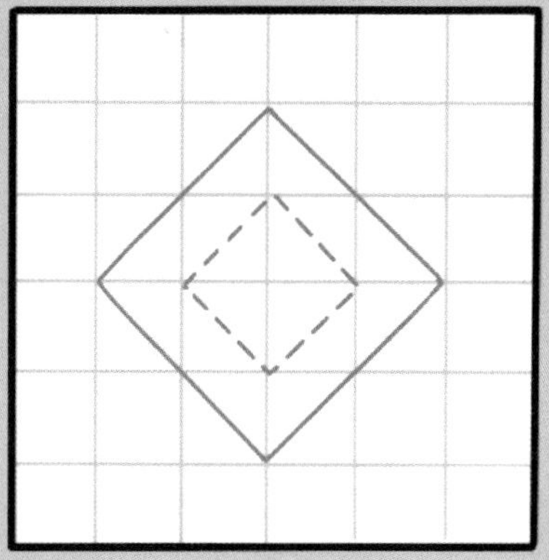

Add a smaller square with valley folds.

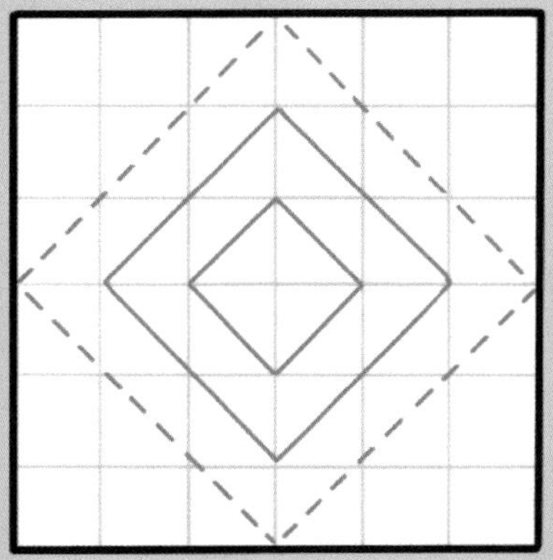

Add a bigger square, also out of valley folds.

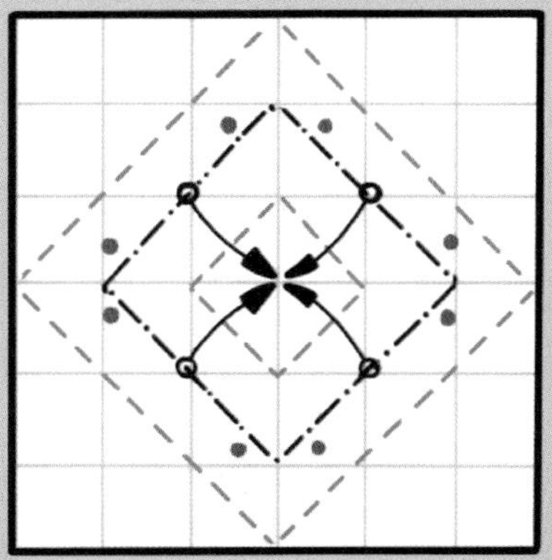

Collapse the first stage as outlined in the Red Flower tessellation (page 75).

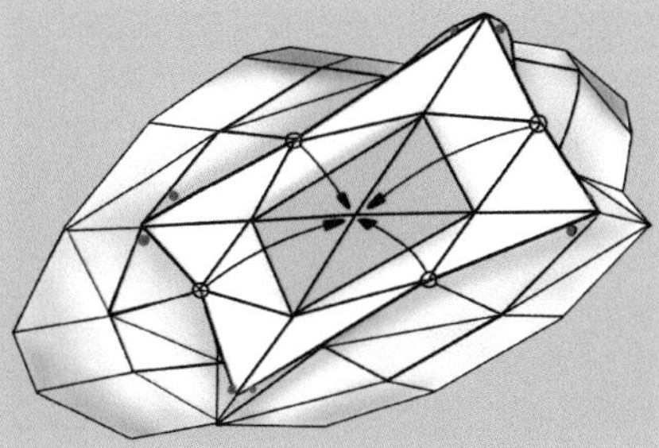

Collapse in process.

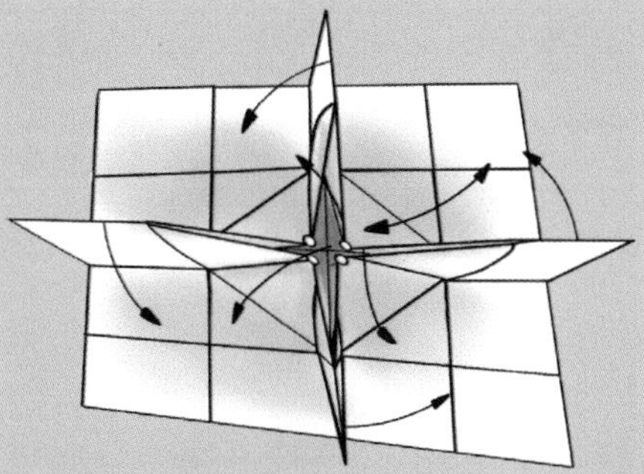

The first stage is fully collapsed.

Pull out the four midpoints and spread out the square.

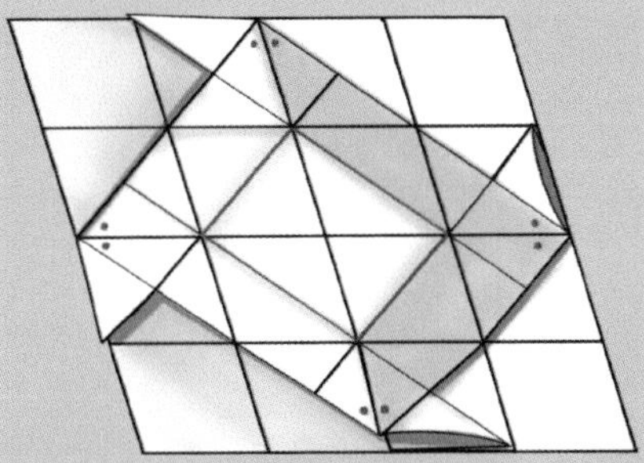

The result. Pinch the four corners (marked with red dots) of the upper square to form a cube. The red square will rise and form a cube shape. You can push it from below, if needed.

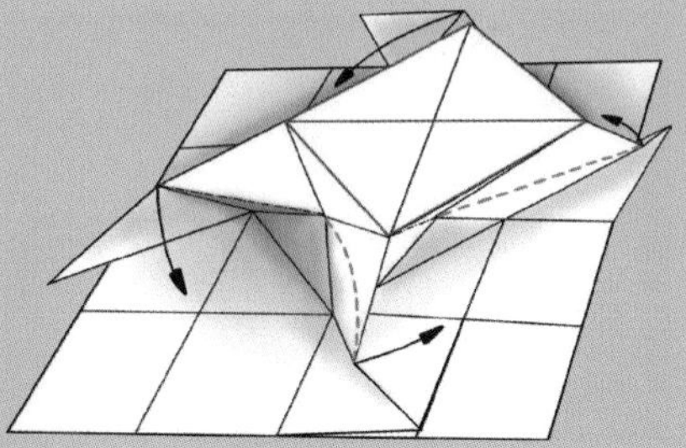

Now flatten the cube again, while relocating the marked flaps. Push the red square down.

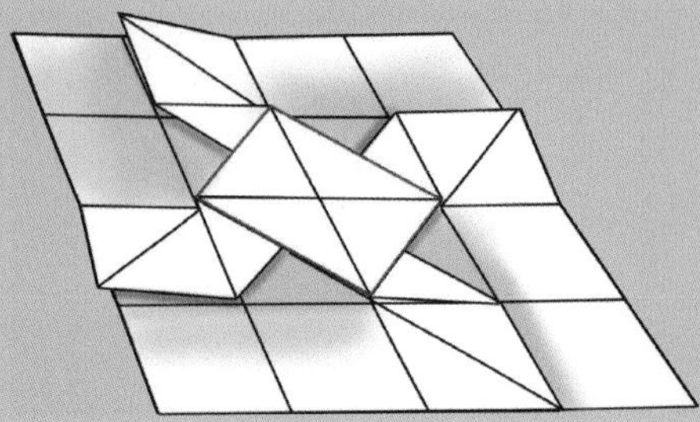

The result.

Note that the red square does NOT rotate during the collapse! It is just lower than before.

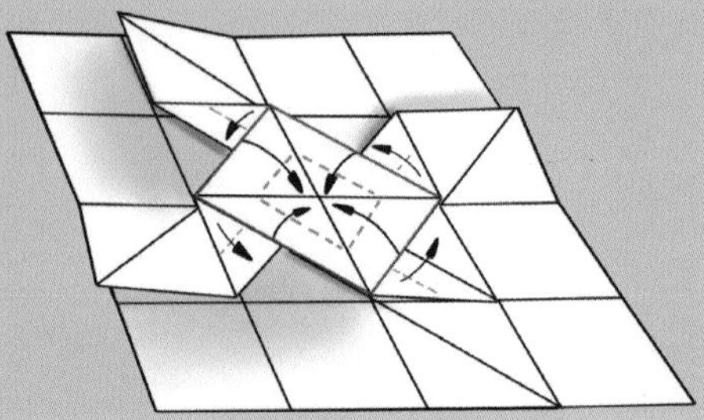

For the second level of the pagoda, fold edges to the center to form a smaller square. At the same time, narrow down the four flaps as shown.

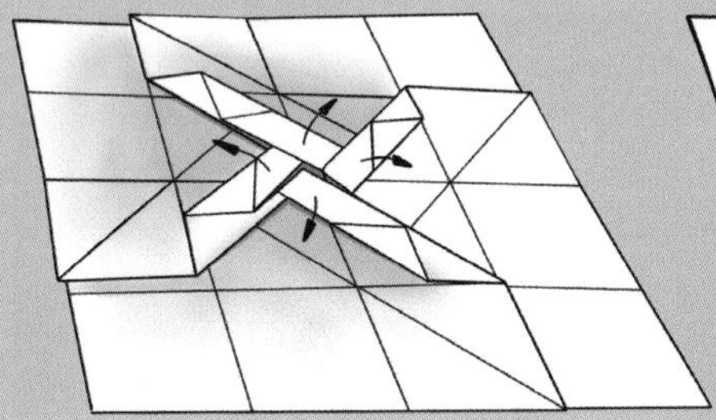

The result.

Unfold the flaps; they were precreases for the next step.

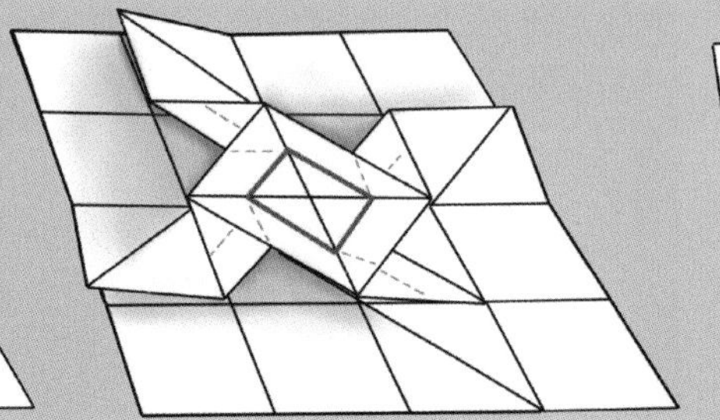

Repeat the process of pinching and raising the central square. You may need to use a long tool to push the paper up from the inside.

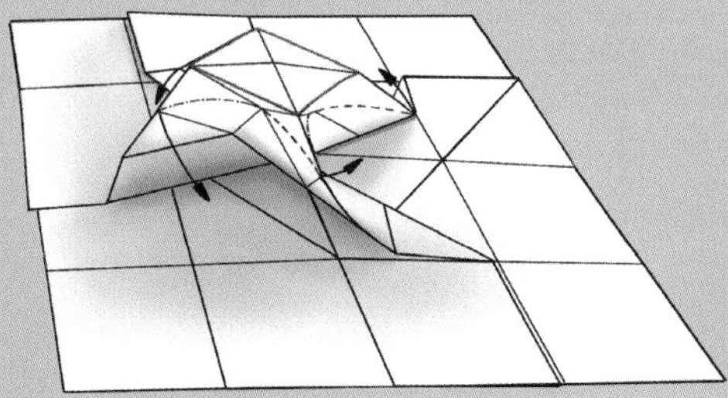

Flatten the square again, while relocating the flaps, as with the first level.

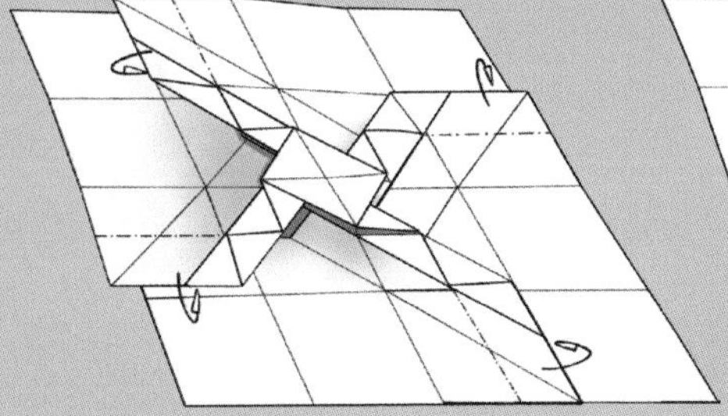

Mountain fold the four flaps as shown to hide them.

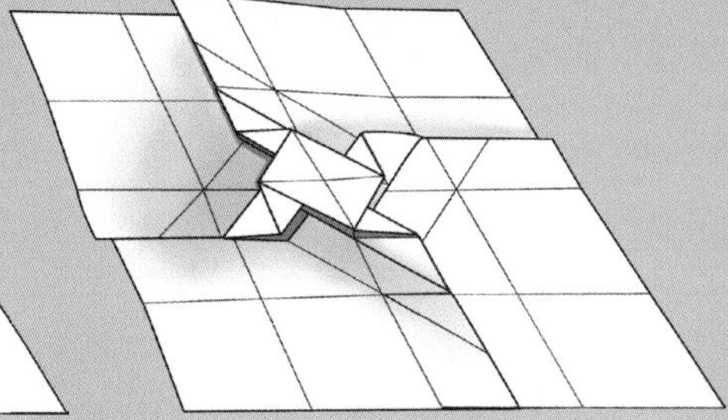

The finished molecule.

2 by 2 Molecules

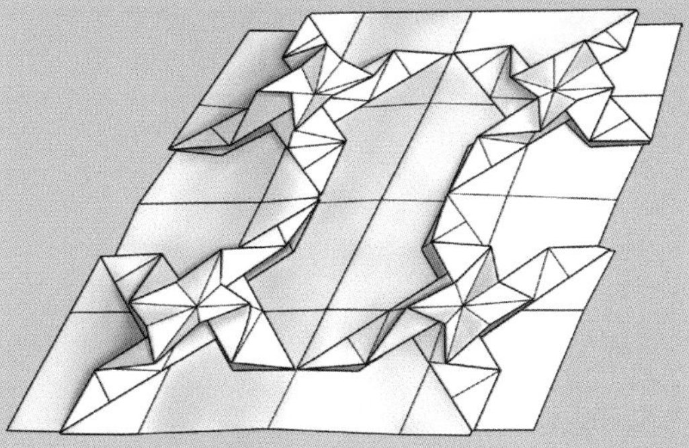

Use a grid of 8 by 8.

Although the single molecule was folded from a 6 by 6 grid, this project is tessellated without an extra column and row, affording a cleaner look.

Add all precreases, following the Red Flower tessellation process on page 76.

After the model is fully collapsed to the un-puffed stage of the Red Flower tessellation, you can work on each molecule separately, and turn it into a Bagan tessellation.

You have to fold this tessellation one level at a time. Complete all molecules to the same level before moving on to the next one.

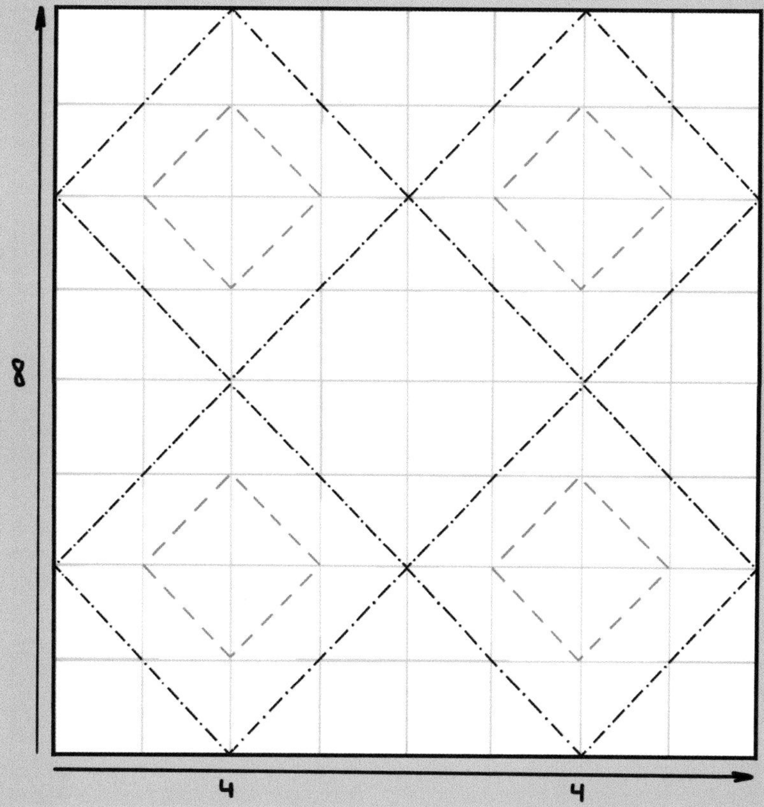

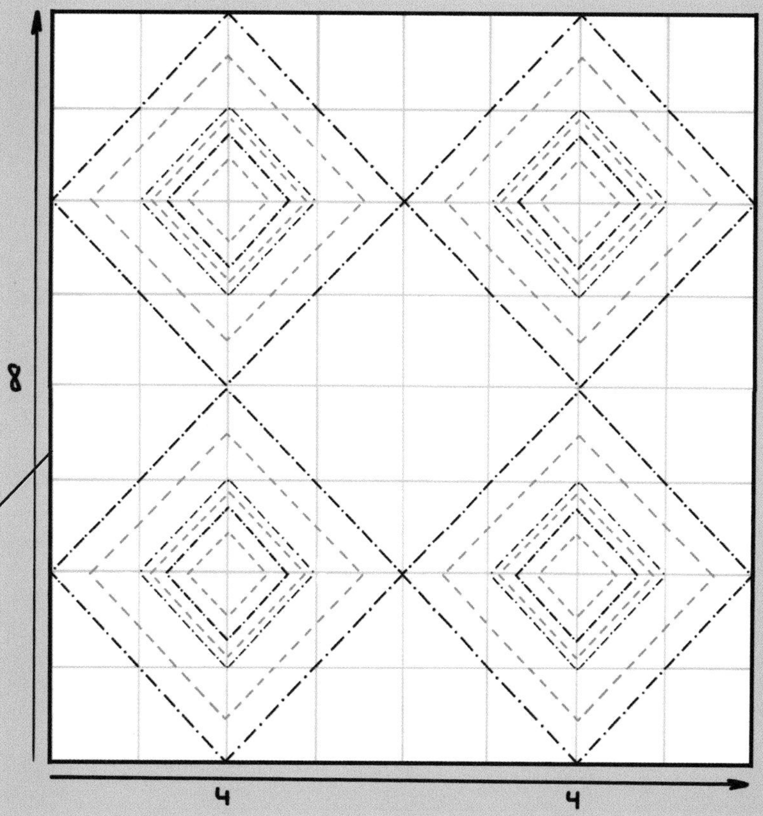

If you want to make the collapse stage easier, follow this CP. The fold lines you have to add to narrow the flaps during the collapse are done beforehand!

4 by 4 Molecules

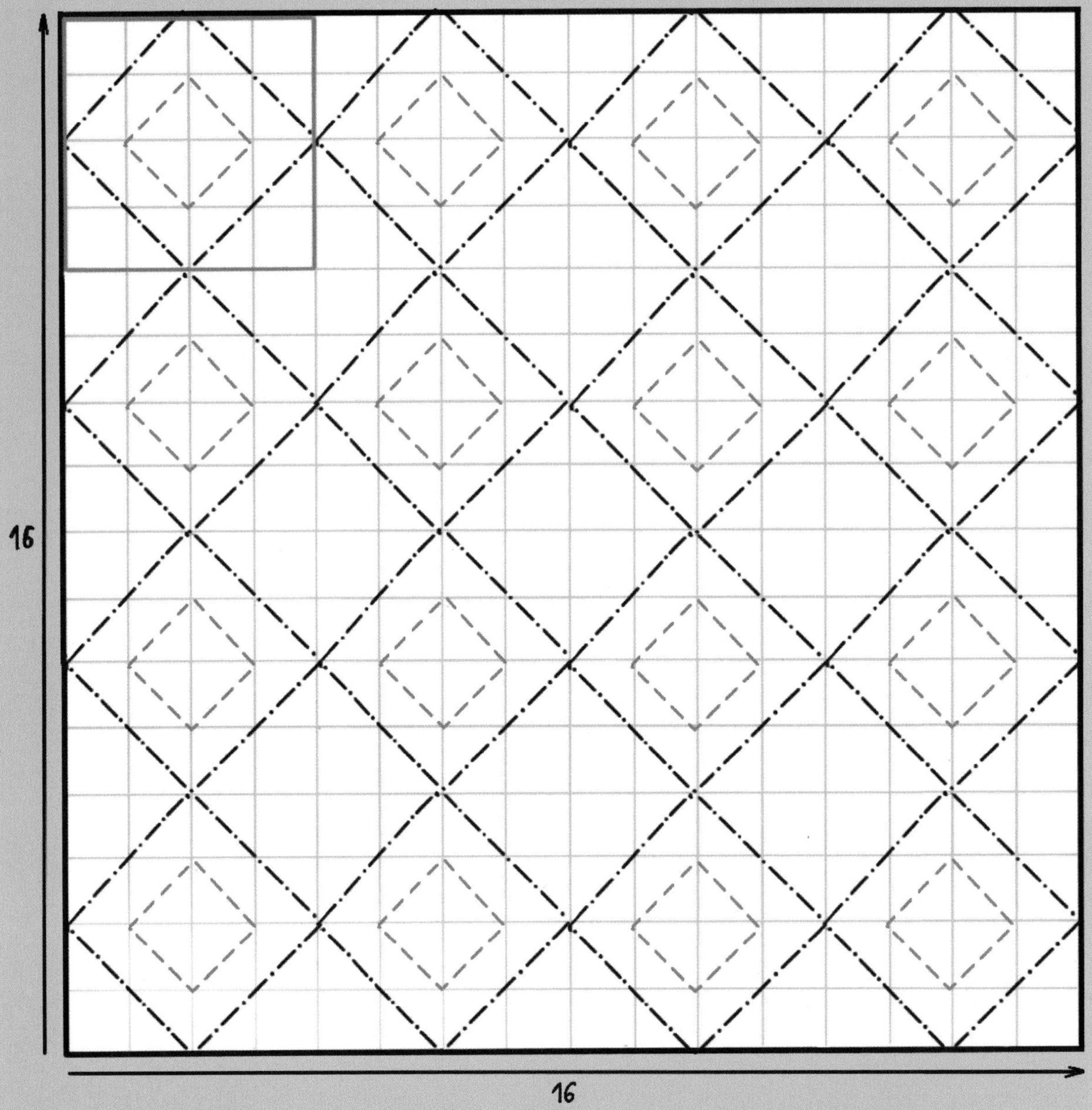

Use a grid of 16 by 16:
4 x 4 = 16.

The final result will be eight squares wide.

Add all precreases; there are shortcuts for the first level of mountain lines only.

You can add all the other creases not shown here beforehand, as with the 2 by 2 project on the previous page.

Collapse row by row.

You have to complete all the molecules to the same level before working on the next one.

3 5 Hexa Flower

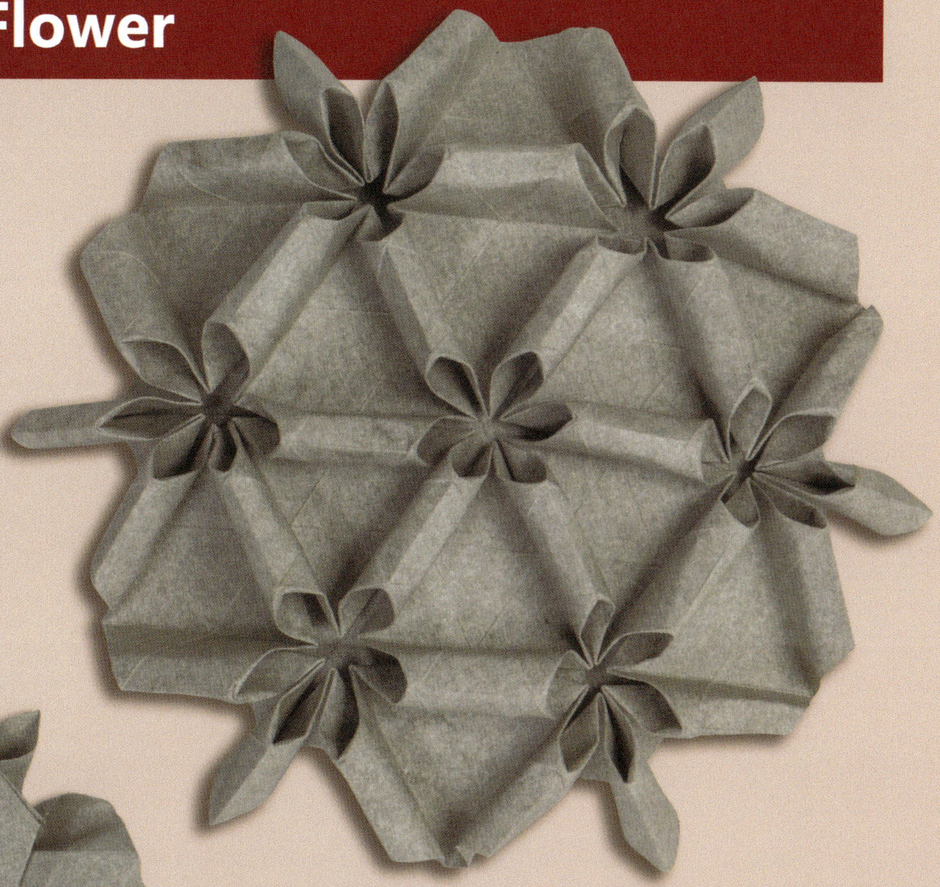

Right: recto view of the Hexa Flower.

Verso view is below.

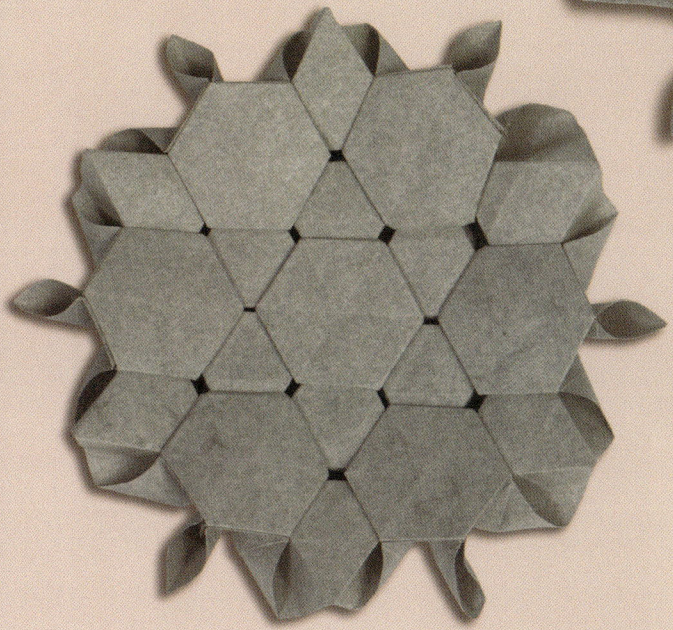

The Single Molecule

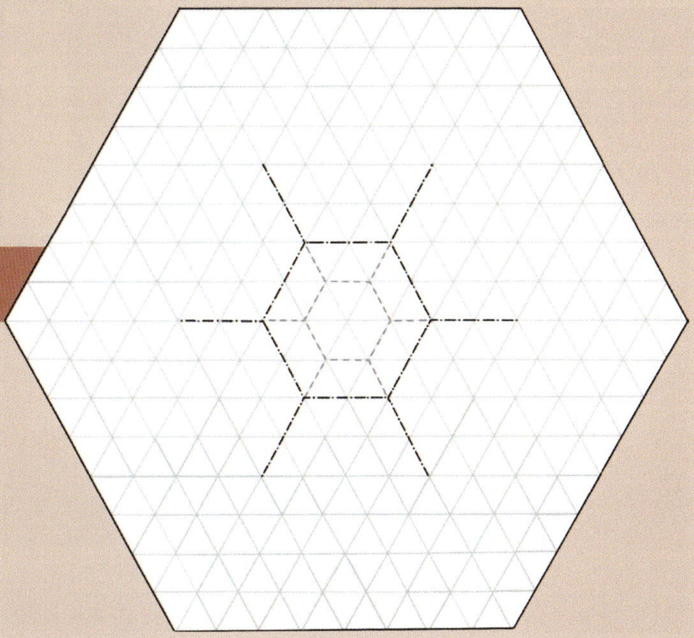

For hexagon grid projects, we start in the center. Following the same approach covered in the square grid projects, we bring the midpoints of the hexagon sides to the center point. This creates the center flower around which more flowers are added.

16 Grid Project

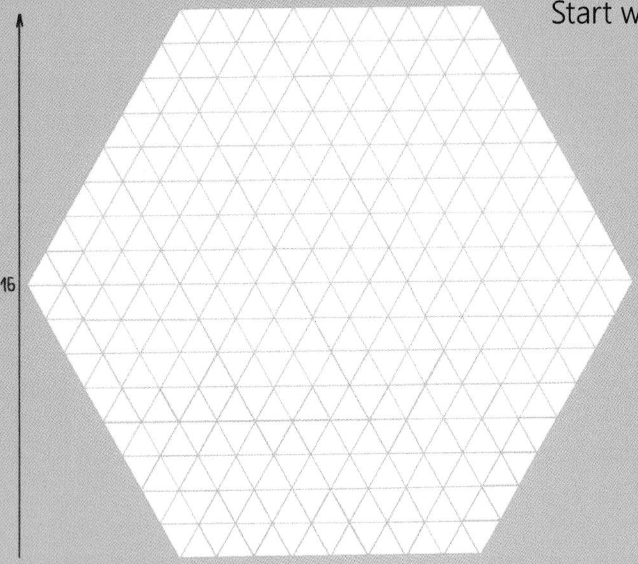

Start with a grid of 16 by 16 by 16.

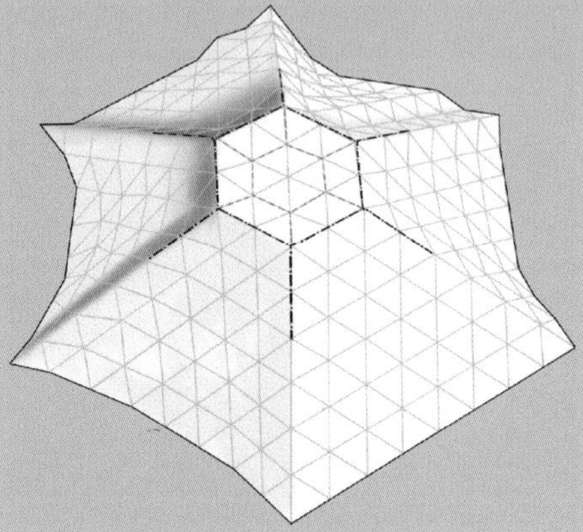

Mountain fold the second inner hexagon and all the fold lines going to the corners of the sheet.

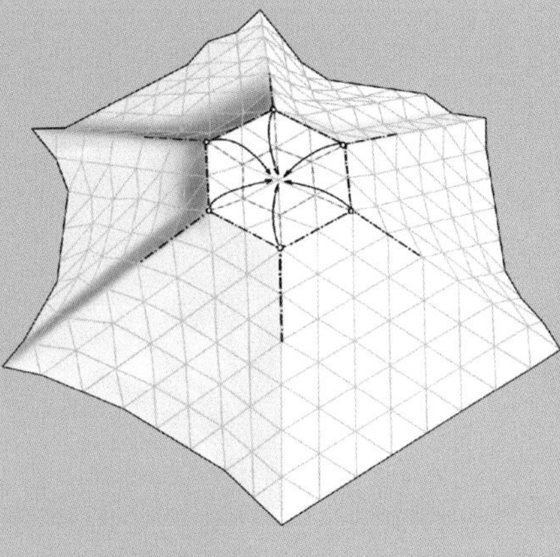

Bring all the corners of the inner hexagon to meet in the center, following the process of the Red Flower molecule, shown on page 75.

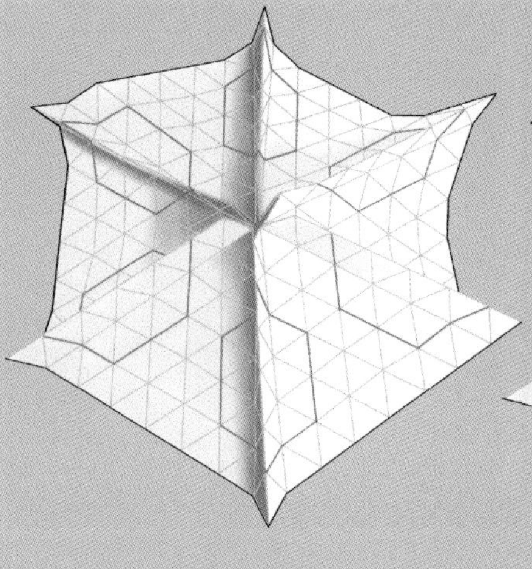

The first flower is collapsed.

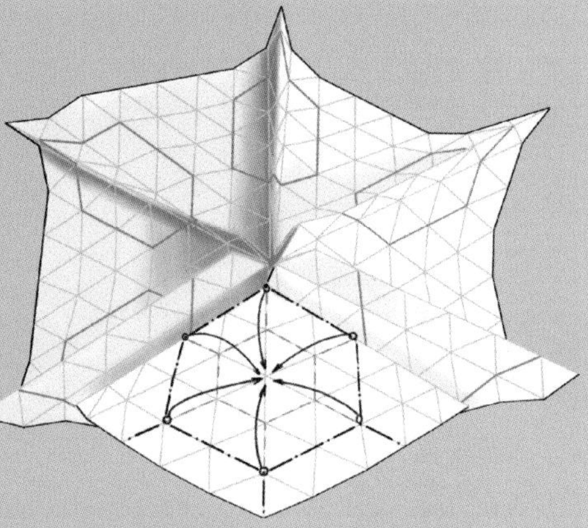

Flatten the paper around the next hexagons and repeat the process. Continue in this fashion until all the flowers are complete.

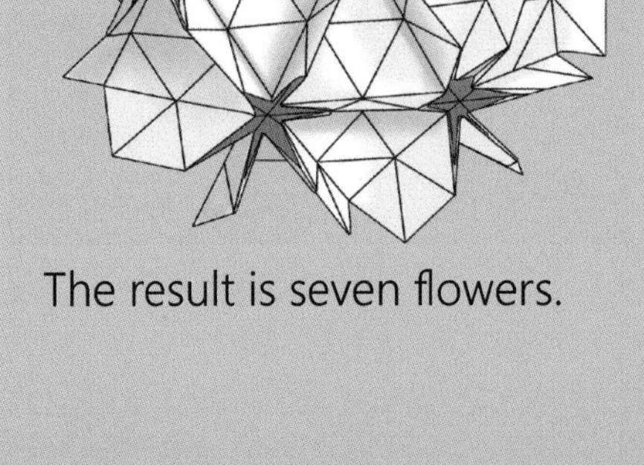

The result is seven flowers.

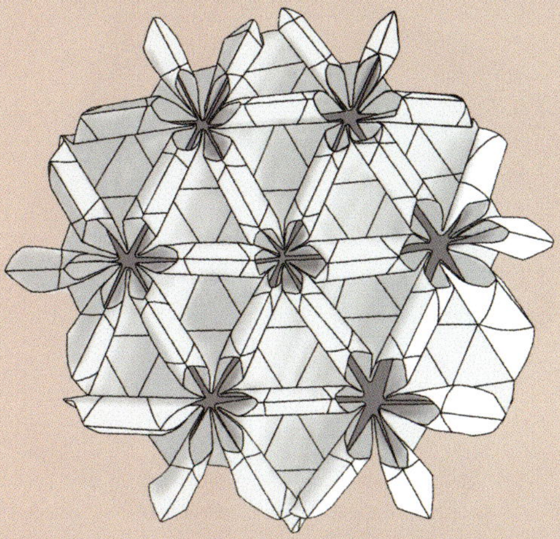

You can puff every petal (or just some) using the same process from the Red Flower tessellation (page 76), squashing the lips slightly with your fingers.

Above and Beyond—A 64 Grid Project

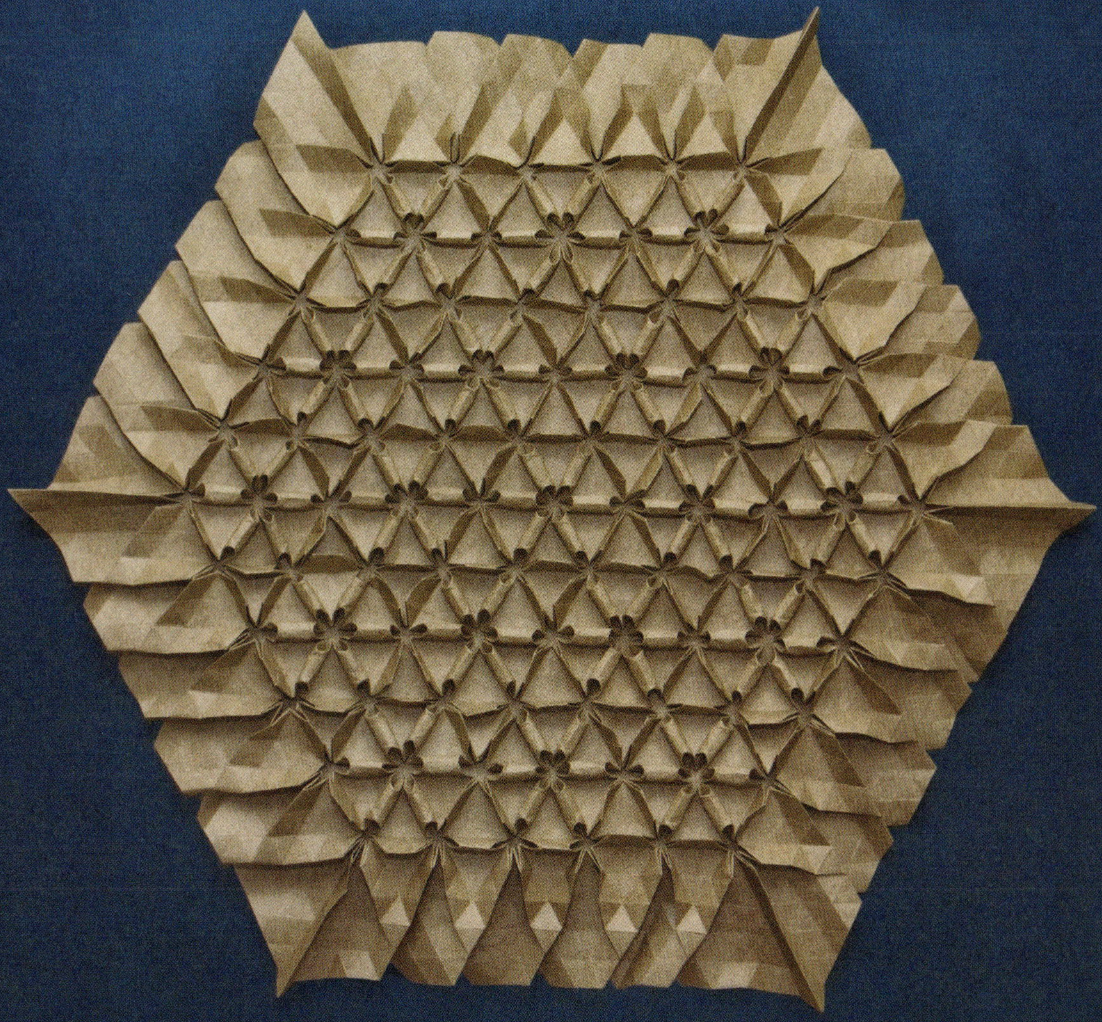

The outer rows are not collapsed to make a wide frame of leaves.

4 The Hood Family

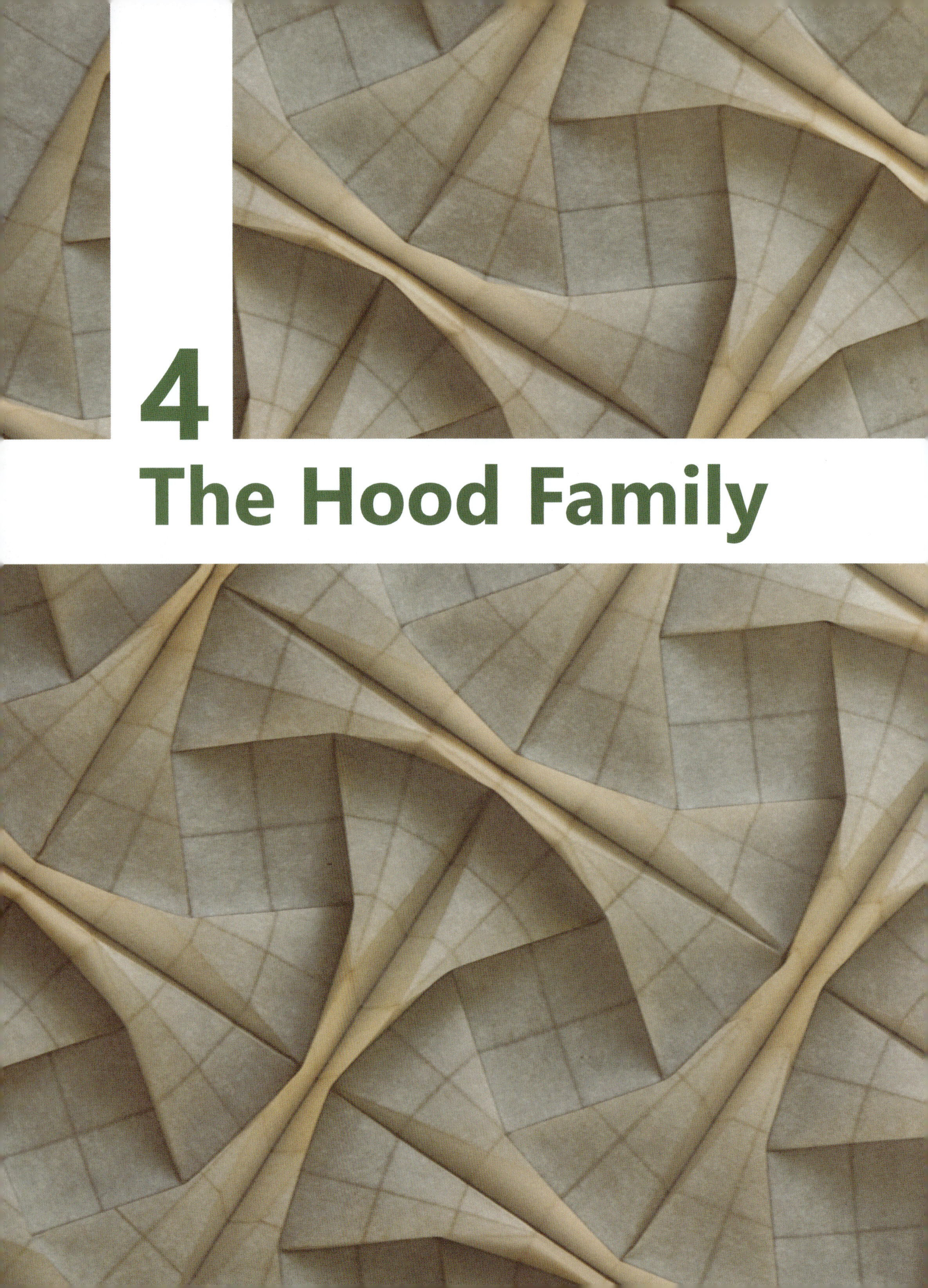

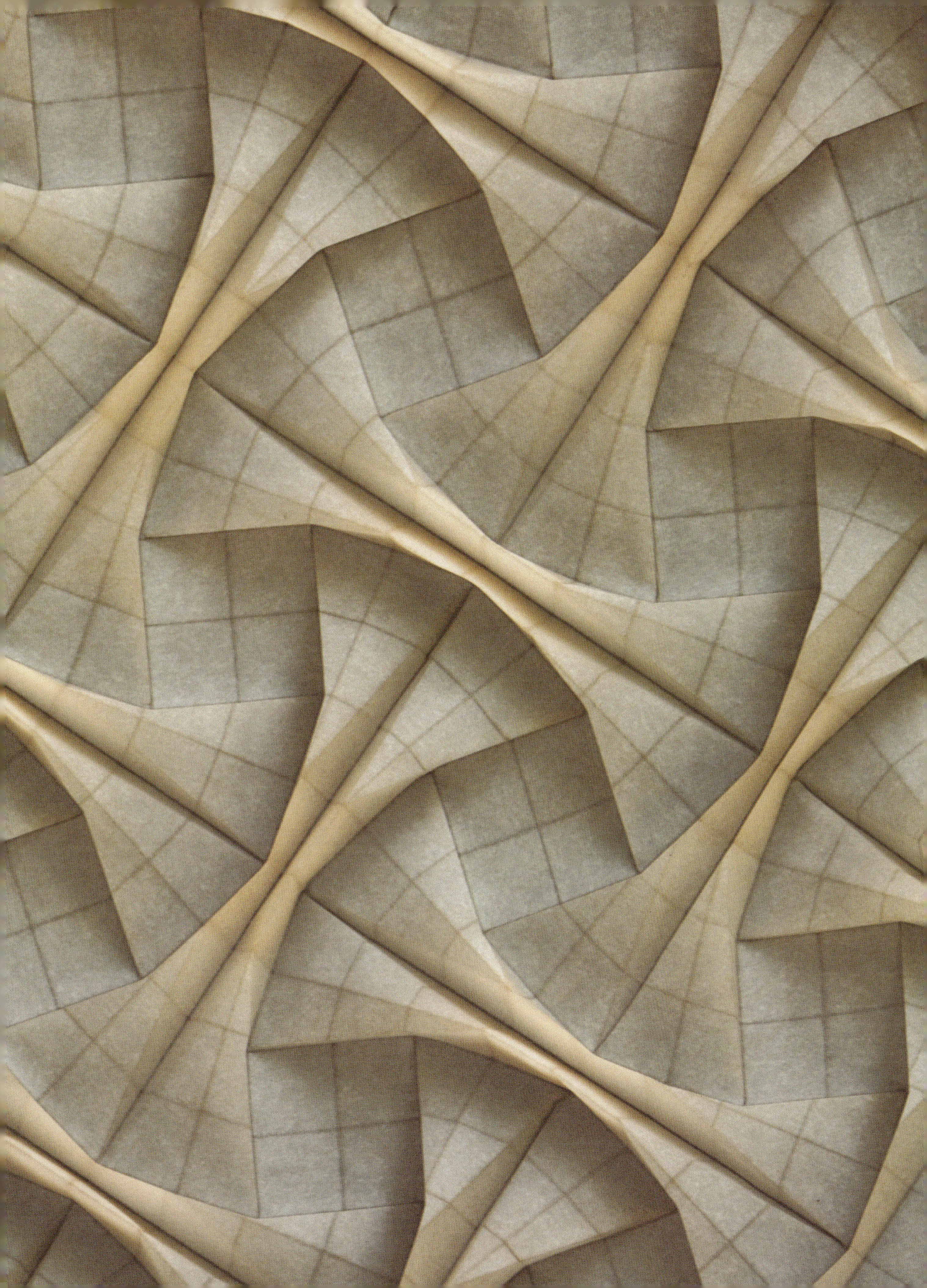

Introduction

The Hood family is based on a square grid. I found it while trying to follow the concept that was presented by Alessandra Lamio (Italy) in her beautiful model, *Square Spaceness*.

The molecule can be easily multiplied or mirrored, as Chagay Golan (a colleague from Israel) and I discovered while working on the concept together.

4 1 Childhood

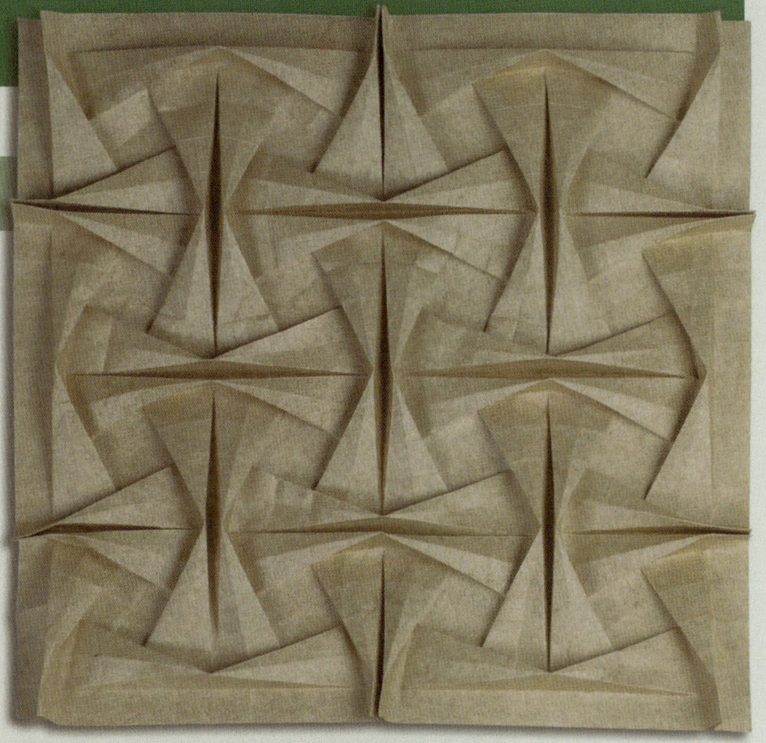

The Single Molecule

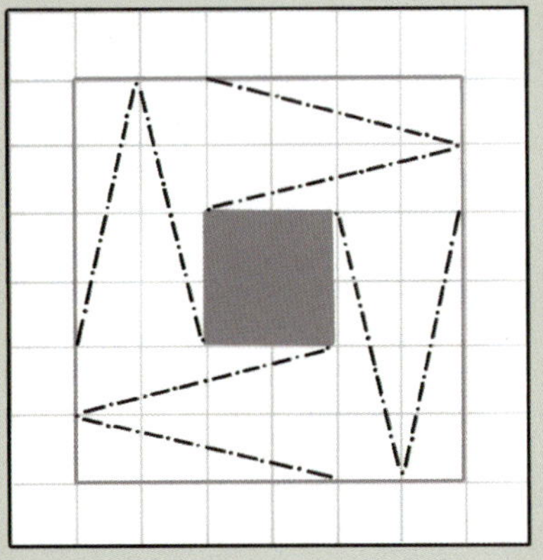

The resemblance to the Cube family is obvious, as you can see from the CP. While the inner folds raise the paper, the outer ones bring it back to the table level.

The molecule is tessellated by mirroring.

The shrinkage ratio is 3:2.

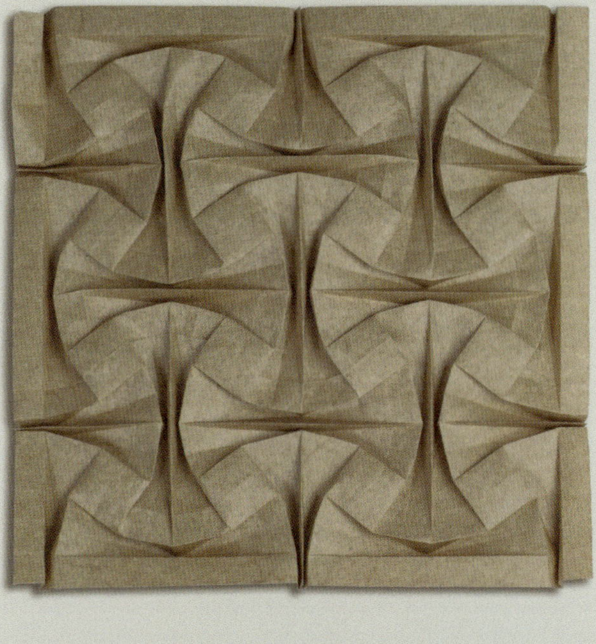

Above: recto view of a 4–molecule by 4 Childhood tessellation.

Verso view is to the left.

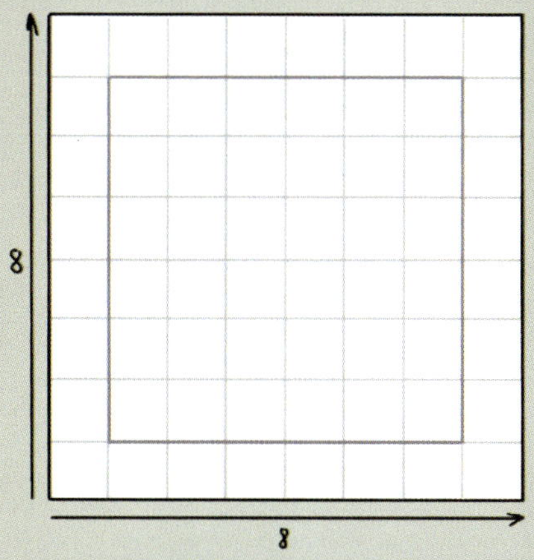

The Childhood molecule is 6 by 6, so start with an 8 by 8 grid. This will give you an extra row so you hold onto the flaps better while collapsing the model.

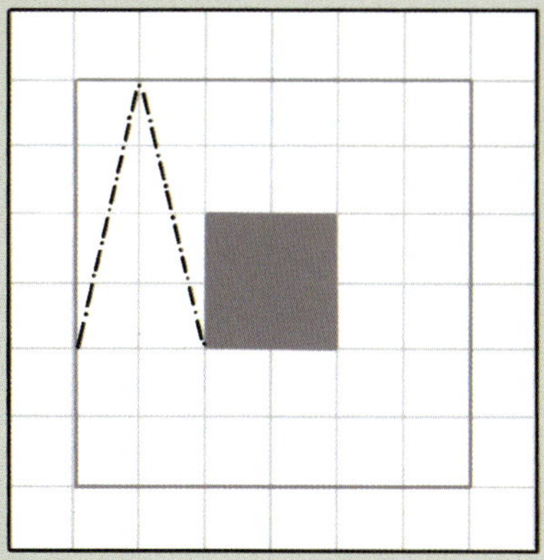

The center four squares (in gray) are left untouched.

Add the precreases as shown.

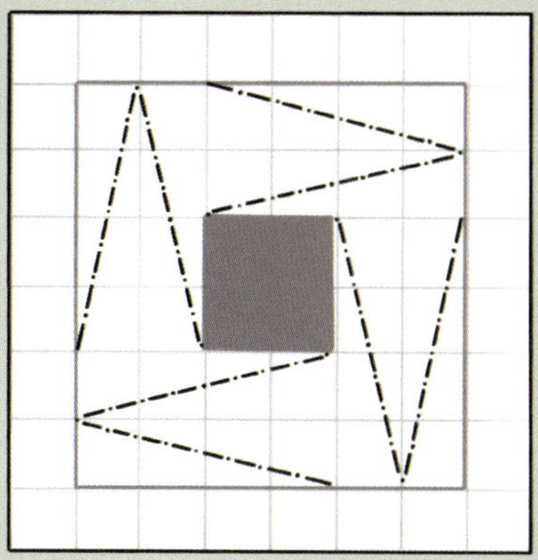

Complete the precreases as shown, all around.

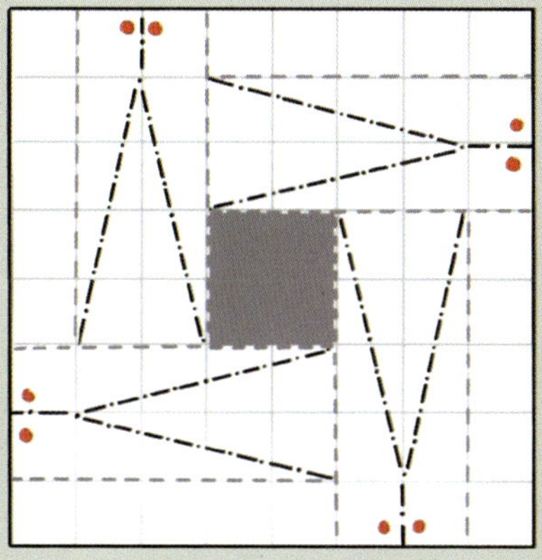

To collapse, pinch the squares together at the dots.

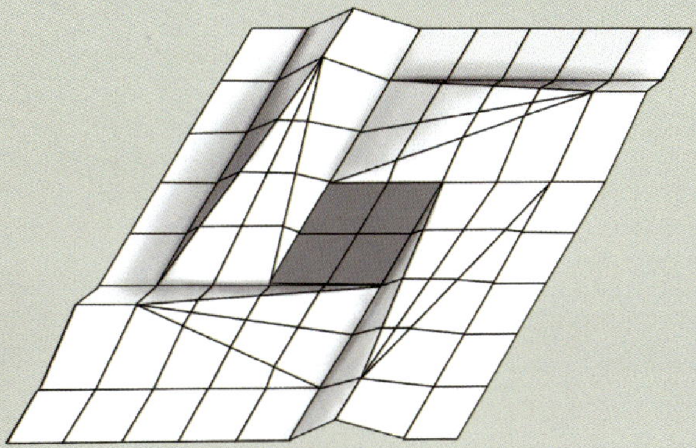

In process. Make sure the center gray area is kept flat on the table!

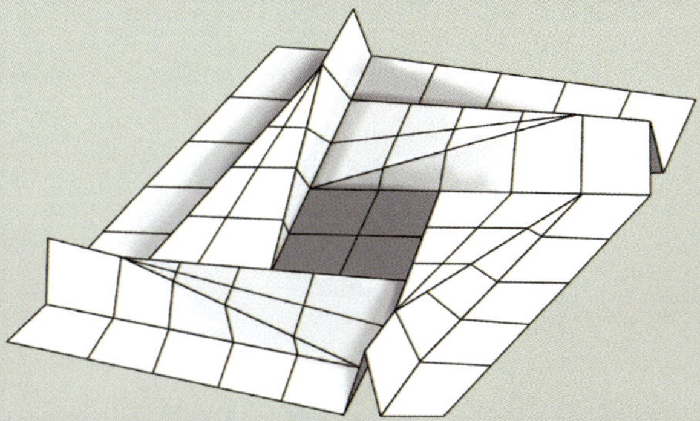

Fully collapsed.

2 by 2 Molecules

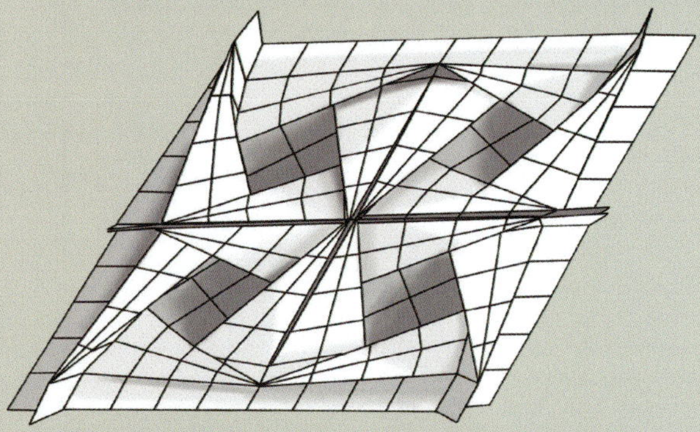

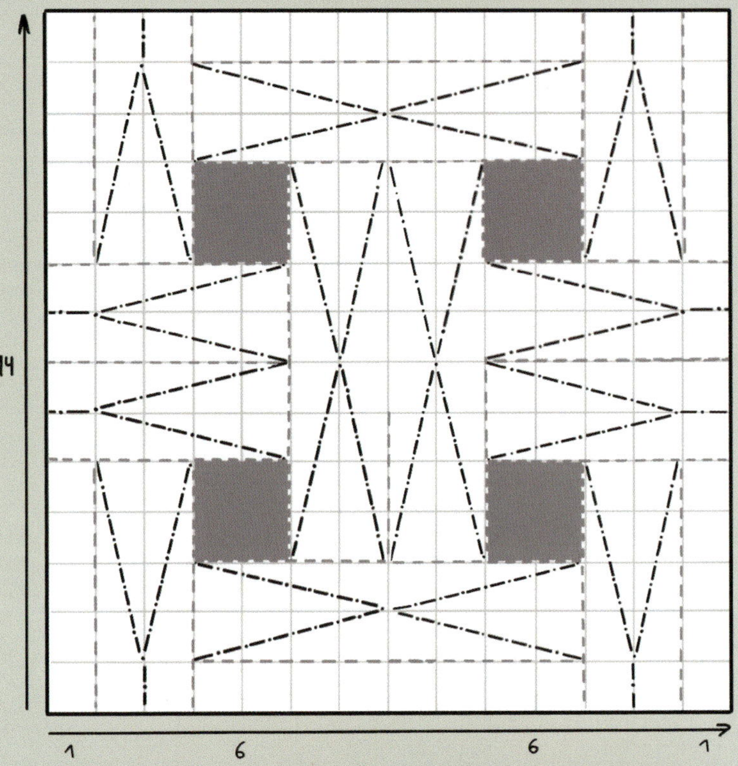

Use a grid of 14 by 14. Add all precreases.

Start with the top left corner molecule, then move to the right molecule.

To complete the project, fold the next two molecules simultaneously.

Use clips to hold the edges in the folded position.

Above and Beyond—A 6 by 6 Project

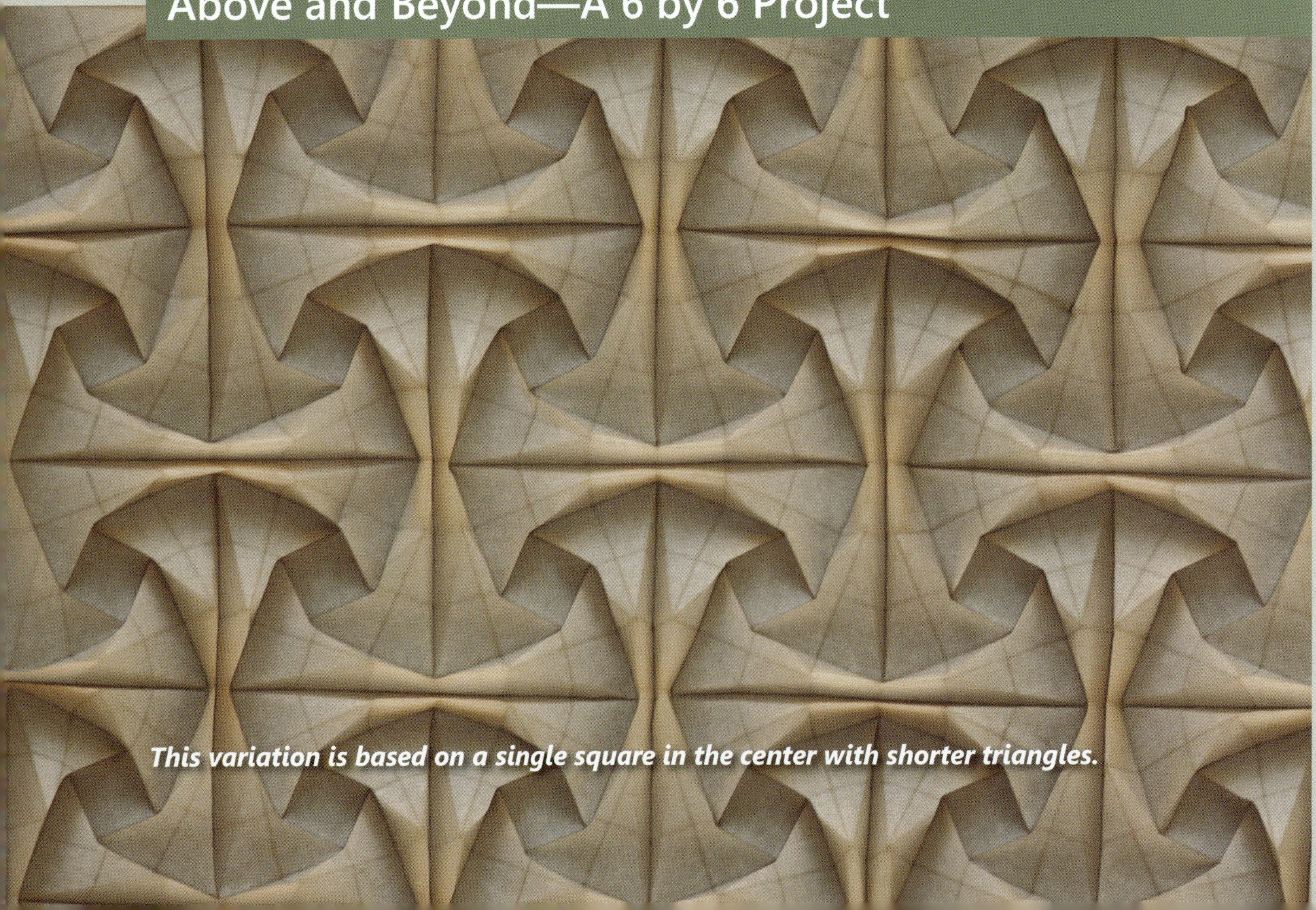

This variation is based on a single square in the center with shorter triangles.

4 by 4 Molecules

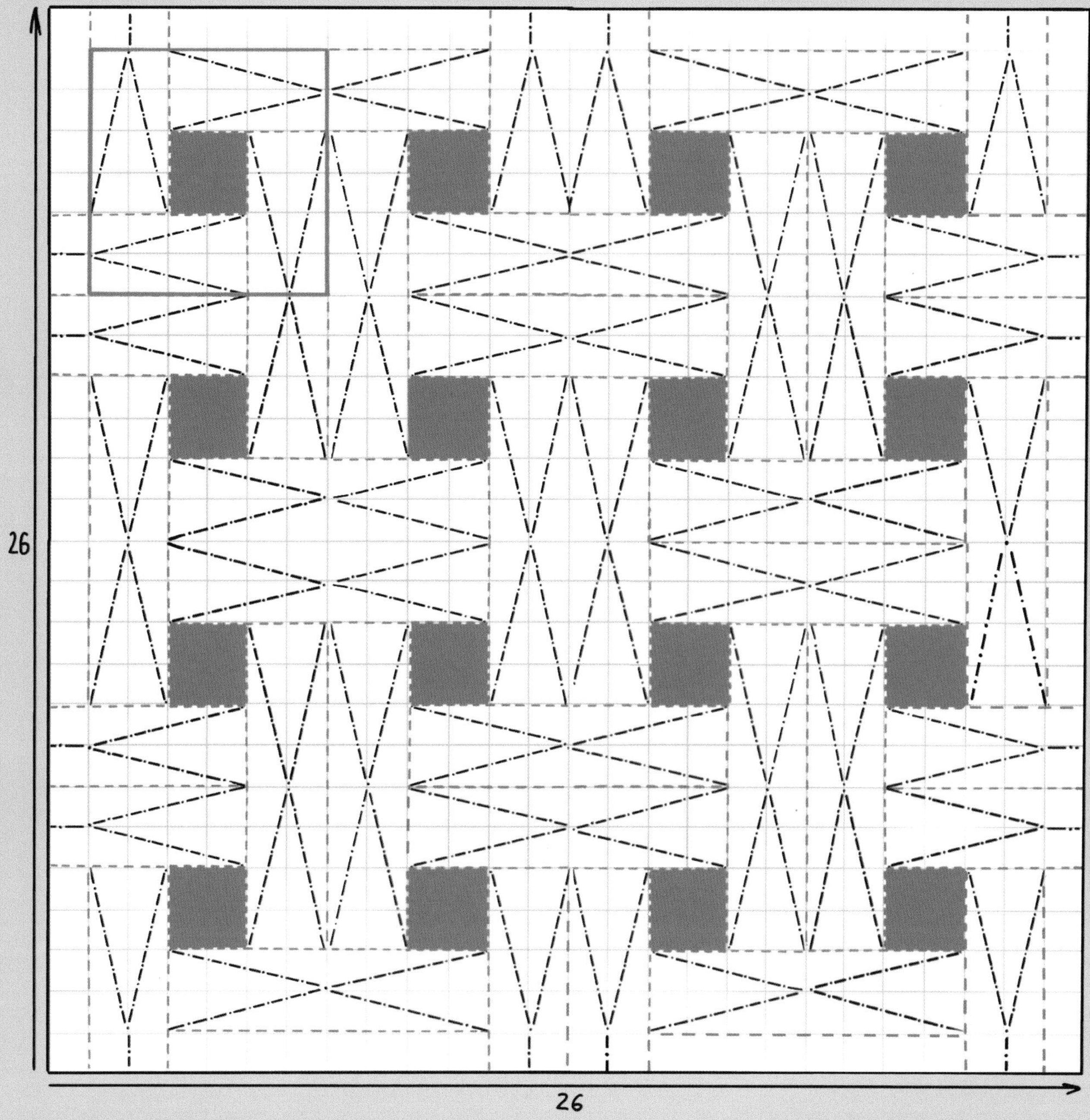

Use a grid of 26 by 26:
1 + 4 x 6 + 1 = 26.

The final result will be 18 squares wide.

Follow the wide Xs to shorten the work time. There are no shortcuts besides that.

Start the collapse with the top left molecule and complete a row of molecules. Continue working *around the edges*. Keeping all the outer molecules collapsed with clips, work inward. If the tension in the center part is too strong, release some clips and push the central molecule into place.

Tip: Turn the paper over during the collapse and rearrange the inner molecules from the other side.

4 2 Childhood Evolved

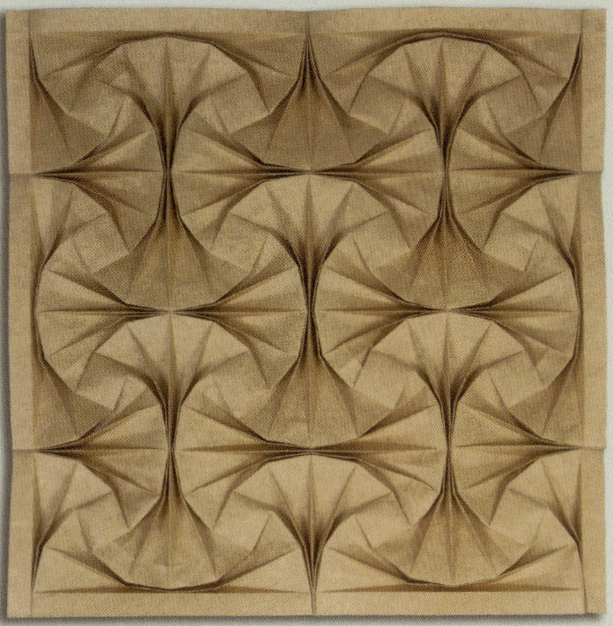

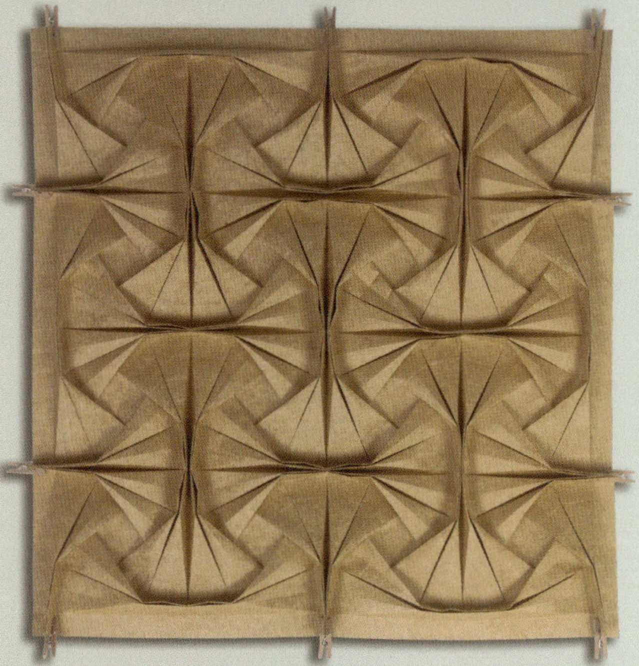

Above: verso view of a 4 by 4–molecule Childhood tessellation with eight triangles per molecule (instead of four). Recto view is to the right.

The Childhood tessellation offers several parameters that can be changed to create many variations.

You can shorten the triangles, which alters the angles of the diagonals. They can be diagonals of 1 by 3 rectangles, 2 by 3, etc.

You can change the center square size from 2 by 2 to a single square.

You can add more triangles around the center of the molecule, making each molecule more packed.

All the changes result in interesting variations. Try to find your own!

Shorter Triangles

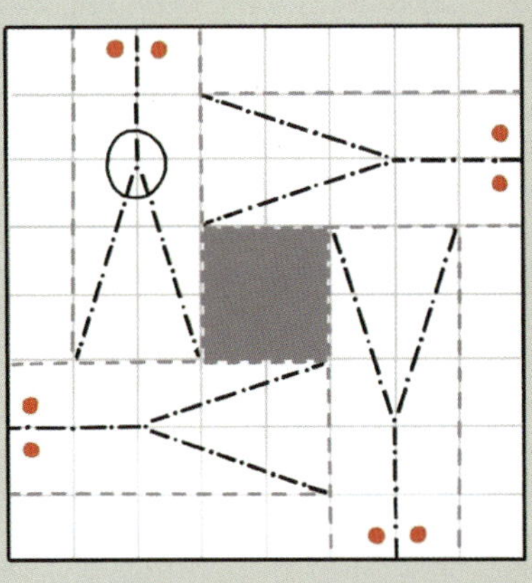

Here the size of the triangle is reduced, based on a diagonal of a 1 by 3 rectangle.

No CP is given, since it is very similar to the original model.

Smaller Center

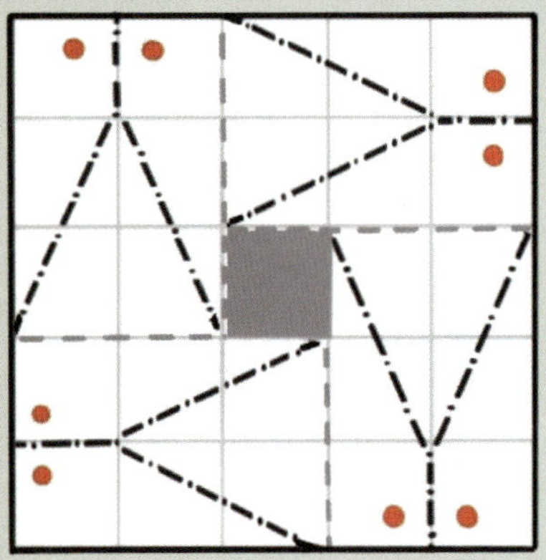

In this variation, the center is now a single square and the triangles are shorter still.

The shrinkage ratio is 2:1.

You can find a CP for a 4 by 4 project with this variation, called Growing Up, on page 105.

More Triangles

You can also add more triangles, and make the molecule more dense.

This example shows how a molecule can have two triangles on each side of the center square.

The molecule size is 10 by 10, so start with a 12 by 12 grid.

The shrinkage ratio is 5:3.

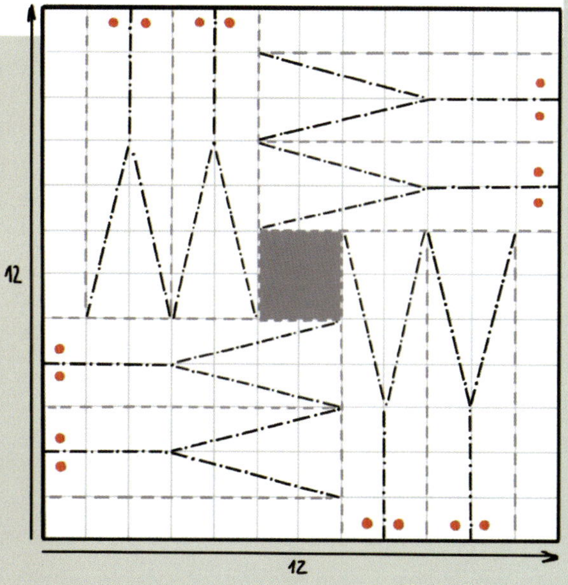

2 by 2 Molecules

Start with a grid of 22 by 22.

Make all precreases.

Collapse the model in two stages. First, collapse all the inner triangles that surround the central square. Only then complete the outer ones.

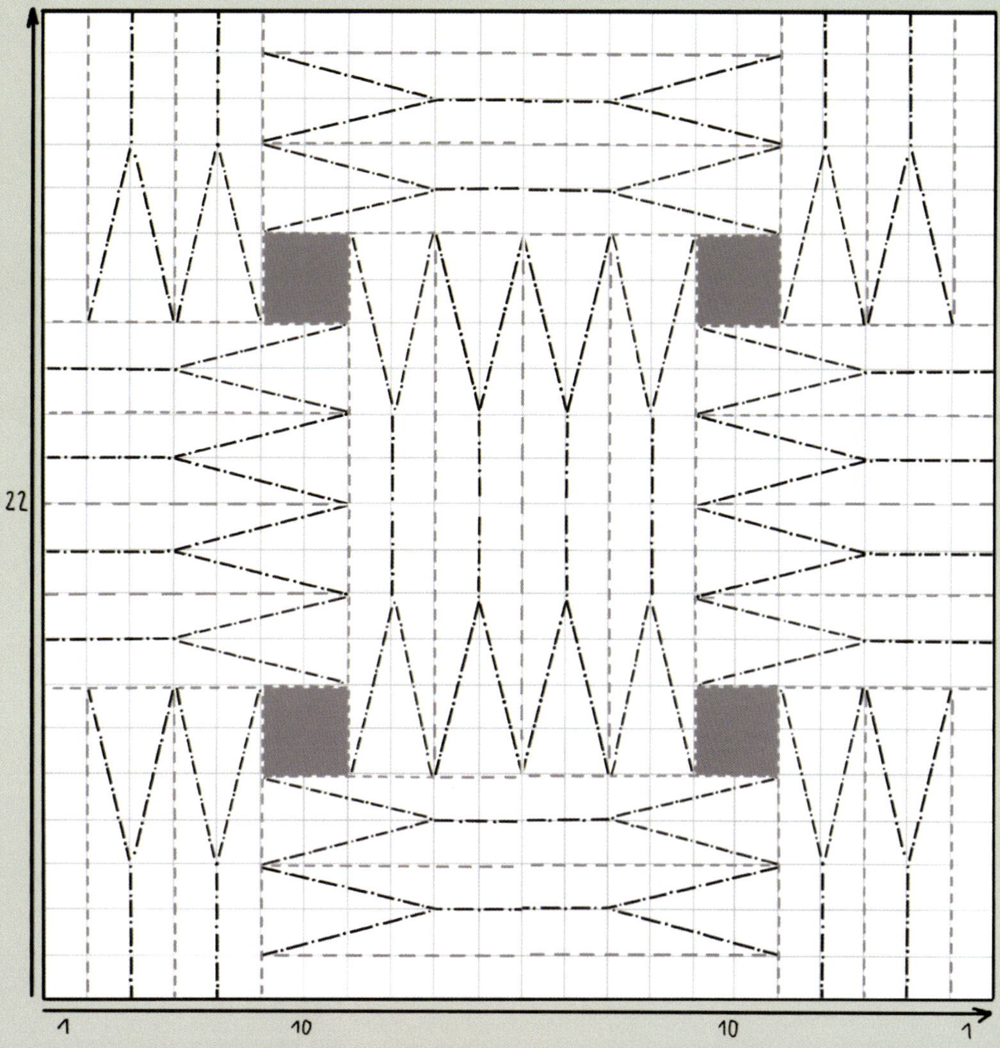

4 by 4 Molecules

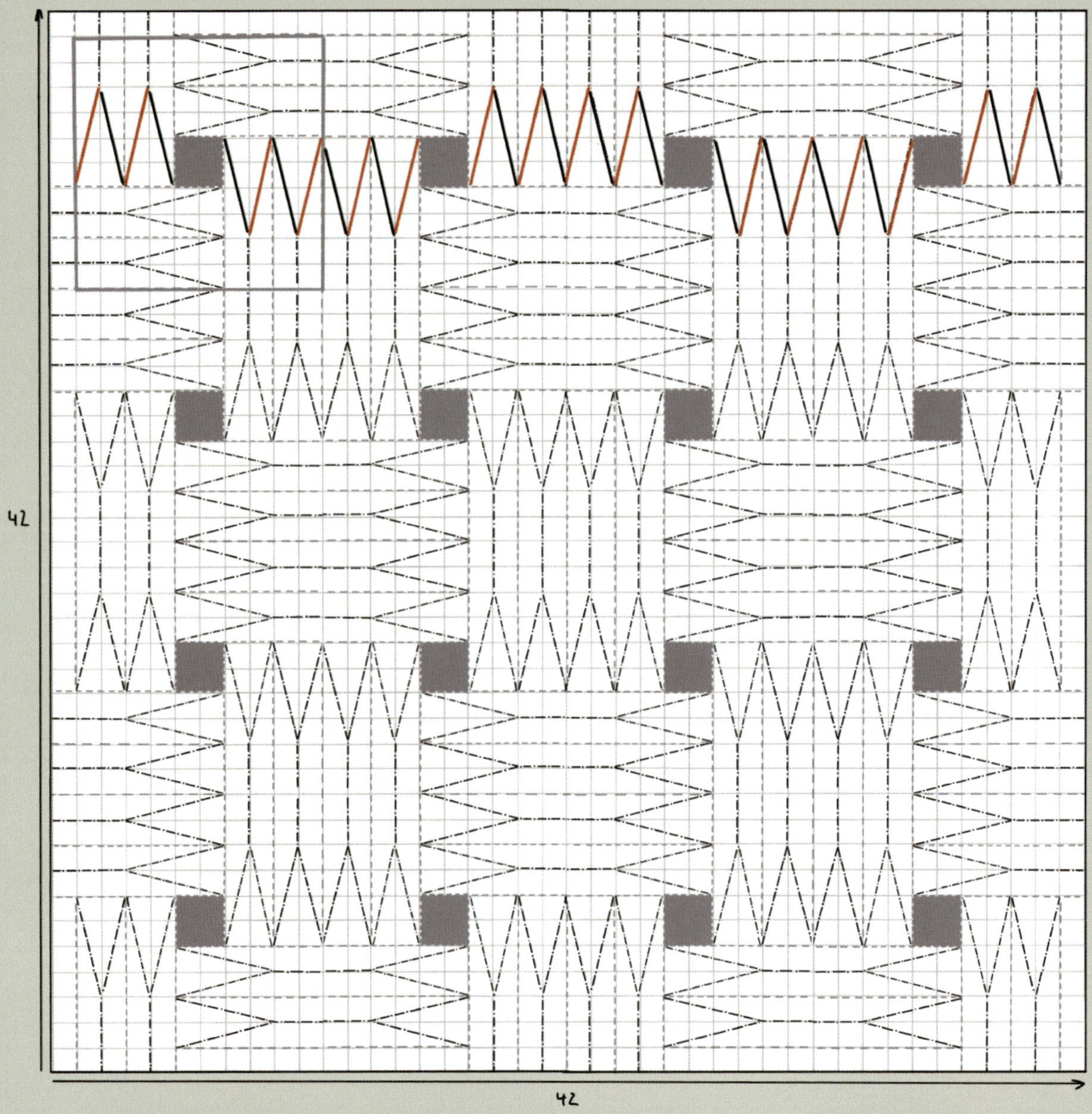

Use a 42 by 42 grid:
1 + 4 x 10 + 1 = 42.

The final result will be 26 squares wide.

The CP above presents a shortcut that will reduce the time needed for the precreases: fold all the diagonals along the top row of molecules at one go. Fold all the right sides of the triangles first (black lines), then fold all the left sides coming back (orange lines). Repeat with remaining rows. You will note that it is hard to fold the long diagonals of 1 by 4 rectangles accurately, especially when the diagonal goes almost in perpendicular to the grain of the paper. Prescoring them would make it much easier.

The collapse is done in two stages. Fold the inner triangles of all the molecules before you fold the outer ones.

For the order of the molecules to collapse, start with the upper left molecule and complete a row. Use paper clips to hold the folded edges. Now it may be better to collapse the molecules *around the edges* first, and not row by row.

Try to find your own best way to work this collapse!

4 3 Growing Up

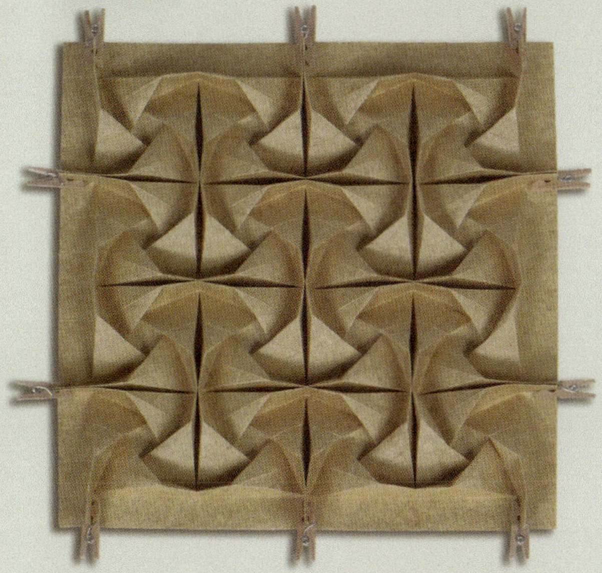

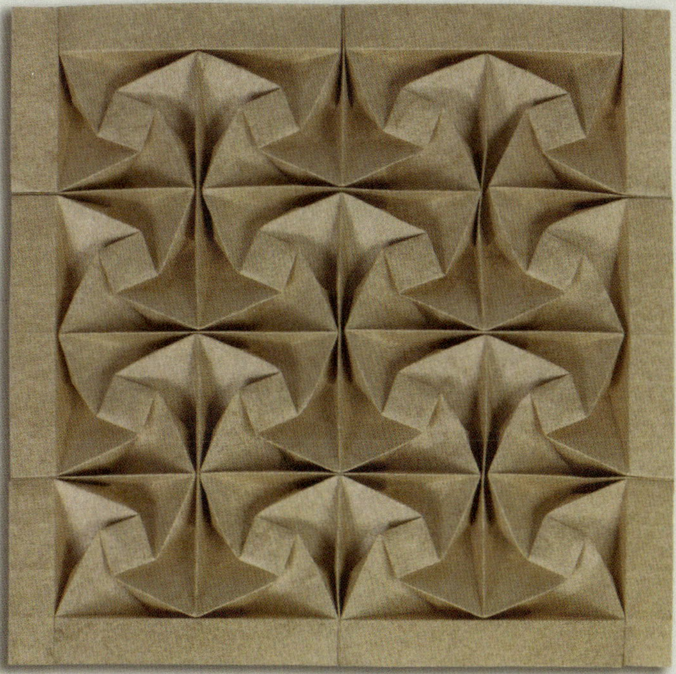

Above: verso view of a 4 by 4–molecule Growing Up tessellation with smaller triangles. Recto view is to the right.

Below is the CP for the Childhood variation I mentioned earlier. This 4 by 4 project has a single square at the center and uses smaller triangles with the diagonals of a 1 by 2 rectangle.

Use a 20 by 20 grid: 4 x 5 = 20.

The final result will be 14 squares wide.

Start with the upper left corner and complete a row of molecules. Use paper clips to hold the folded edges together. Collapse the molecules around the edges first; don't go row by row.

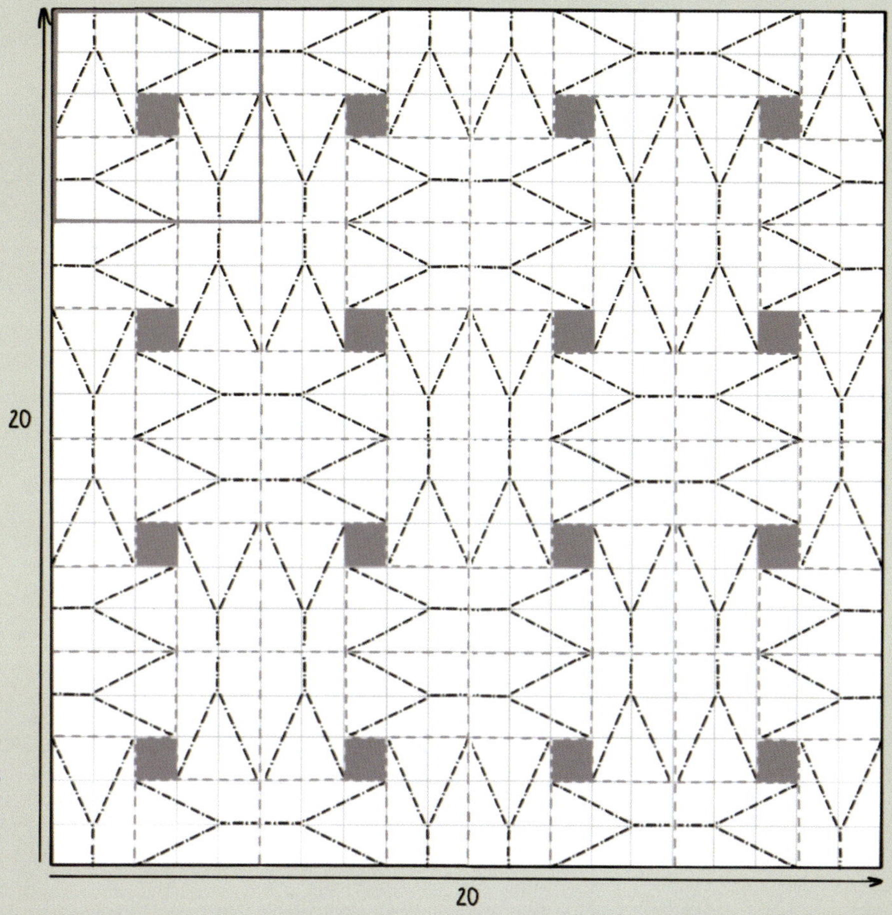

4 4 Adulthood

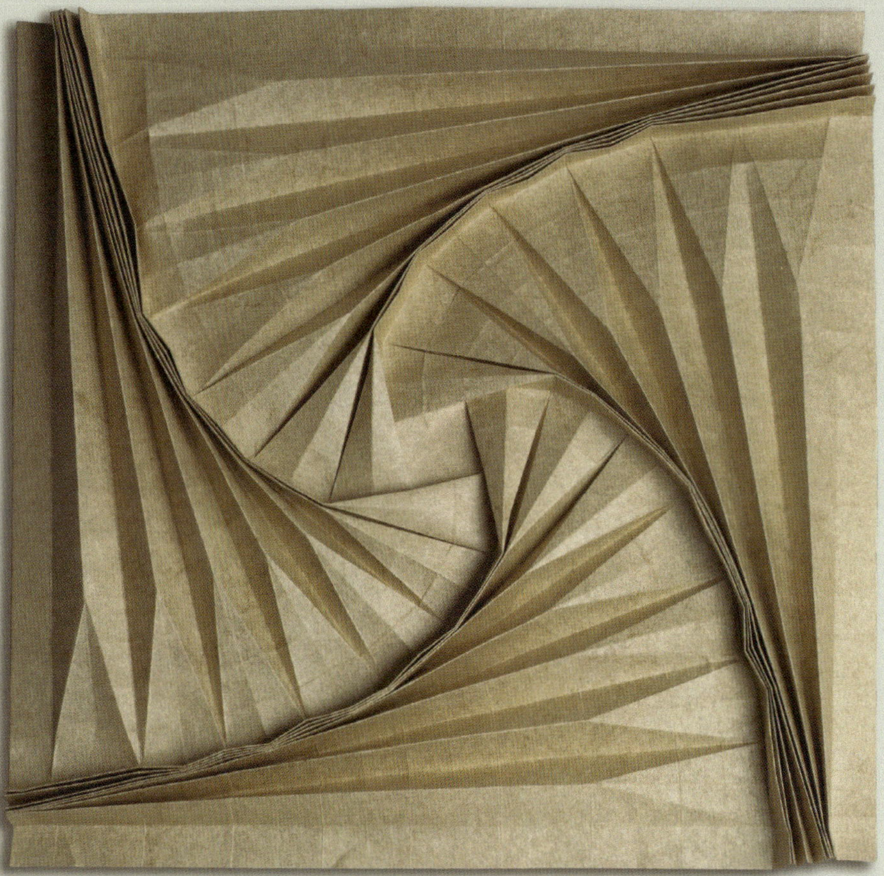

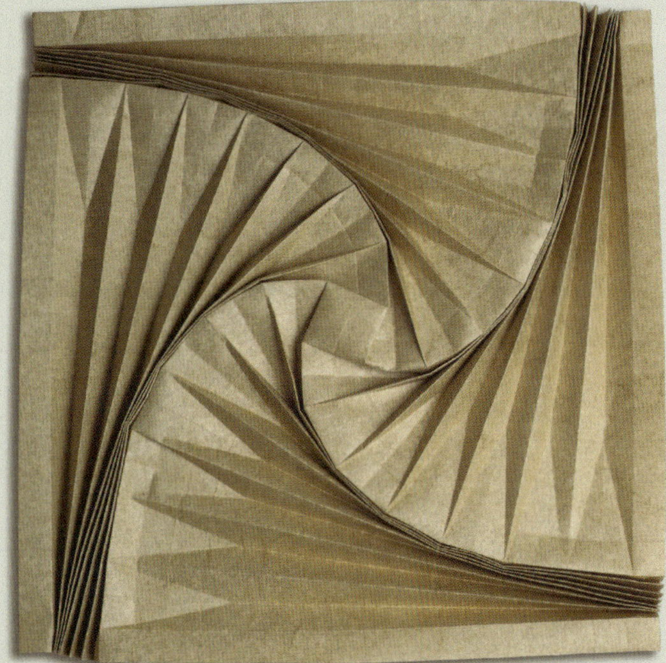

Above: recto view of a single molecule of Adulthood tessellation.

Verso view is to the left.

The Single Molecule

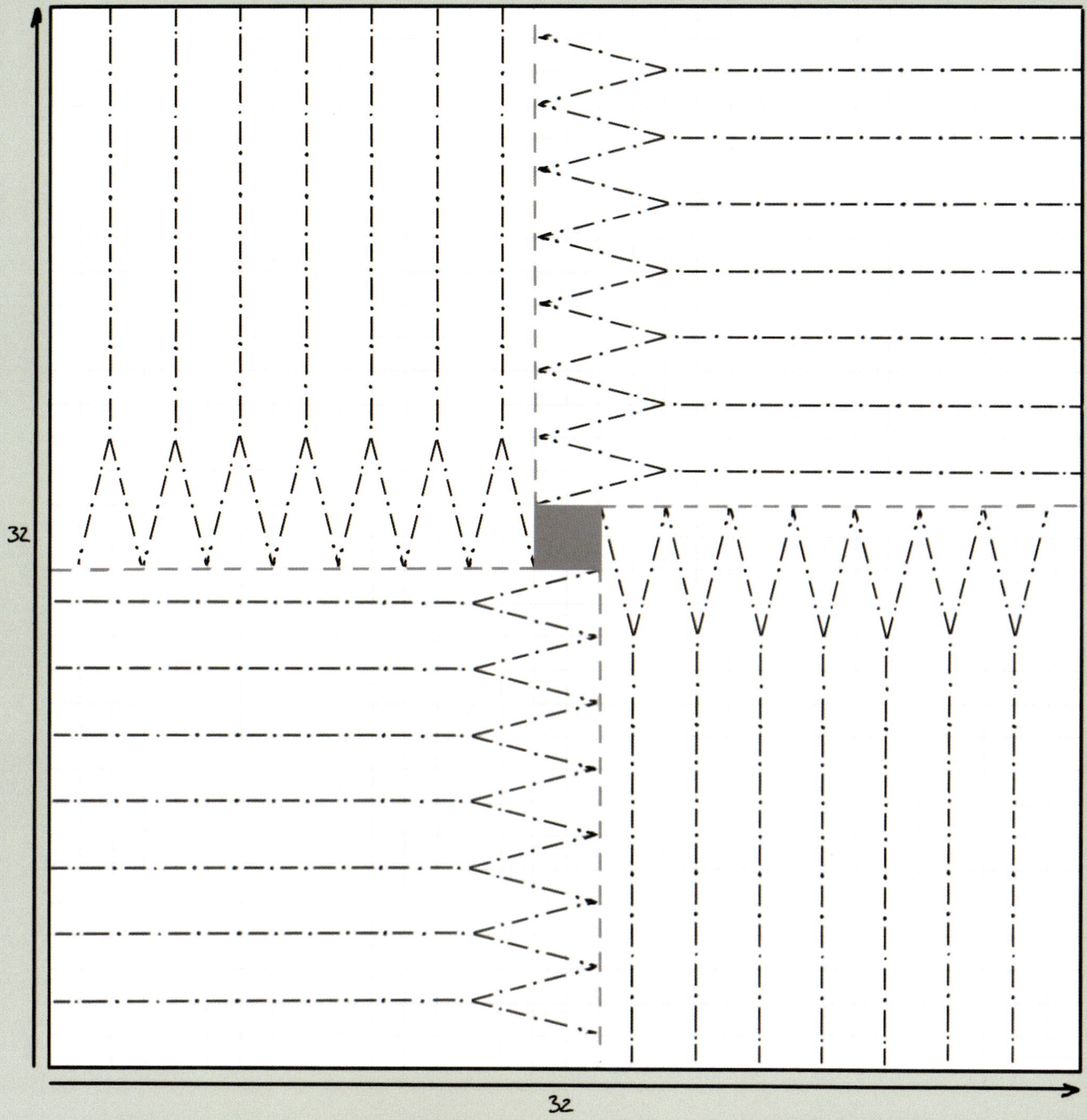

Adding triangles to the basic molecule and fanning them out results in this spiral model.

Here is a CP for a single molecule of Adulthood tessellation. It has seven triangles on each side of the center square, using a 32 by 32 grid.

The shrinkage ratio is 2:1.

2 by 2 Molecules

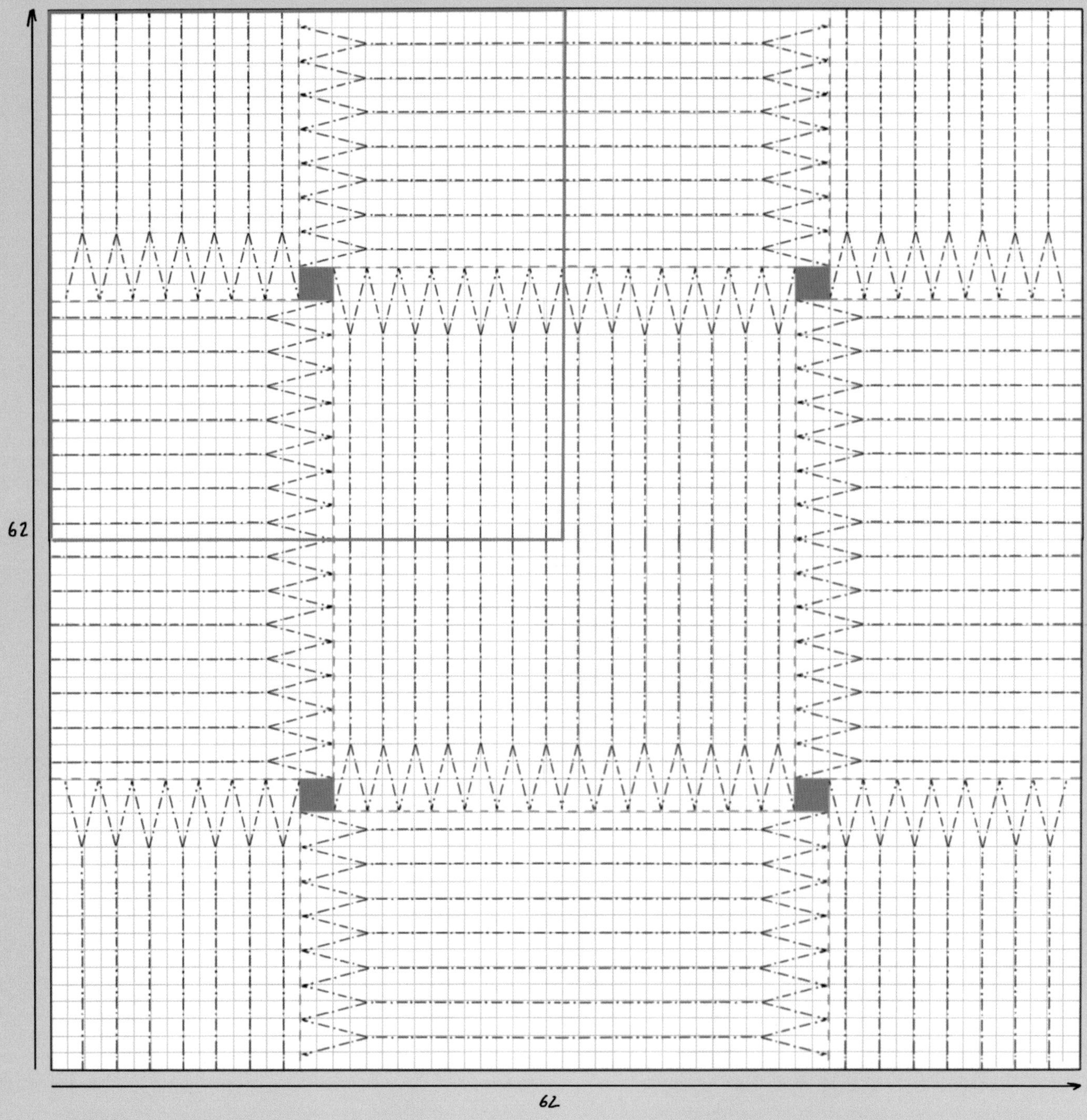

This is an advanced project.

Use a grid size of 62 by 62: 1 + 2 x 30 + 1 = 62.

It is easier to make a grid of 64 by 64 and leave two rows on each edge. You can also cut it down to 62 by 62.

The final result will be 42 squares wide.

For the precreases, fold all the diagonals along the top row of molecules at one go; the right sides of the triangles first, then all the left sides coming back (this is the same process used on page 104).

Fold this project only after you've mastered the single molecule of Adulthood.

The collapse is done in seven stages: first, collapse the innermost triangles for all the molecules (start from the top left, complete a row, then continue to the next row). Move to the next triangle all over the model and repeat the process. Keep going until all seven triangles on each side are collapsed.

Above and Beyond—A 4 by 4 Project

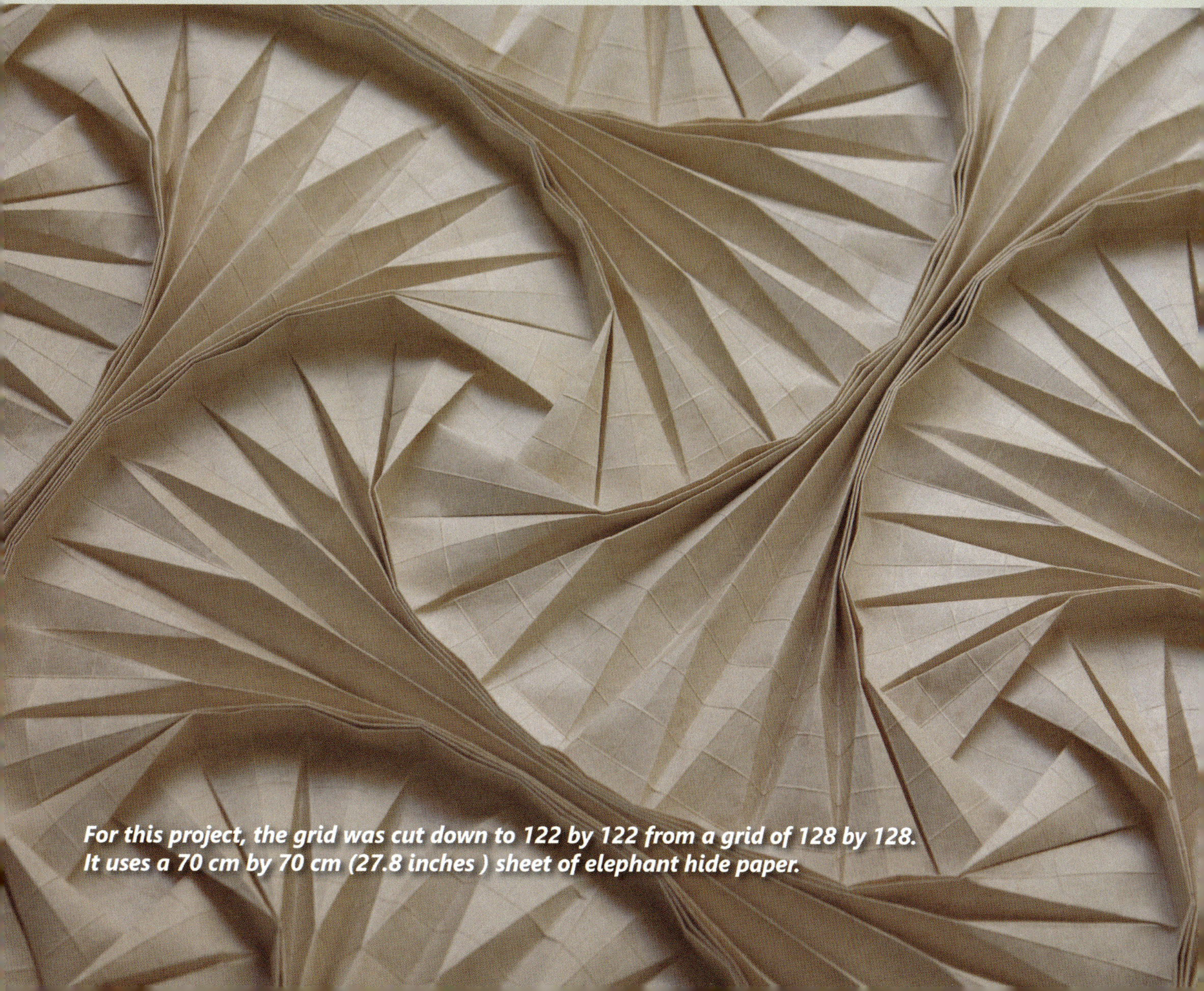

For this project, the grid was cut down to 122 by 122 from a grid of 128 by 128. It uses a 70 cm by 70 cm (27.8 inches) sheet of elephant hide paper.

5 The Twister Family

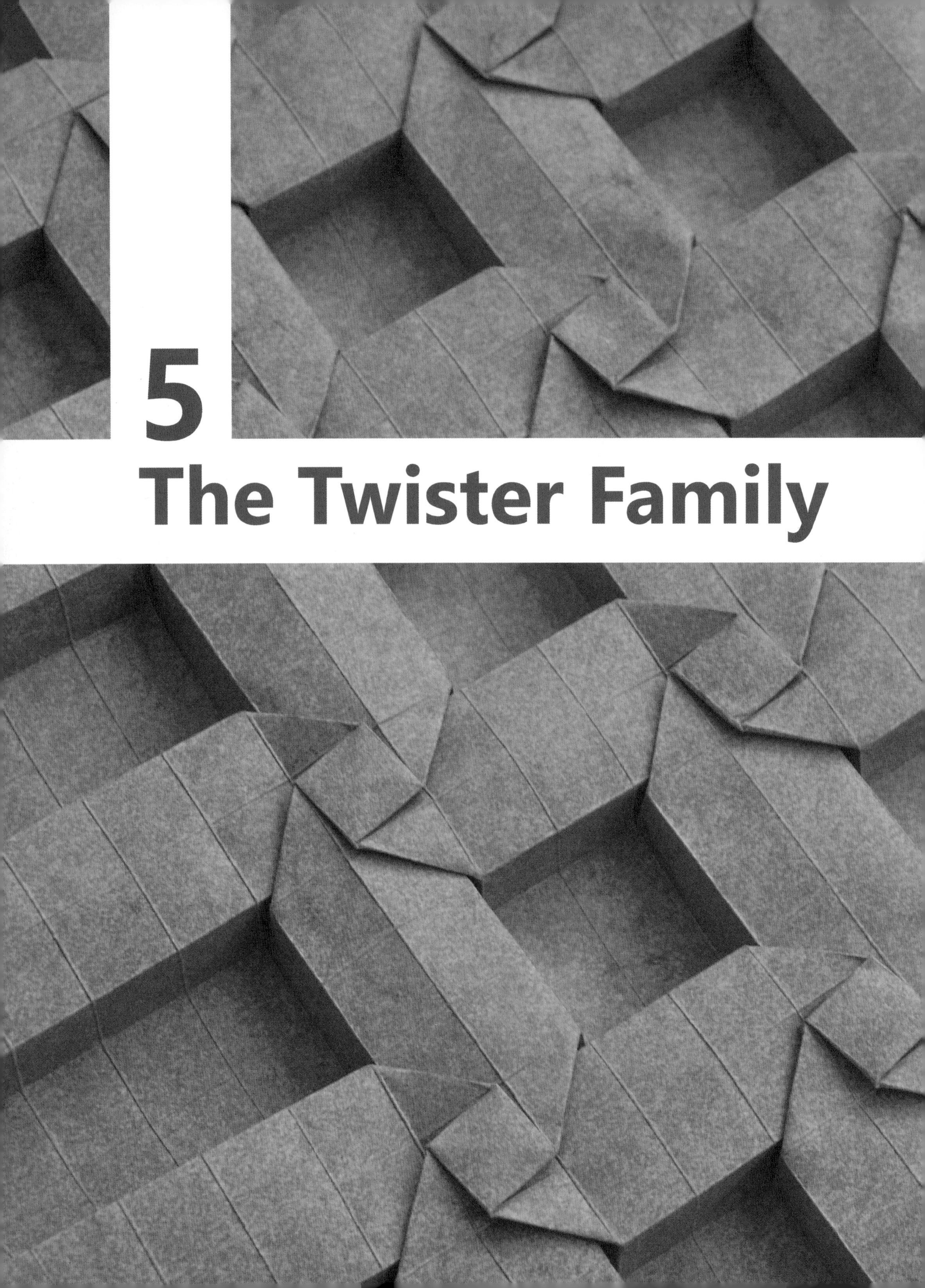

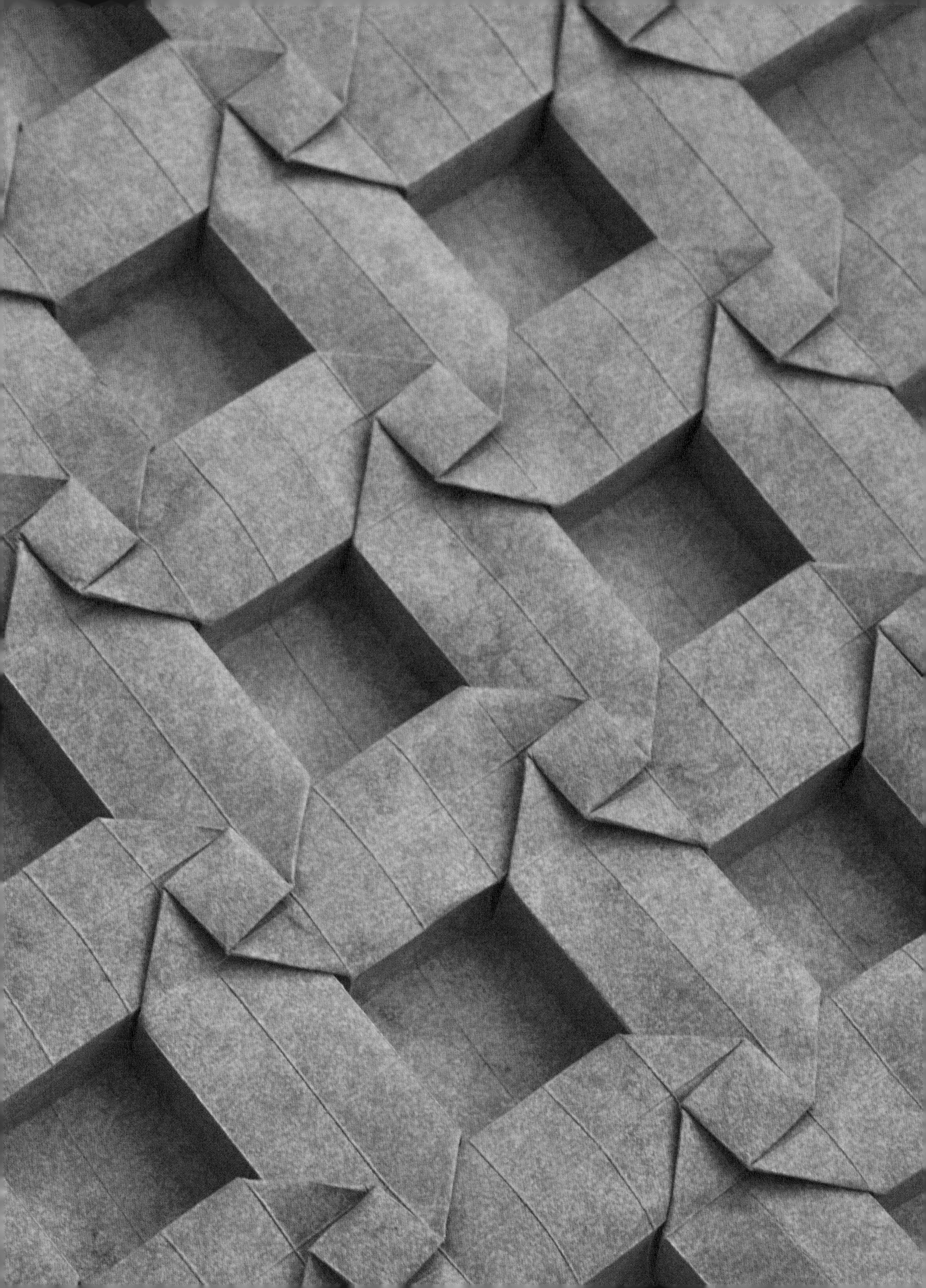

Introduction

The Twister family is based on a square-twist. Unlike the classic twist (the basis for the Kawasaki Rose, for example) that stays flat after the rotation of the middle part, the twist here can create volume.

Variations can be achieved by adding spaces between molecules and changing the size of the middle square.

You can tessellate this family by either mirroring or shifting molecules.

5 1 Twister A

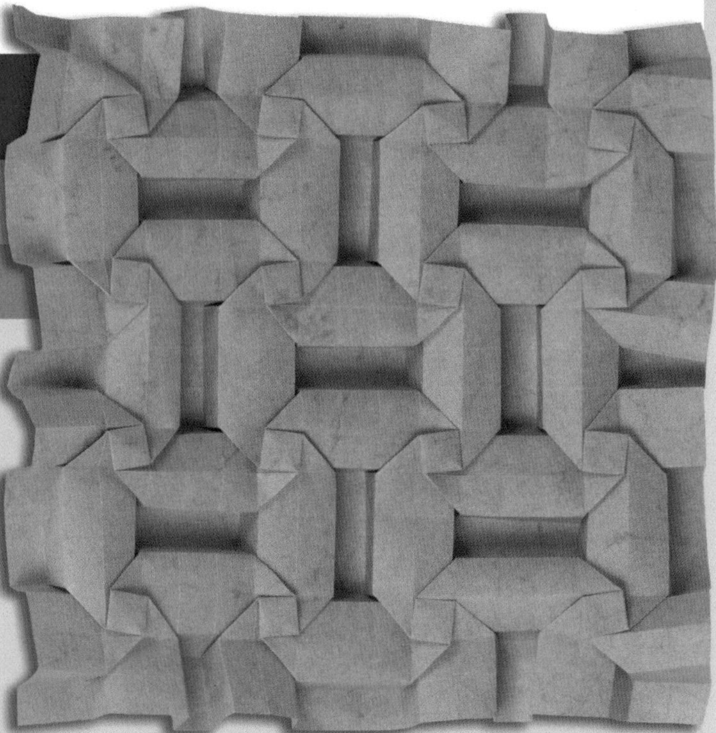

Above: recto view of a 4 by 4–molecule Twister A tessellation. Verso view is below.

The Single Molecule

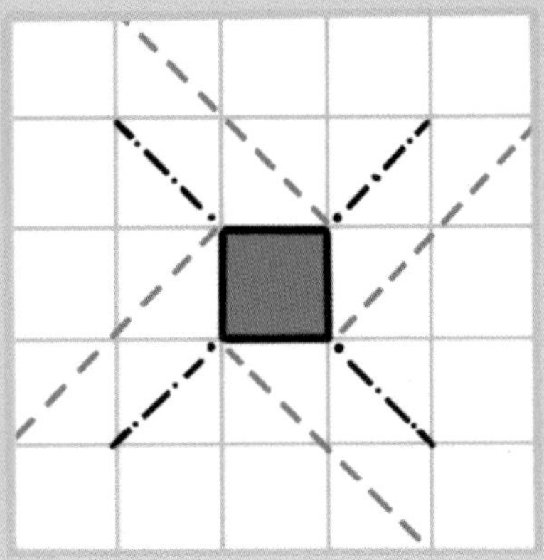

As with all twisting steps, you have mountain and valley folds coupled on each side of the central square.

The molecule size is 5 by 5 squares.

The shrinkage ratio is 5:3.

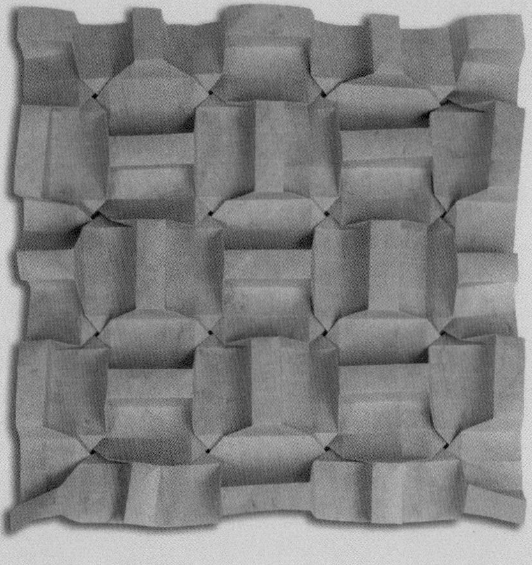

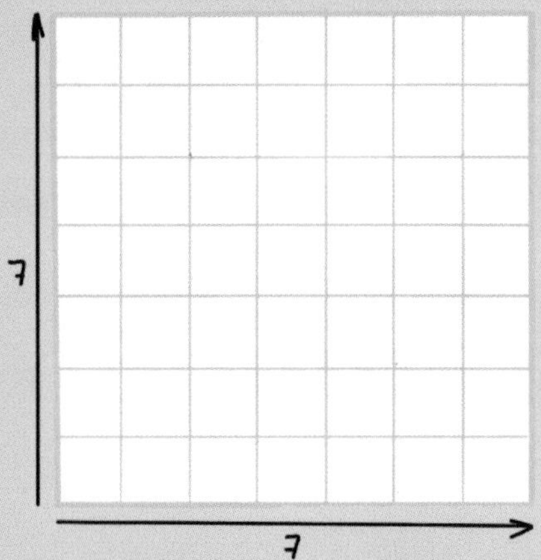

Start with a 7 by 7 grid.

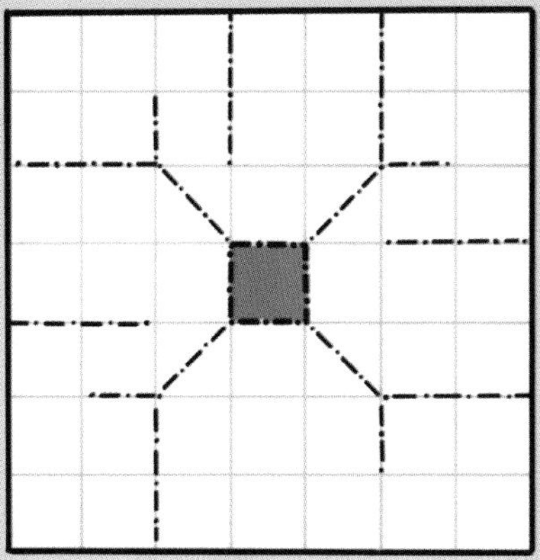

Add four diagonal mountain creases, going from the center-square corners out. You can also reinforce the mountains that follow the grid lines.

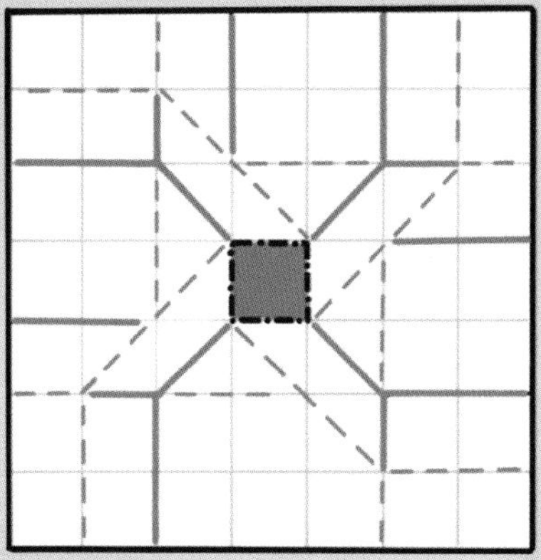

Add four valley folds going in parallel to the mountains. You can also reinforce the valleys that follow the grid lines.

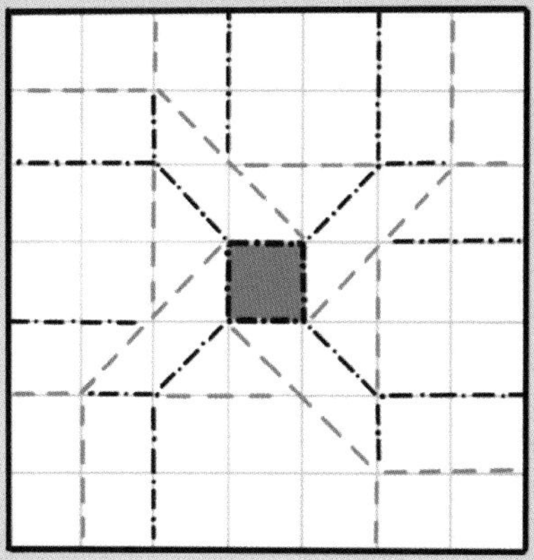

The complete CP.

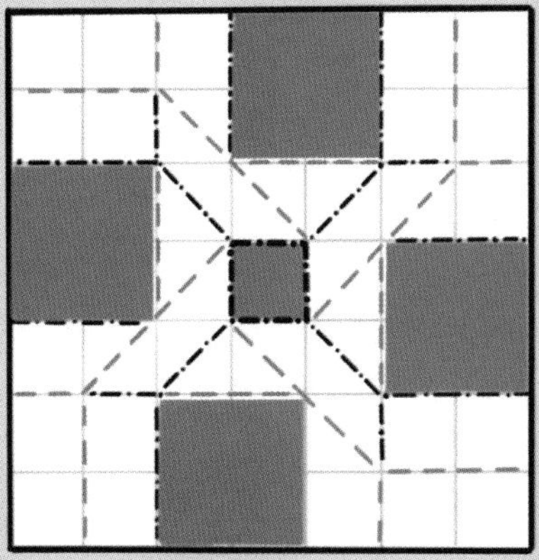

Start by pushing the gray squares up. As the collapse progresses, the central square will rise above all.

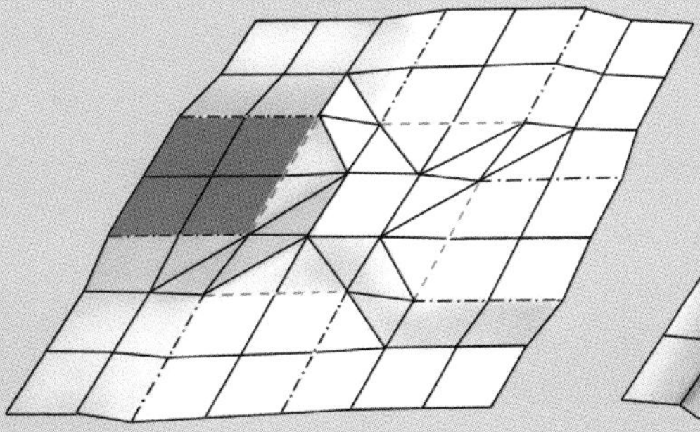

Collapse in process. Two sides of the big gray square are mountains, the inner one is valley.

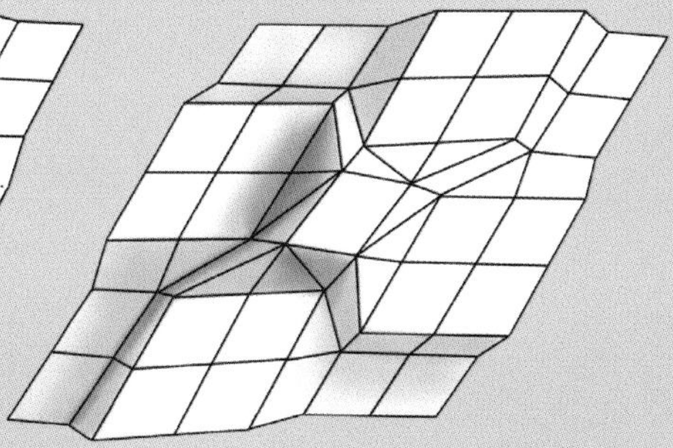

In process.

Twist to continue the collapse. The central square will form a cube.

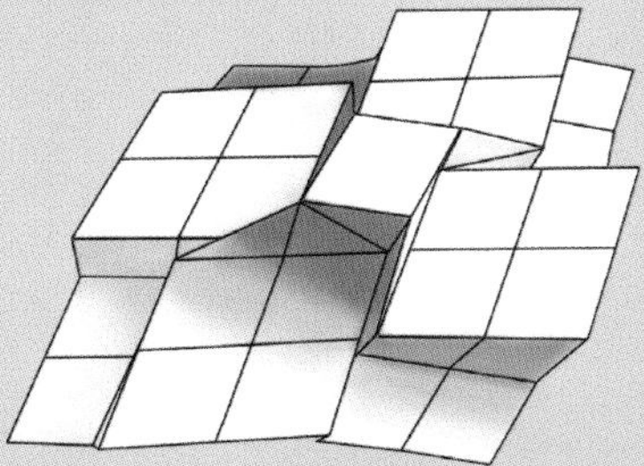

The first step of the twist is done.

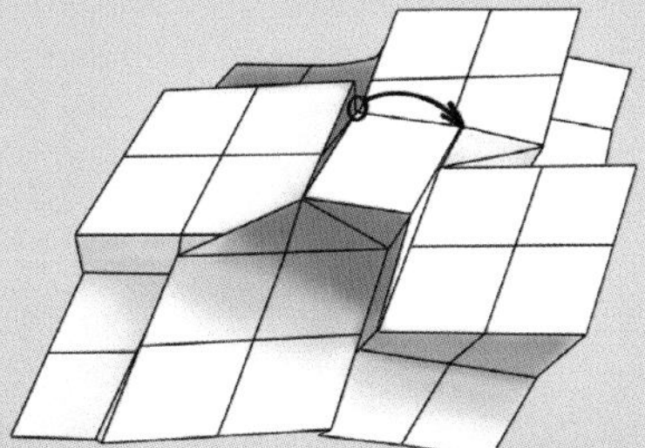

If you want, continue the collapse. Twist the square even further, going clockwise. Follow the direction of the arrow at the marked corner.

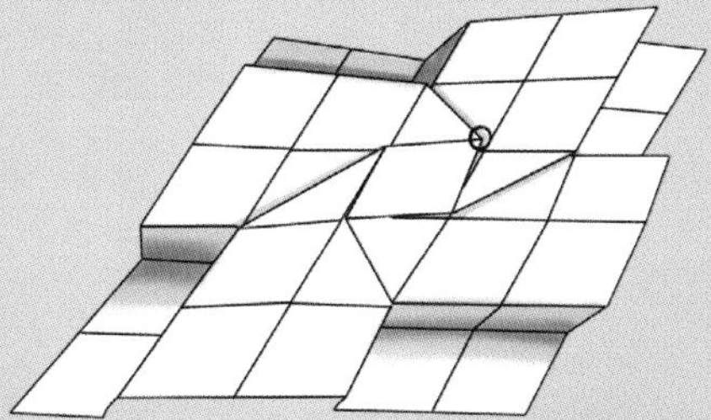

Fully twisted!

2 by 2 Molecules

Mirrored (with Spacing)

The light gray area represents the space we created between the molecules.

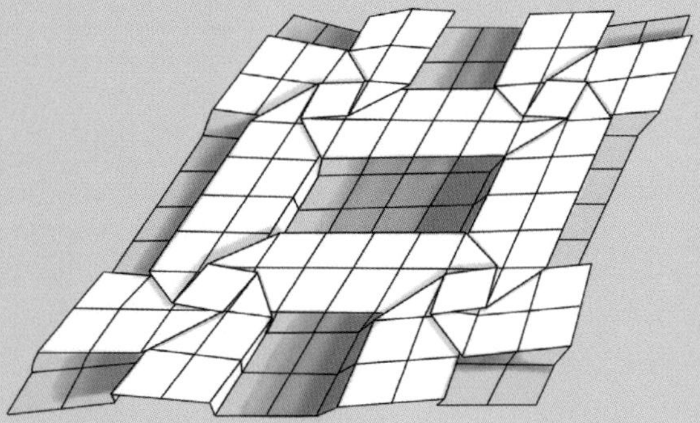

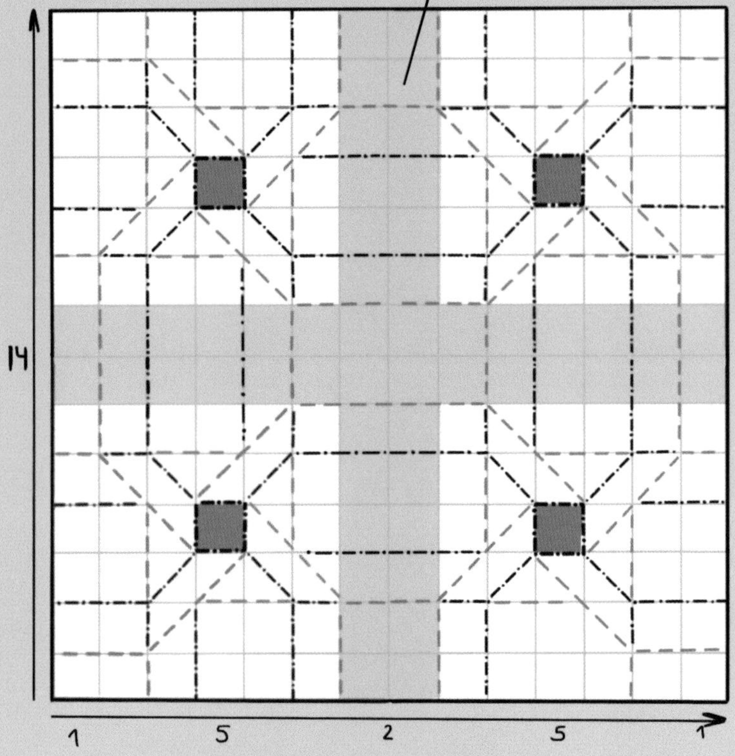

Use a 14 by 14 grid to make this 2 by 2–project of mirrored molecules.

Between every two molecules there is a spacing of two squares (shown as gray strips).

Don't complete the twists until you erect all the molecules. Twisting the top square of each is the last step.

Shifted (with Spacing)

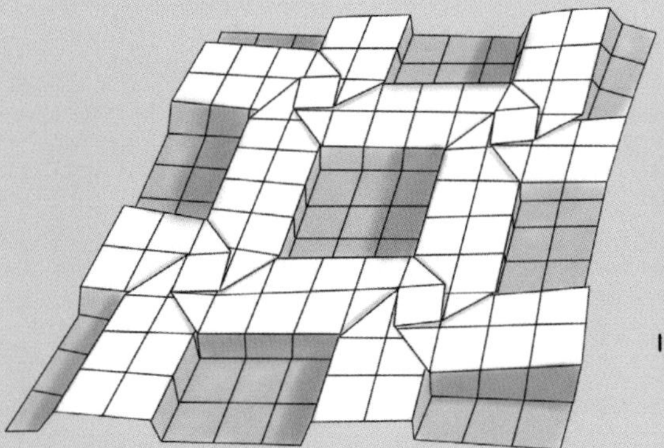

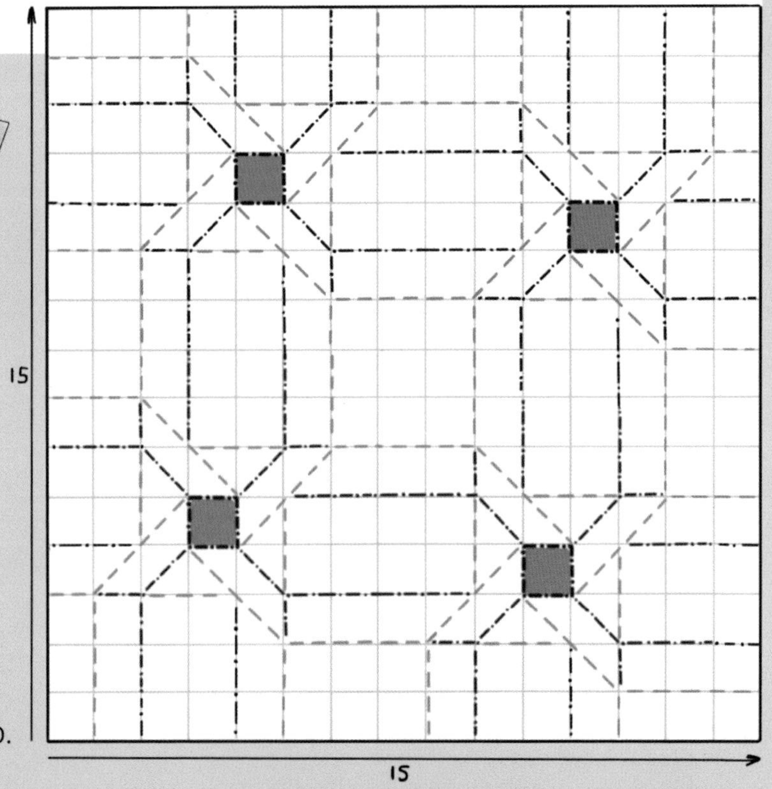

This project—2 by 2 shifted molecules—calls for a 15 by 15 grid.

As with the mirrored project, don't twist each molecule completely until you erect all the molecules. Twisting the top square of each is the last step.

4 by 4 Molecules

Mirrored (Single Spacing)

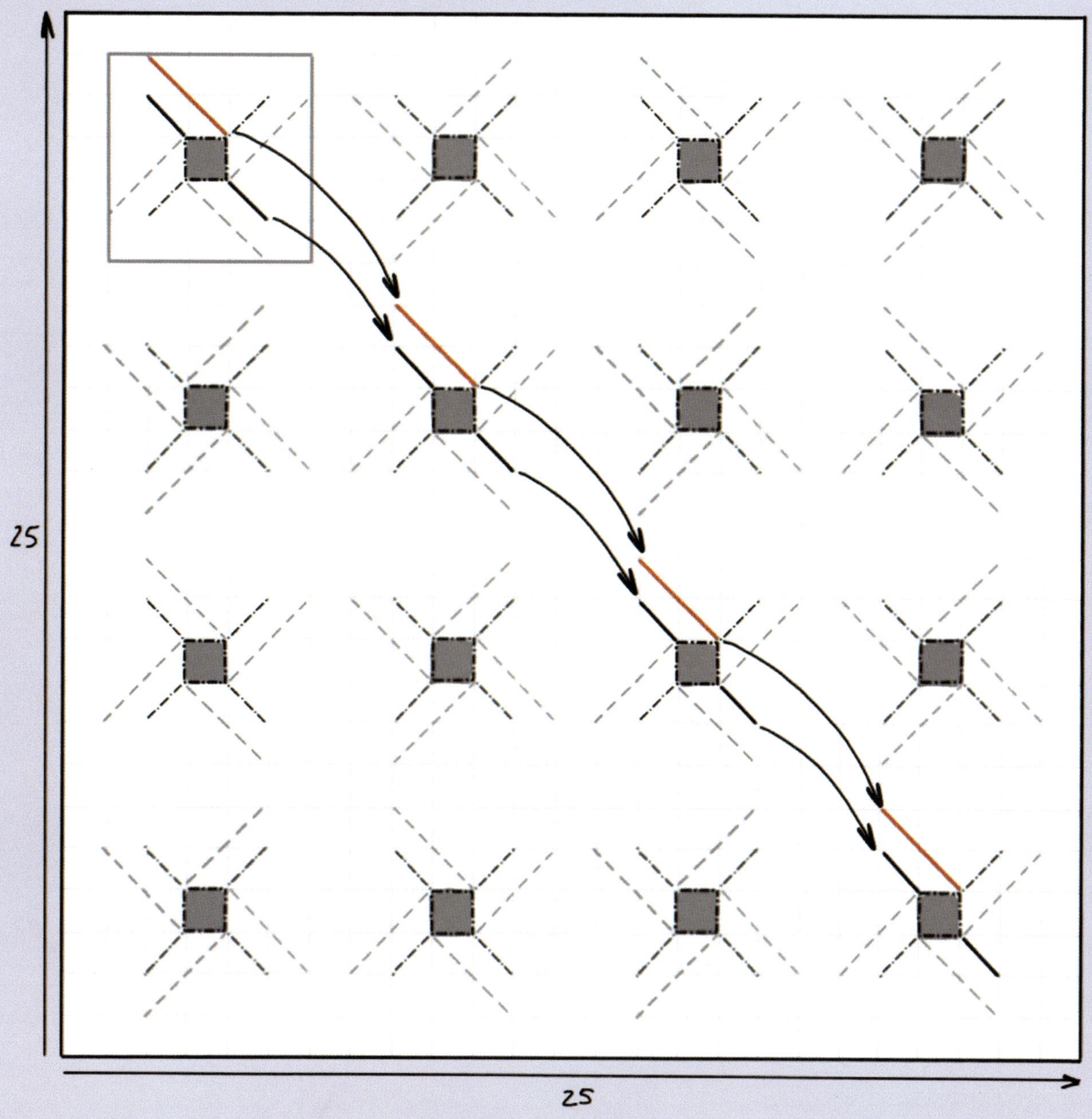

For a 4 by 4 project with ***single-square*** spacing and mirrored molecules, use a 25 by 25 grid: 5 x 1 + 4 x 5 = 25.

The final result will be 17 squares wide.

For easier precreasing, follow the diagonal mountain creases shown in bold black: fold one square, skip one square, fold one square, then skip three squares, and move on to the next molecule.

Fold the valleys (orange) next: fold two, skip four, fold two in one direction, then go back and fold the diagonals in the opposite direction.

The next CP shows the complete creases needed for the collapse. All creases are in now.

Collapse row by row.

Don't twist each molecule completely until you erect all of them. Twisting the top square of each is the last step.

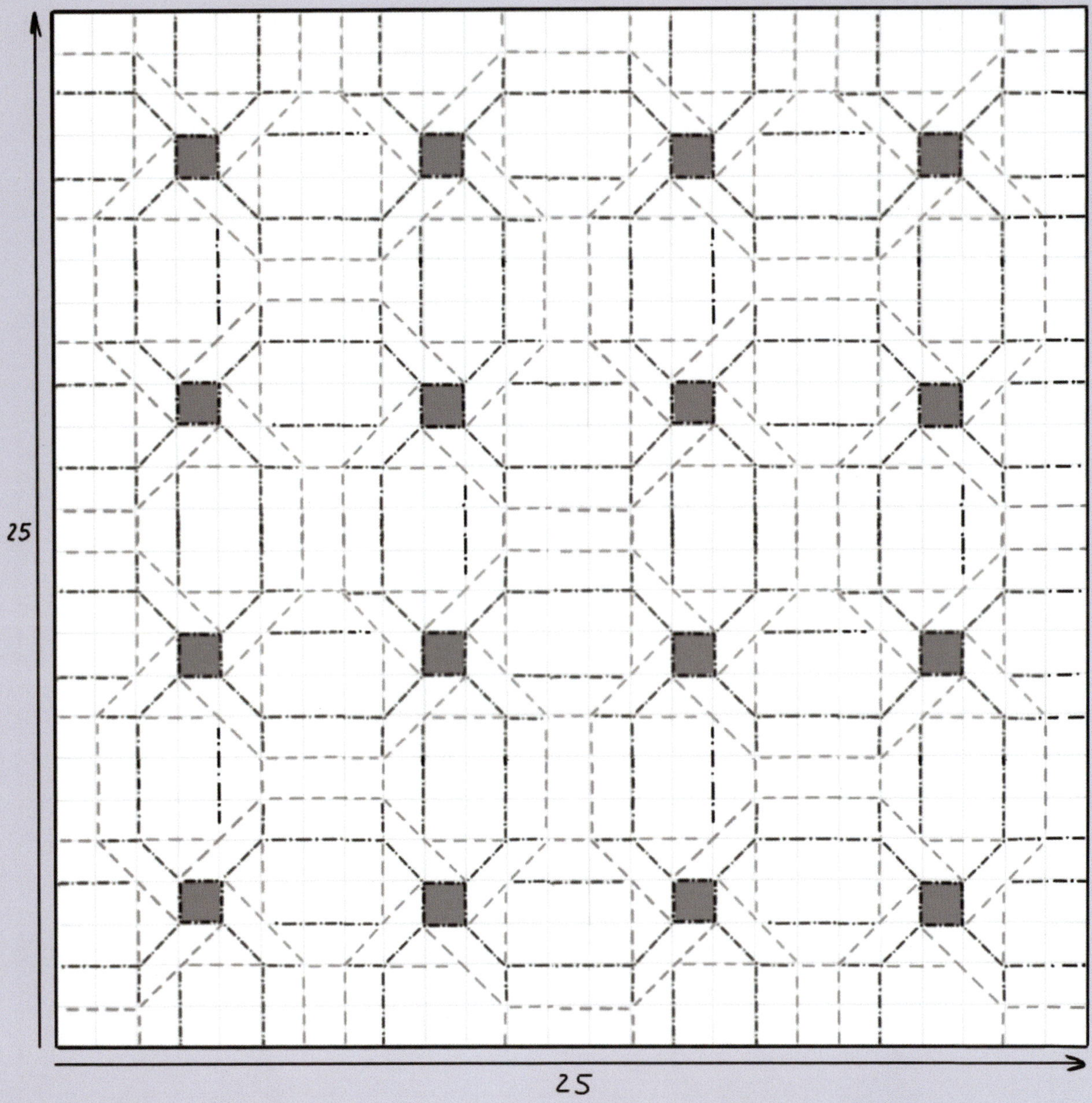

Above and Beyond—A 6 by 6 Project (detail)

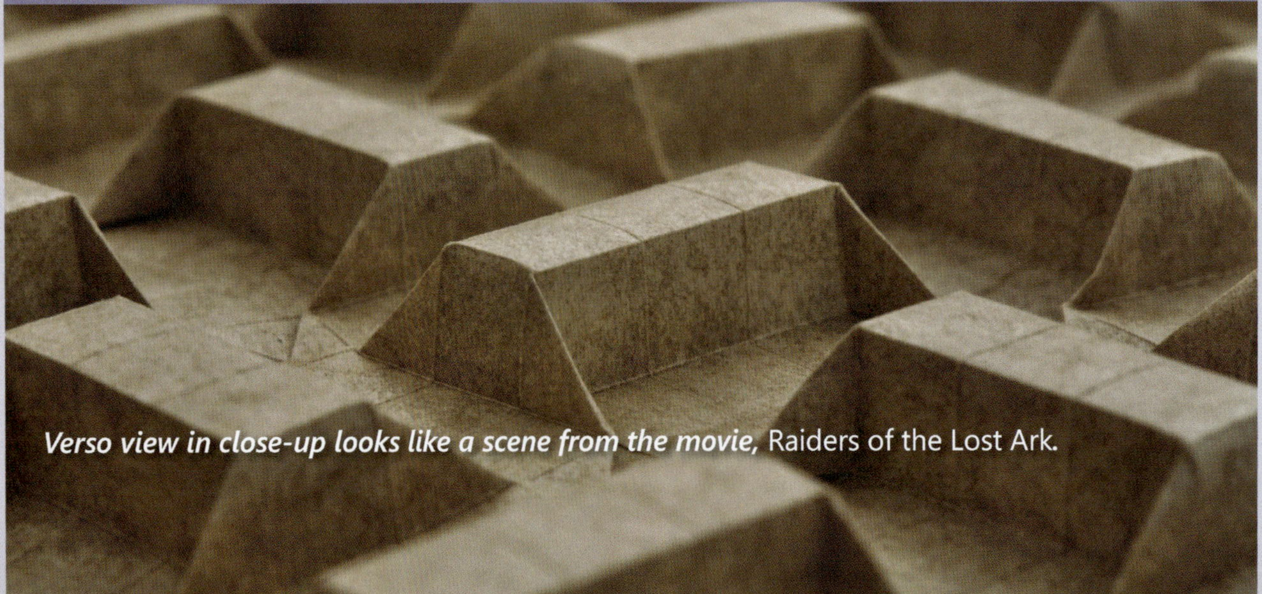

Verso view in close-up looks like a scene from the movie, Raiders of the Lost Ark.

5 2 Twister B

The Single Molecule

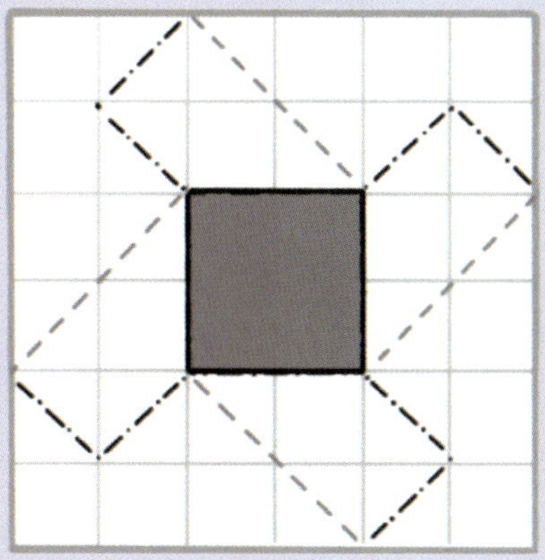

Having a larger square in the center means we must increase the grid size for this molecule. In order to twist the center square completely, you will need a grid of 8 by 8.

Again, the mountain and valleys come in parallel pairs.

The shrinkage ratio is 2:1.

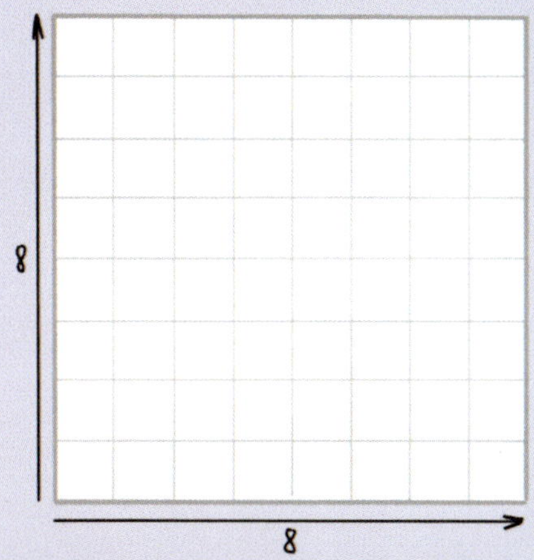

Start with an 8 by 8 grid. This creates a fully twisted molecule without an extra row or column.

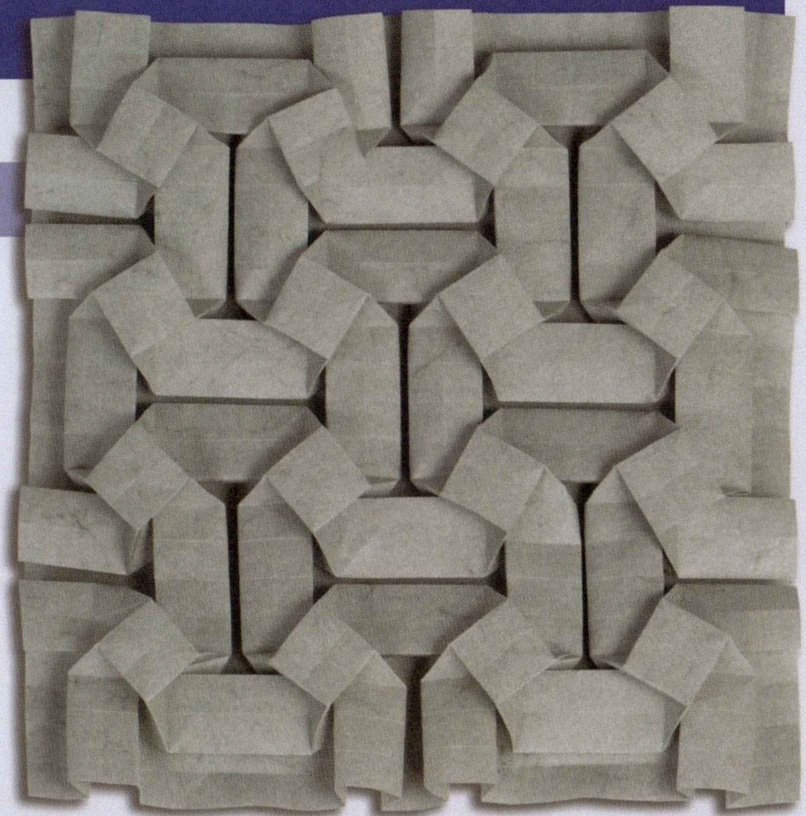

Above: recto view of a 4 by 4–molecule Twister B tessellation. Verso view is below.

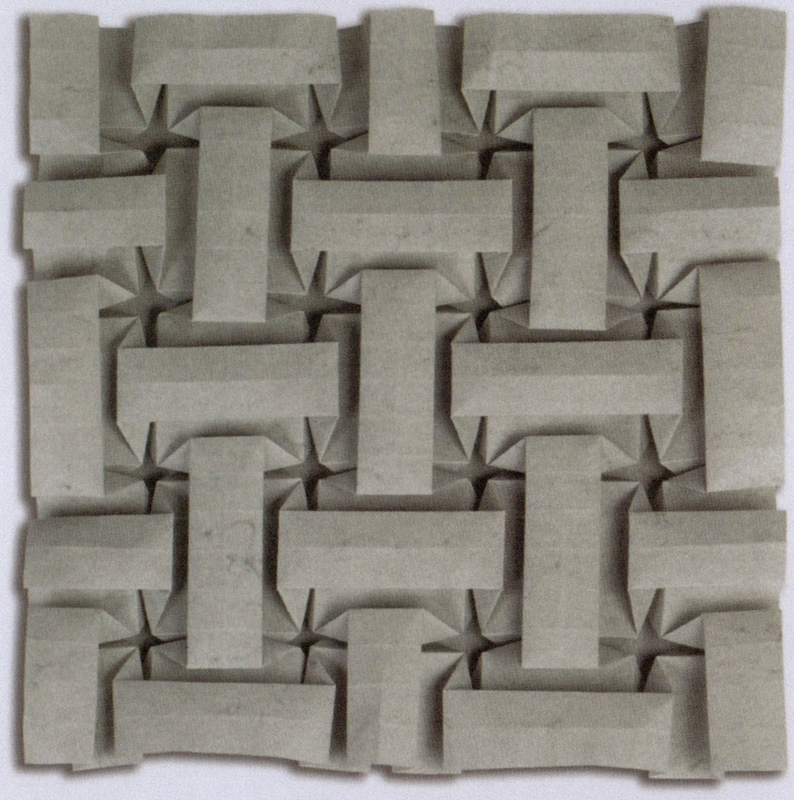

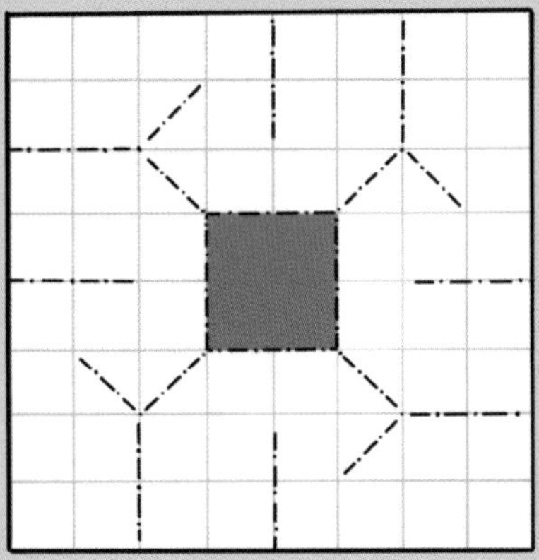

Form all the mountains as indicated.

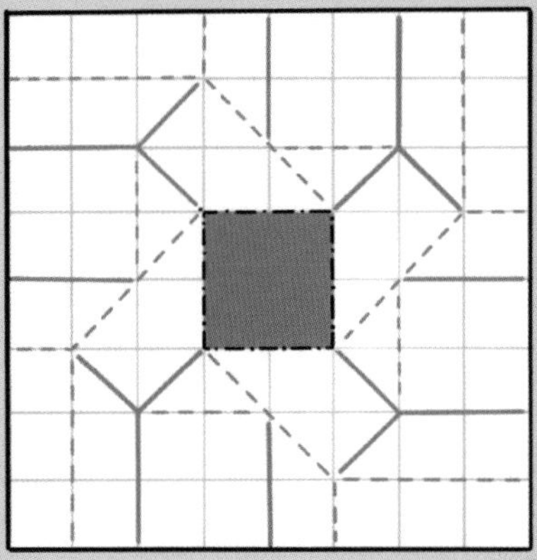

Add all the valleys as indicated.

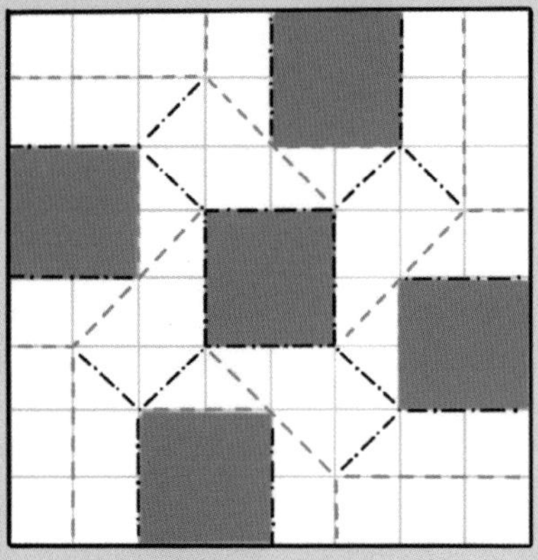

Start the collapse by forming squares around the center.

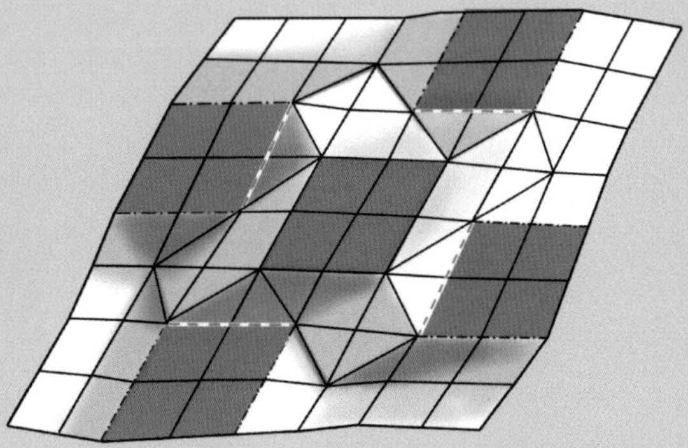

In process.

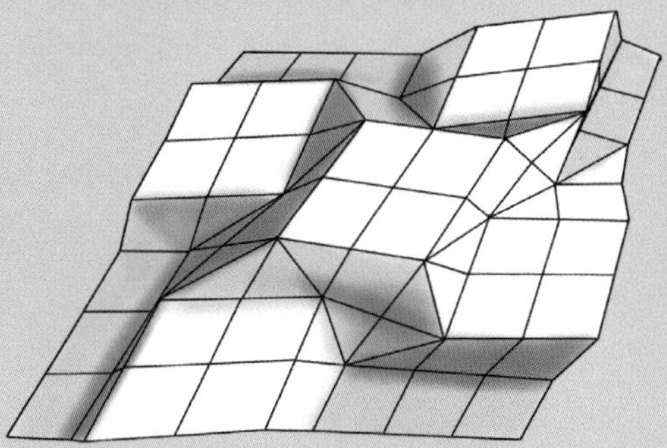

In process. The center starts to lift up.

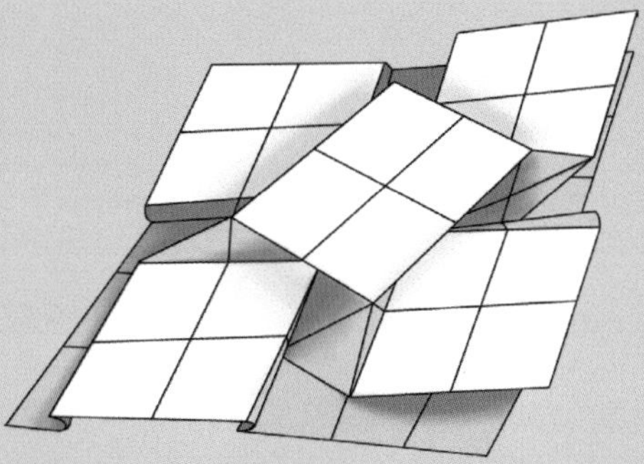

In process.

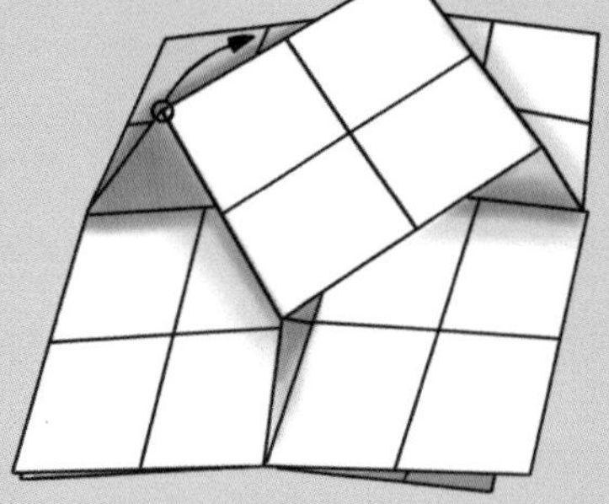

Note that the molecule uses the entire grid. You can continue to twist the top clockwise.

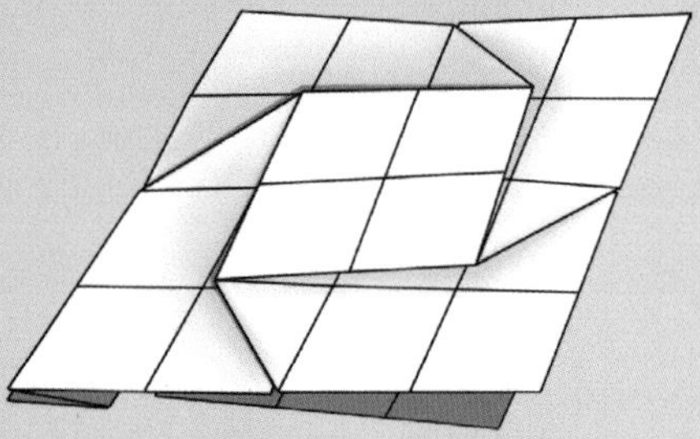

Fully collapsed, fully twisted.

2 by 2 Molecules

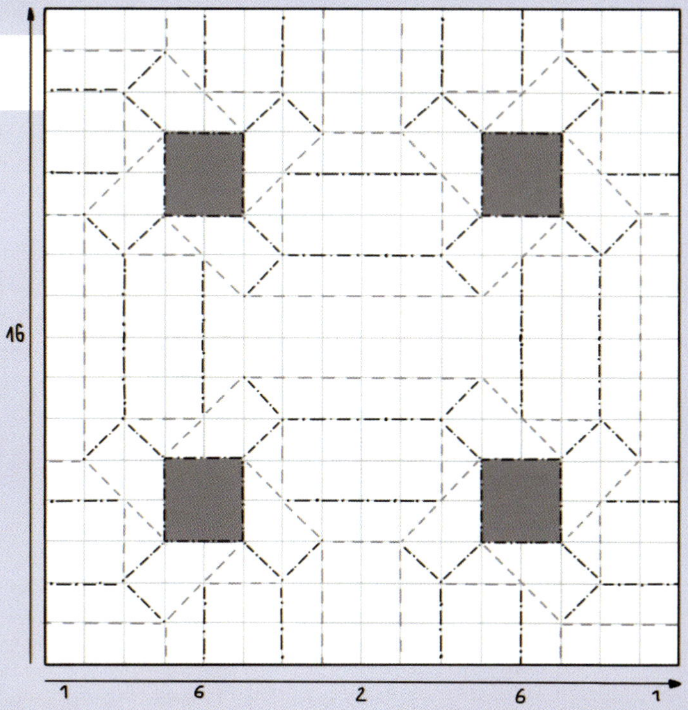

Mirrored (no Spacing)

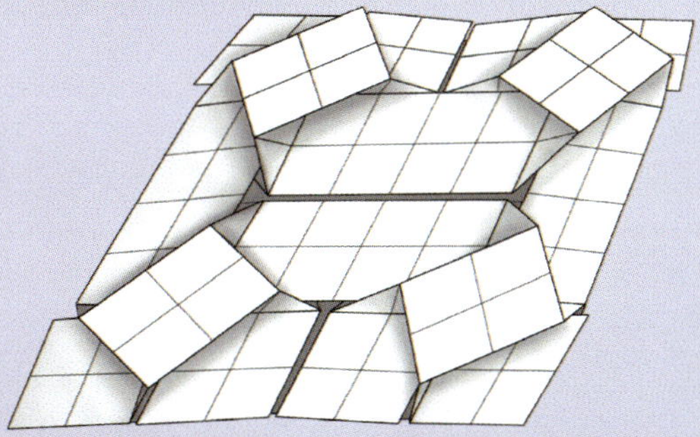

This project has no extra rows or columns.

You can decide to flatten it totally or leave the inner square raised and partially twisted.

Use a grid of 16 by 16.

Start to collapse the top left molecule and then complete a row.

Complete the last two molecules at one go.

Shifted (no Spacing)

If you shift molecules, you will need a bigger grid.

There is an extra row and column all around, so use a 20 by 20 grid.

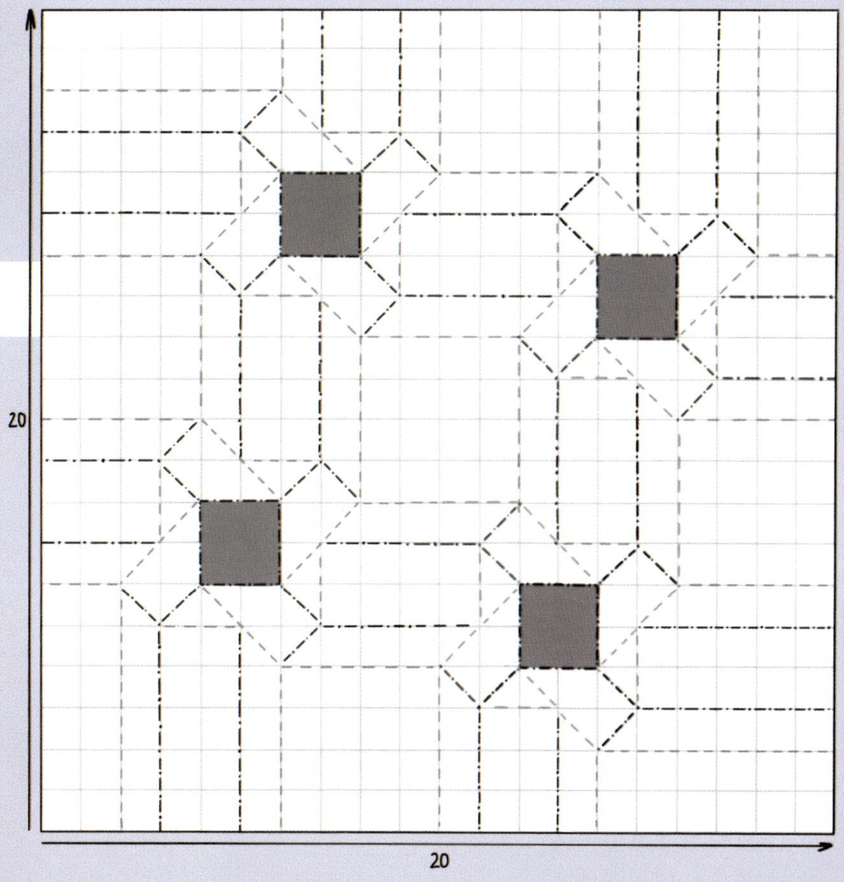

4 by 4 Molecules

Mirrored (no Spacing)

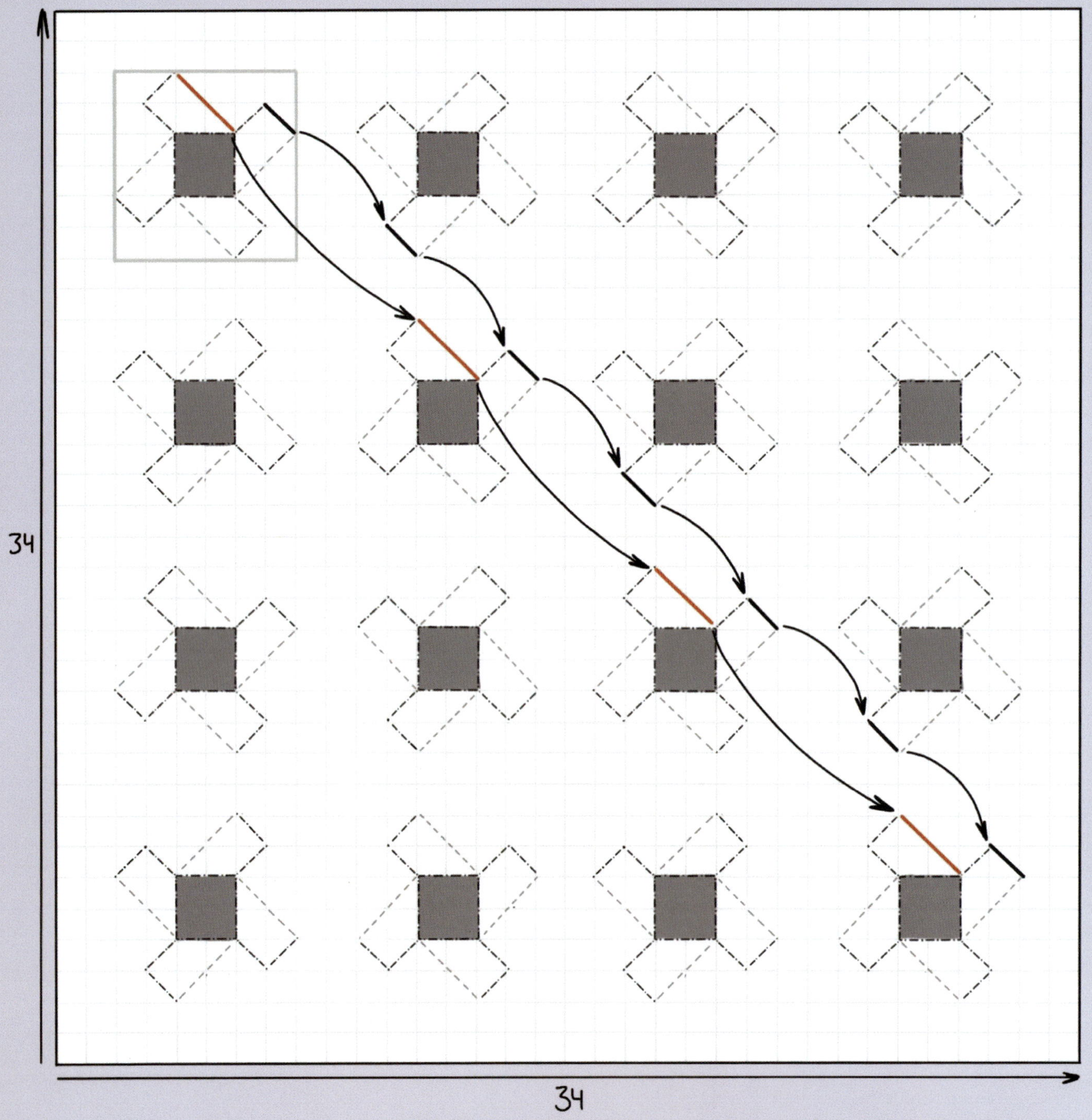

Use a grid size of 34 by 34: 1 + 4 x 8 + 1 = 34.

The final result will be 18 squares wide.

Start by marking all the central squares.

The shortcut for the mountain precreases follows this pattern: fold one square, skip three, fold one, skip three, repeating until all the diagonals in one direction are creased. Then fold the diagonals going in the opposite direction.

The pattern for the valleys (in red line) is fold two squares, skip six, repeat.

Start to collapse from the top left molecule and complete a row after that. Do not try to fully twist a molecule until all are collapsed halfway through. The final twist locks down the molecule.

But there is beauty in the open state, as well, so locked or untwisted—the choice is yours.

Above and Beyond—A 6 by 6 Project (detail)

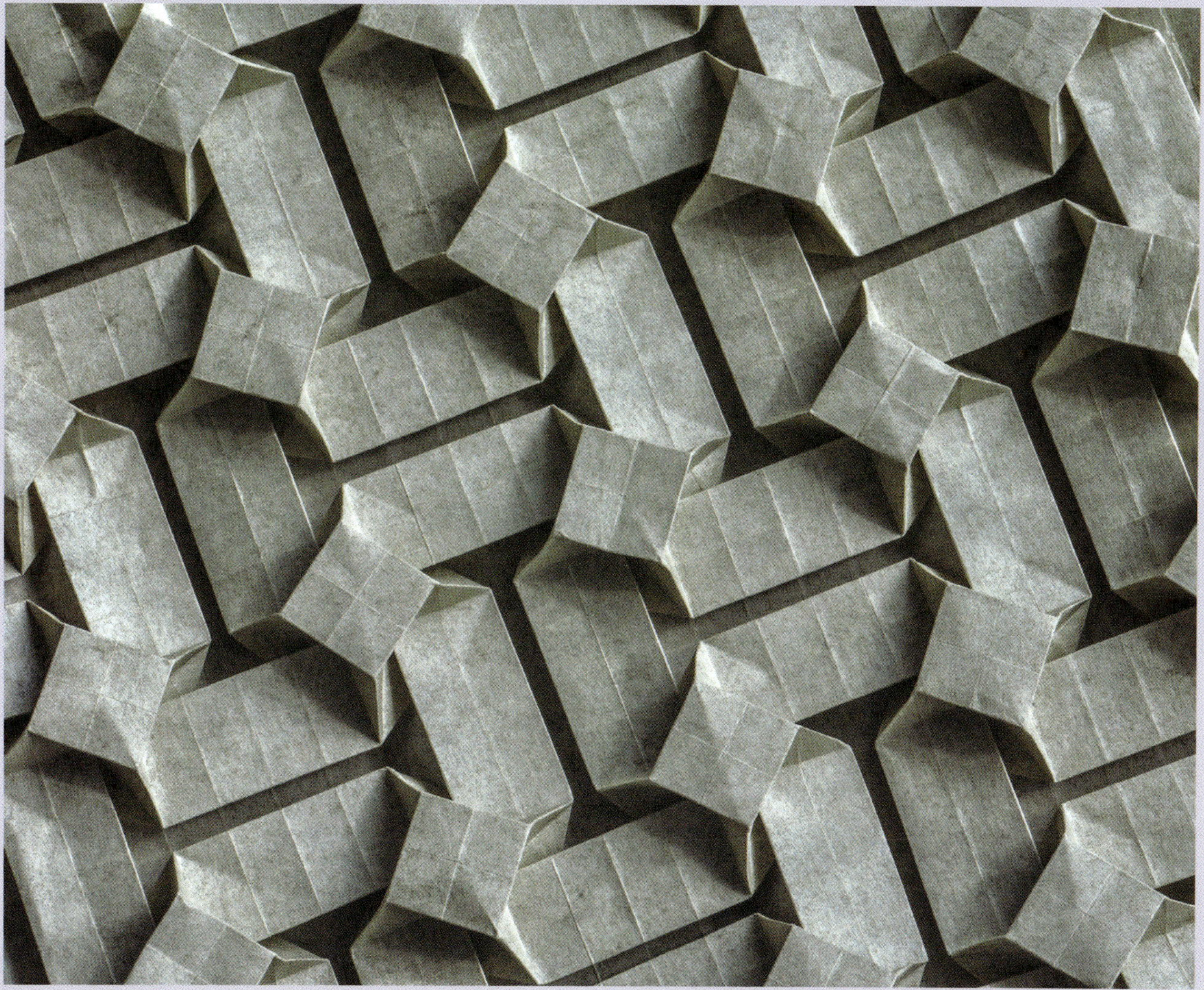

This version has no spacing between the molecules and the central squares are untwisted, so the model has three layers.

5 3 Twister C

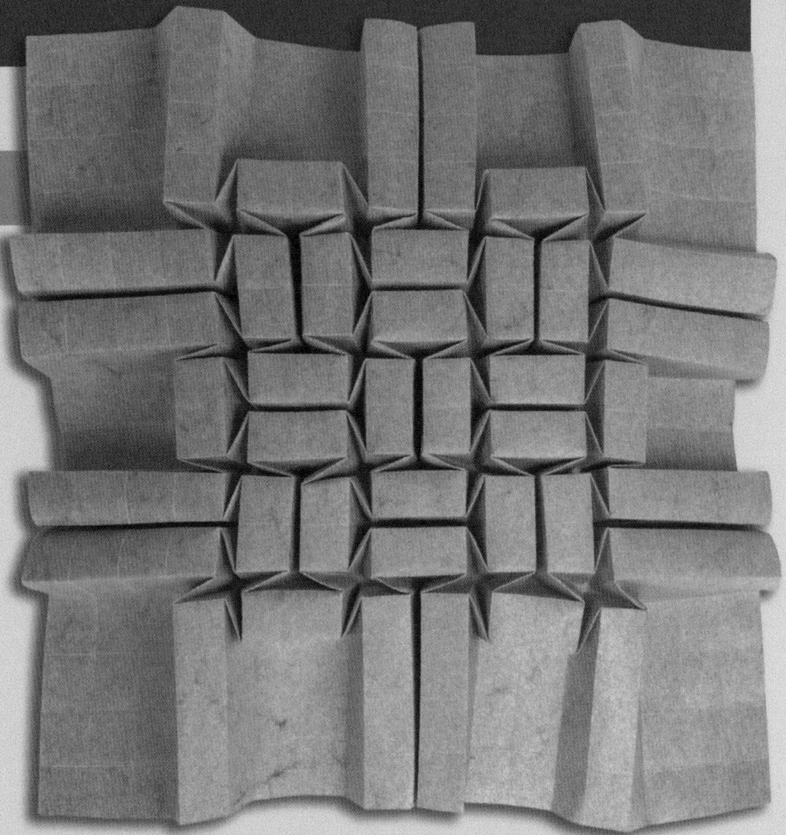

The Single Molecule

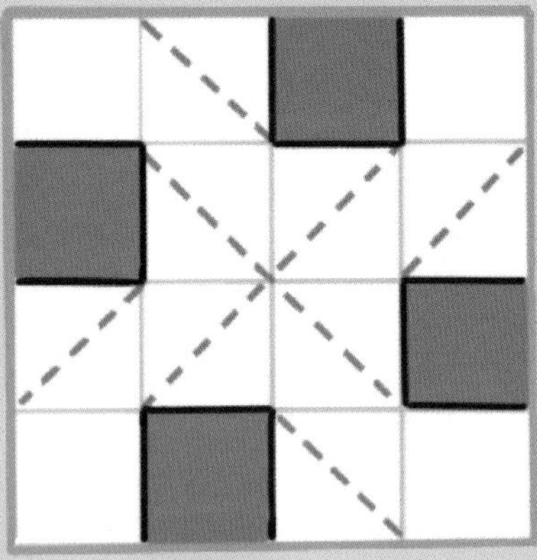

This molecule has its inner square minimized to a point. The parallel folds are still there, although both now are valleys.

The molecule size is 4 by 4.

The shrinkage ratio is 2:1.

Above: recto view of a 4 by 4–molecule Twister C tessellation.

Verso view is to the below.

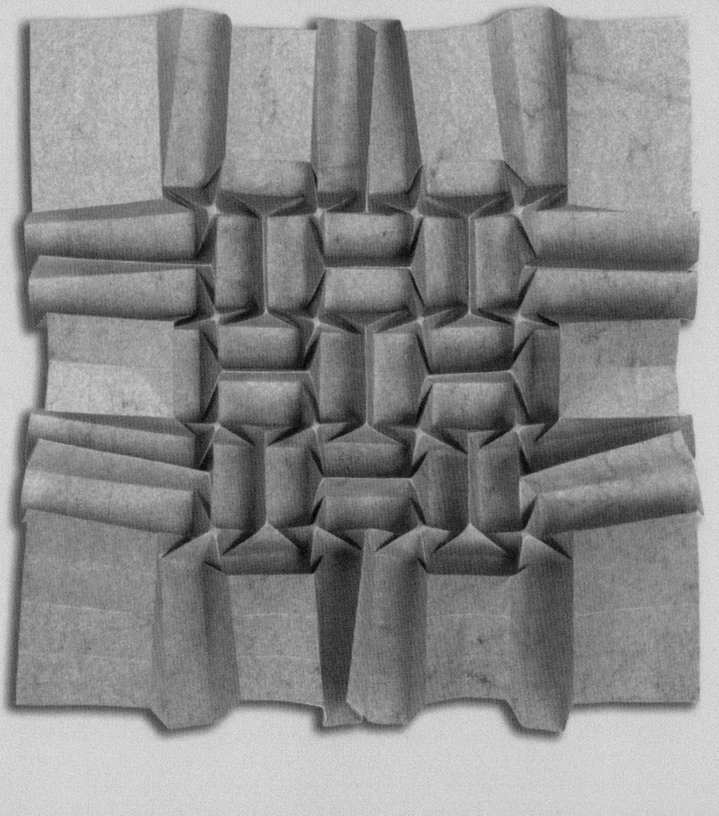

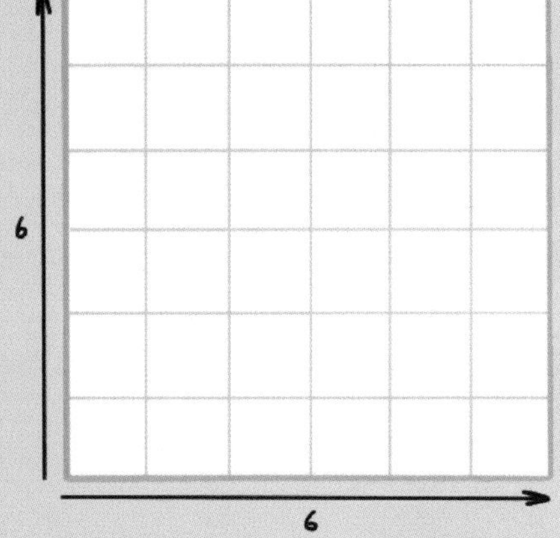

Start with a 6 by 6 grid.

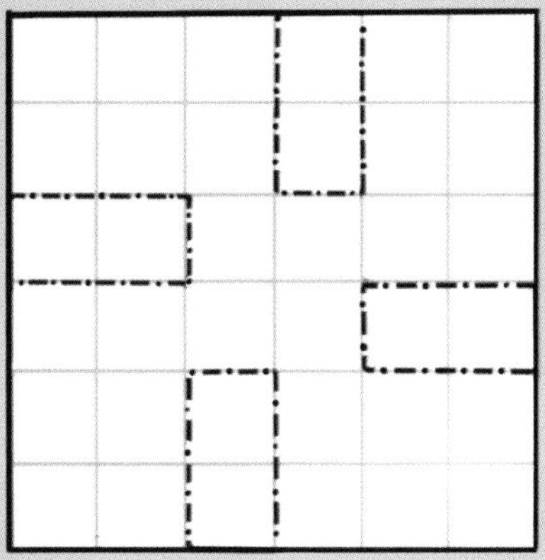

Crease the four rectangles with mountains.

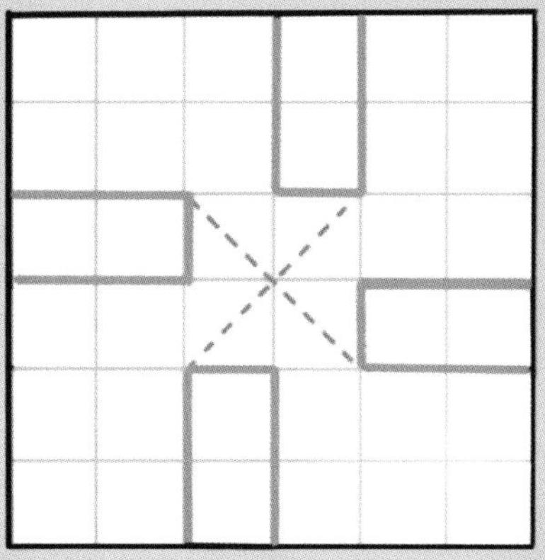

Valley fold an X in the middle.

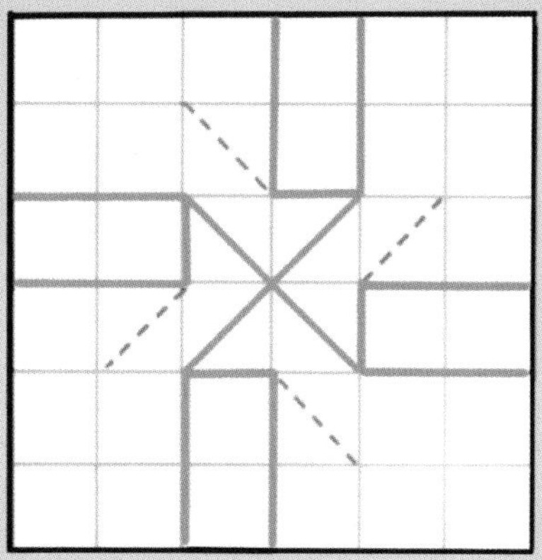

Add four valley folds as shown.

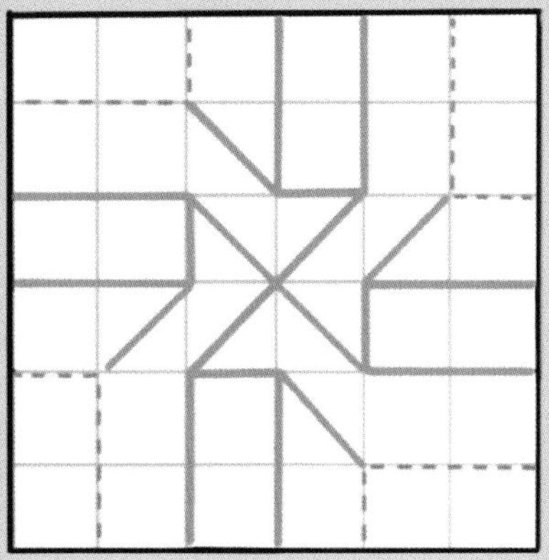

Crease the rest of the valley folds to complete the molecule.

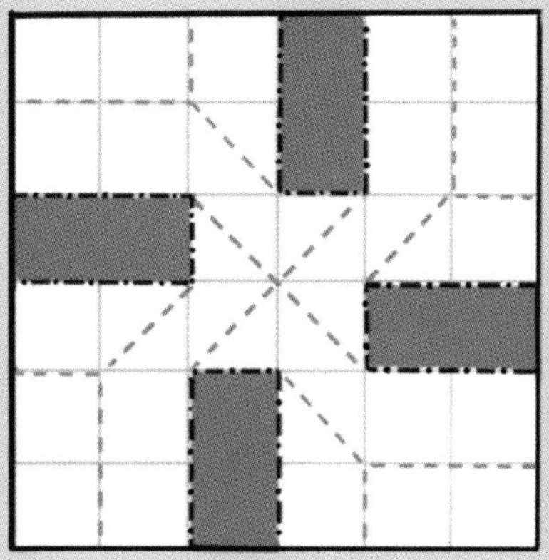

The complete CP. The gray rectangles indicate the raised areas.

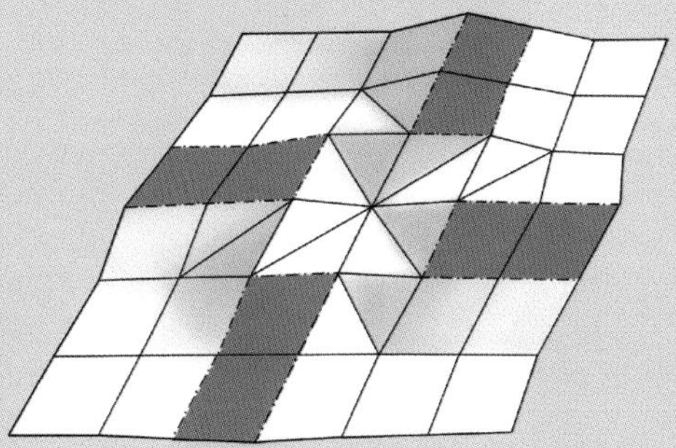

Start the collapse by forming a water bomb base in the center. Raise the gray parts while doing so.

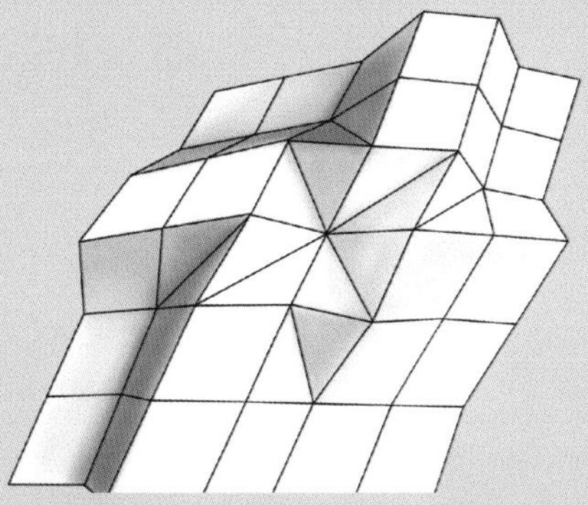

In process.

The final form is becoming evident.

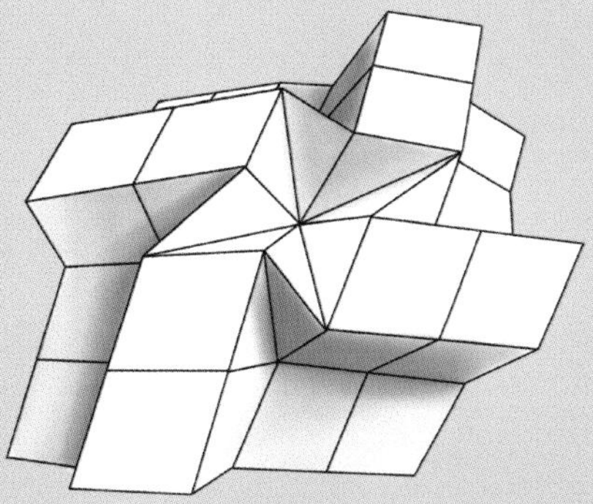

Almost finished.

Note how the water bomb base in the center is twisting.

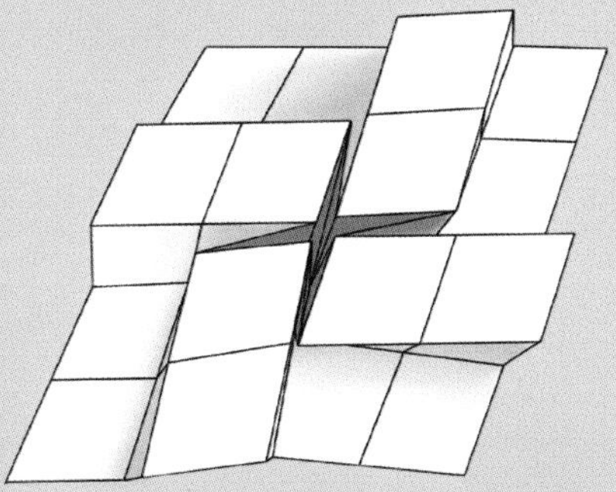

Fully collapsed.

2 by 2 Molecules

Mirrored (no Spacing)

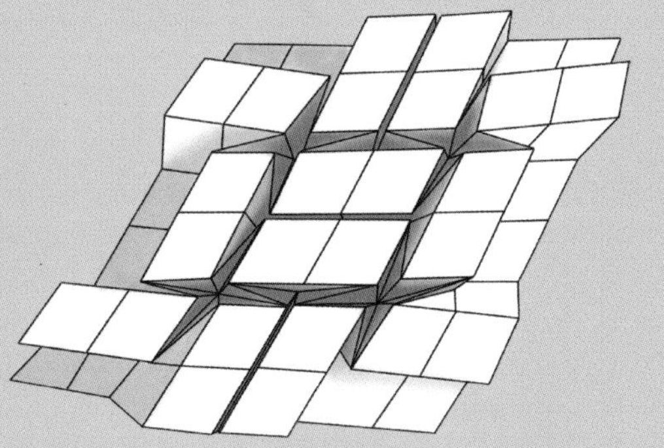

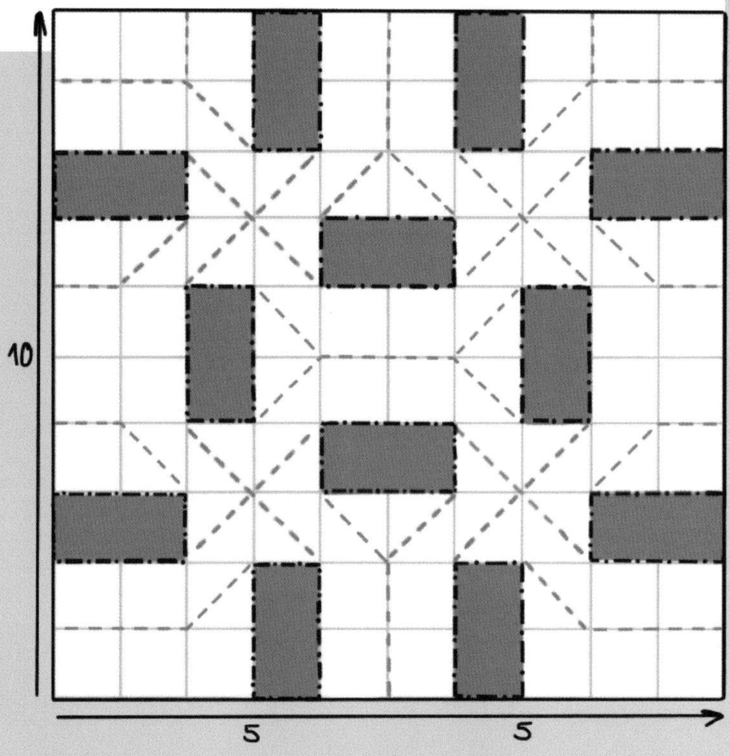

Use a 10 by 10 grid.

Collapse the molecules row by row.

For each molecule, arrange the outer gray areas first, and then try the inner ones.

While collapsing, it helps to reinforce the water bombs from the other side.

Shifted (no Spacing)

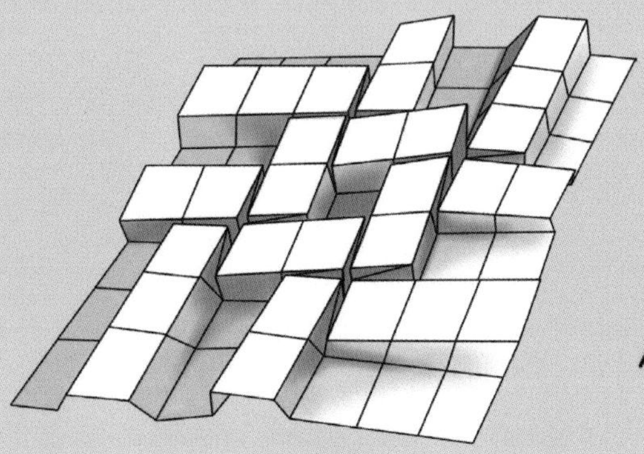

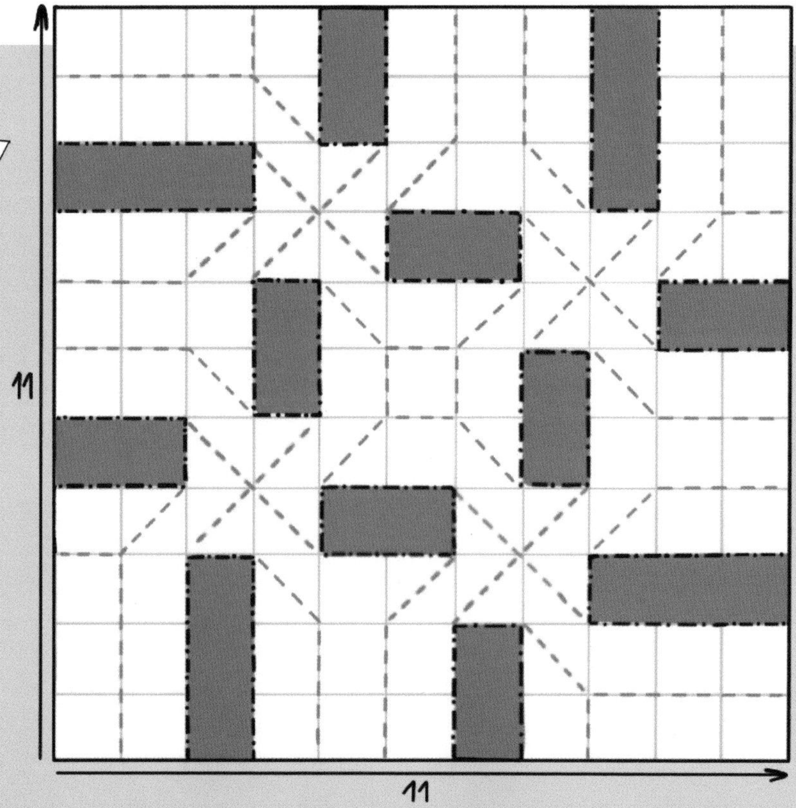

Shifting the molecules increases the grid you will need to 11 by 11.

You will also need to extend the gray rectangles that are on the edges by one square. This will give the model a cleaner, more finished look.

4 by 4 Molecules

Mirrored (no Spacing)

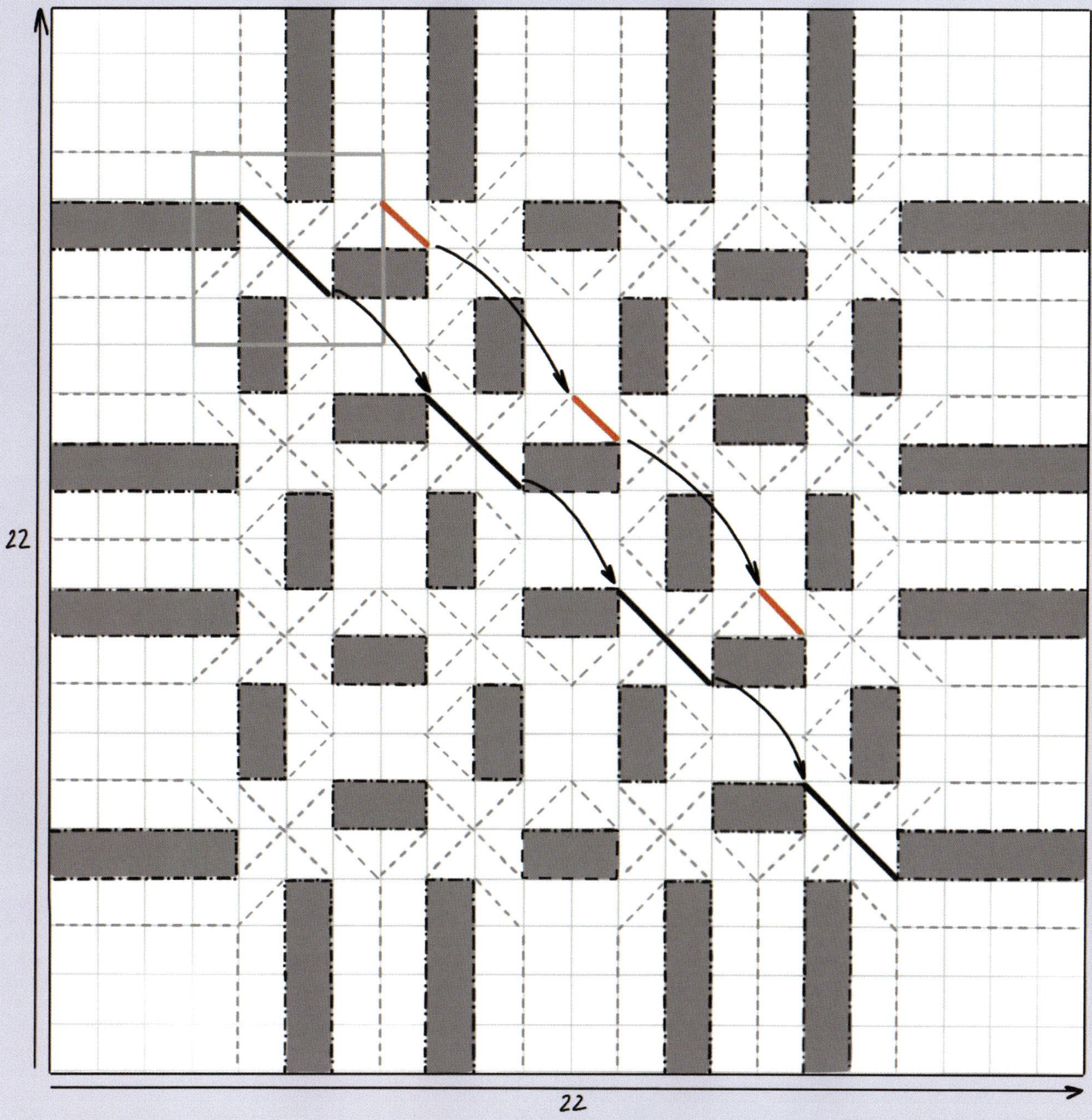

This project calls for a 22 by 22 grid. You will make a massive border of three extra rows and columns on all sides: 3 + 4 x 4 + 3 = 22.

The final result will be 14 squares wide.

Start with making Xs all around, following a fold two, skip two pattern. Crease all top-left to bottom-right diagonals first, and then rotate the paper to complete the Xs.

For all the extra valleys that aren't part of the Xs (in orange), the pattern is fold one, skip three.

As always, start the collapse at the corner and complete a row of molecules before moving to the next one.

Note that the outer gray areas are extended to reach the edges of the paper.

While collapsing, it helps to reinforce the water bombs from the other side.

Above and Beyond—A 6 by 6 Project

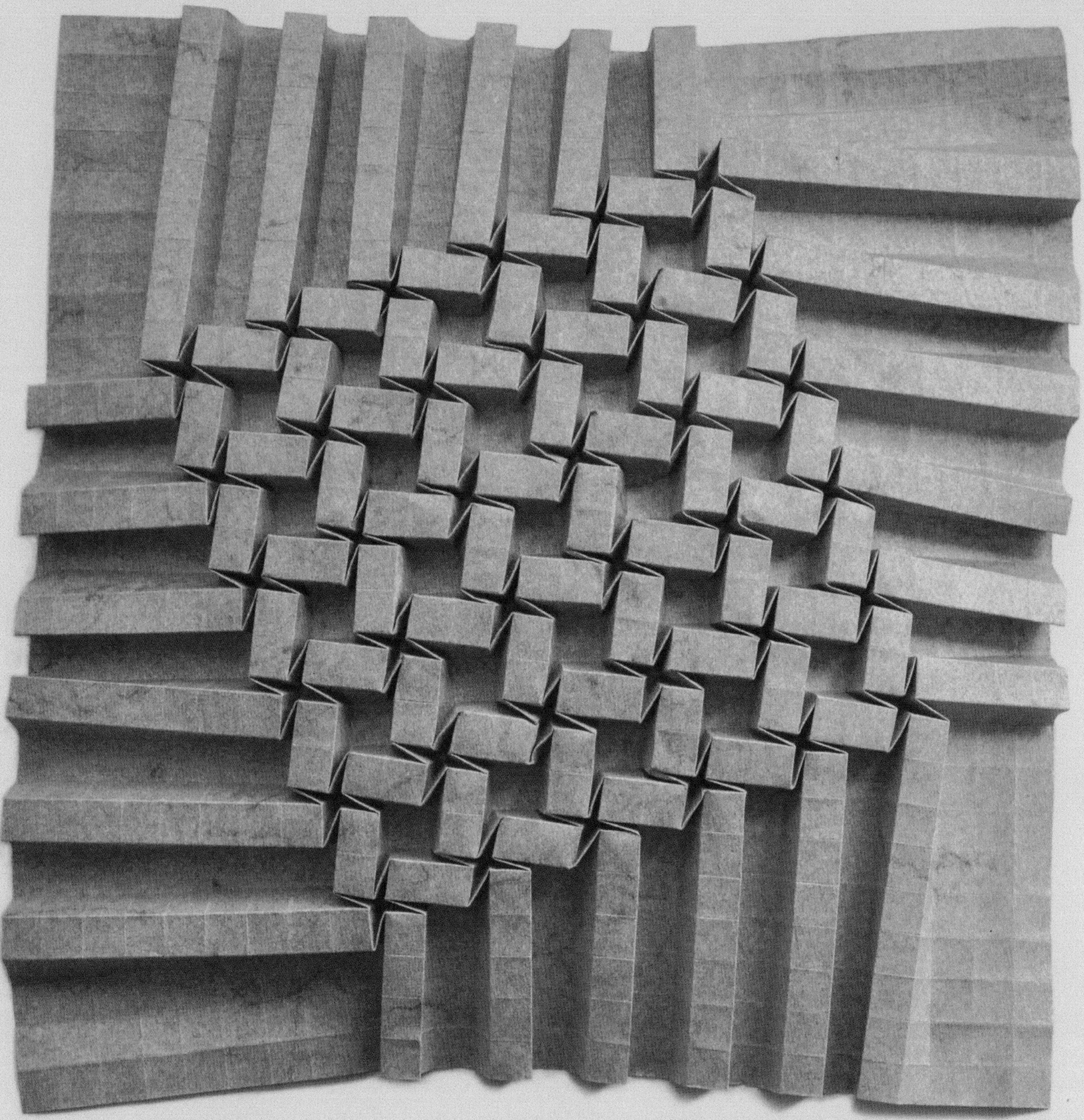

Recto view of a 6 by 6 molecule project (shifted, no spacing) that was made on a 35 by 35 grid. Molecules are shifted and the border is three squares wide.

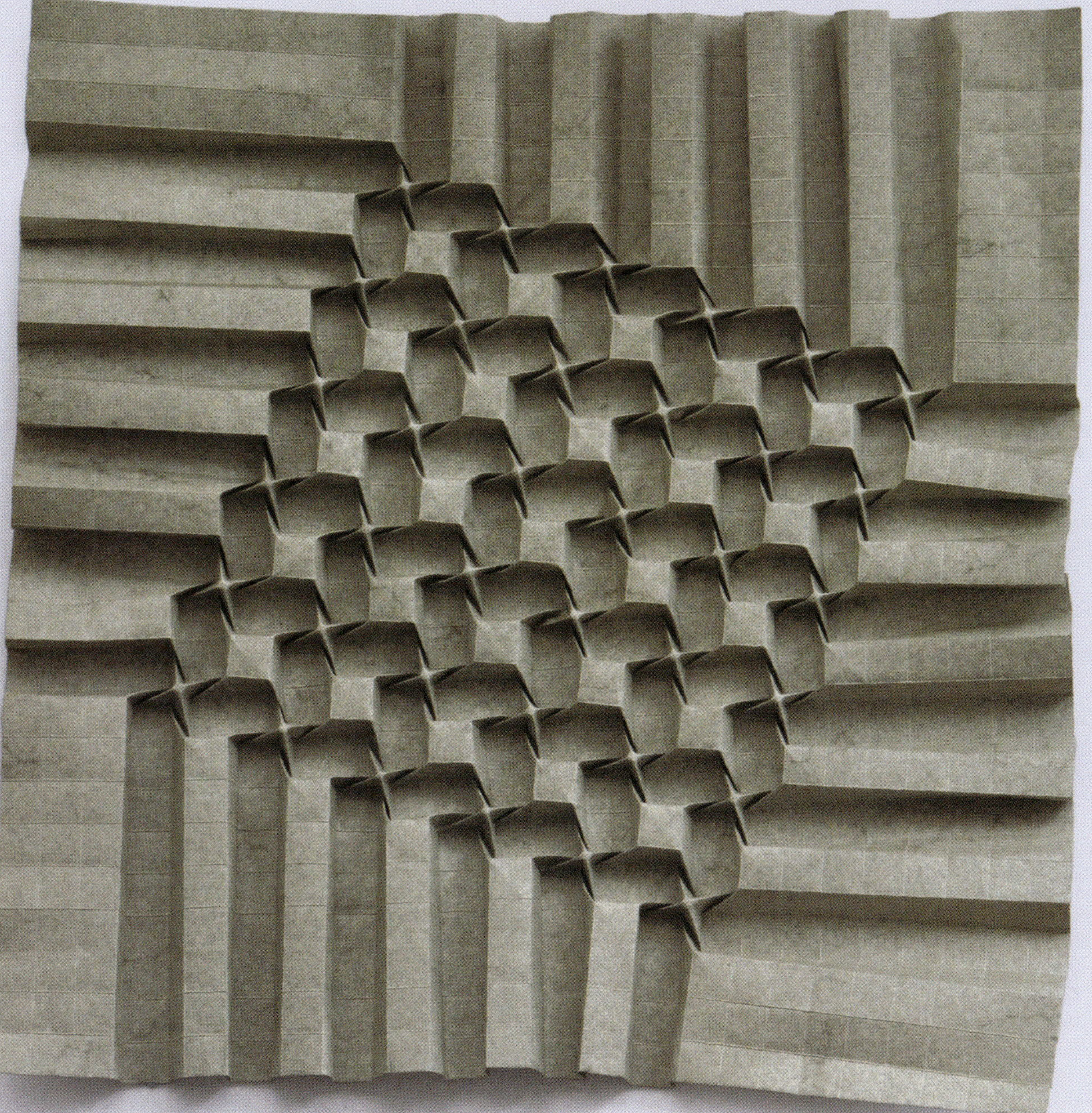

Verso side of the same project.

6 The Complex Family

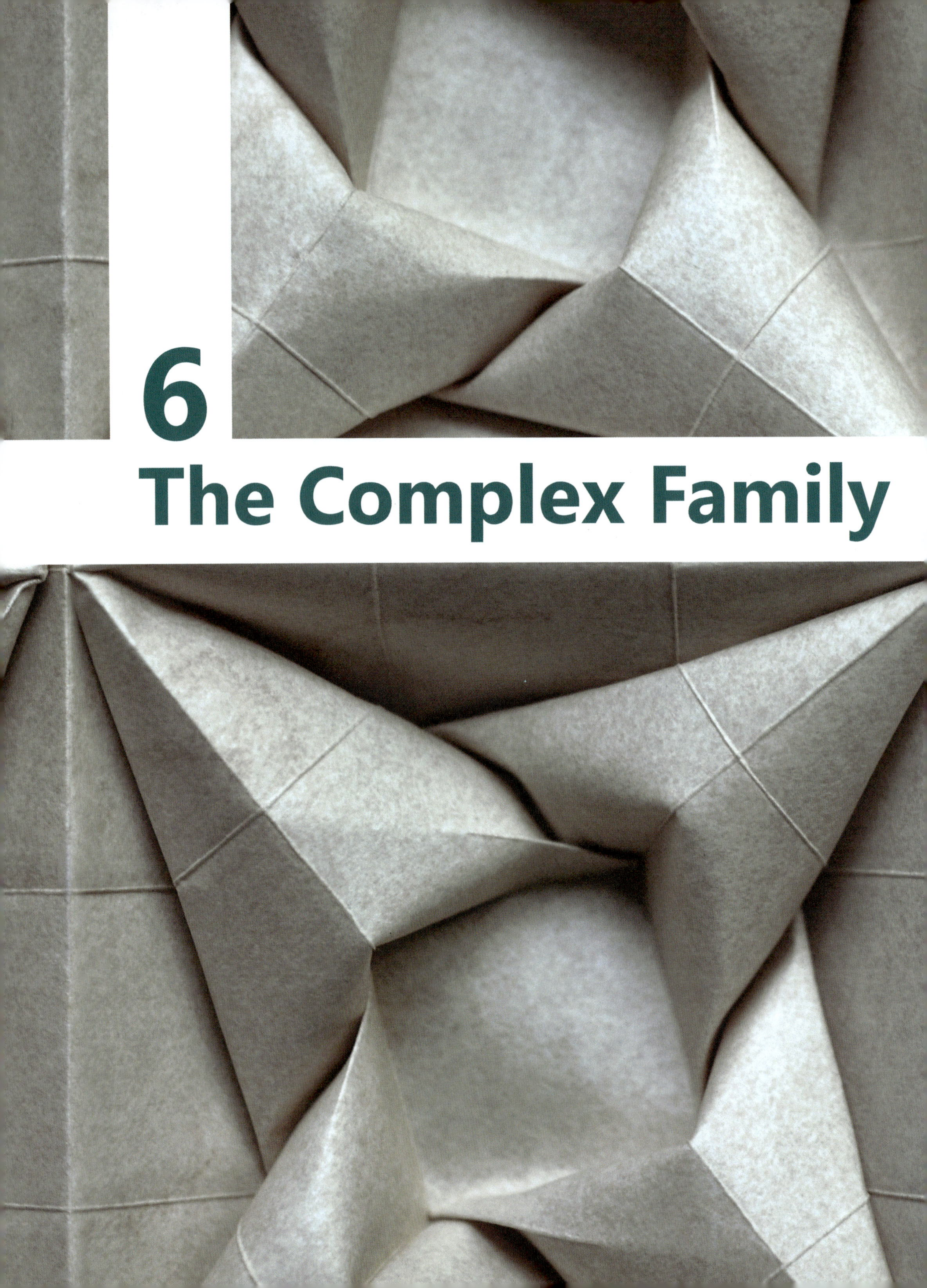

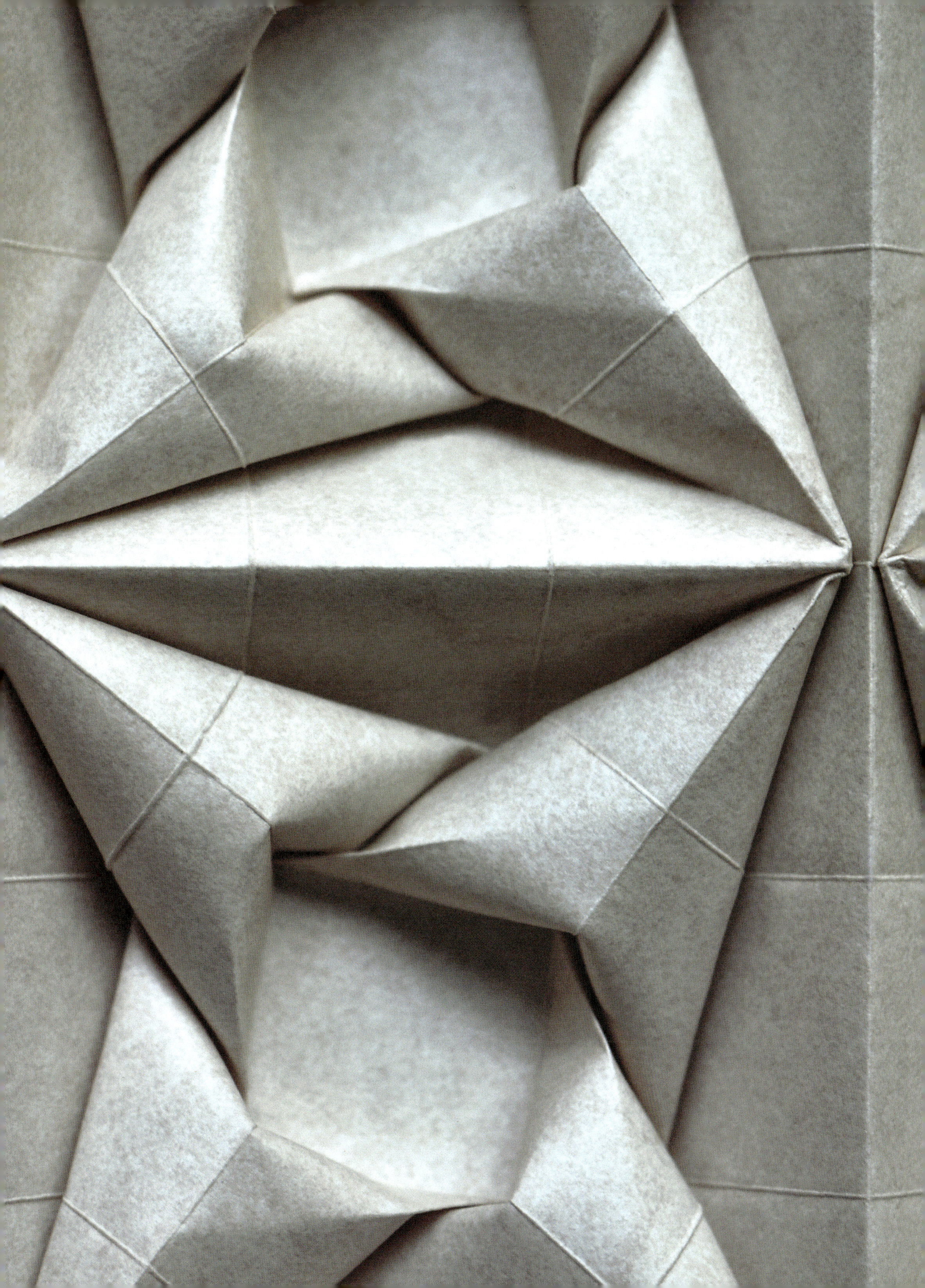

Introduction

In this chapter are a few stand-alone models, yet they share some common lines. All are based on a central square, and have four-way symmetry. They are grouped together under the title Complex, as they all tend to be difficult to collapse.

Although all the creases are straight lines, two of them have curves, unusual in this field. The curves appear because the collapse is stopped before you flatten the creases all the way through. This raises the difficulty level of those models.

6 1 Hilula

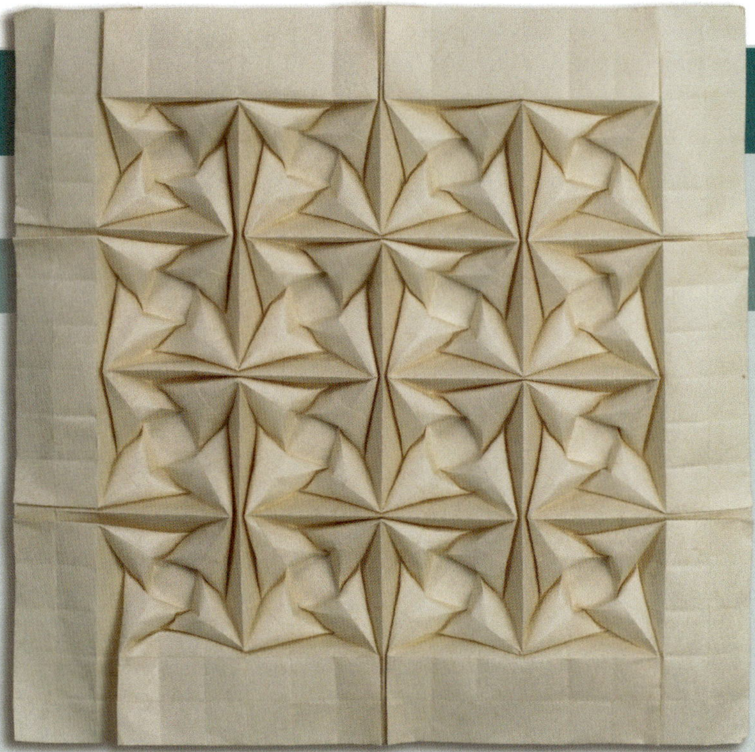

The Single Molecule

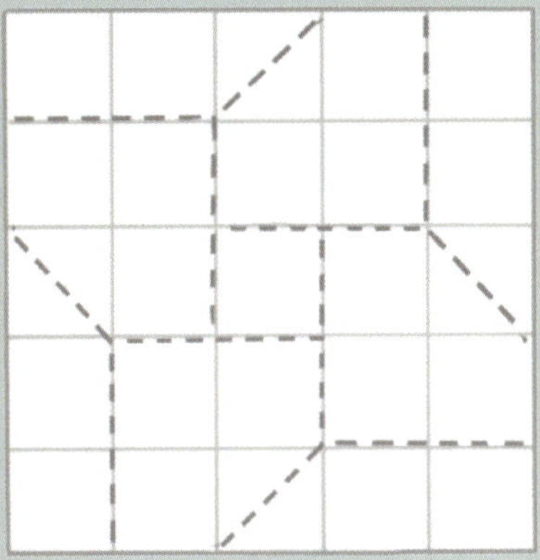

This molecule looks a lot like the Cube tessellation CP but the valley fold lines are spread out by one square. This calls for a 5 by 5 grid instead of a 3 by 3.

Surprisingly, this small change results in one of the most unique molecules in this book. The tension in the paper from the shaping causes such an interesting dimensional look.

The shrinkage ratio is 5:3.

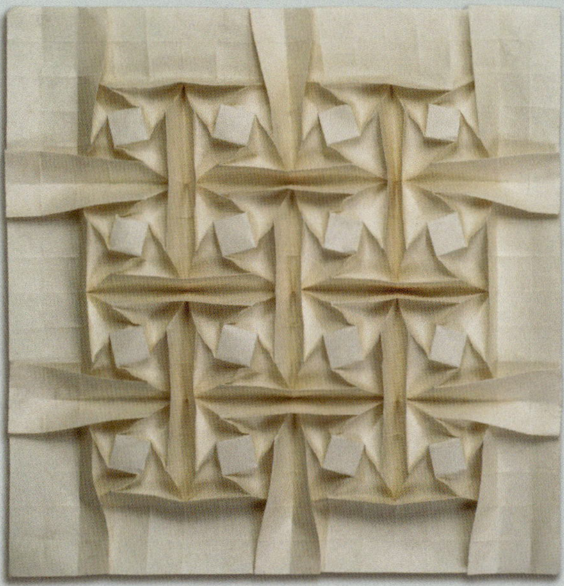

Above: recto view of a 4 by 4–molecule Hilula tessellation.

Verso view is shown to the left. The relationship between Hilula and Cubes is more obvious in this view.

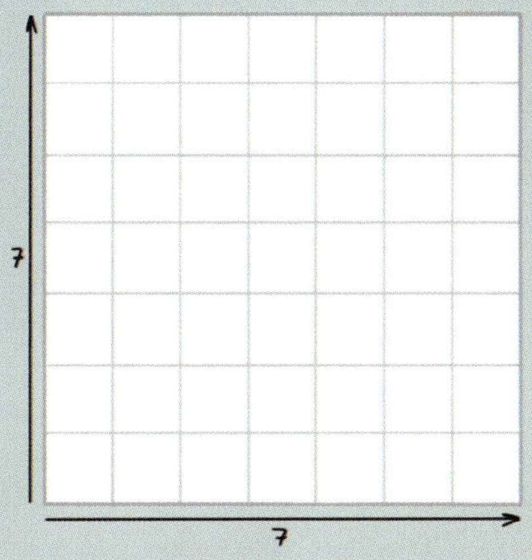

Use a 7 by 7 grid (a 5 by 5 grid with an extra row and column all around), mountain creases side up.

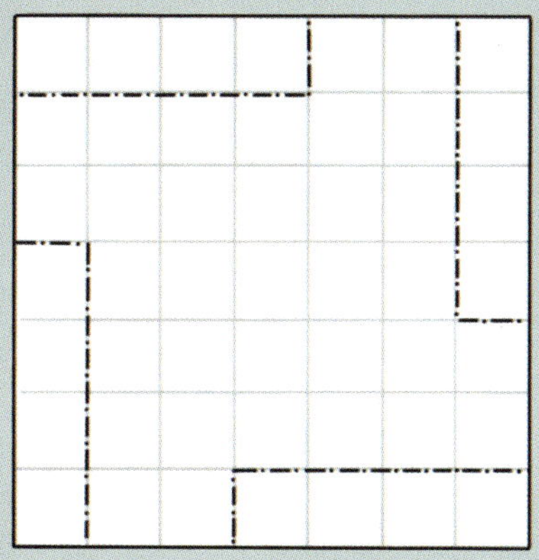

Reinforce the mountain creases, as marked.

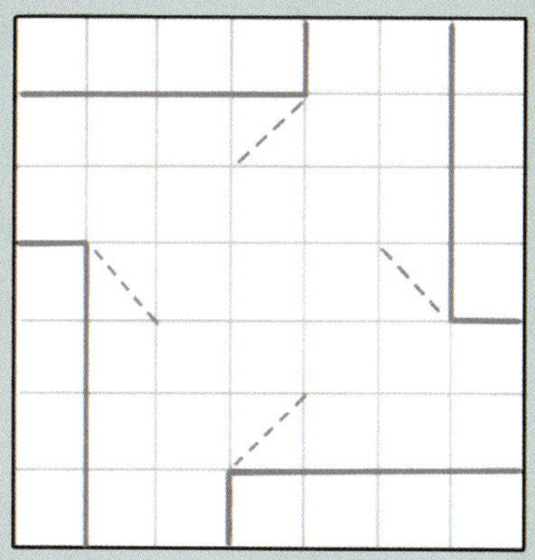

Add four valley creases.

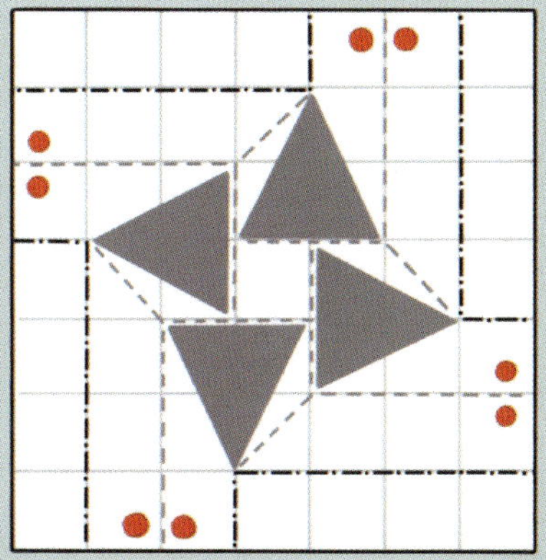

Pinch the long valleys (three squares in length) that go from the diagonals to the edges. Note the gray triangles, as they will help you through the collapse process.

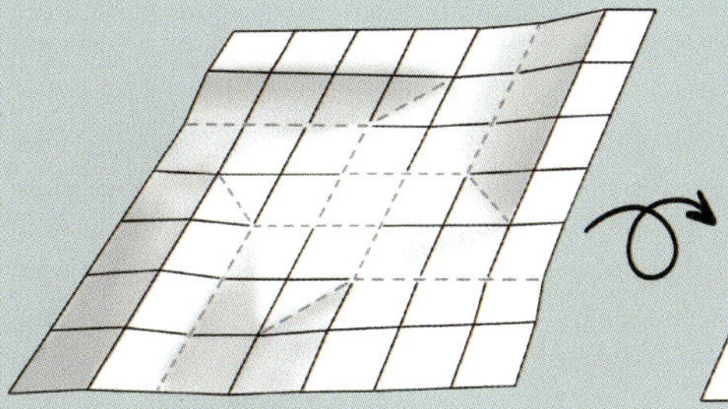

Note the triangles start to curl. Make sure the central square is flat on the table.

Turn the paper over.

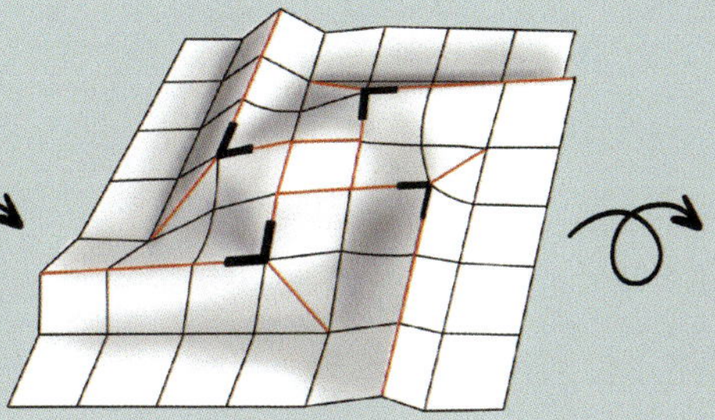

Pinch together the mountain lines (in red) that form the Vs shown in bold. This will help to establish the puffed-up triangles. Turn the paper back over.

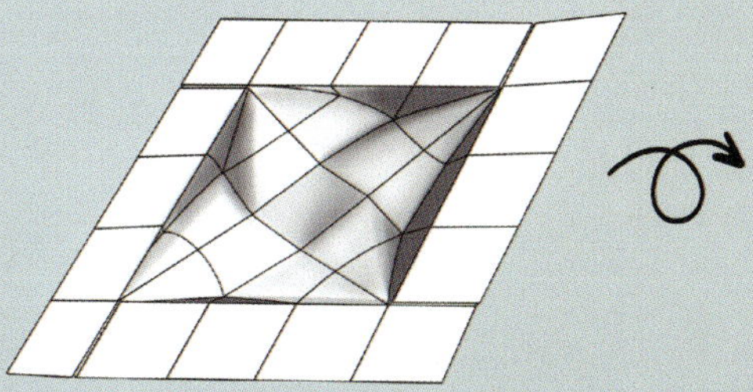

Front view. The triangles are starting to emerge. We are halfway there. Turn over.

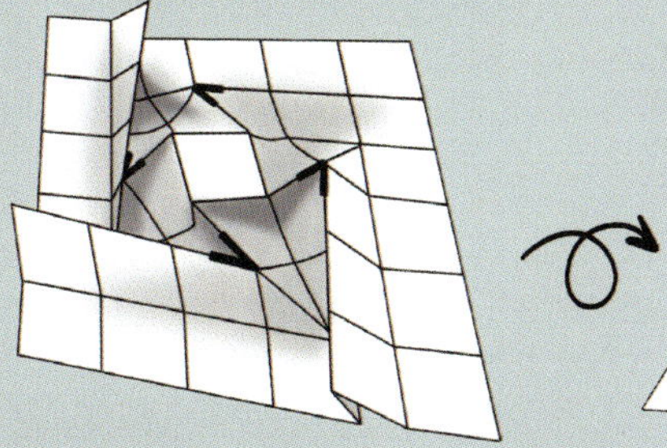

This side shows the Vs again. Find those Vs and squeeze them during the collapse to push the molecule into its final shape more easily. Turn over.

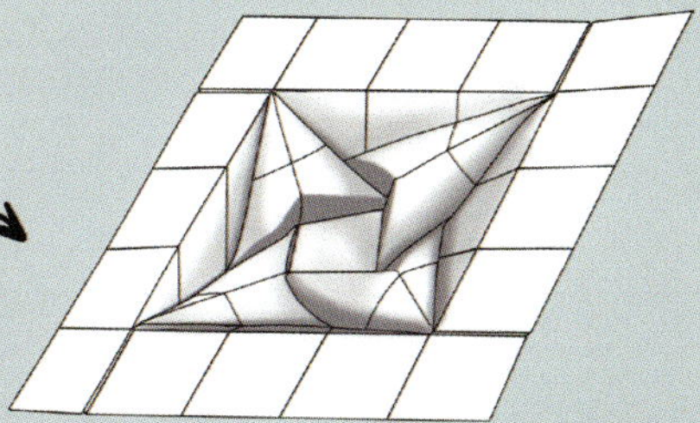

Fully collapsed.

2 by 2 Molecules

Use a grid of 12 by 12.

Start with the long mountains, as with the single molecule. Form the valleys beside them as shown.

Start the collapse in the corner and complete one row at a time.

Once you understand how this models works, try and collapse it while working from the other side, looking for the Vs to pinch.

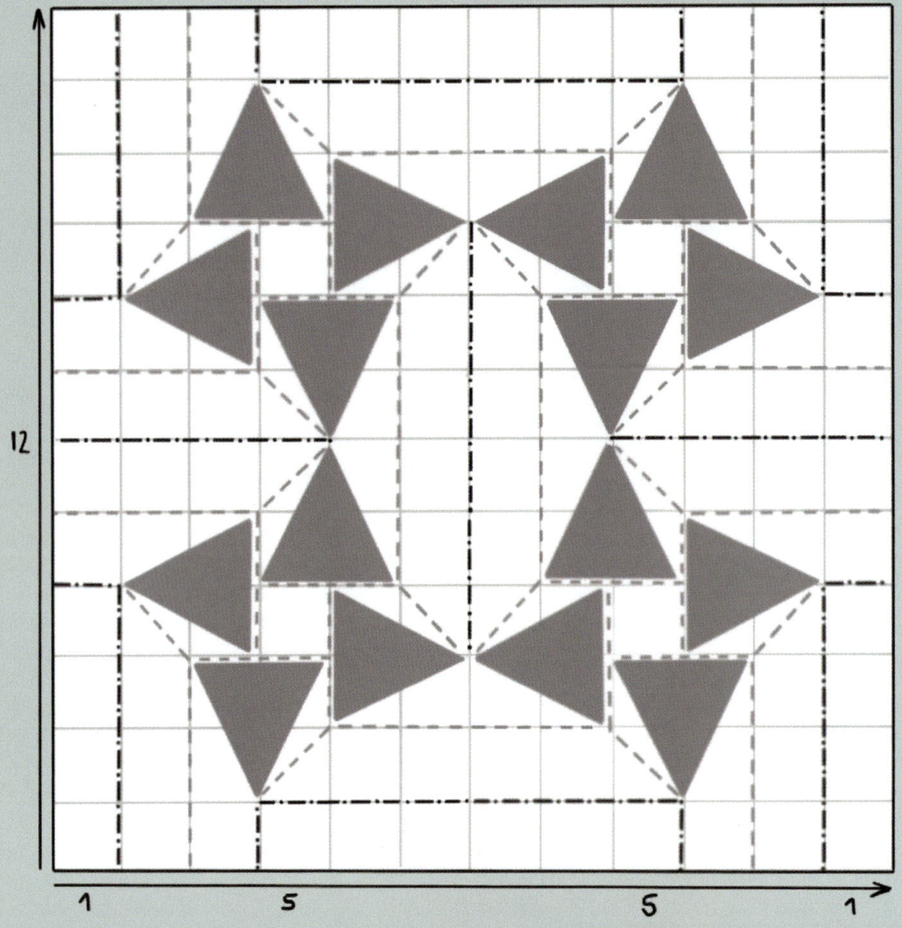

Above and Beyond—Pendant

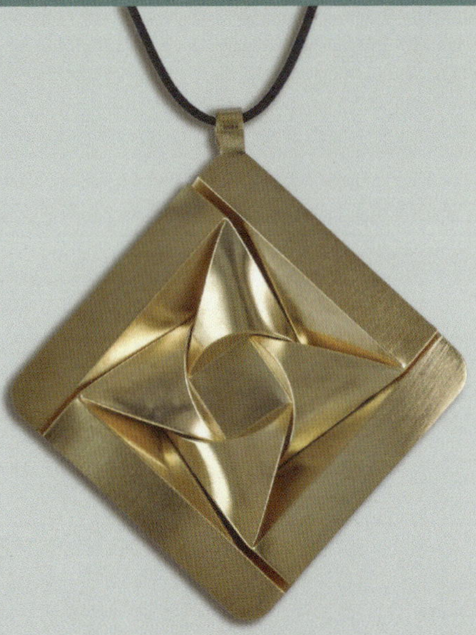

Even a single molecule of Hilula can be spectacular when folded from a sheet of metal. The curves around the center must be formed before you can execute the collapse. This step isn't necessary in paper, which is much more malleable than brass (the metal used to make this pendant).

4 by 4 Molecules

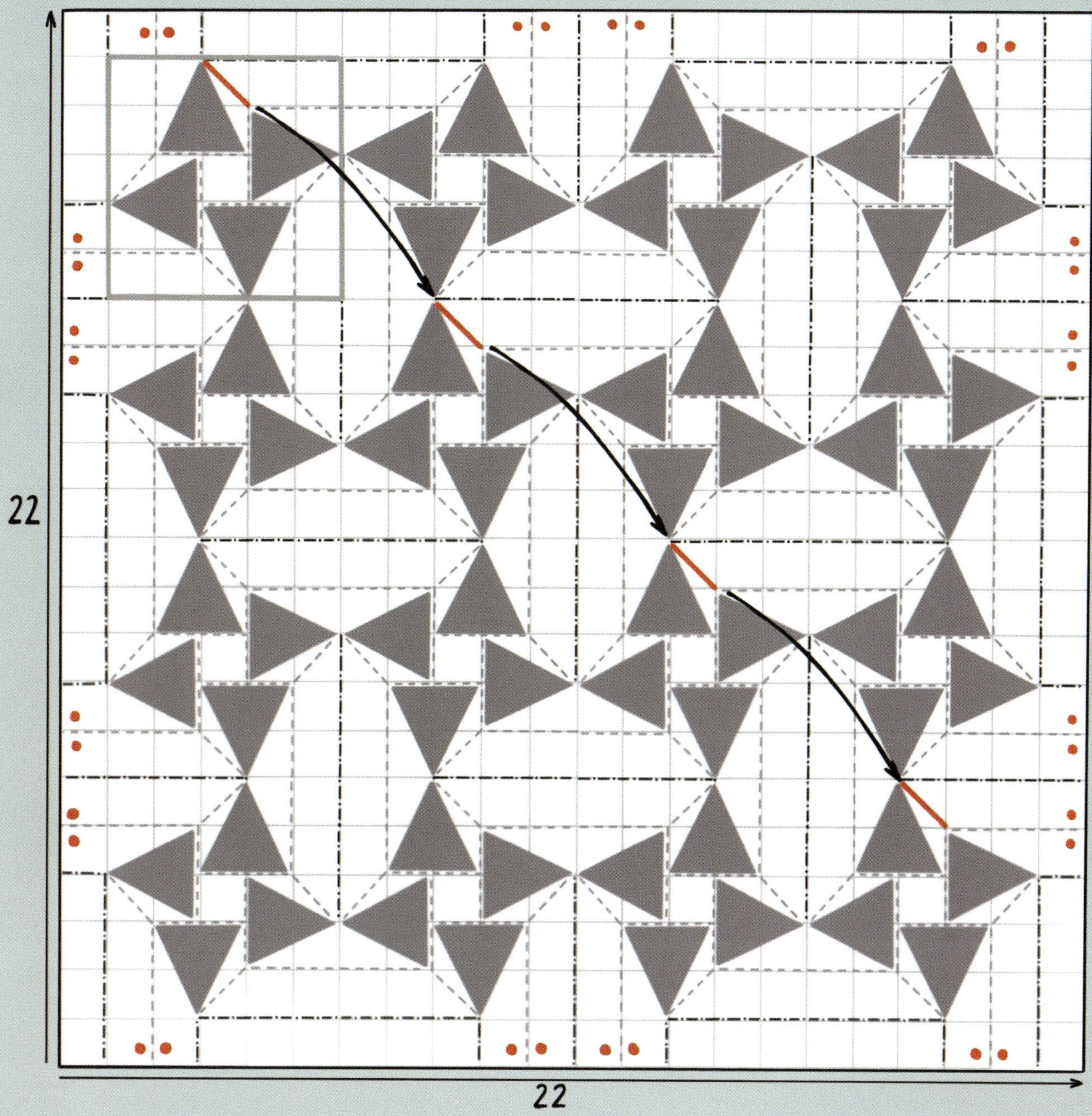

Use a 22 by 22 grid for this project: 1 + 4 x 5 + 1 = 22.

The final result will be 14 squares wide.

There is a shortcut for this size: working diagonally from the top left, fold one, skip five, repeat. You can use a 24 or even a 26 grid to give you more to hold onto. Then you can use the extra rows and columns to lock all the folds in place by mountain folding them backward.

As always, start the collapse in the corner and complete one row at a time. Pinch at the pairs of red dots for an easier collapse, and hold them in place with clips.

It is also helpful to work on the collapse from the other side as well, looking for the V created by the diagonal fold.

6 2 Amsterdam

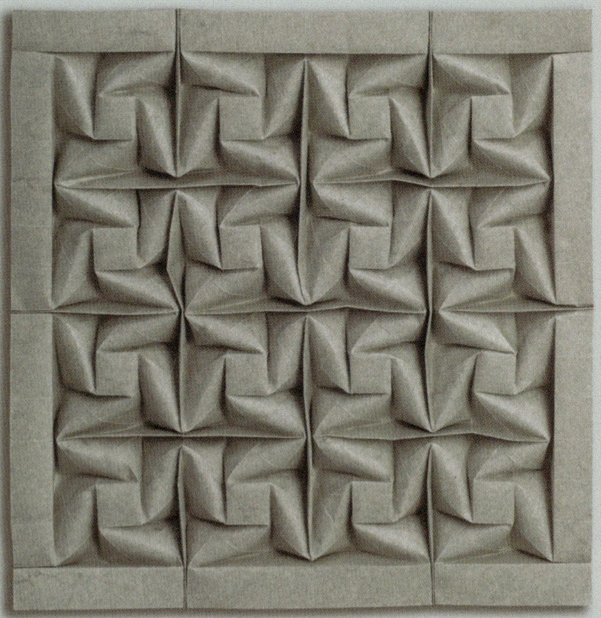

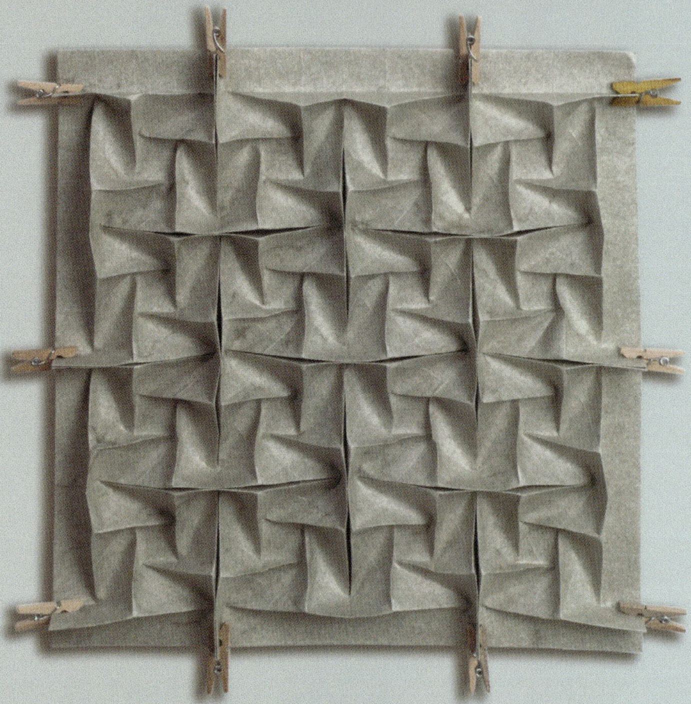

Above: recto view of a 4 by 4–molecule Amsterdam tessellation. The verso view is shown to the right.

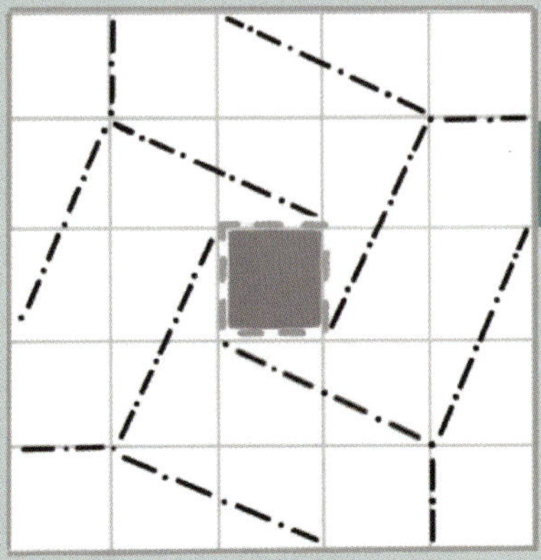

The Single Molecule

The molecule size is 5 by 5.

What makes this molecule unique is the curve that forms between every pair of parallel mountain folds.

The name came from the fact I found the design while I was visiting the city.

The shrinkage ratio is 5:3.

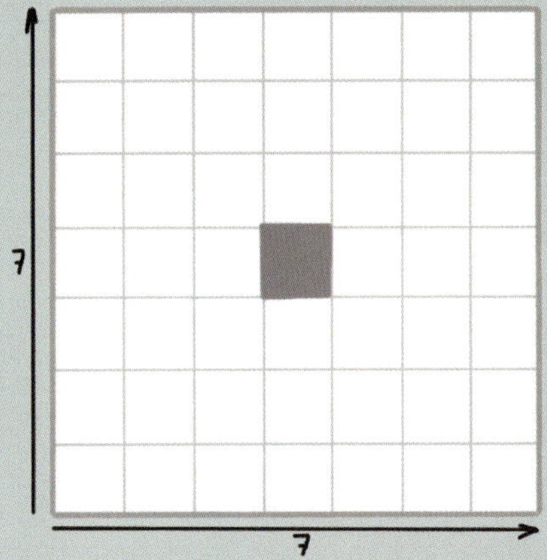

Start with a 7 by 7 grid. Mark the center square.

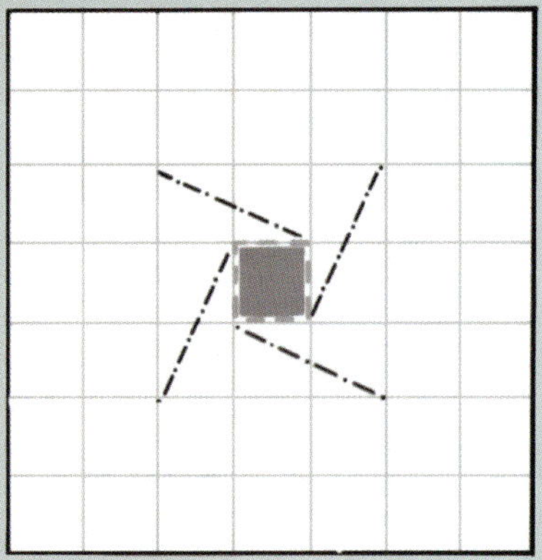

Mountain fold the inner diagonals first.

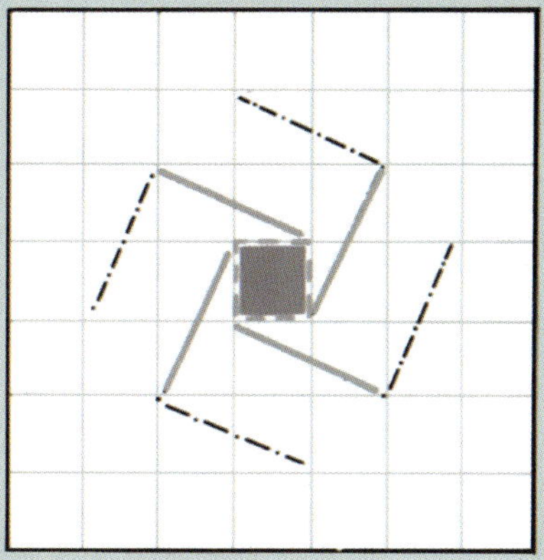

Add more diagonals perpendicular to the first ones.

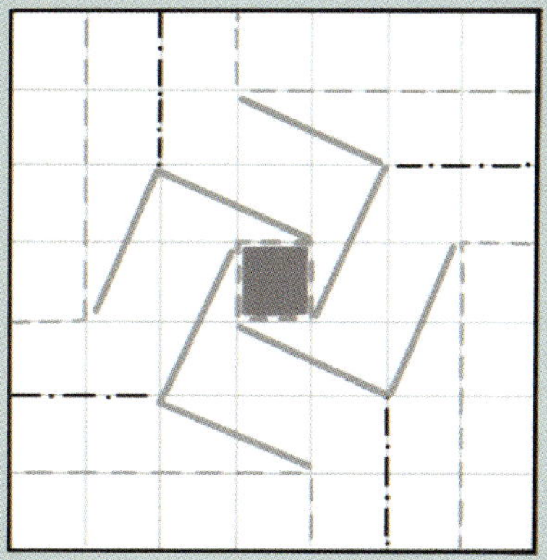

Now reinforce the valleys and mountains on the grid.

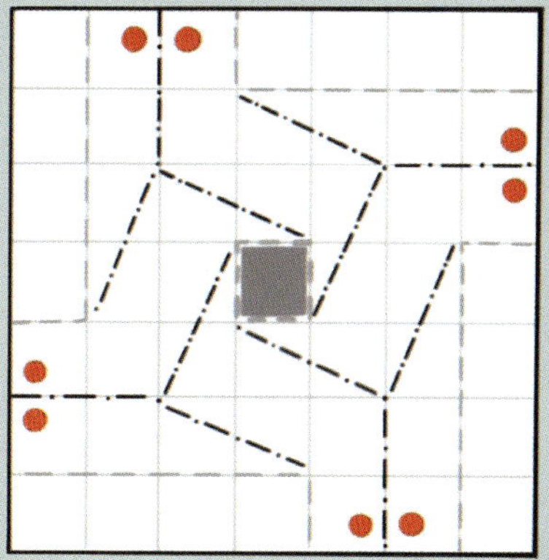

The complete CP of the molecule.

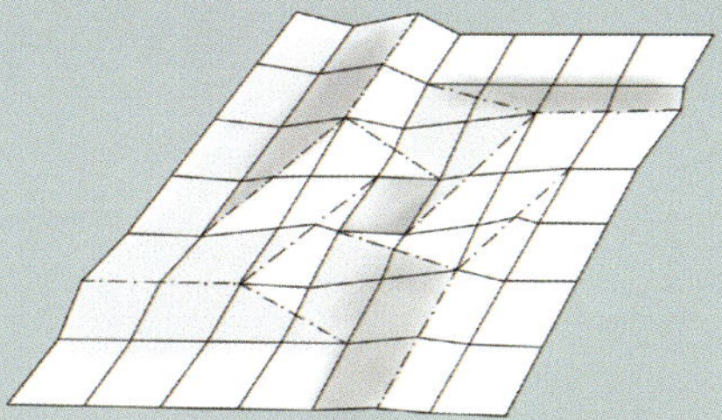

Start the collapse by pinching the mountain folds. The center square should stay flat and down.

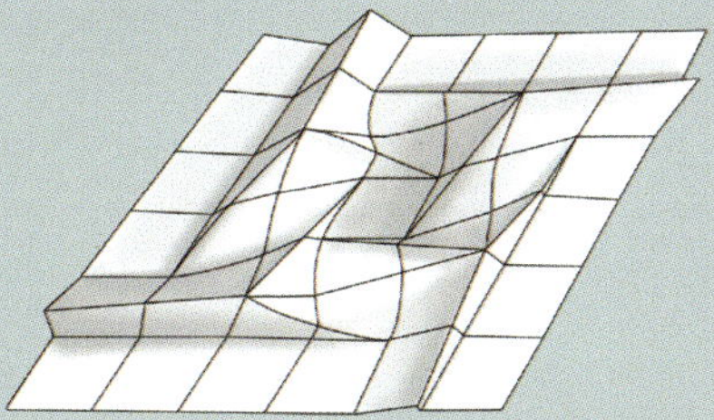

In process. Note the concave surface that emerge between the pairs of mountains.

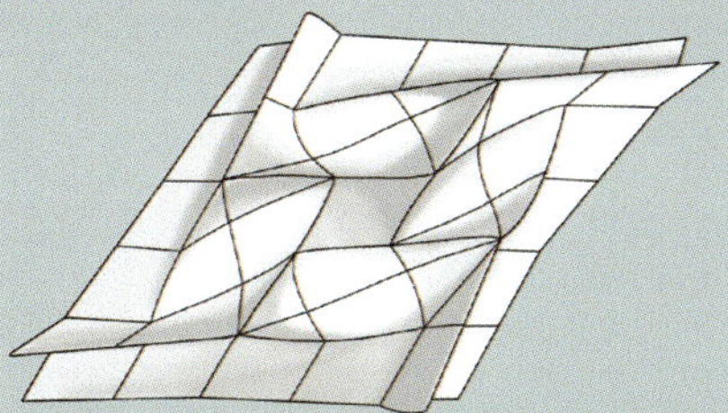

When the pinch is complete, the molecule is fully collapsed. In other words, the molecule is held together only at the edges.

2 by 2 Molecules

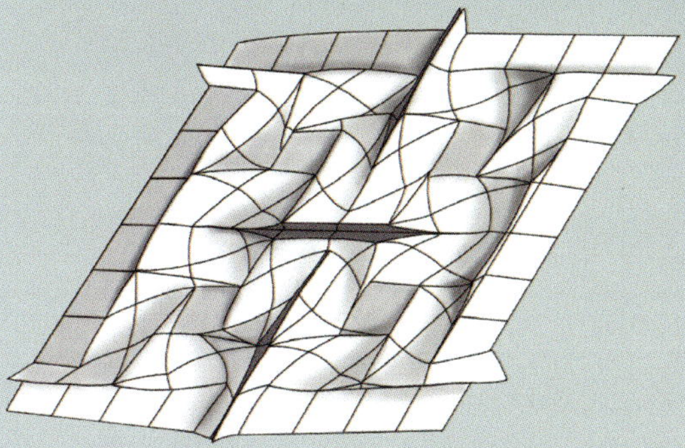

Use a grid of 12 by 12.

Mark off the squares.

Add all precreases as shown.

Work from the edge of the paper inward. Pinch the mountains; the valleys will form on their own.

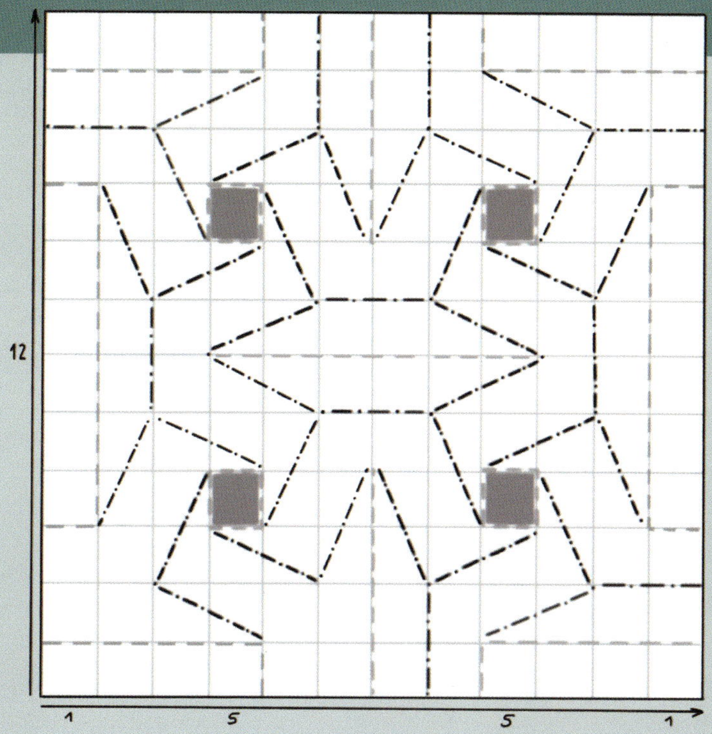

4 by 4 Molecules

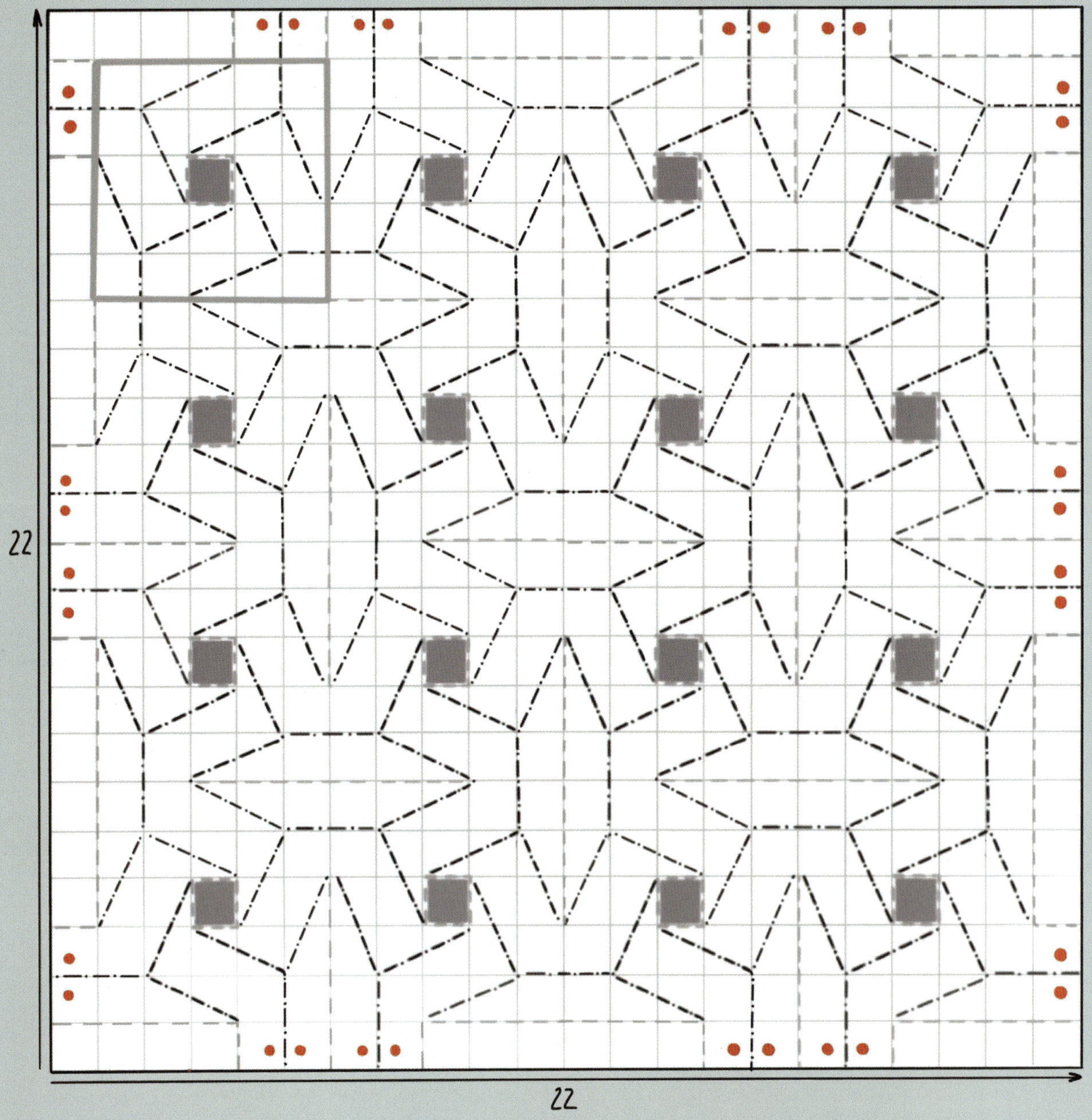

For a 4 by 4–molecule project, start with a 22 by 22 grid: 1 + 4 x 5 + 1 = 22.

The final result will be 14 squares wide.

Put in all the precreases marked above.

There is no way to cut the folding time for this project; your best bet is to be efficient. You can make all the inner diagonals for all the molecules and then complete each molecule with the outer lines.

Follow the collapse process outlined for the single molecule. Start from the top left corner and collapse row by row.

Pinch at the pairs of red dots for an easier collapse, and hold them in place with clips.

It is easier to collapse if you work on both sides (recto and verso) of the model.

Above and Beyond—A 5 by 5 Project

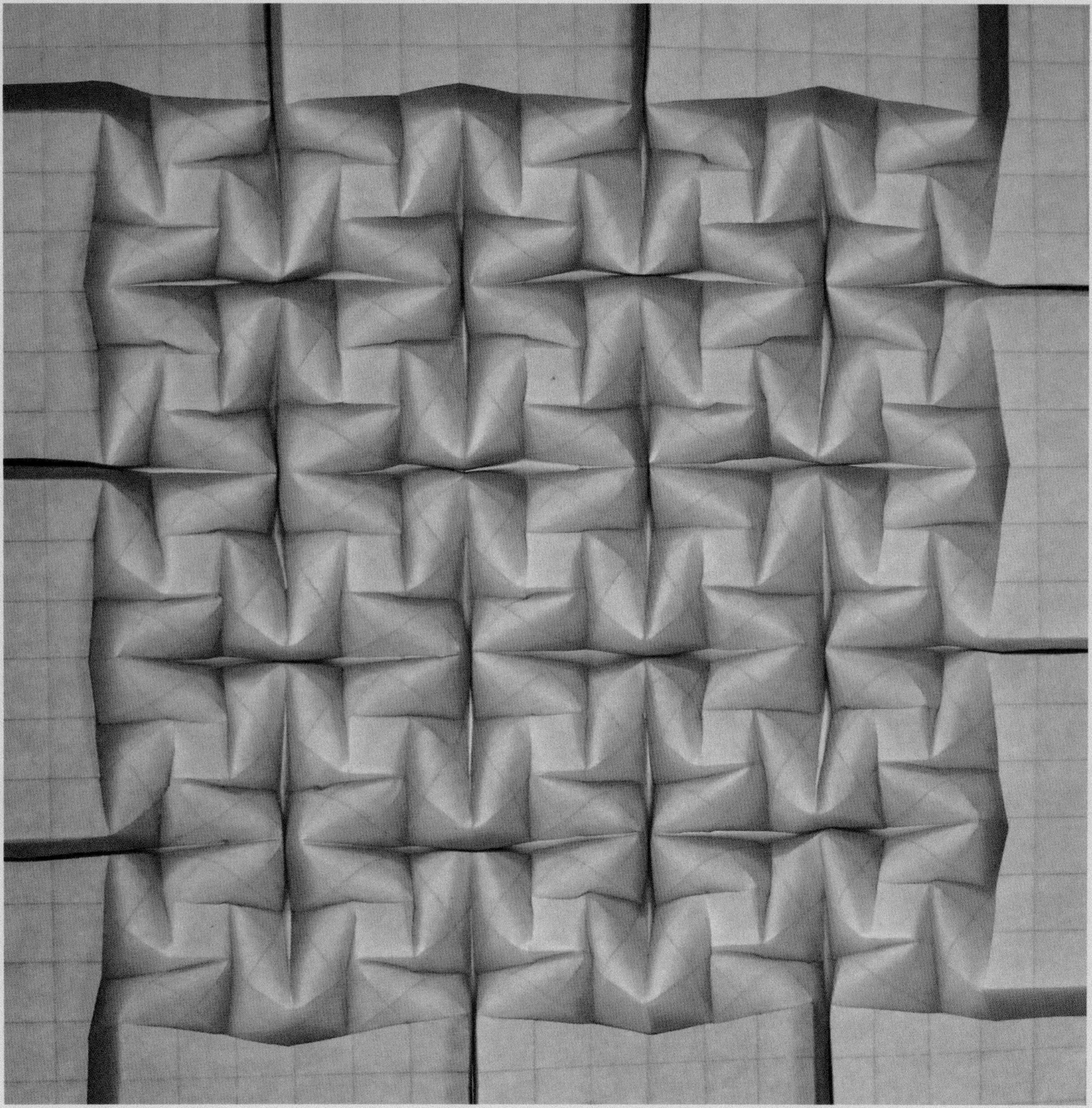

Backlighting puts the focus on the unique curves of this molecule, especially with a field this large.

6 3 NSNS

The Single Molecule

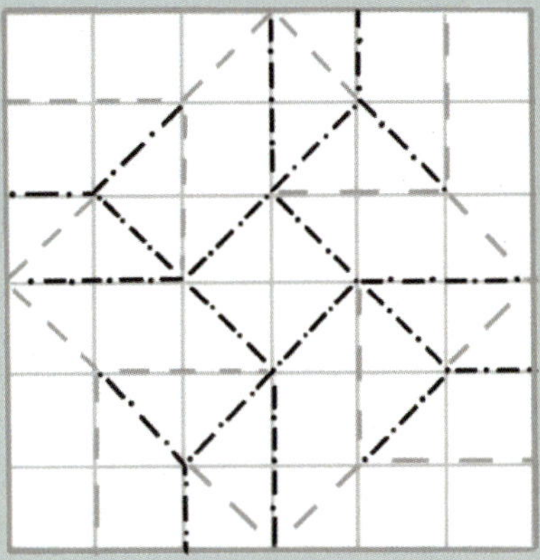

NSNS stands for North/ South Negative Space: the empty area creates a four–pointed star, pointing to the four directions.

This 6 by 6 molecule is a variation on the Cubes tessellation, in which the center square is rotated by 45°.

It resembles Amsterdam, as well—it has the same 90° angles formed by mountain folds that surround the central square.

The shrinkage ratio is 3:2.

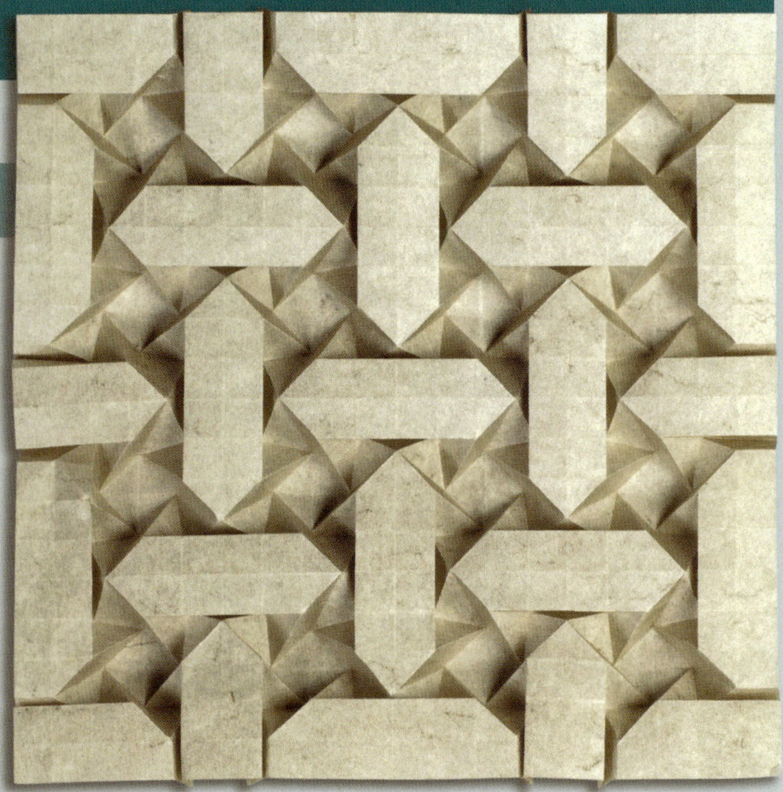

Above: recto view of a 4 by 4–molecule NSNS tessellation. The verso view (below) shows the similarity to Cubes.

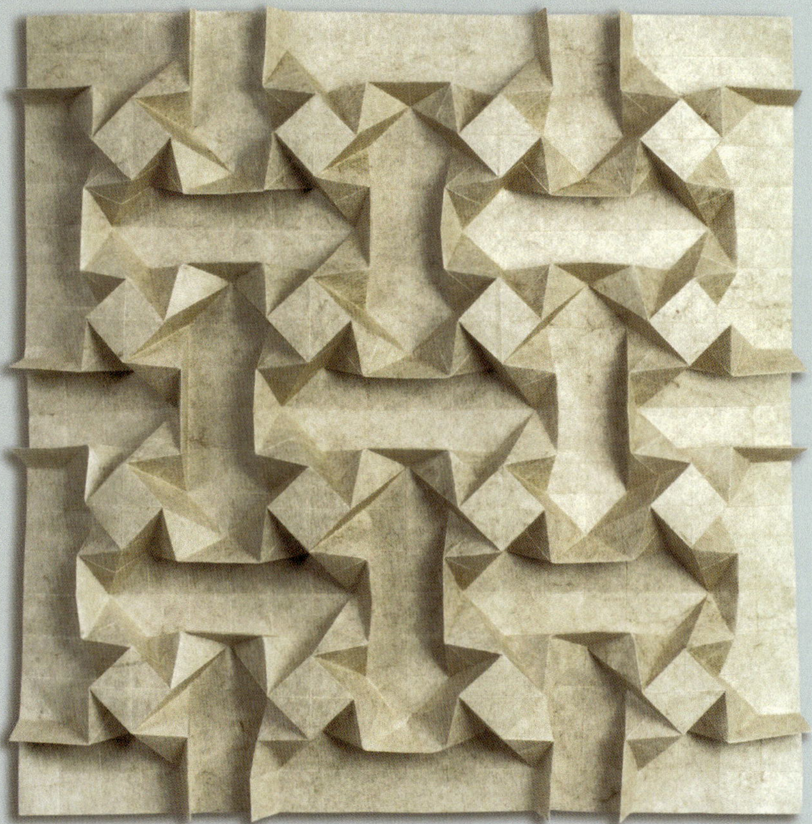

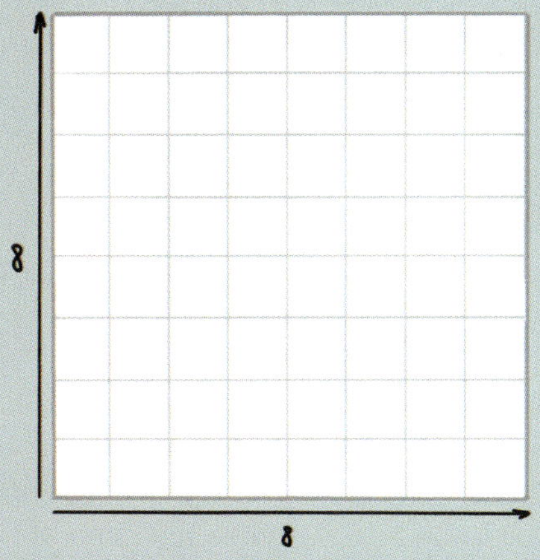

Start with an 8 by 8 grid (a 6 by 6 grid with an extra row and column all around).

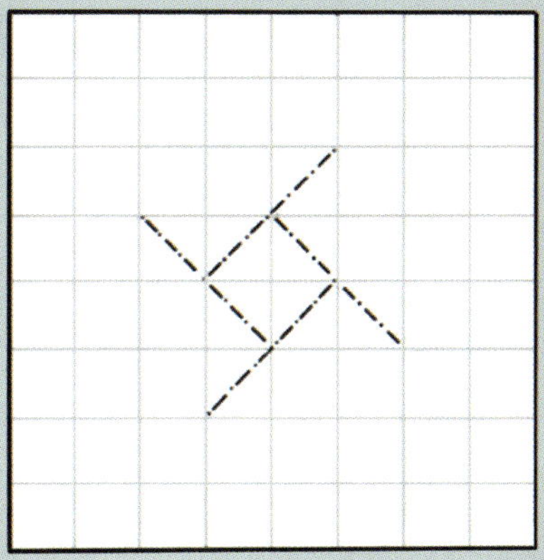

Mountain fold the inner diagonals first.

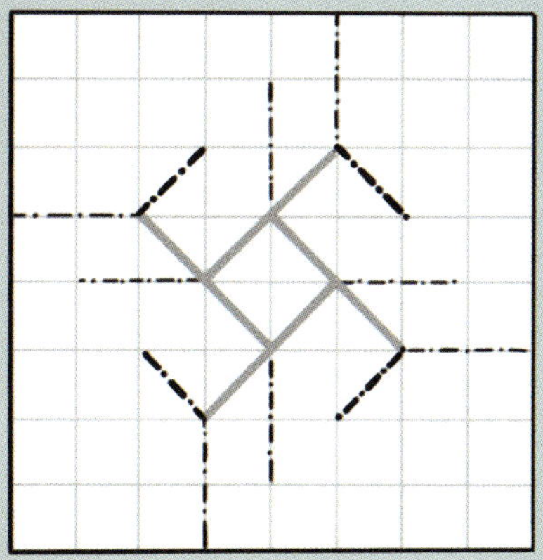

Add more diagonals, at 90° angles to the first ones.

Reinforce the mountains on the grid lines.

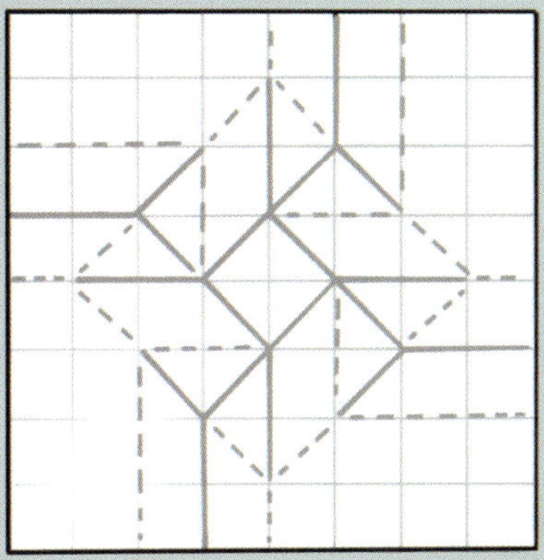

Continue with the valleys shown. Note that all the diagonals complete another tilted square around the inner one.

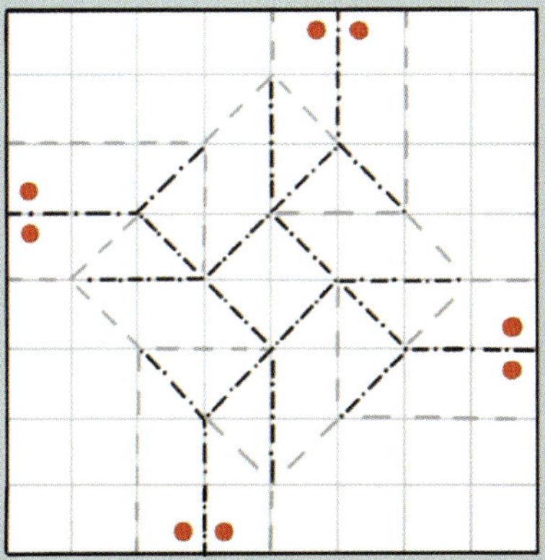

The complete CP of the molecule.

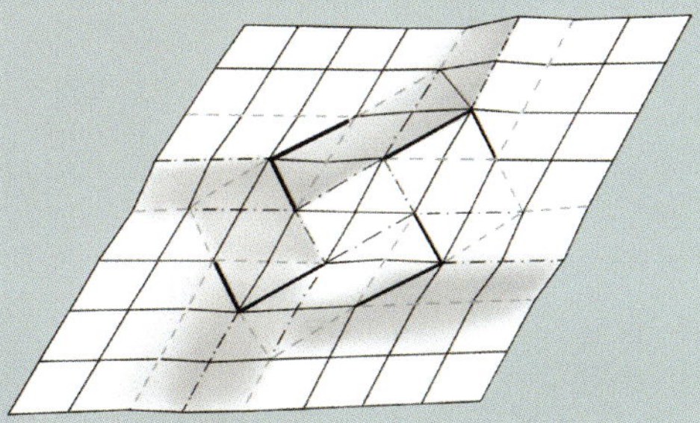

Start the collapse by pinching the mountain folds that goes from the V (created by the two diagonal mountain fold lines) center point to the edge of the paper. The center square should stay level and raised up.

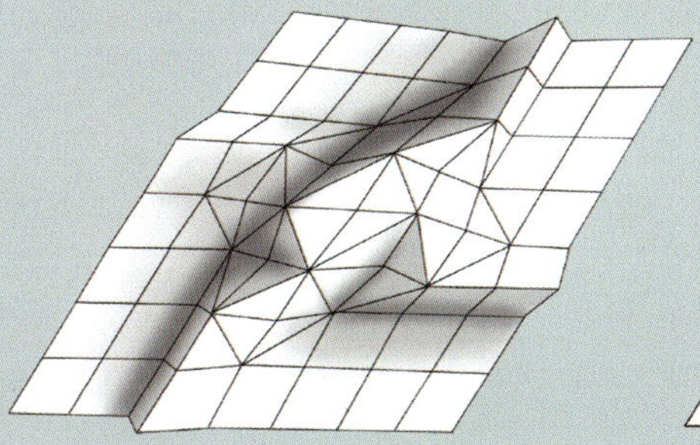

In process. Make sure every precrease folds the right way!

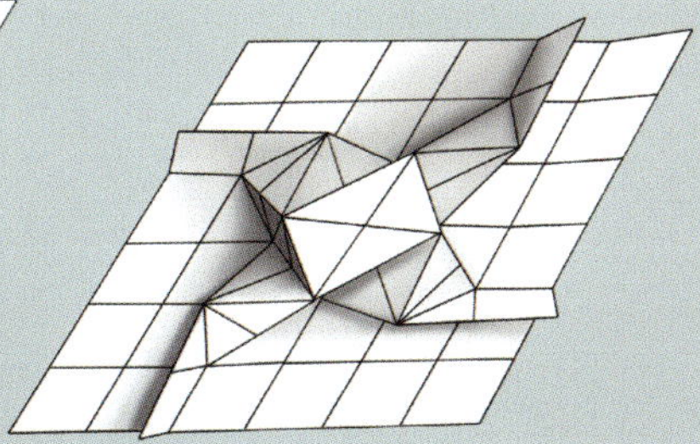

Fully collapsed.

2 by 2 Molecules

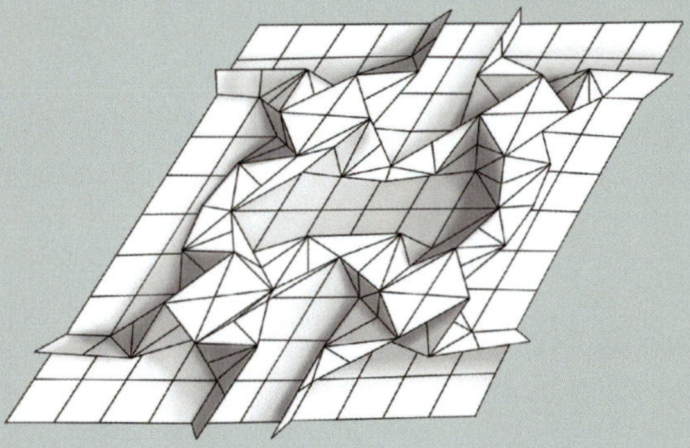

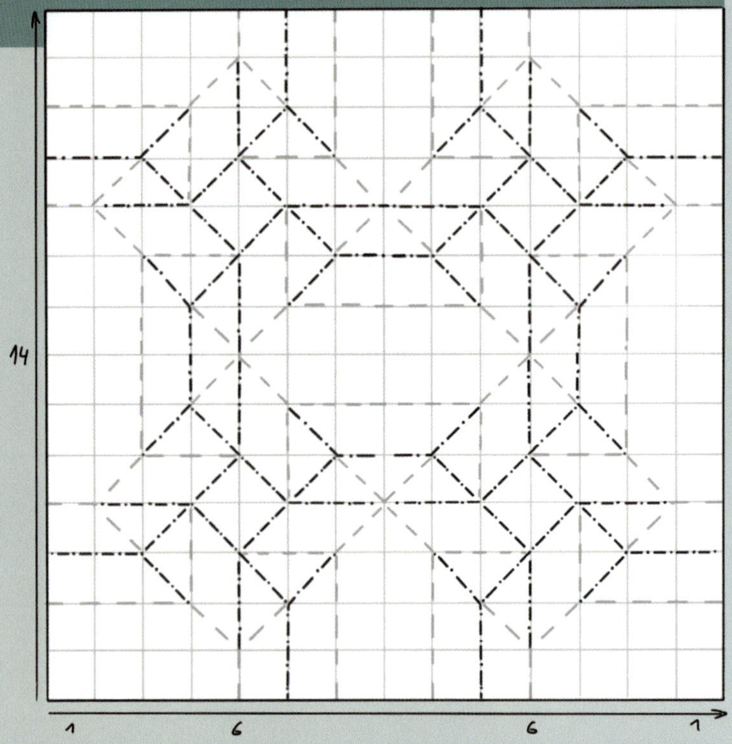

Use a grid of 14 by 14.

Adjacent molecules mirror each other. Add all precreases.

Start the collapse in the corner and complete one row at a time.

Pinch the mountains; the valleys will form on their own.

Above and Beyond—Pendant

A single NSNS molecule folded from a sheet of brass, verso side up.

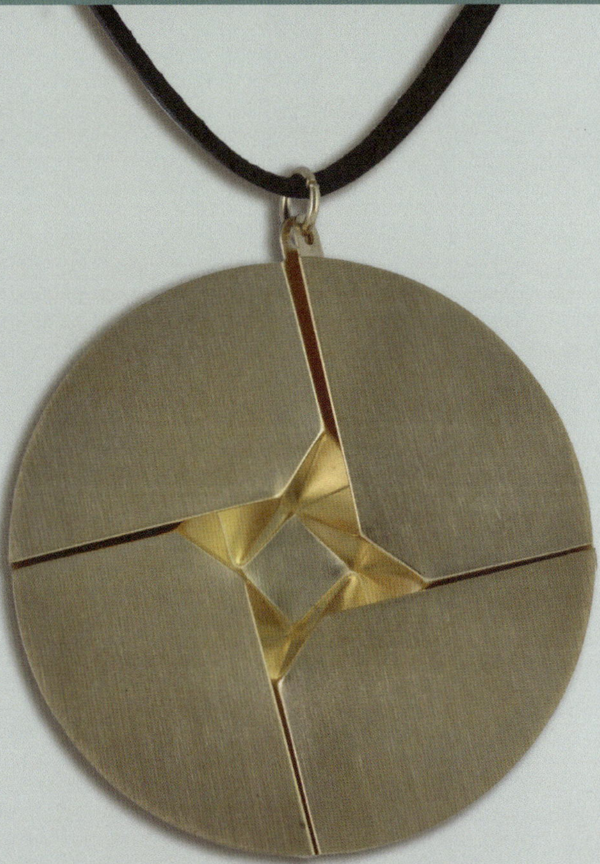

4 by 4 Molecules

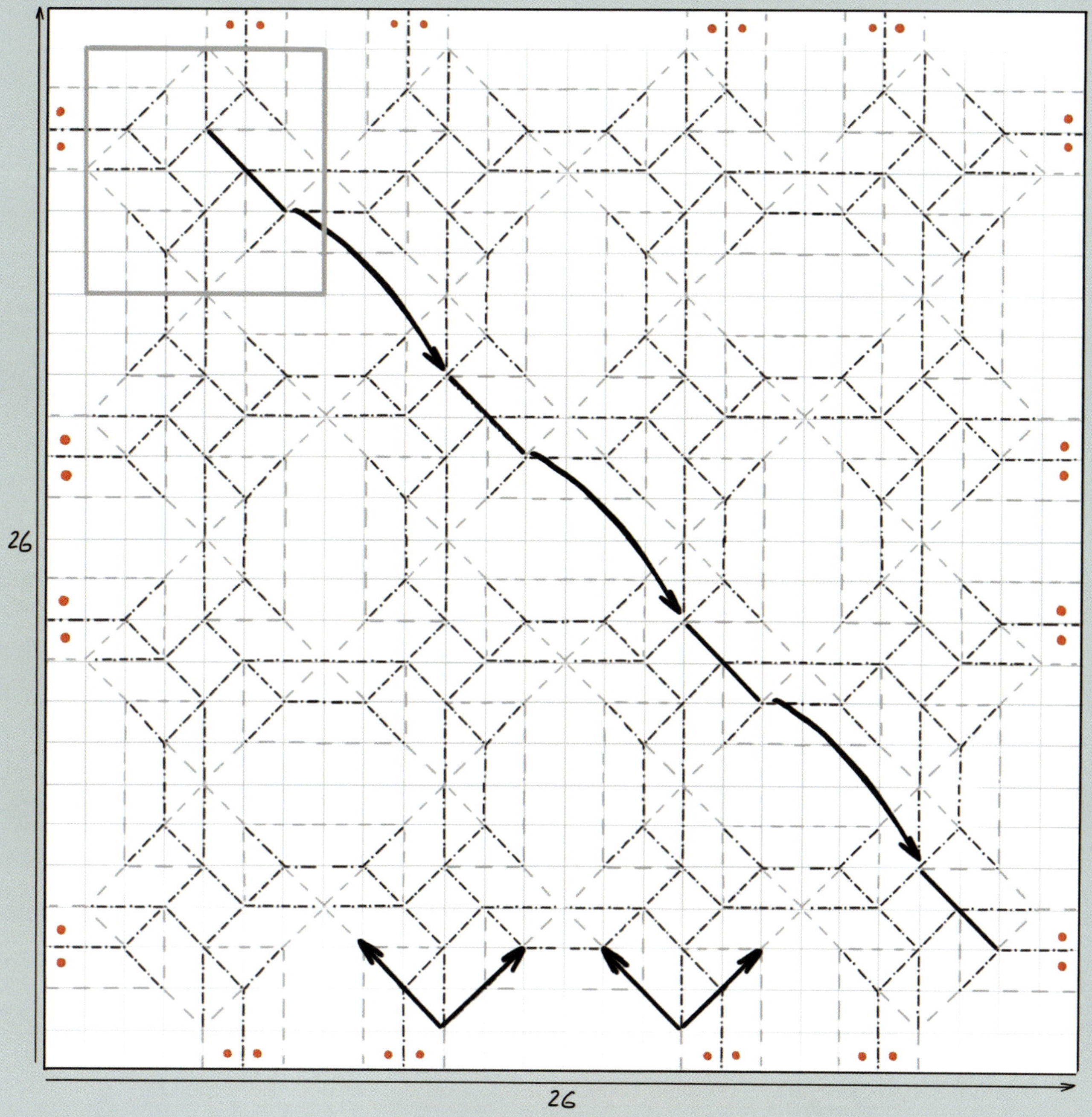

For a 4 by 4–molecule project, start with a 26 by 26 grid: 1 + 4 x 6 +1 = 26.

The final result will be 18 squares wide.

Make all the precreases as shown above.

There are two important shortcuts. First, the outer edges of the big tilted squares align to create straight lines (see the arrows at the bottom). Although the middle part of each is a mountain, you can crease them in one valley stroke, then reverse the middle part to mountain.

The second shortcut is for the smaller squares: fold two diagonals, skip four, repeat.

The collapse works best row by row. Also, it is easier if you work on the model from both sides (recto and verso).

6 4 Templar Garden

The Single Molecule

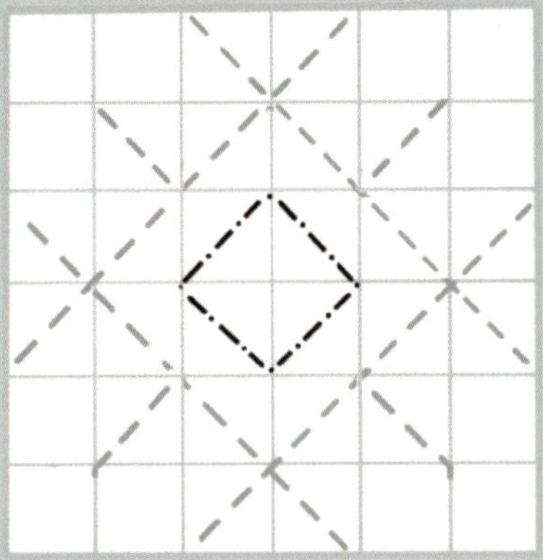

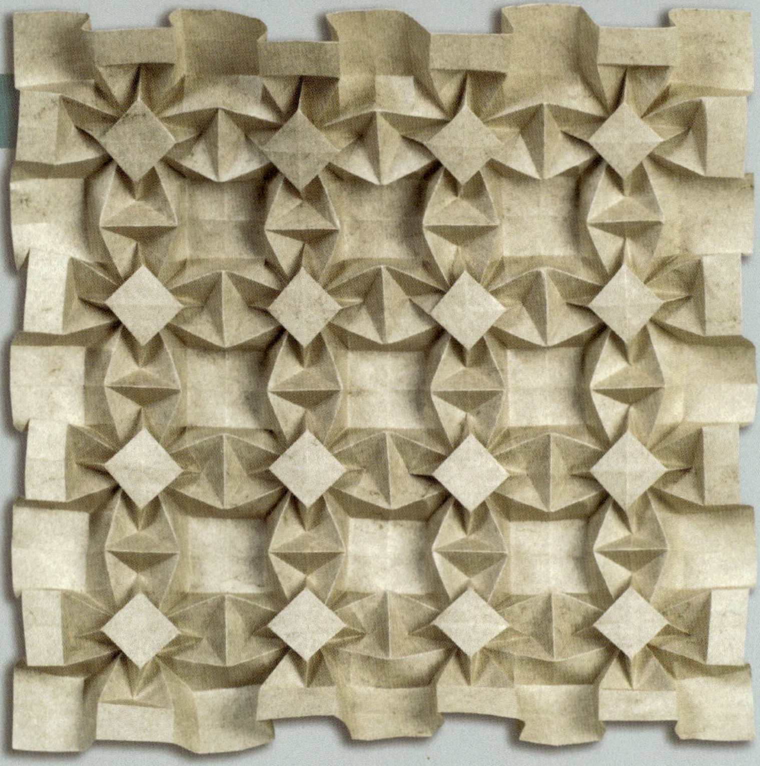

This single molecule has a strong resemblance to the cross of the Knights Templar when collapsed. Tessellating it gave me the sense of a garden—hence the name.

The molecule size is 6 by 6.

The shrinkage ratio is 3:2.

Above: recto view of a 4 by 4–molecule Templar Garden tessellation.

Verso view is shown below.

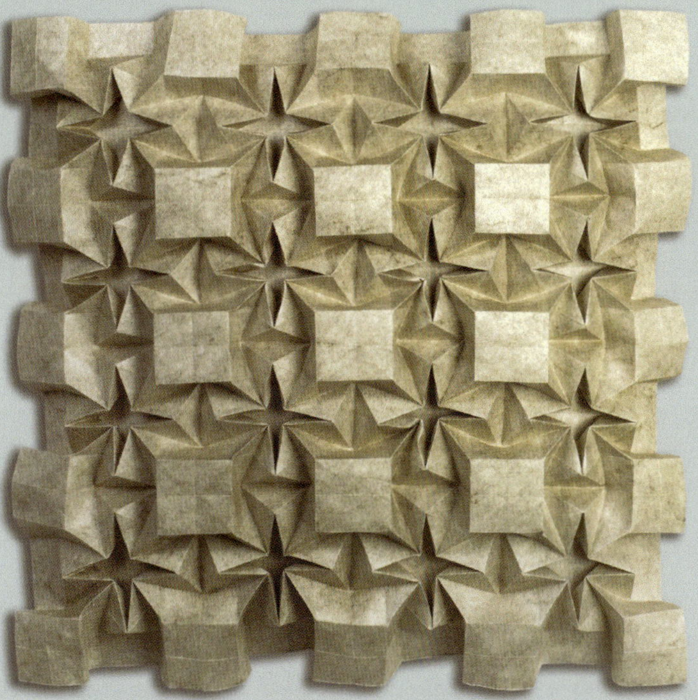

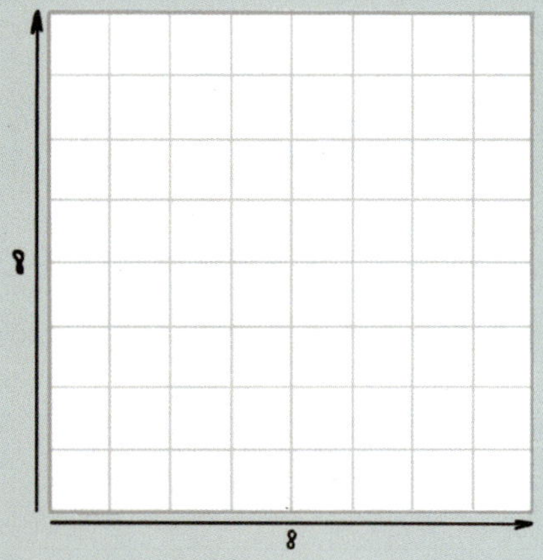

Start with an 8 by 8 grid (a 6 by 6 with an extra row and column all around).

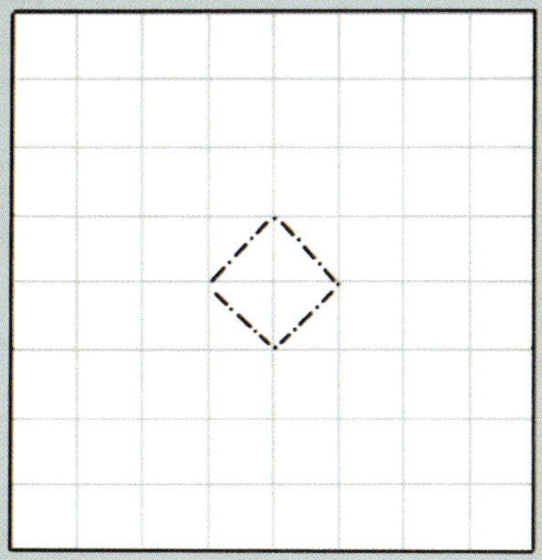

Create a tilted square in the center with mountains.

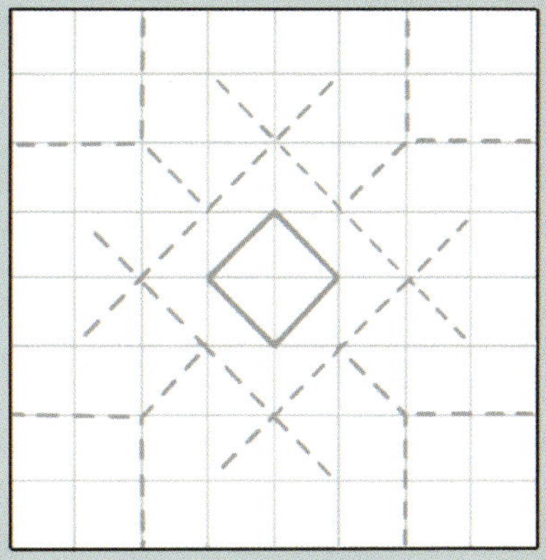

Add the valleys shown, leaving the center clear.

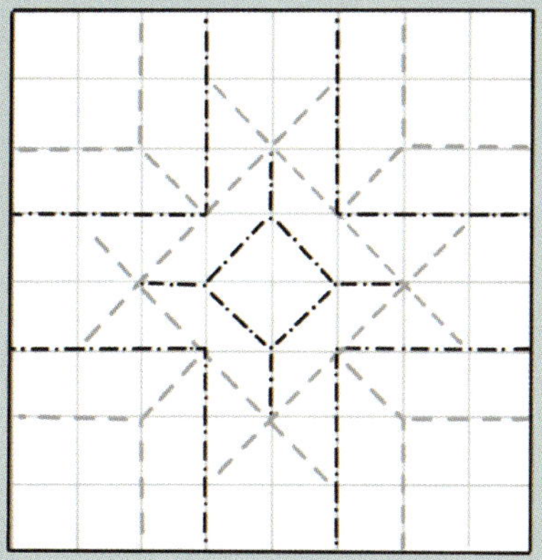

The complete molecule CP.

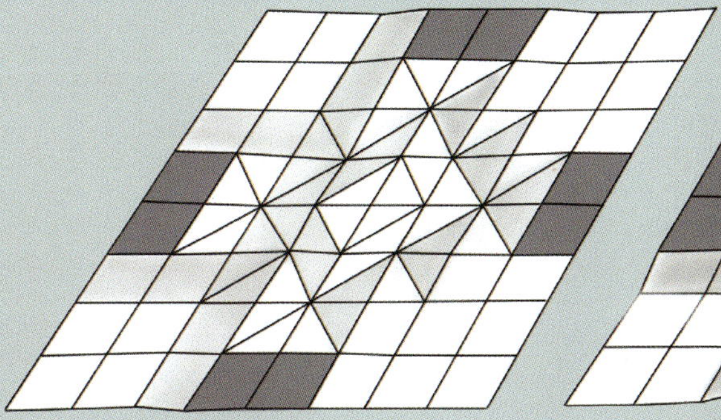

Start the collapse by reinforcing the mountains that elevate the marked dark gray areas.

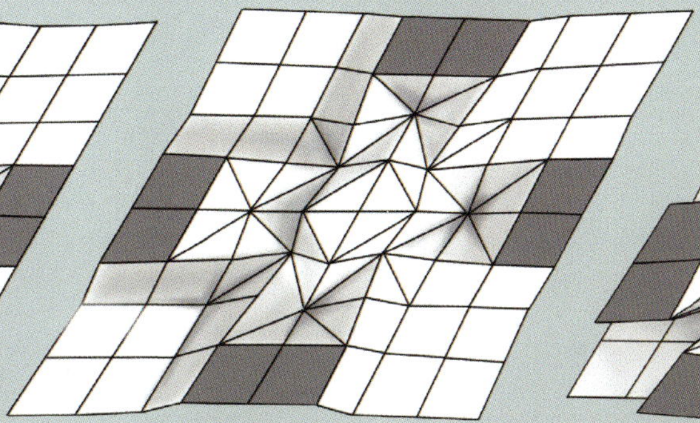

In process. Make sure the inner square is elevated and surrounded by valleys. The gray parts should be elevated, as well.

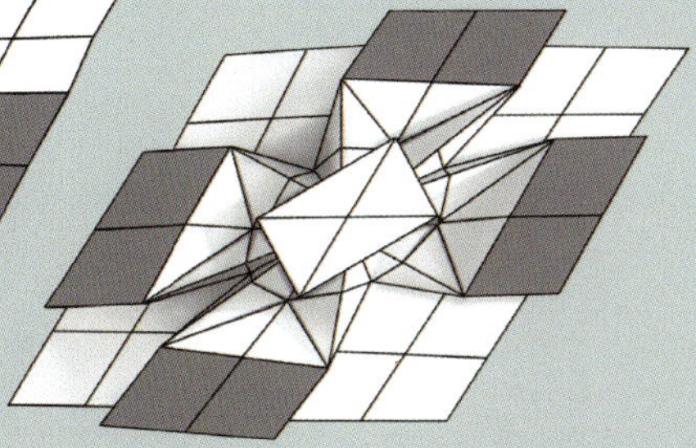

Fully Collapsed.

2 by 2 Molecules

Use a grid of 14 by 14. Add all precreases.

Handle carefully. The lack of space around the molecule makes it hard to create the inner sides of each cross.

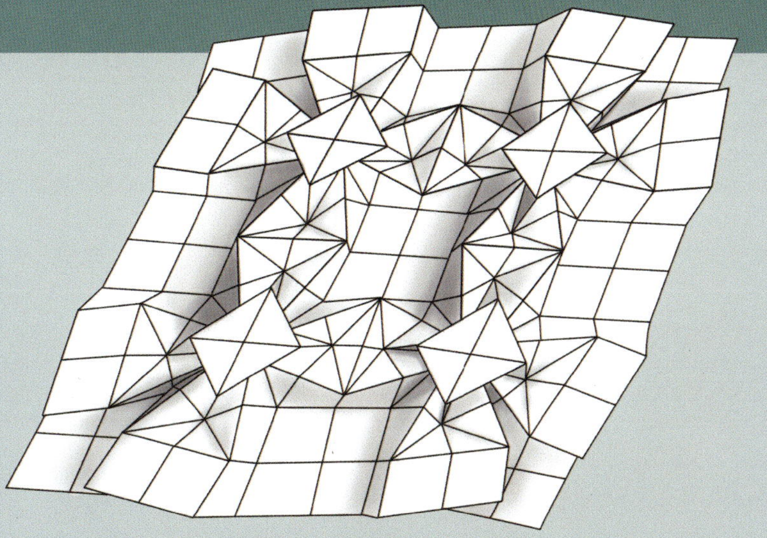

Use the outer rim to shape the molecule and force the edges marked in bold to be elevated while collapsing the inner parts—the edges each cross shares with the other crosses.

See the top left molecule as an example. The top and left sides are on the edges of the paper and can be manipulated easily. The bottom and right sides are shared with other molecules, and the only area that should be elevated is the marked thick line, the shared edge.

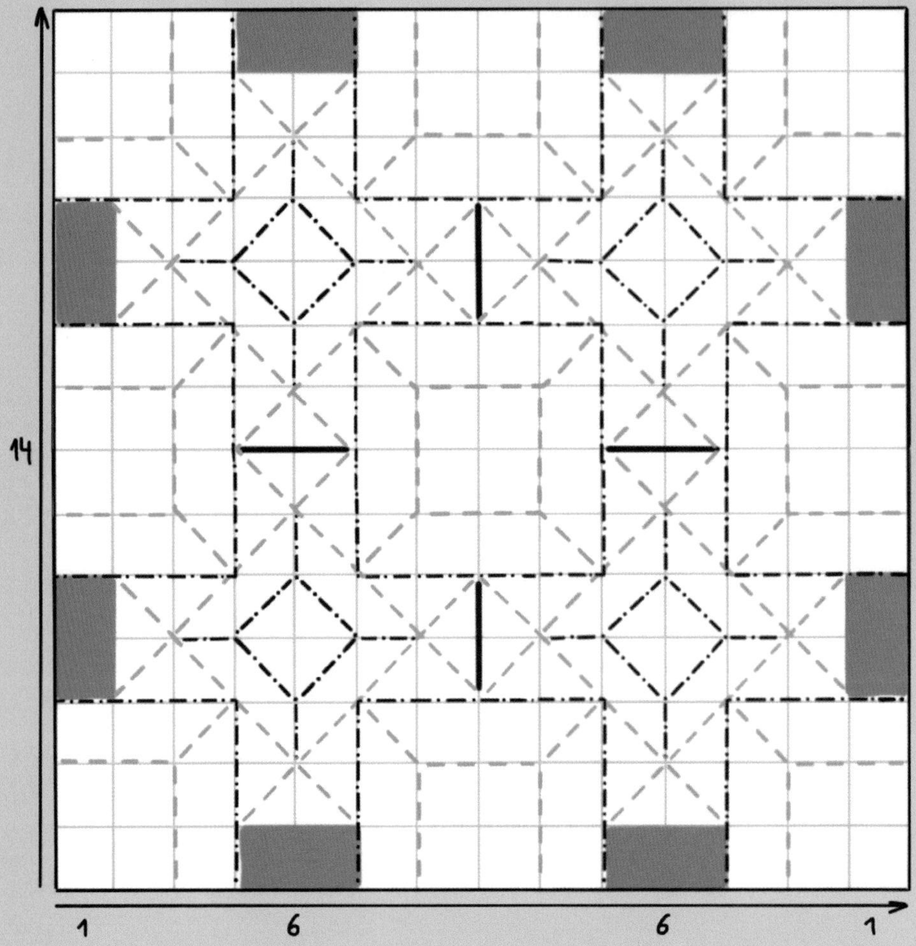

4 by 4 Molecules

For a 4 by 4–molecule project, start with a 26 by 26 grid: 1 + 4 x 6 +1 = 26.

The final result will be 18 squares wide.

Make all the marked precreases.

There are three shortcuts for this model.

Make the inner mountain squares first. Mark them all, then fold a diagonal (marked in a bold black line). Skip five squares and then repeat the sequence. Complete the inner squares before starting on the long valley creases.

For these, fold along four squares (marked by long orange lines), skip two, and continue the sequence for the remaining long valleys.

Lastly, put in the small valleys (marked by short orange lines) to complete the CP. The pattern here is fold one, skip two, and repeat.

The collapse is easiest if you work row by row. It is better to work on the model from both sides (recto and verso).

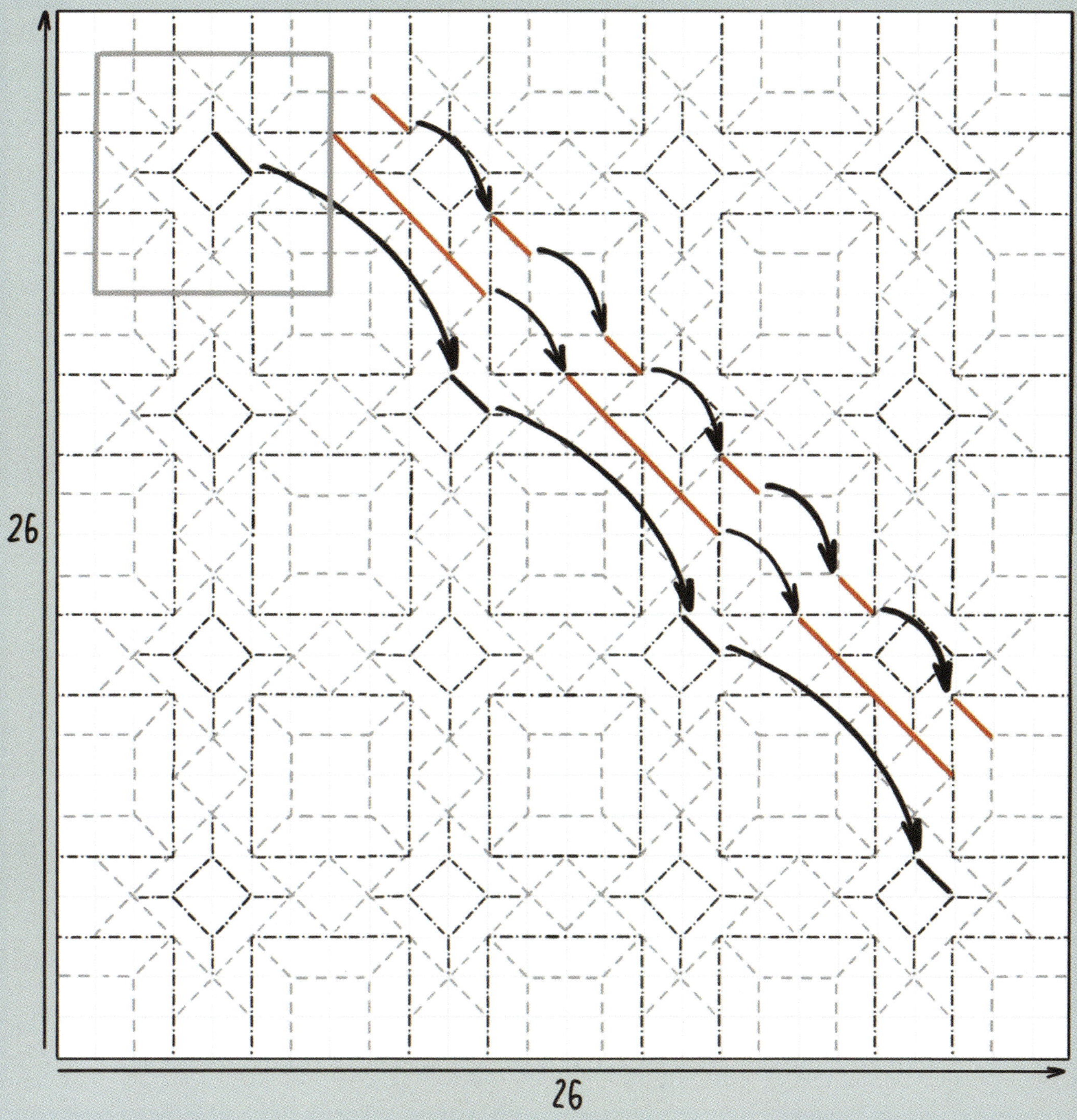
26
26

Above and Beyond—An 8 by 8 Project

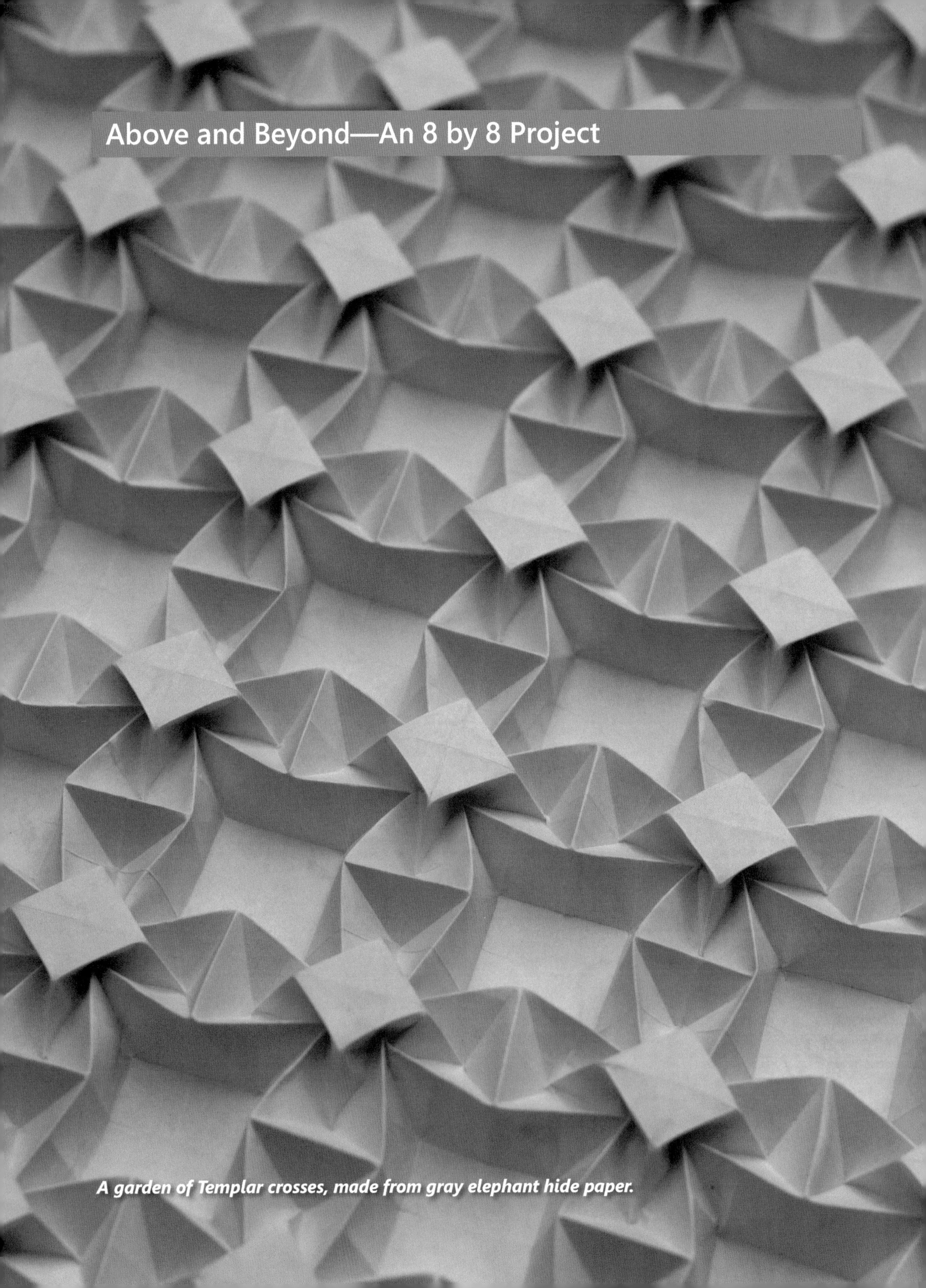

A garden of Templar crosses, made from gray elephant hide paper.

6 5 Mushroom Field

Mushroom Field is only one small step forward from Templar Garden. But what an interesting difference this step makes!

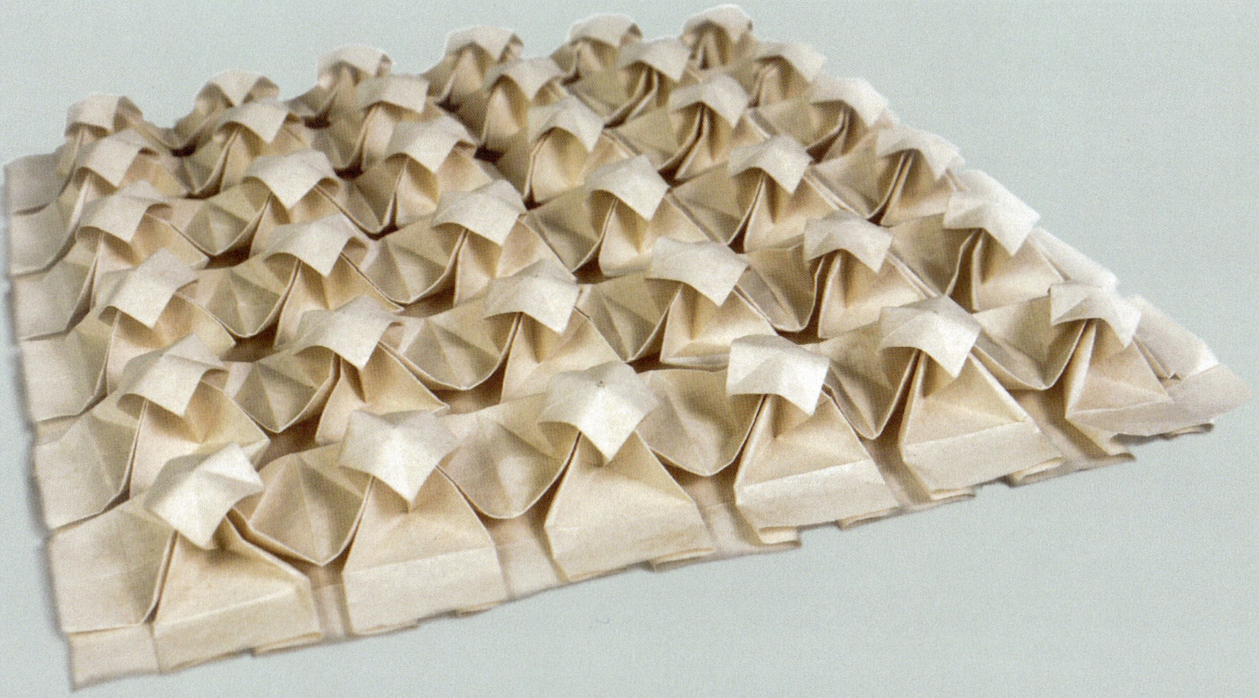

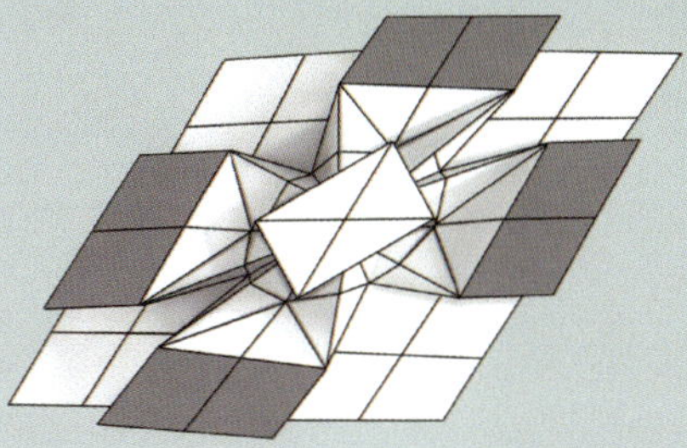

Start with a single molecule of Templar Garden (page 142), fully collapsed. Flatten all the edges completely.

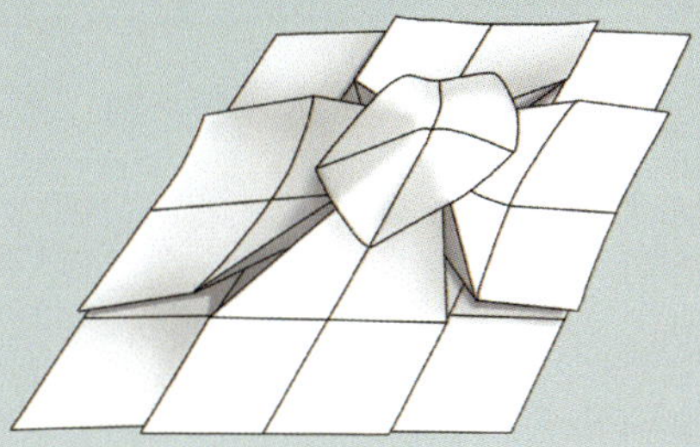

Stretch the center square over the cross in the middle. Suddenly it looks like the head of a mushroom—hence the name.

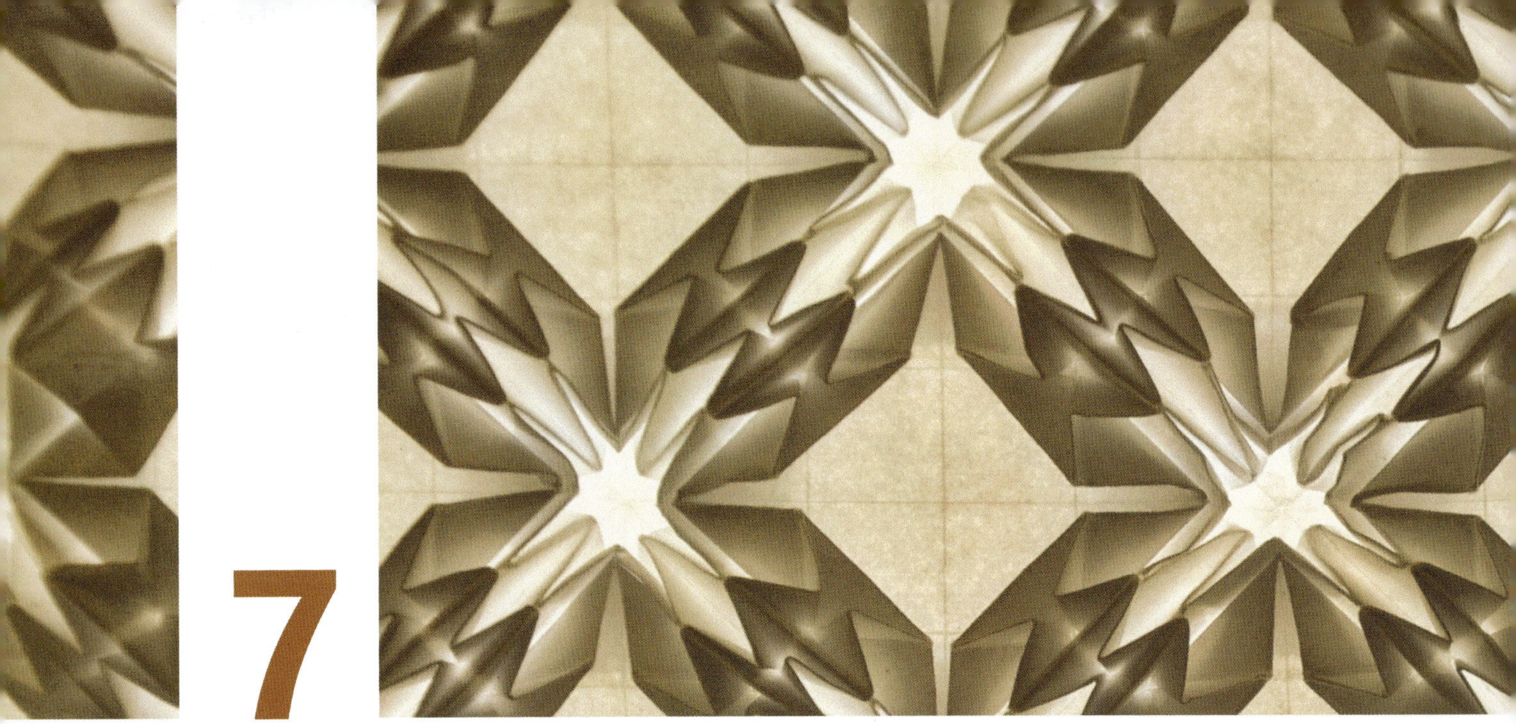

7 The Pineapple Family

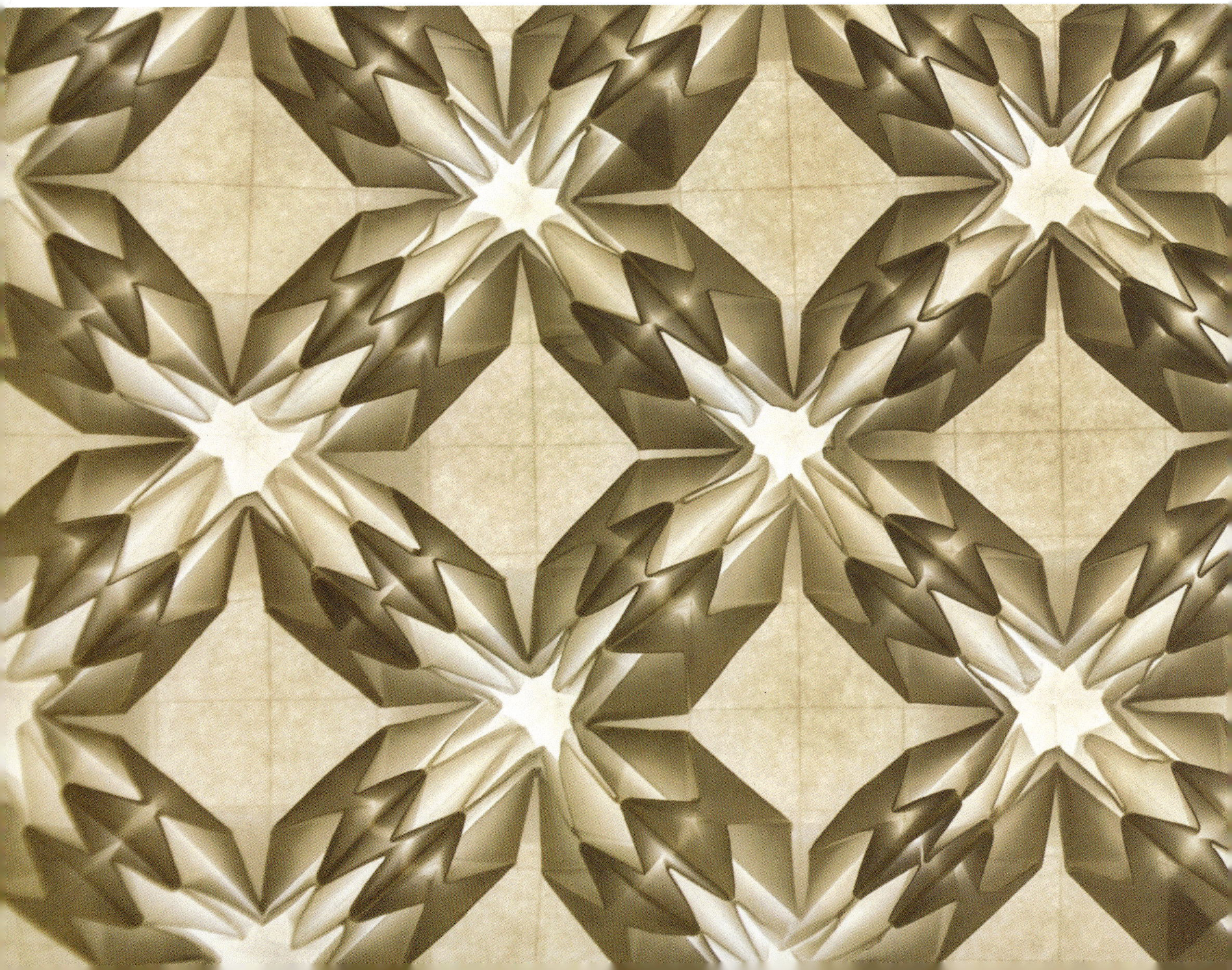

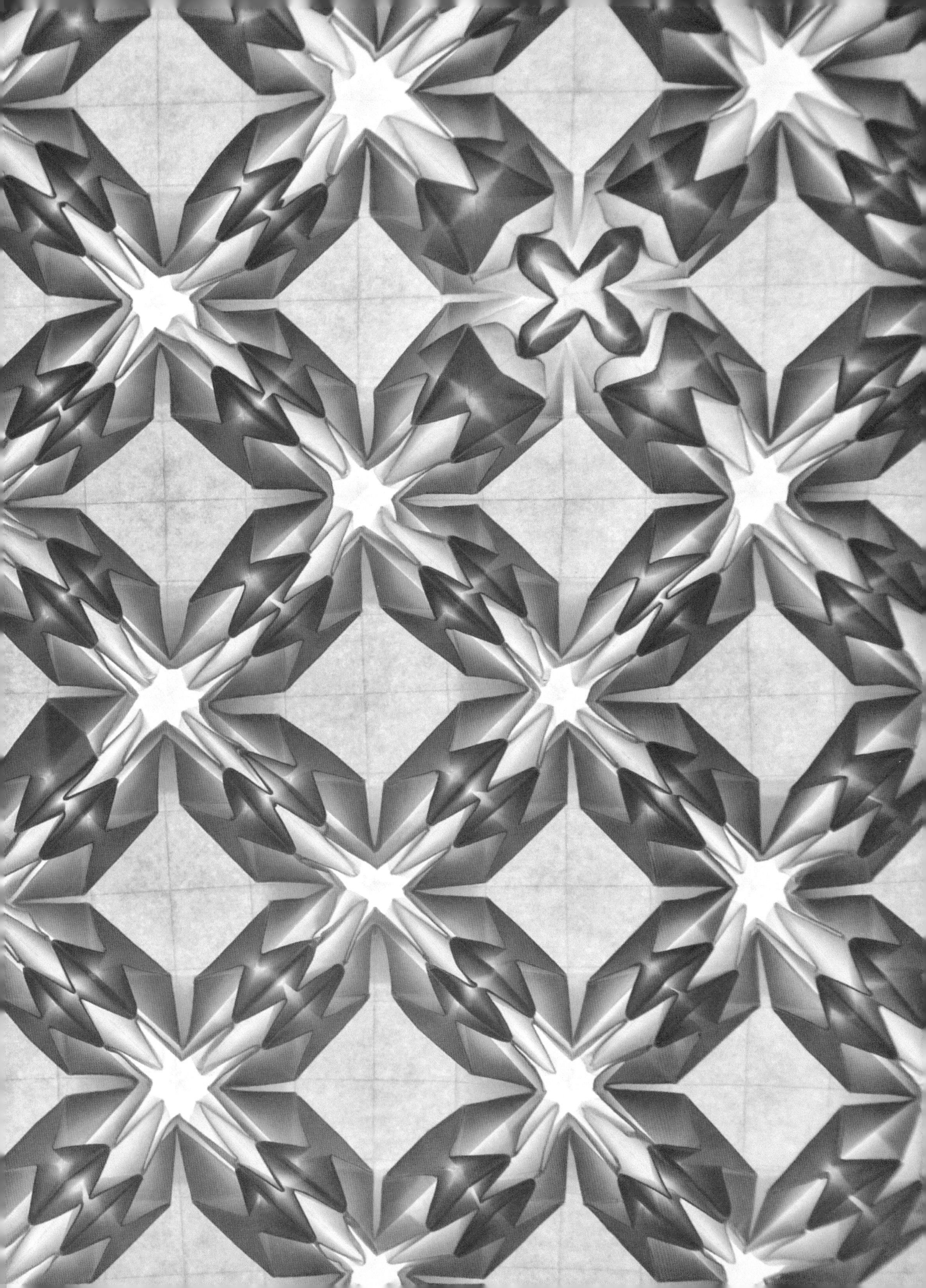

Introduction

The Pineapple family is based on a diagonal pattern. A large rectangle is stretched from top right to bottom left in the single molecule. When you put several together, the overall look is spiky, like the outside of a pineapple (see the photo on the previous page).

The Pineapple Family was built around the Criss Cross molecule shown below. The basic Pineapple molecule has the same diagonal rectangle, but with added layers. The advanced variations are further extensions of the Pineapple molecule, made by lengthening the molecule or increasing its number of layers.

For all but Criss Cross, the collapse is done in two stages. Some have even more.

7 1 Criss Cross

The Single Molecule

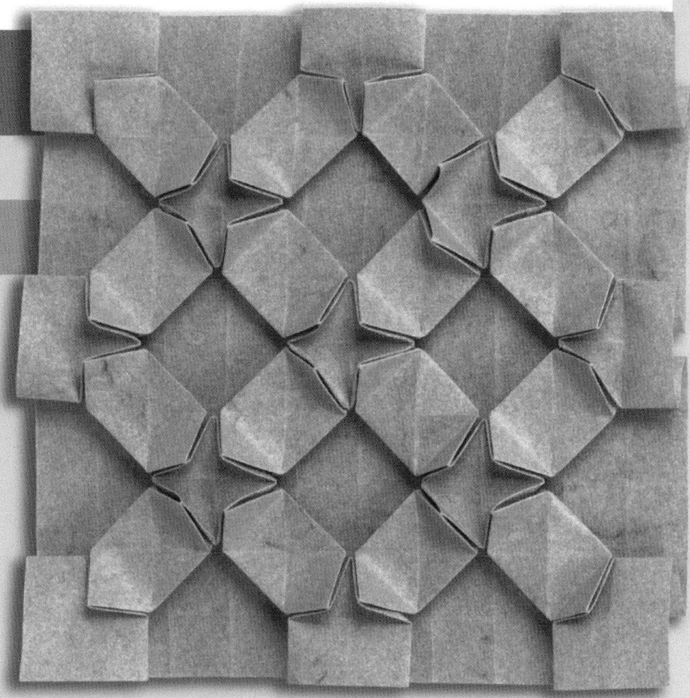

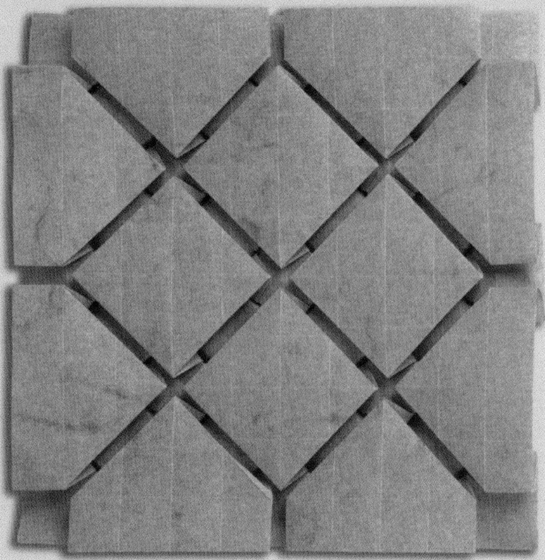

Above: recto view of a 4 by 4–molecule Criss Cross tessellation.

Verso view is to the left.

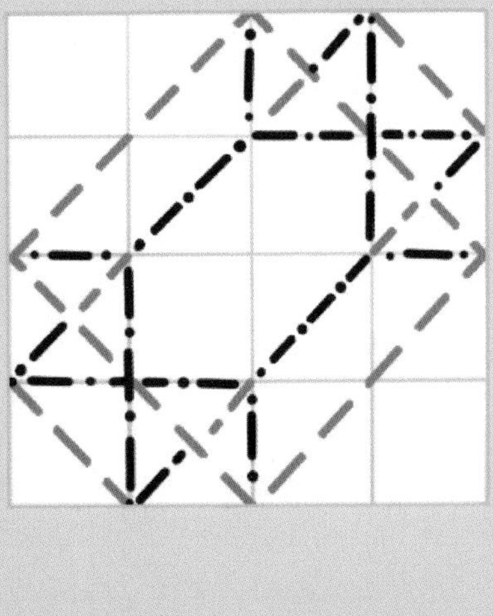

This model is the basis for the entire Pineapple family. It exploits the idea of a diagonal-based molecule.

The shrinkage ratio is 2:1.

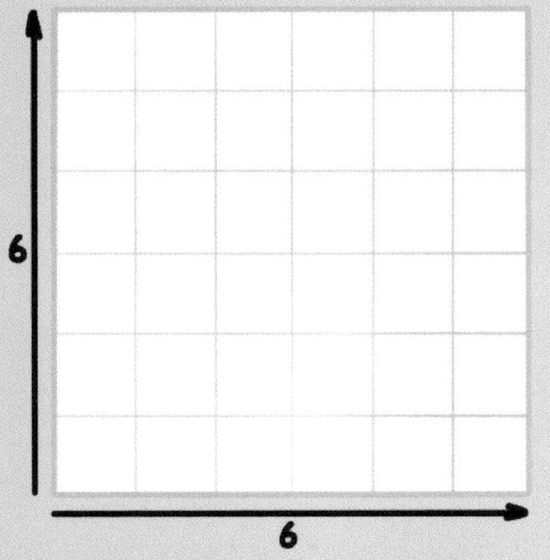

Start with a 6 by 6 grid, with the mountain creases side up.

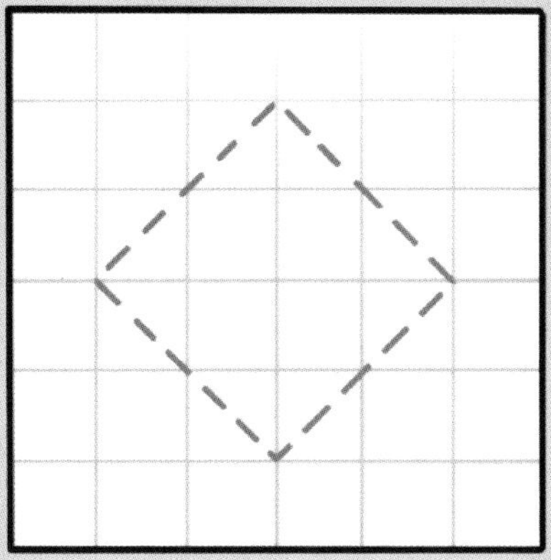

Valley fold the square first.

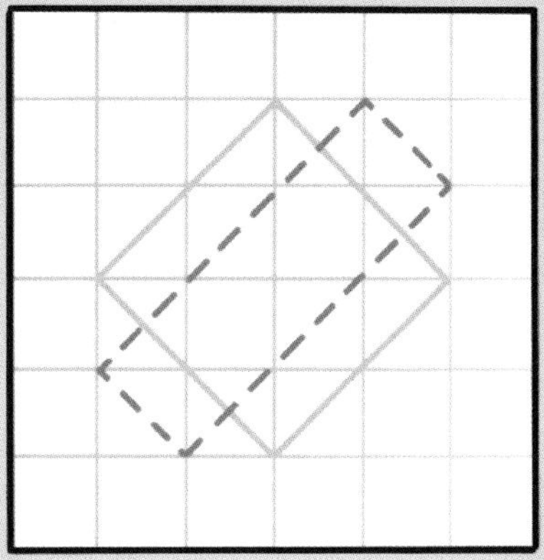

Add the rectangle.

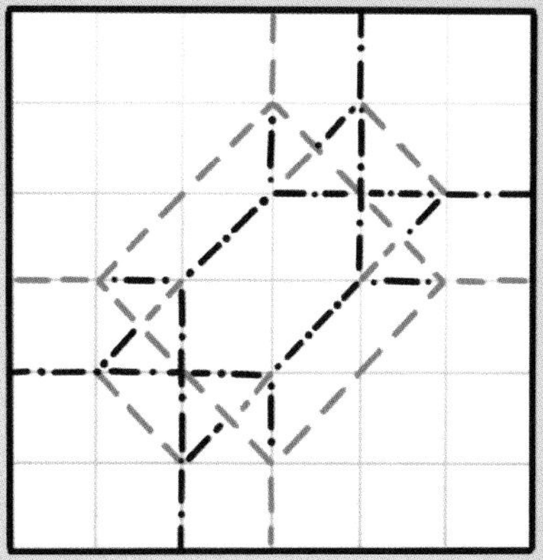

Now mountain crease as shown. You will fold along some existing creases and add new ones, too.

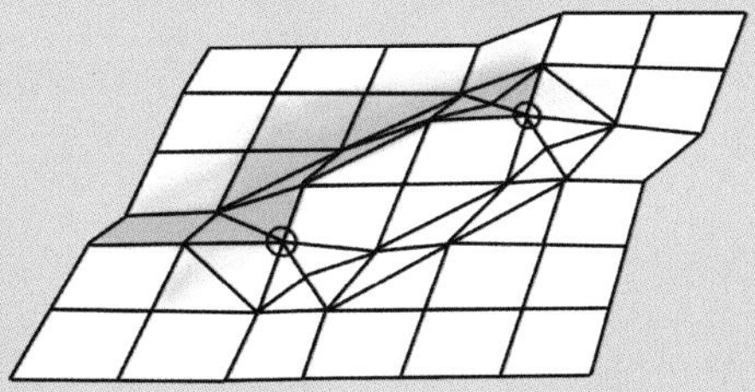

Start the collapse by making a preliminary base at the circled corners.

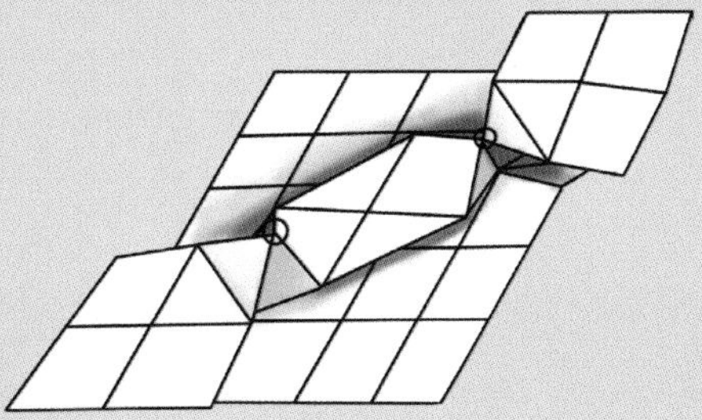

The two preliminary bases are beginning to emerge.

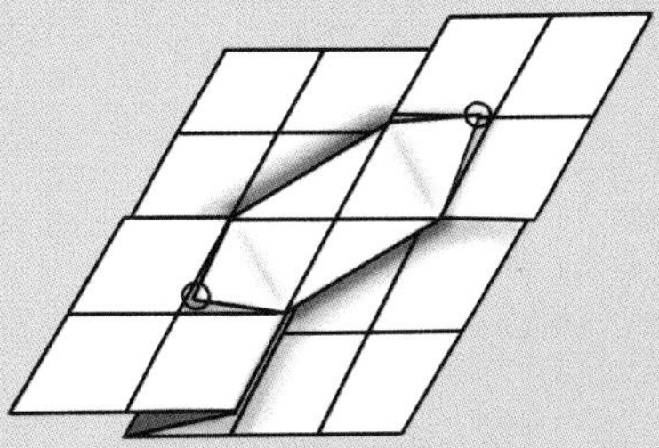

The fully collapsed single molecule.

Note the spikes at the circled corners now.

2 by 2 Molecules

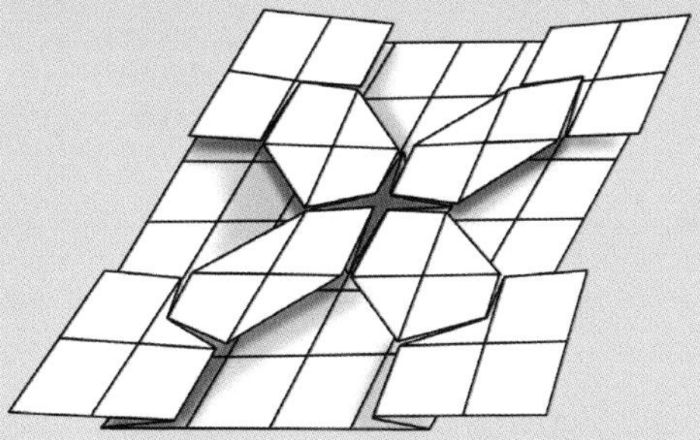

Use a grid of 10 by 10. Add all precreases.

First collapse only the top left molecule, extending all the creases to the edges of the paper.

Now collapse the top right molecule.

On the next row of molecules, collapse both into place at the same time.

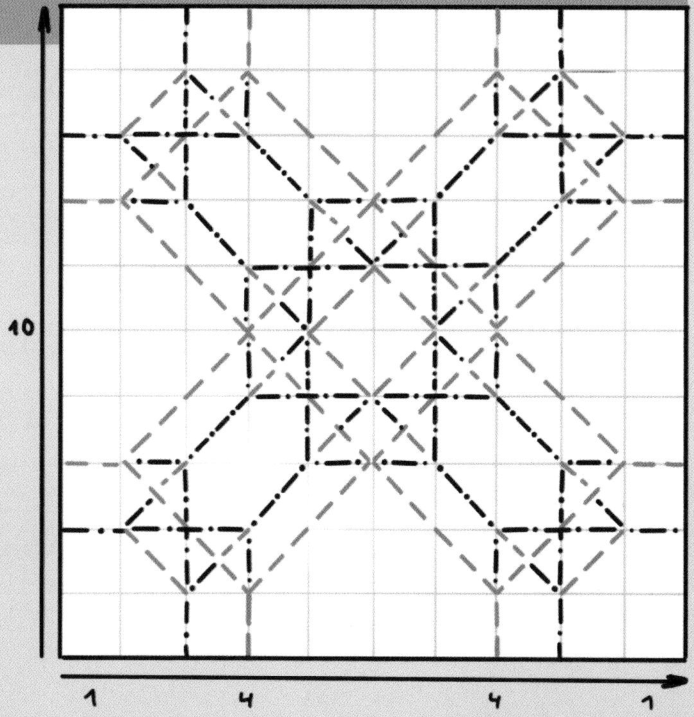

4 by 4 Molecules

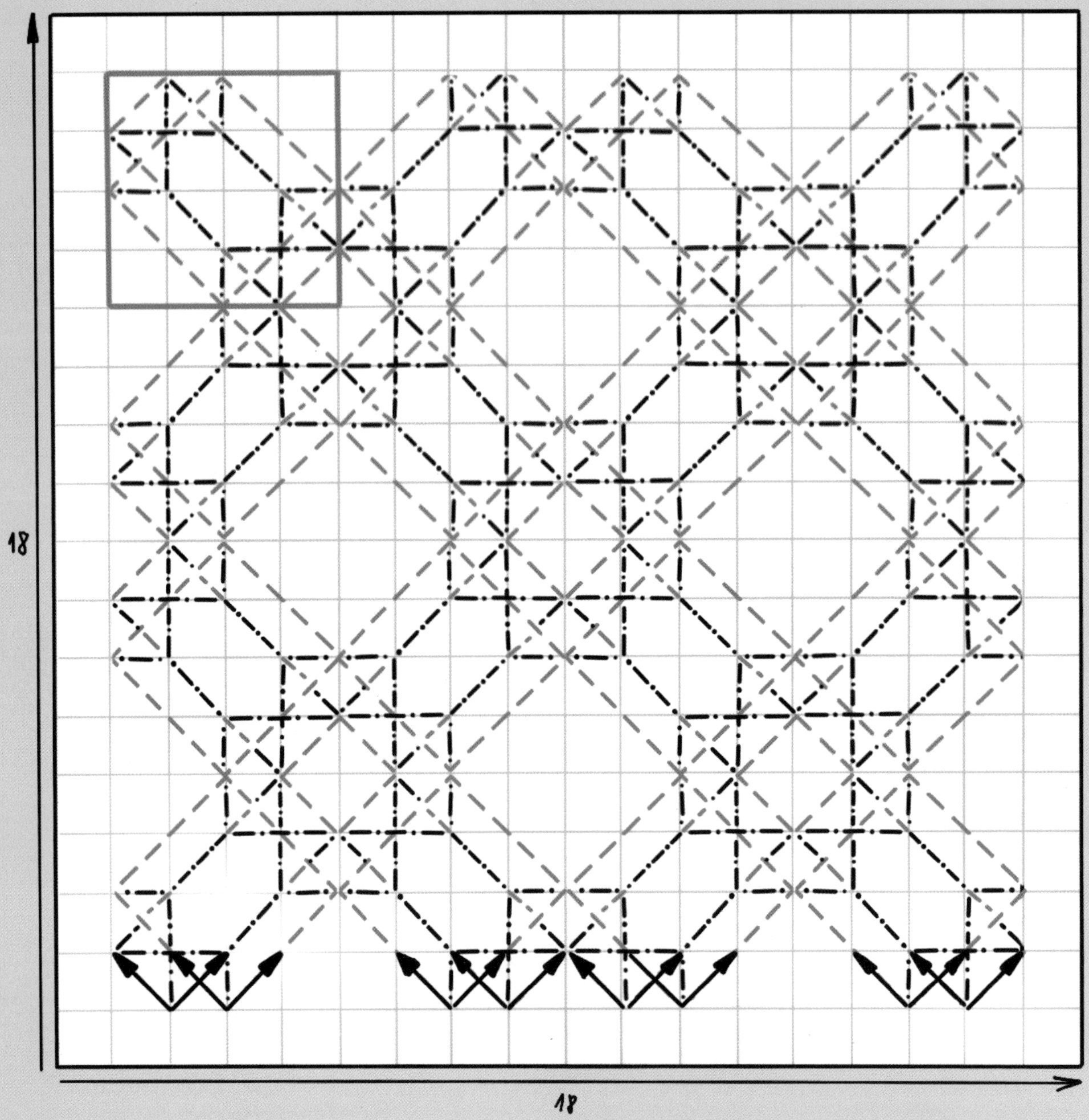

For this 4 by 4–molecule project, start with an 18 by 18 grid: 1 + 4 x 4 + 1 = 18.

The final result will be 10 squares wide.

There are shortcuts for the precreases. The edges of the tilted squares, as well as all the tilted rectangles, line up and can be folded in a single stroke. Those long diagonals come in pairs; one square and two squares away from every molecule corner (marked by the arrows on the bottom of the diagram).

Collapse the top left molecule first, and continue to complete a row of molecules. On the second row of molecules, collapse the left-most one after you arranged the creases of the molecule to the right.

7 2 Pineapple

The Single Molecule

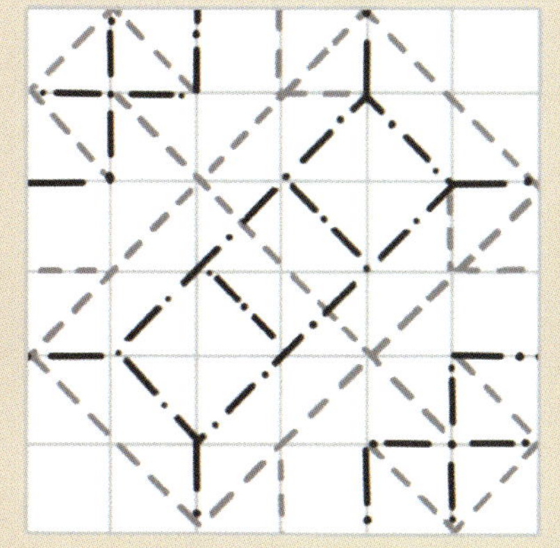

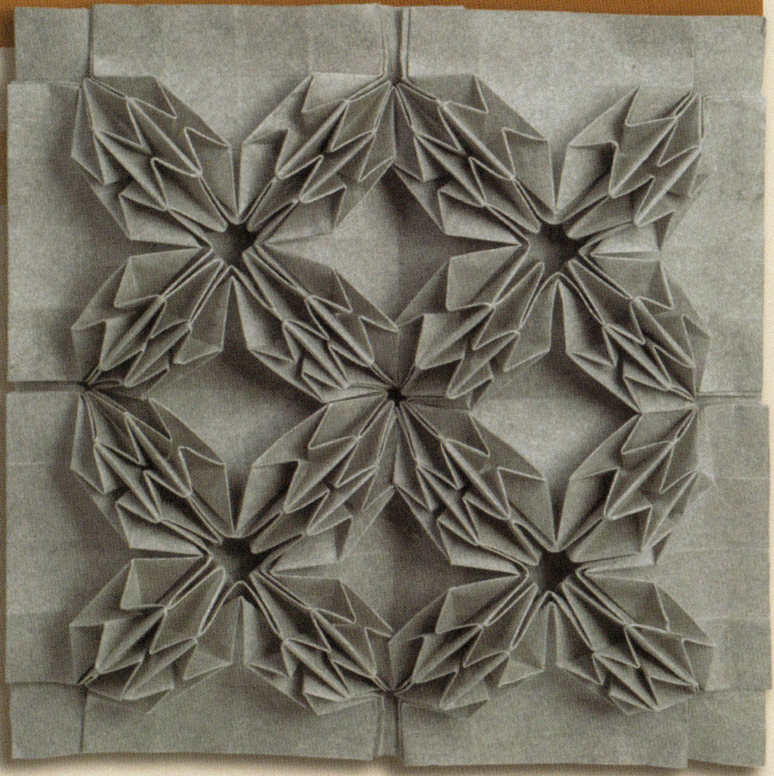

The basic Pineapple molecule employs the same collapse process as Criss Cross (see page 150).

If you think of the grouping of four molecules as one large molecule, you can see the resemblance to the famous Hydrangea model by Fujimoto.

The collapse is done in two stages. You collapse all molecules to the first stage, and then continue to collapse all to the finished position.

The single molecule CP lacks some fold lines that will be made later. In addition, some changes in orientation of lines are not shown here to make the diagram easier to read.

The shrinkage ratio is 3:1.

Above: recto view of a 4 by 4–molecule Pineapple tessellation. Verso view is below.

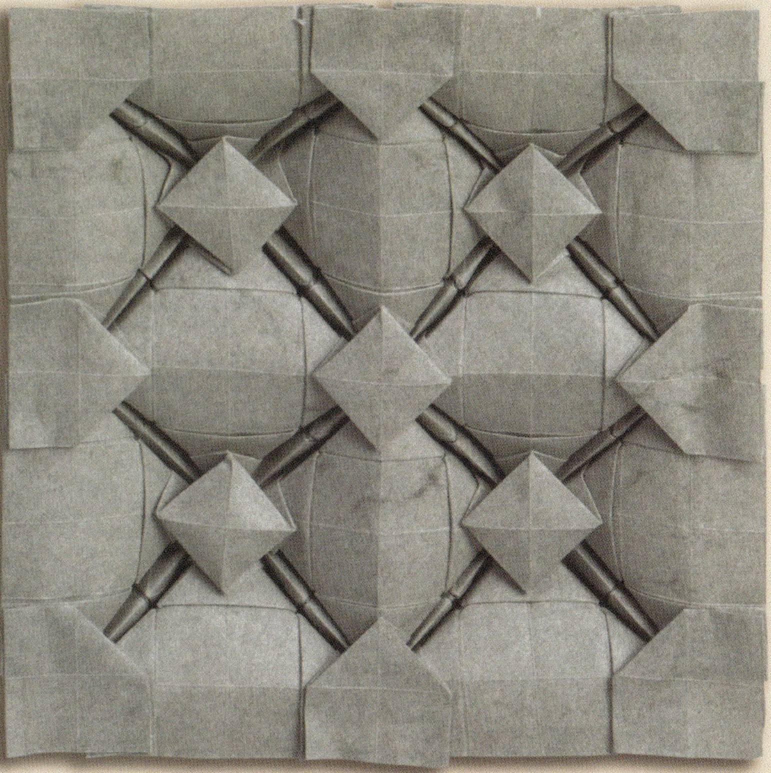

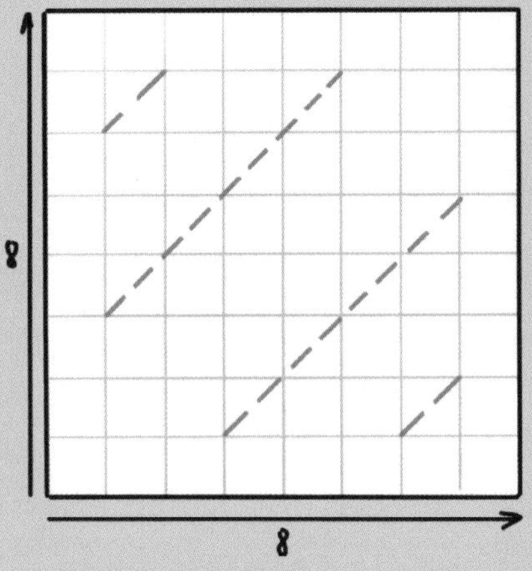

Start with an 8 by 8 grid, the mountain side up. Valley fold all diagonal lines shown.

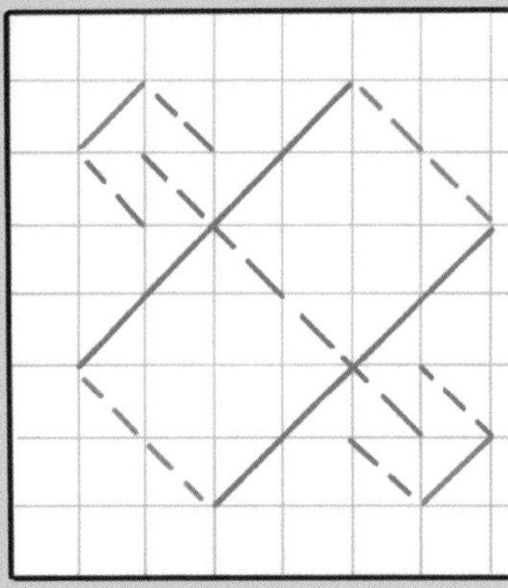

Crease the additional valley folds. Note the U-shaped creases around the ends of the long diagonal fold.

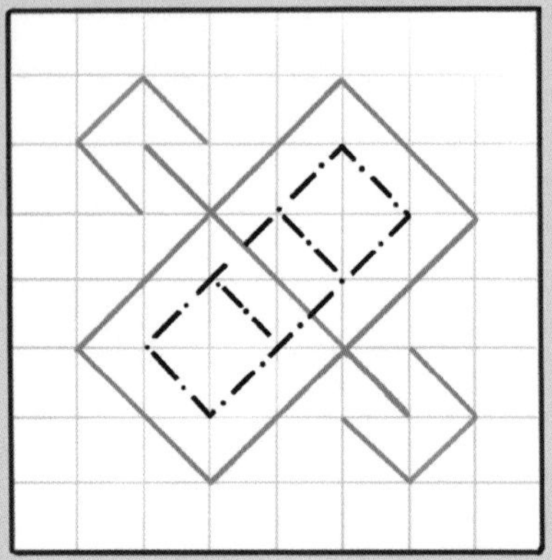

The last precreases are mountains.

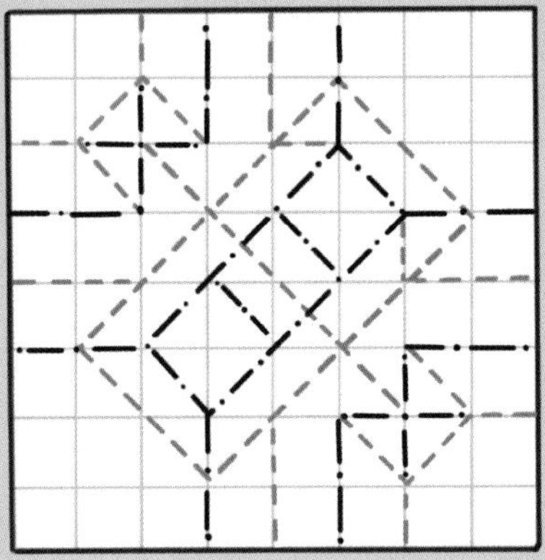

Reinforce all the precreases to the orientation shown here.

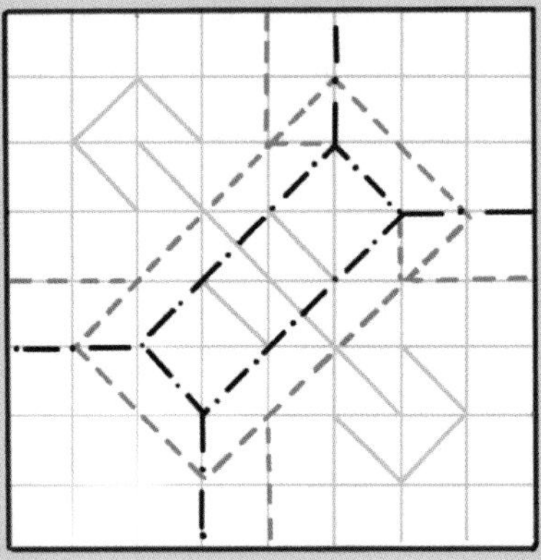

For the first stage of the collapse, follow only the crease lines shown here (NOT shown in light gray).

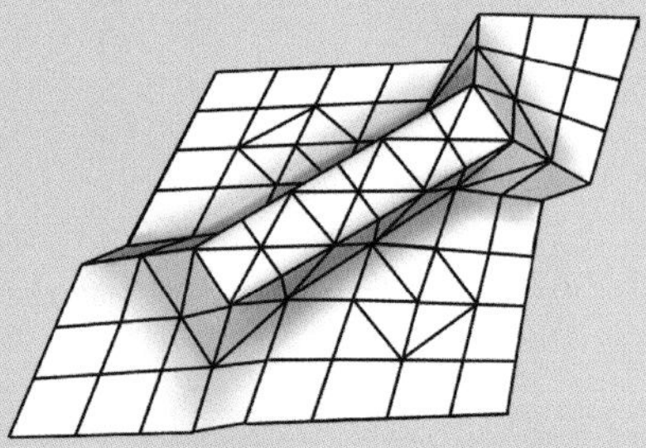

In process.

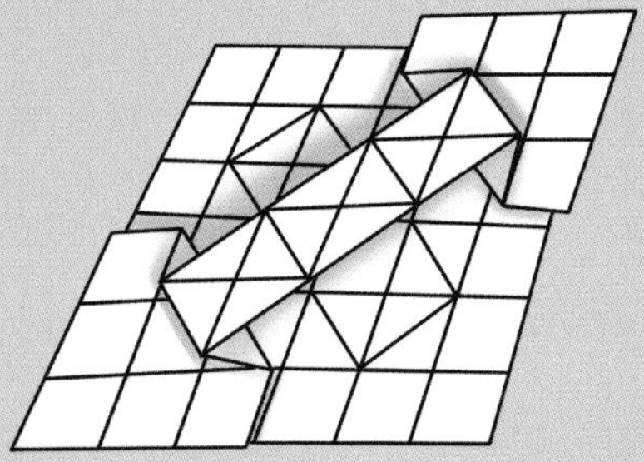

The result.

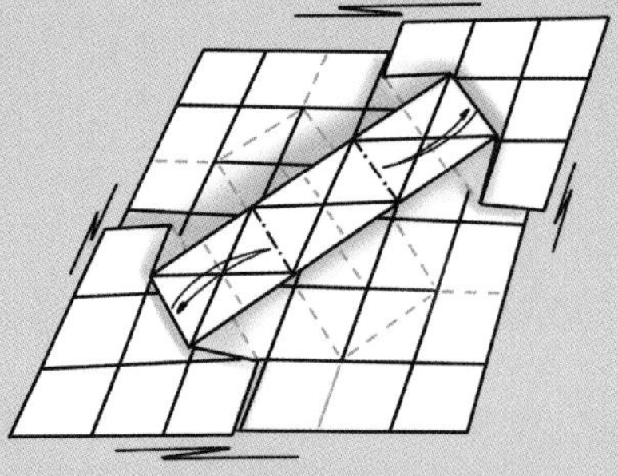

Reinforce the precreases for the second stage of the collapse. Fold and unfold the two squares at either end.

Note the pleated edges near the two corners.

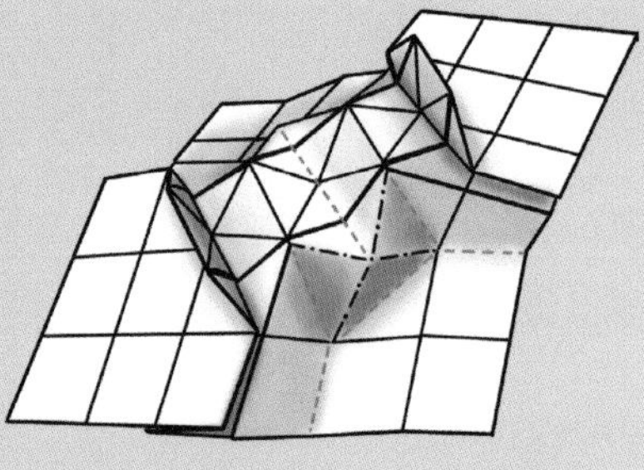

Collapse further by following the U-shaped valleys. This will create more pleats.

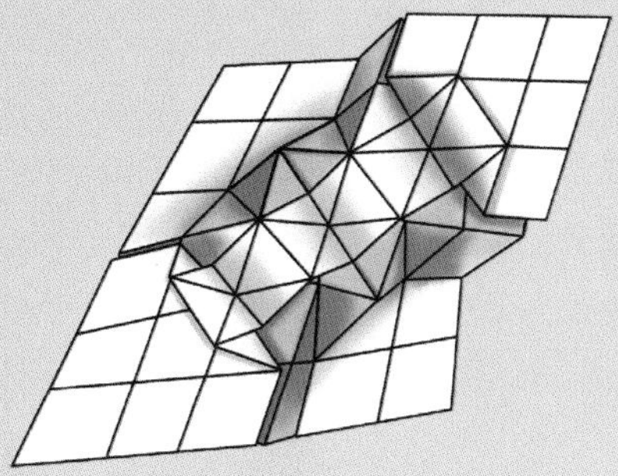

In process. The pleats are about to be doubled!

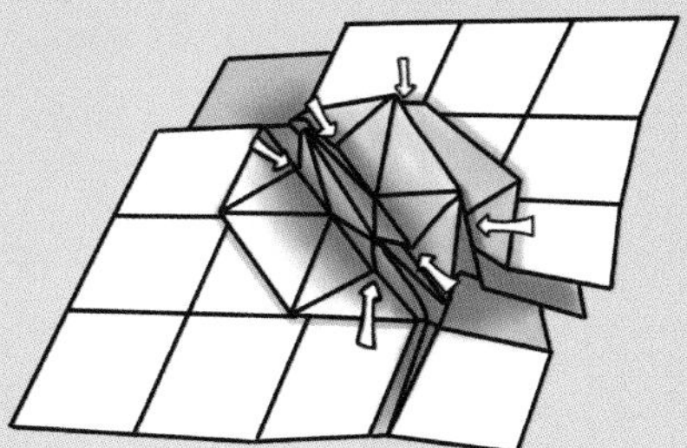

Fully collapsed.

Note the pleated edges near the two corners have double the layers.

Complete the molecule with six inside reverse folds.

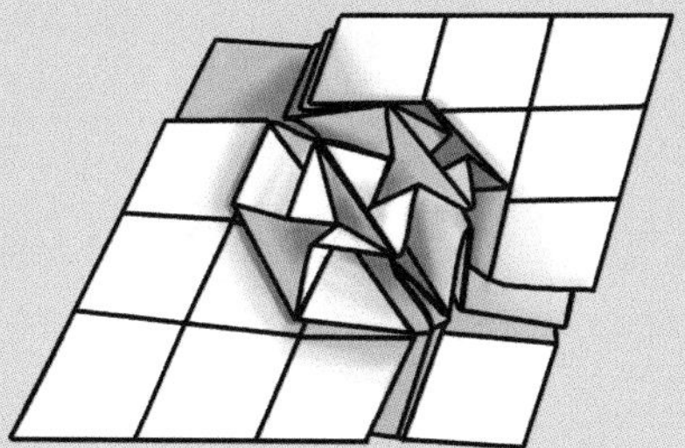

The finished single molecule.

2 by 2 Molecules

X-Shaped

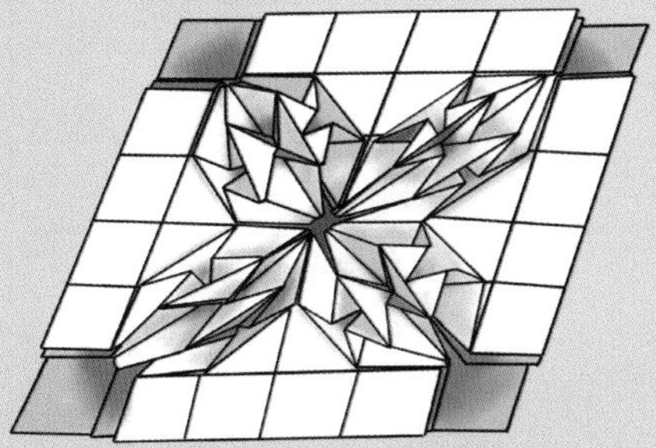

Since the molecule is slanted, four molecules can either be arranged as an X or as an O. Both projects call for a 14 by 14 grid.

This is the CP for the X-shaped version.

Collapse all the molecules to the first stage. Start the second stage only when the first is complete and go row by row.

The collapse is not simple, so take it slow! Look for the pleats on the edges. They are a helpful landmark.

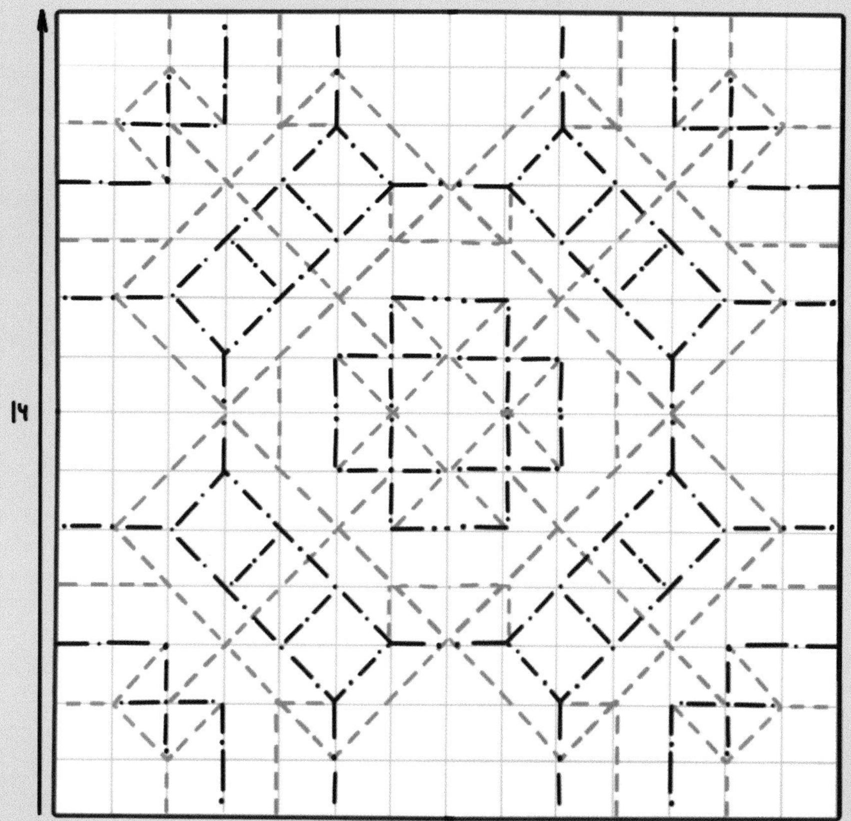

2 by 2 Molecules

O-Shaped

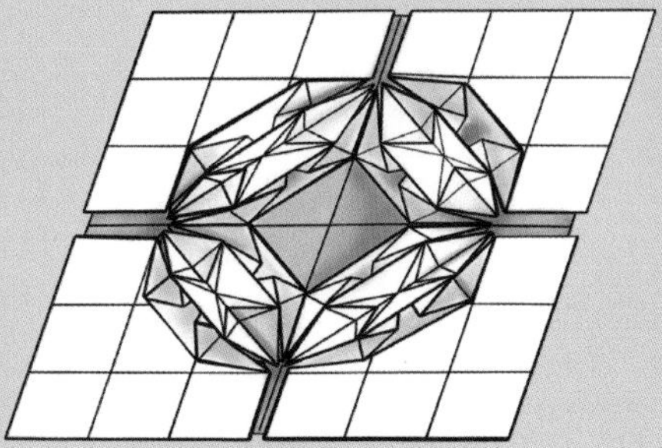

To make an O-shaped model, change the orientation of the molecules.

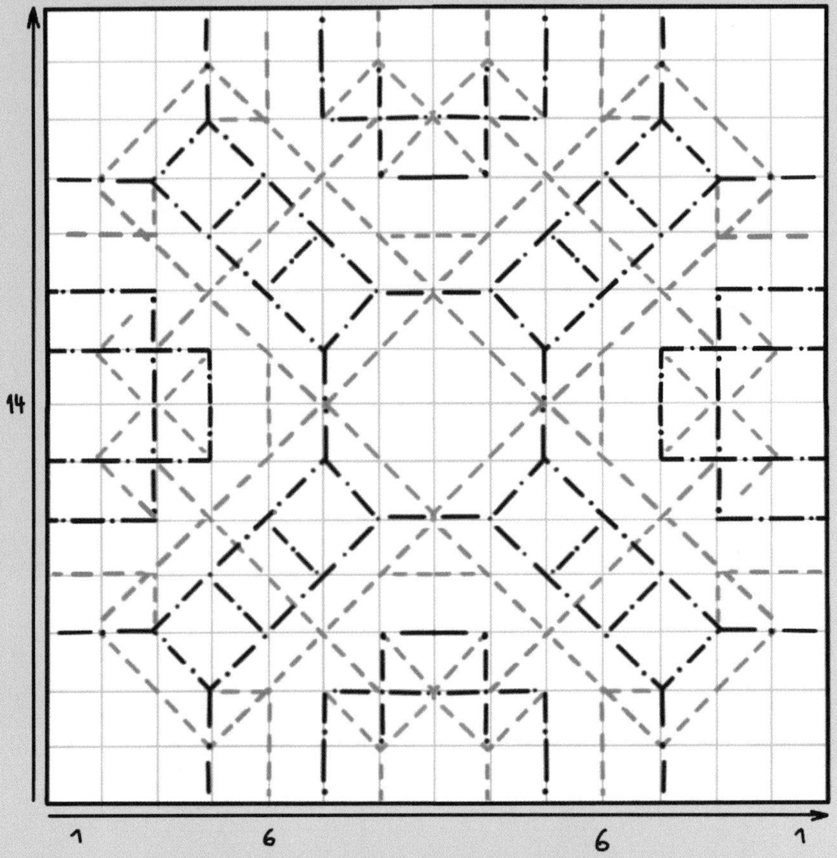

Above and Beyond

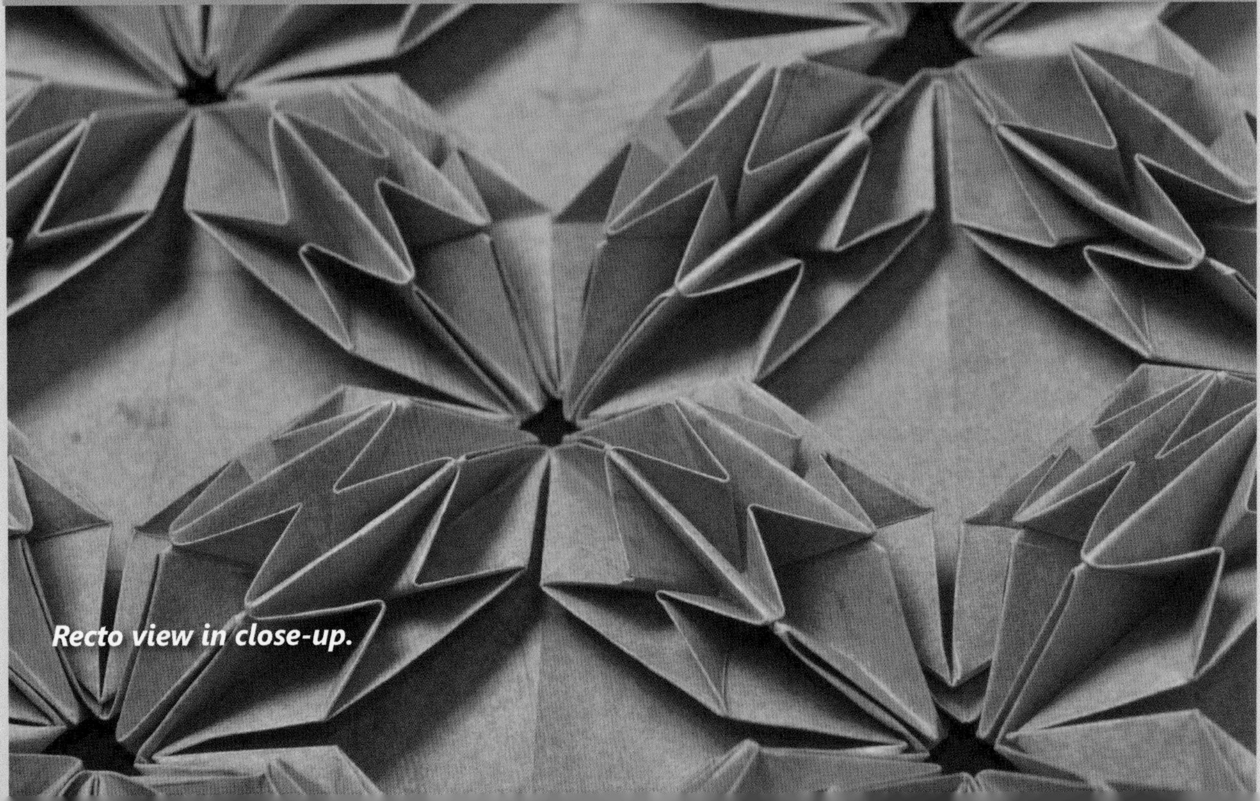

Recto view in close-up.

4 by 4 Molecules

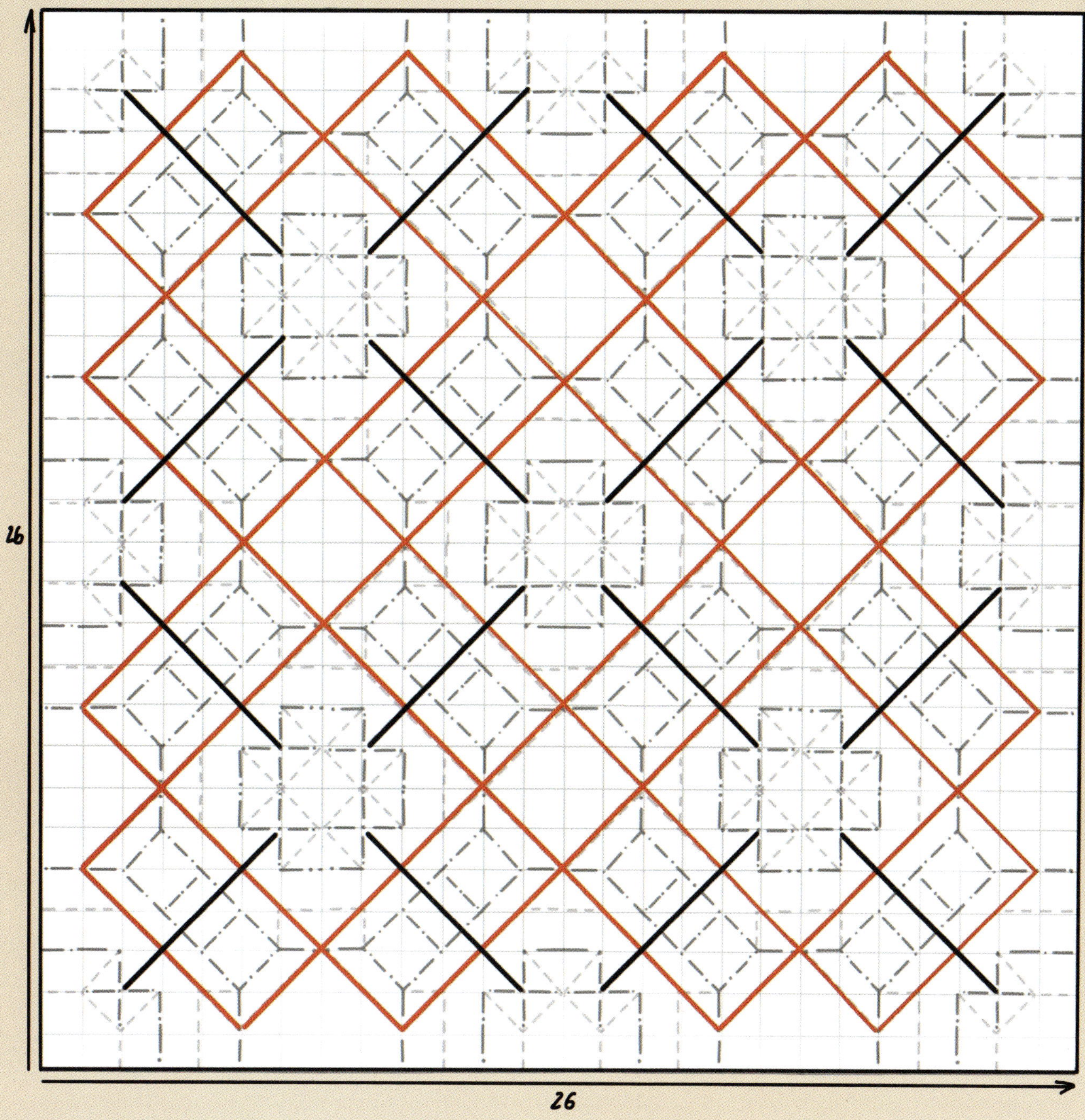

For a 4 by 4 molecule project, start with an 26 by 26 grid: 1 + 4 x 6 + 1 = 26.

The final result will be 10 squares wide.

Start to precrease all the valleys.

First follow the rectangles (in orange) with valley creases. Note how their edges align!

Next add all black diagonals as valleys (bold black lines), using this shortcut: fold four and skip two.

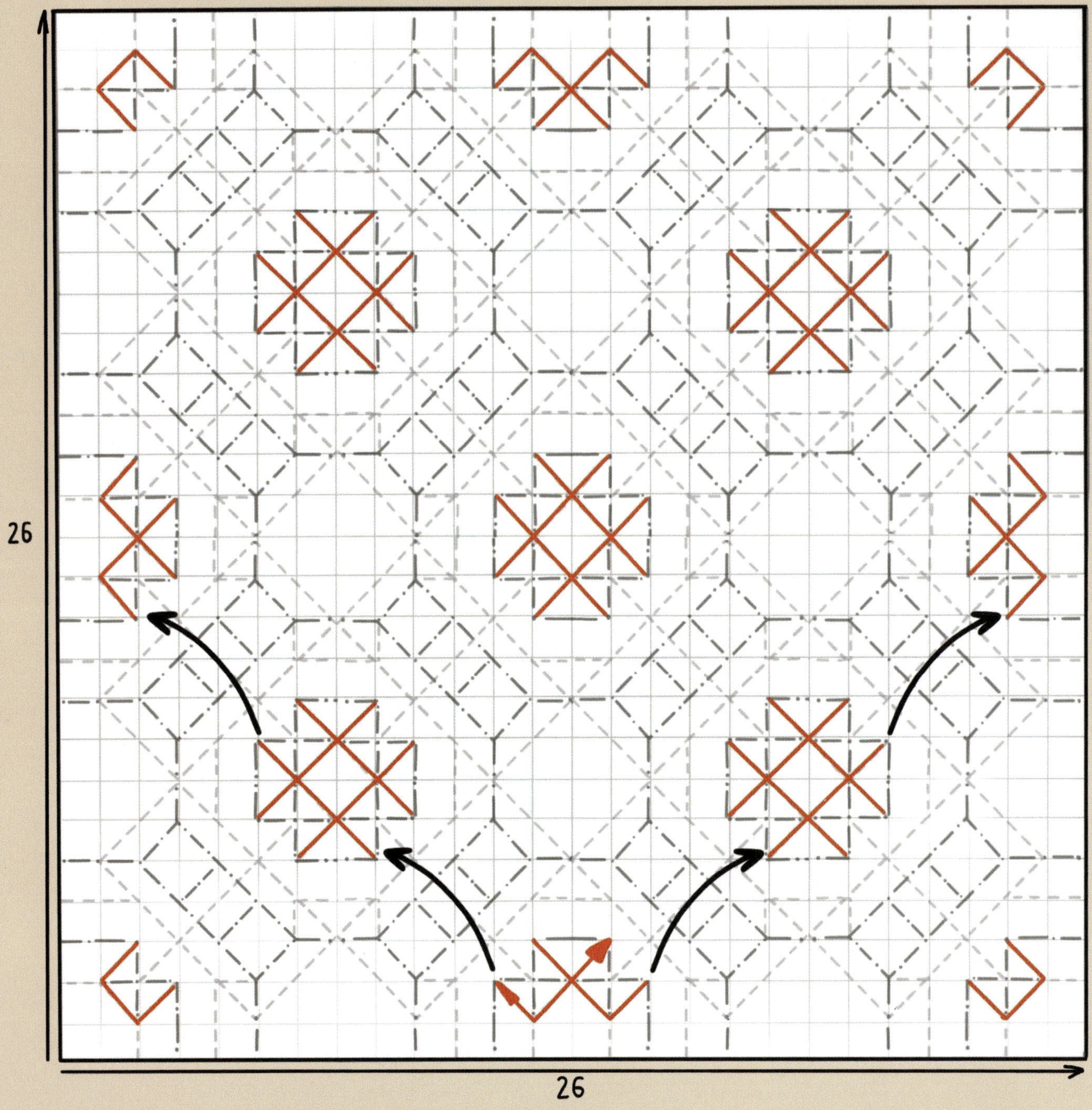

Continue precreasing—add the tic-tac-toe pattern as valleys. It has a shortcut as well!

Starting from the edges, fold one (following the short orange arrow pointing left) or two (following the arrow pointing to the right), skip three, fold three, skip three, and so on until you reach the other edge, where you once again fold only one (or two, if you started with two).

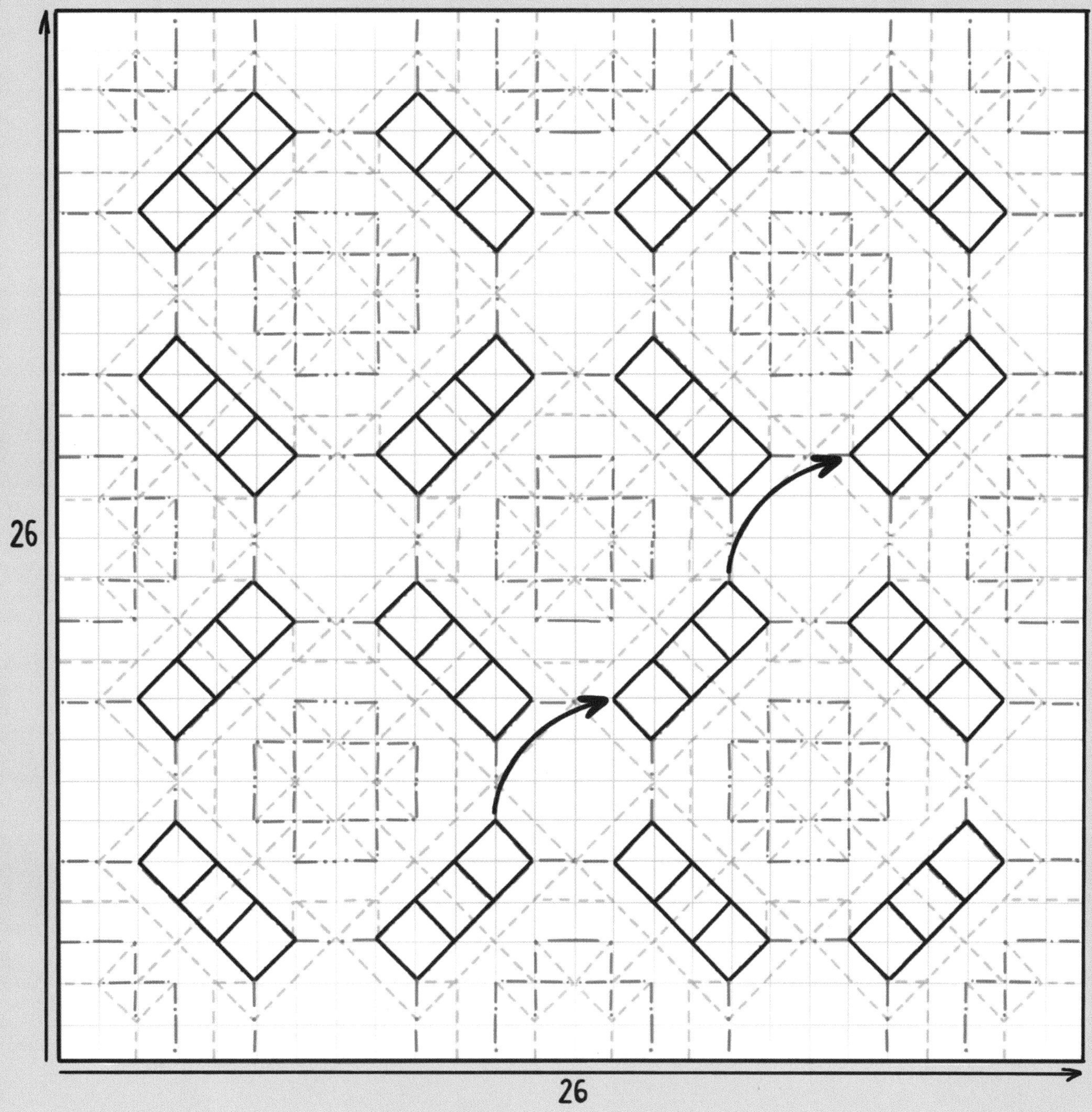

Finish the precreases. Add all the mountains folds (shown in bold black lines). Fold three, skip three is the shortcut here.

Now we are ready to collapse! This is one of the hardest projects to collapse. The inner molecules give very little free paper to hold, and are highly challenging.

Collapse all the molecules, row by row, to the first stage. Only then continue to the second stage. Unlike most other square based tessellations, it may be better to collapse all the outer molecules before approaching the inner ones.

Check the edges of the paper to make sure the pleats overlap properly, as with the single molecule. And don't forget to inside-reverse all the flaps when you finish the collapse!

Above and Beyond—A 10 by 10 Project

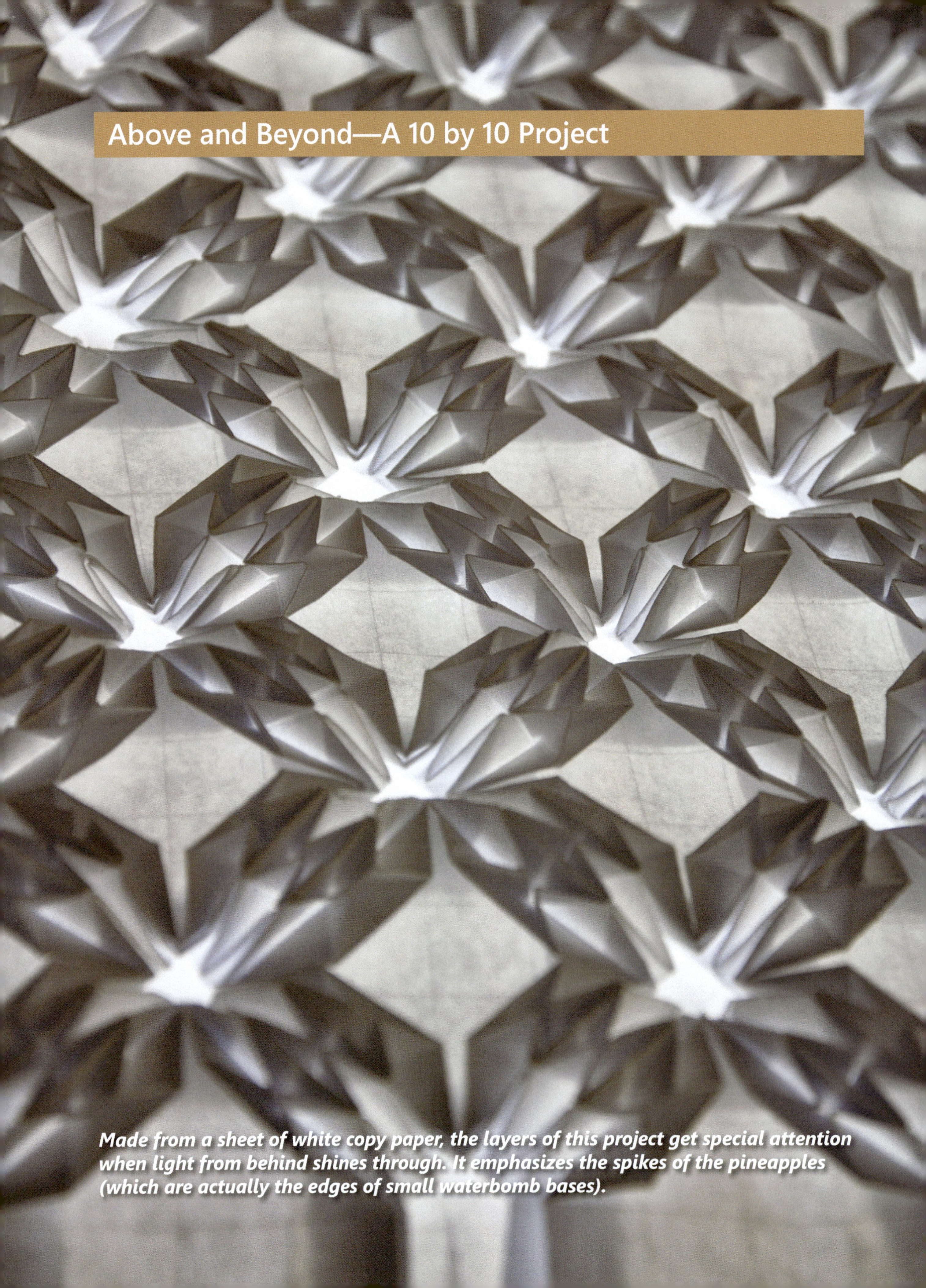

Made from a sheet of white copy paper, the layers of this project get special attention when light from behind shines through. It emphasizes the spikes of the pineapples (which are actually the edges of small waterbomb bases).

7 3 Pineapple Bowl

The Pineapple Bowl uses four molecules with some spacing in between to create the inner space and the legs.

Make sure to practice folding the single molecule (page 153), then complete the 2 by 2 project before you start on this one.

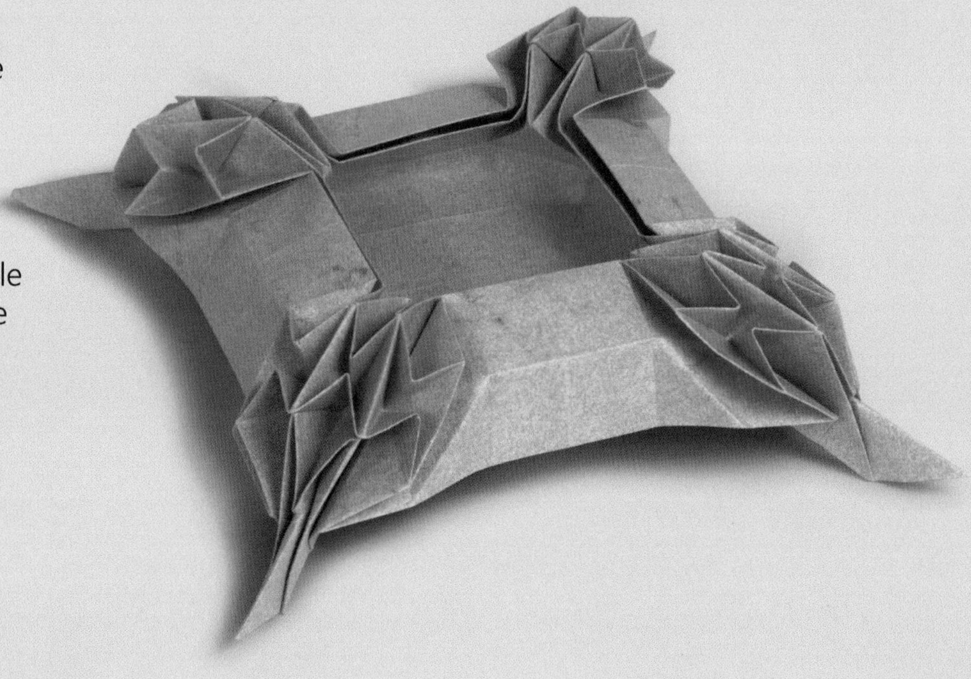

The four molecules form a big X.

Two rows and columns in between create the extra area needed for the bowl's interior.

Collapse the four molecules in two stages.

Some lines are not shown in the CP for easier reading.

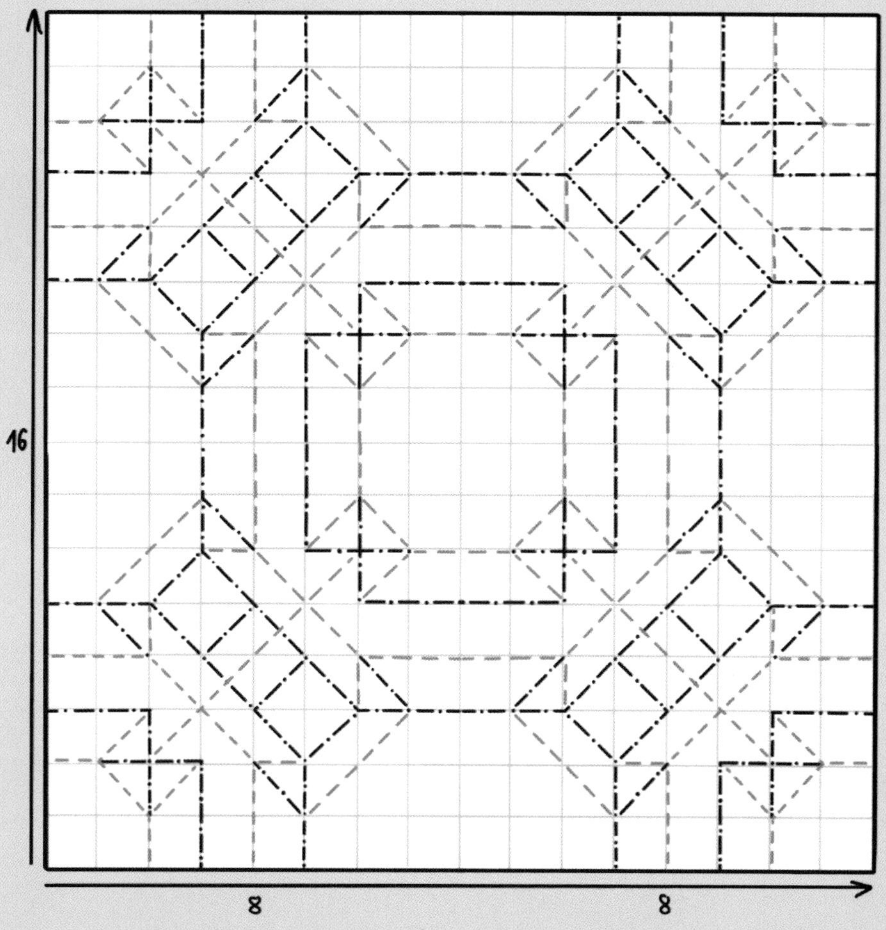

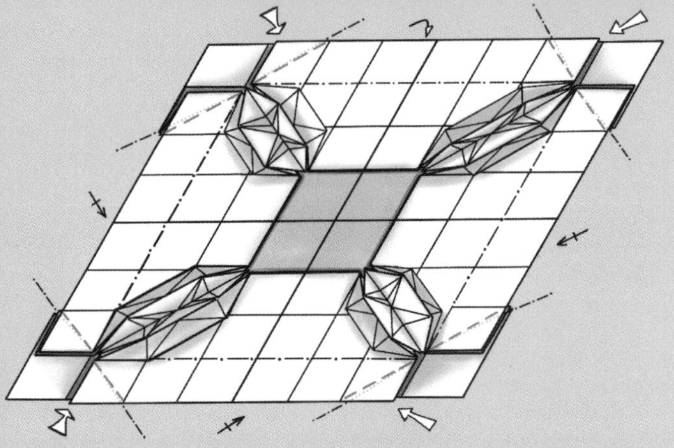

Mountain fold the outer rows and columns while pushing in the corners marked with white arrows. Fold the upper layer only!

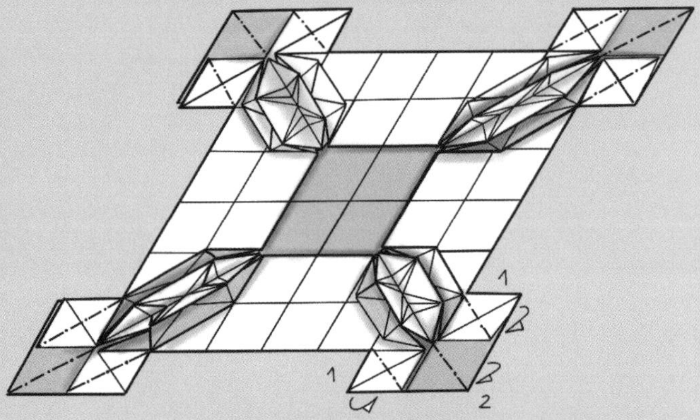

Narrow down the legs. Fold the opposing corners under (1), then fold in half as shown (2).

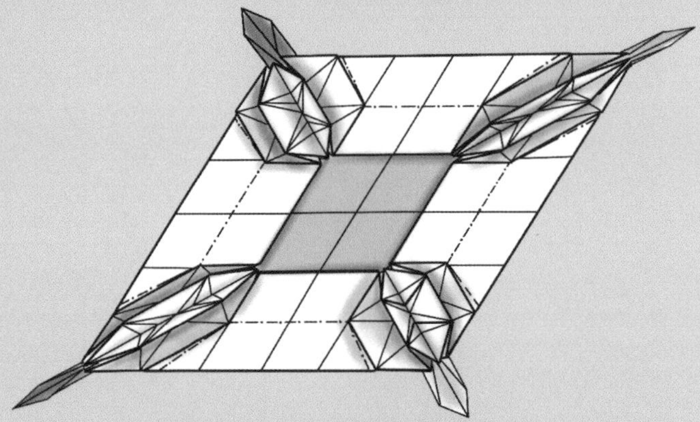

Give the bowl dimension: add the mountain folds all around, then push the center down to form the side walls.

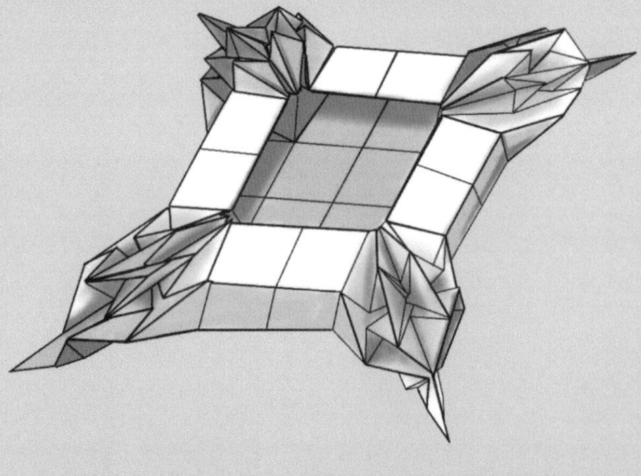

The finished model.

7 4 Extreme Pineapple

The Single Molecule

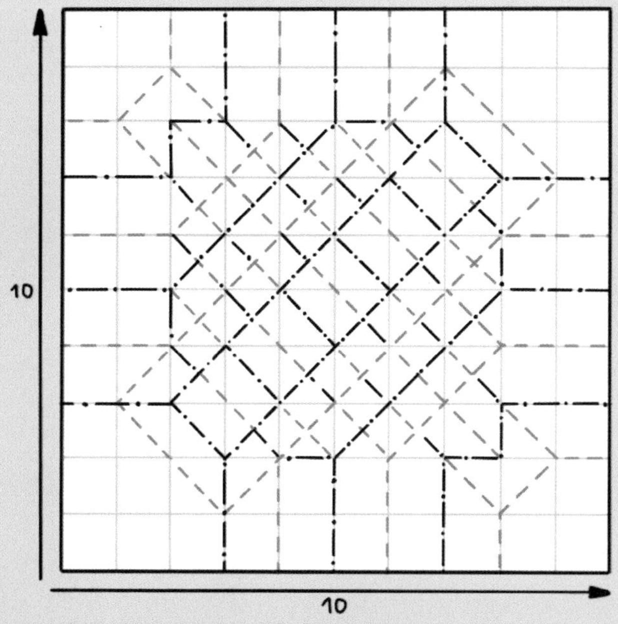

I call this one Extreme Pineapple because of all the layers. The molecule size is 8 by 8, so start with a grid of 10 by 10.

The number of layers is determined by the length of the inner rectangle. On the original molecule it is stretched over three square diagonals, creating four flaps. Here it is stretched over five diagonals so the molecule has six flaps. The collapse is done in three stages; two flaps are joined together at every stage.

The shrinkage ratio is 4:1.

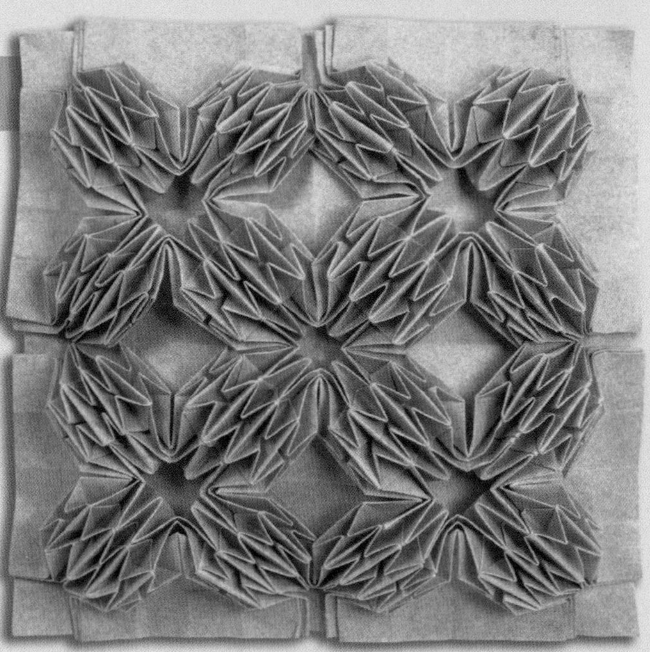

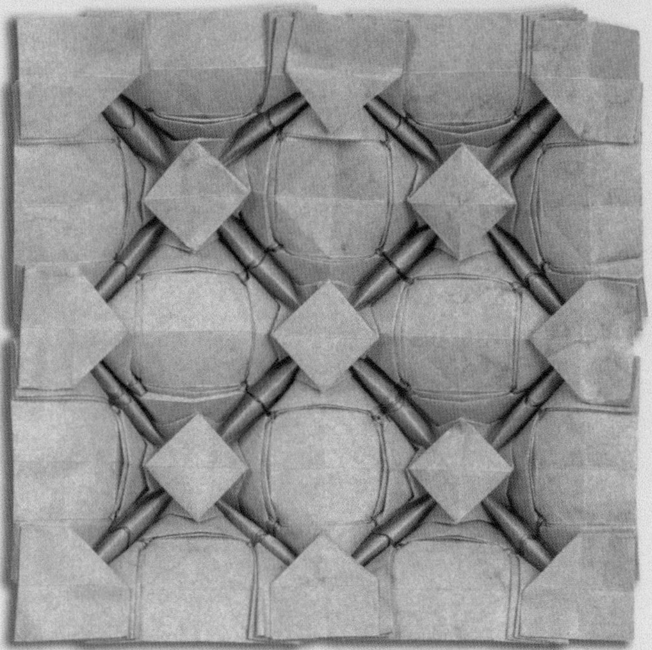

Top: recto view of a 4 by 4–molecule Extreme Pineapple tessellation.

Verso view is shown at bottom.

2 by 2 Molecules

Start by collapsing the longest inner rectangle (1) on the top left molecule.

Repeat that with the other three molecules.

Next, collapse all the second rectangles (2), which are actually squares.

Finally, collapse the U-shaped corners (3) as you did with the basic molecule on page 154.

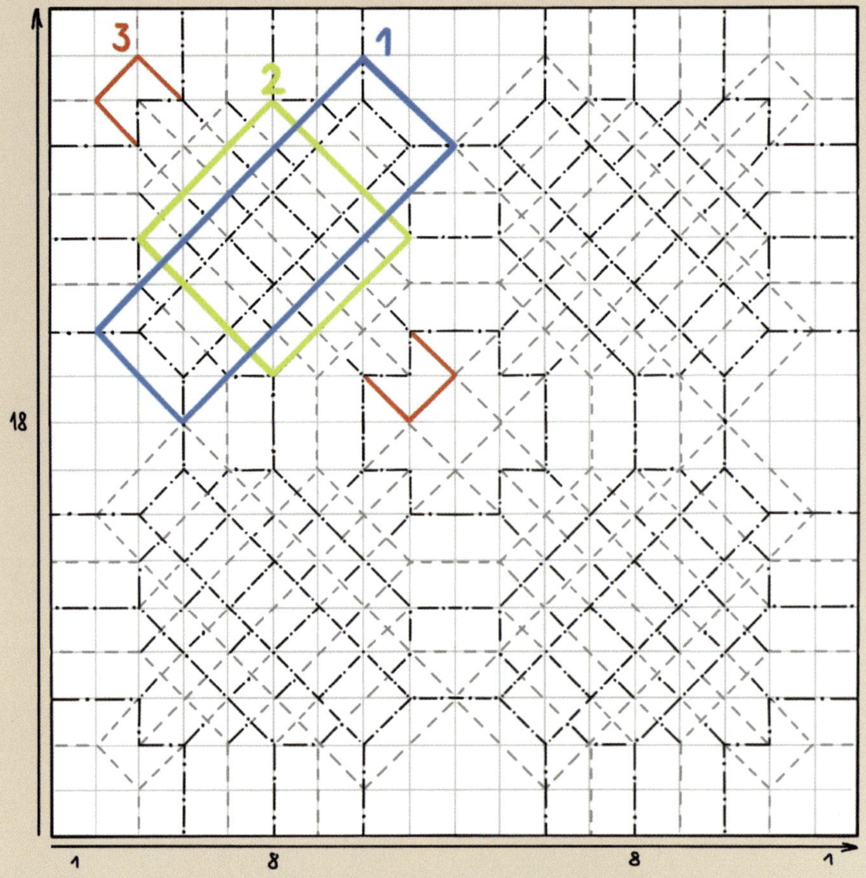

Above and Beyond

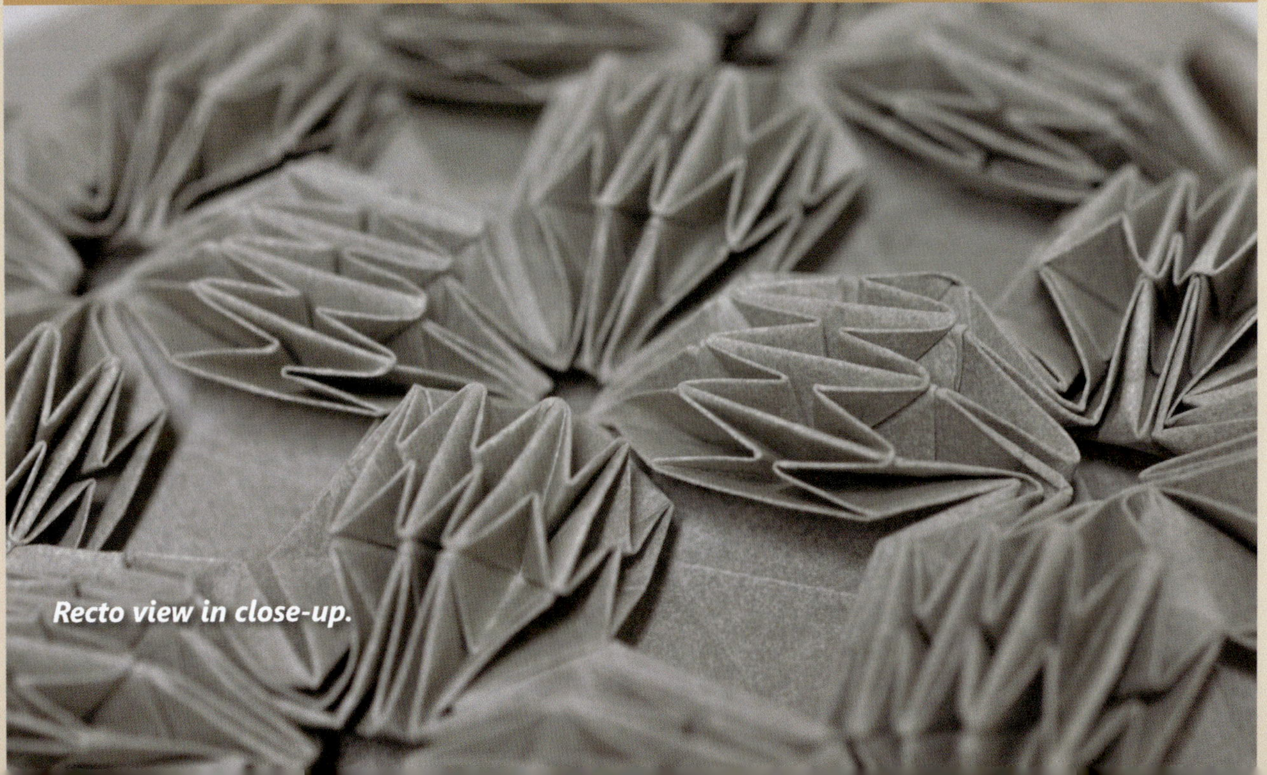

Recto view in close-up.

4 by 4 Molecules

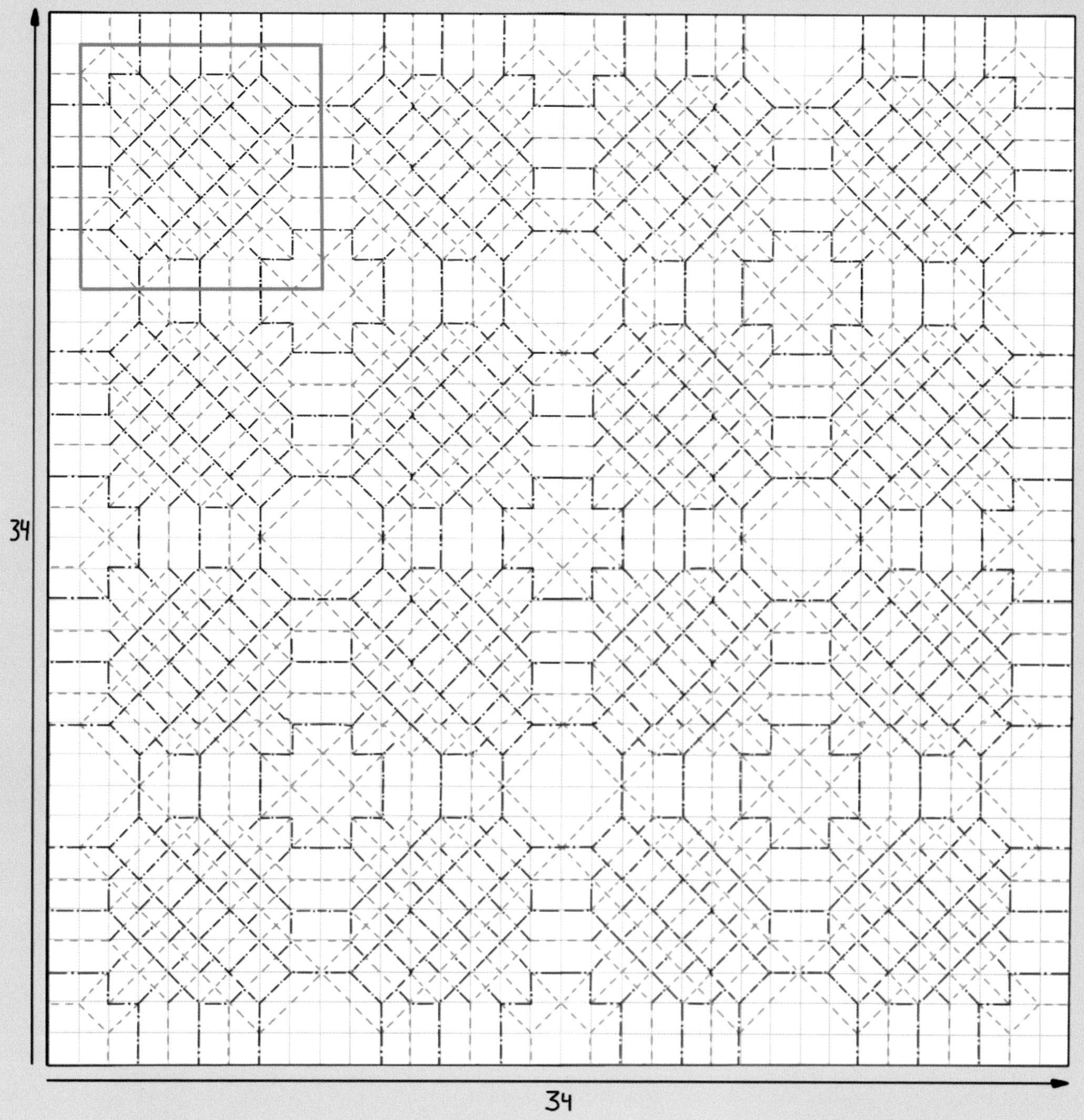

For a 4 by 4-molecule project, start with a 34 by 34 grid: 1 + 4 x 8 + 1 = 34.

The final result will be 10 squares wide.

This is not a project for the faint of heart! There are many precreases, and the collapse is tedious. Still, the result is extremely satisfying.

Remind yourself of the collapse process outlined in the 2 by 2 project on page 155, from the innermost rectangle to the outside one.

Don't forget that there should be a zigzag pattern (pleats) at the edge of each molecule.

7 5 Extreme Double Pineapple

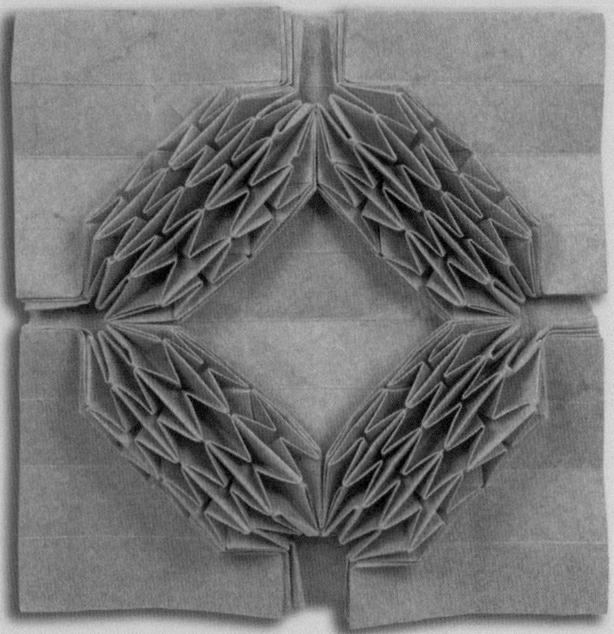

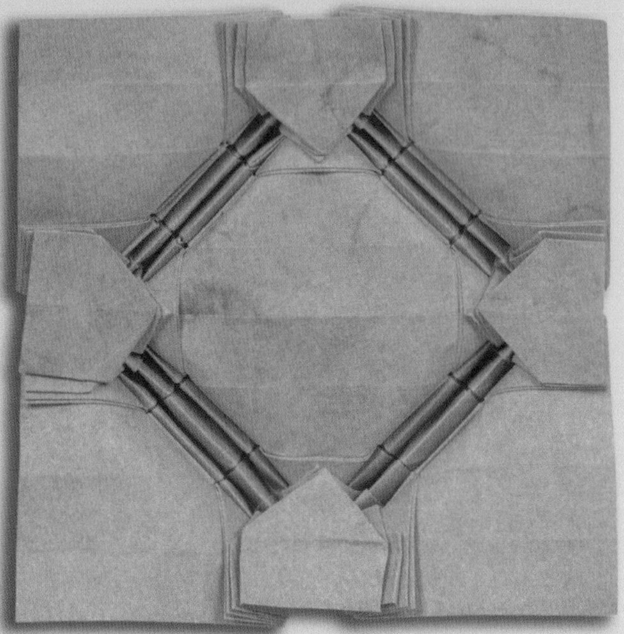

Above: recto view of a 2 by 2-molecule Extreme Pineapple tessellation.

Verso view is to the right.

The Single Molecule

This extreme version was designed by Michał Kosmulski. It is by far the most difficult and time-consuming molecule in this book.

The molecule size is 11 by 11, so start with a grid of 13 by 13.

By increasing the grid size and duplicating the inner rectangle, we double the number of spikes rows. It is done by creating two inner rectangles and hiding the extra paper that is formed between them.

The shrinkage ratio is 11:3.

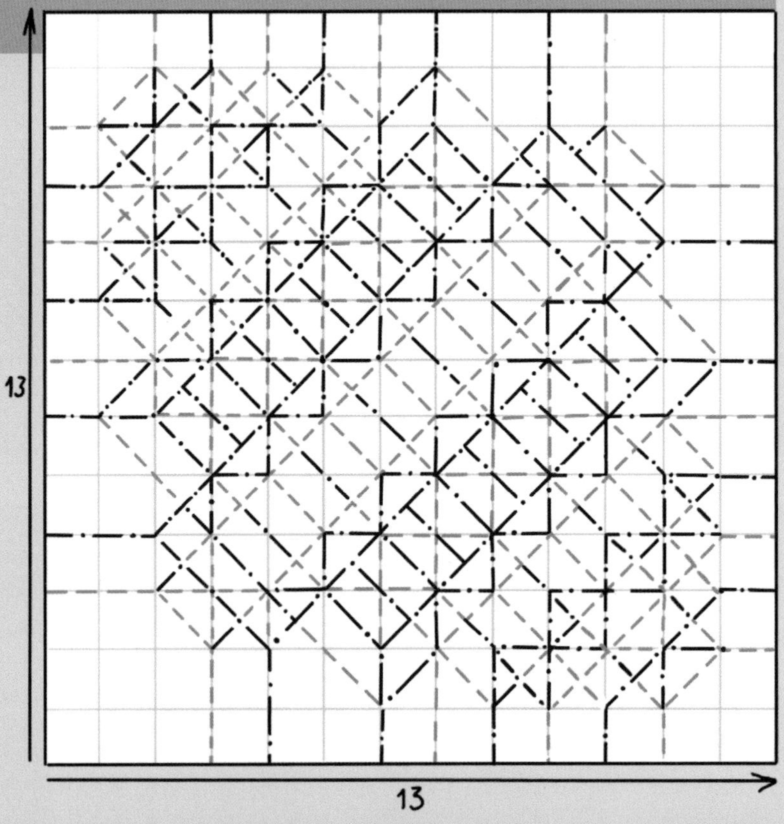

Start with the inner rectangles. Follow the CP carefully.

Collapse the two black rectangles, so they are positioned side by side. Use only the valleys marked in orange.

Now continue to form the rows of spikes, as it is done with the basic molecule (see page 154). Form the pleats on the edges as a guiding line.

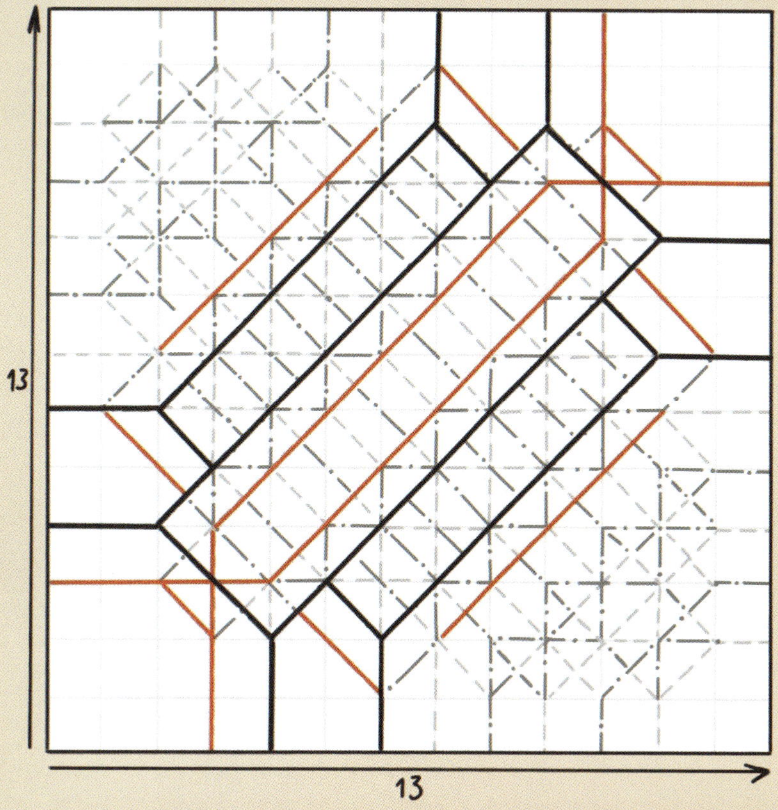

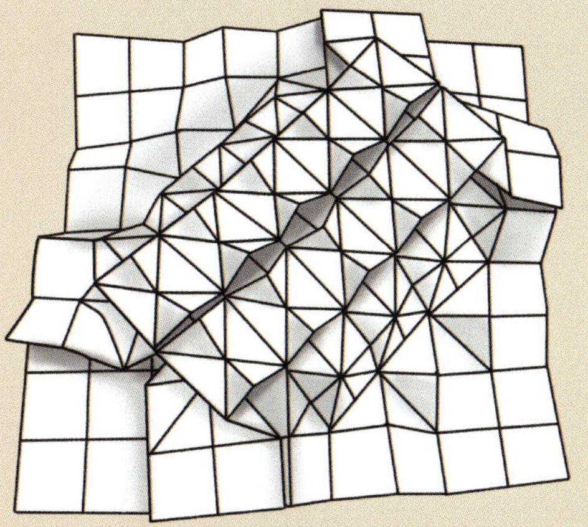

Above and Beyond

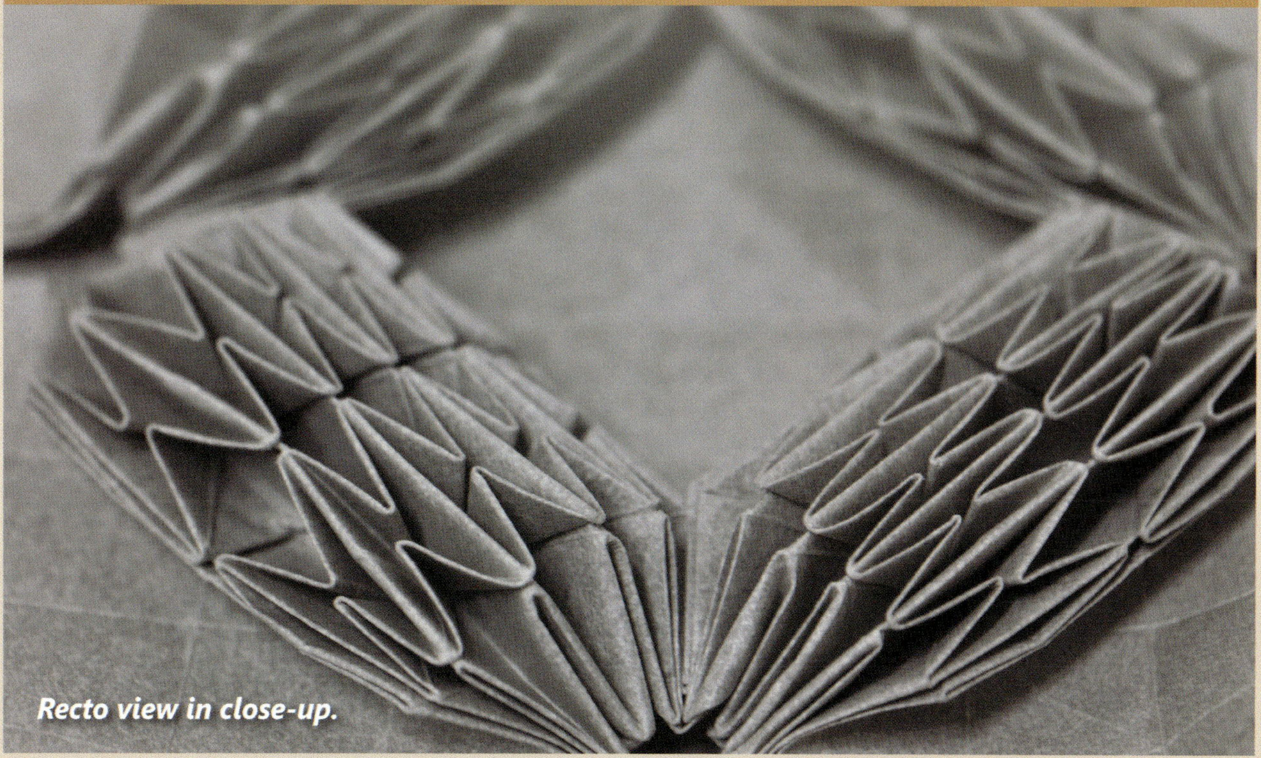

Recto view in close-up.

2 by 2 Molecules

X-Shaped

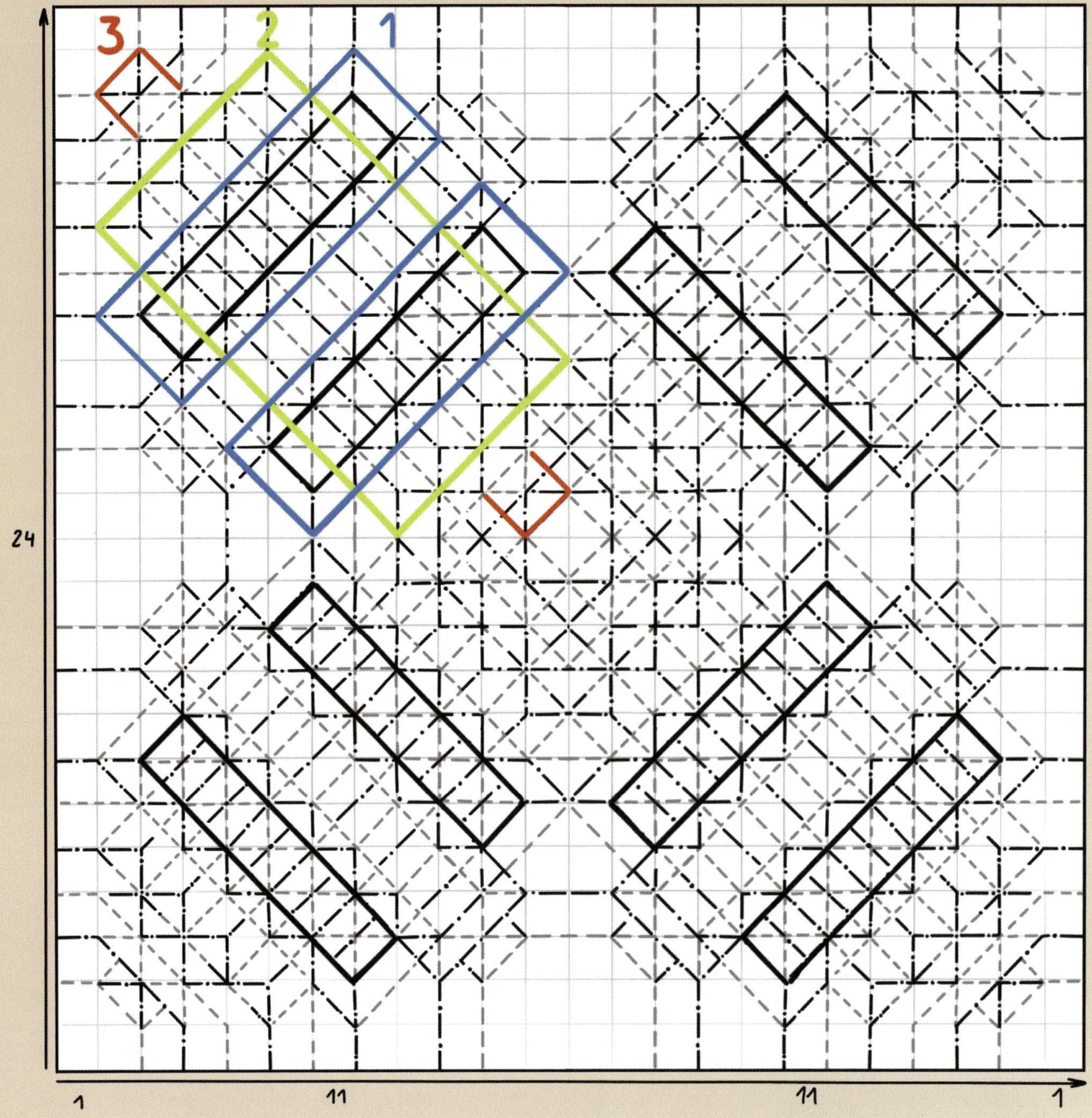

For a 2 by 2-molecule project, start with a 24 by 24 grid: 1 + 2 x 11 + 1 = 24.

The final result will be 8 squares wide.

Take it slow and follow the CP closely, collapsing in three stages as indicated before.

Start with the inner rectangles all around (1), and when finished, move to the next, outer rectangles (2). Finish with the U-shaped folds (3).

2 by 2 Molecules

O-Shaped

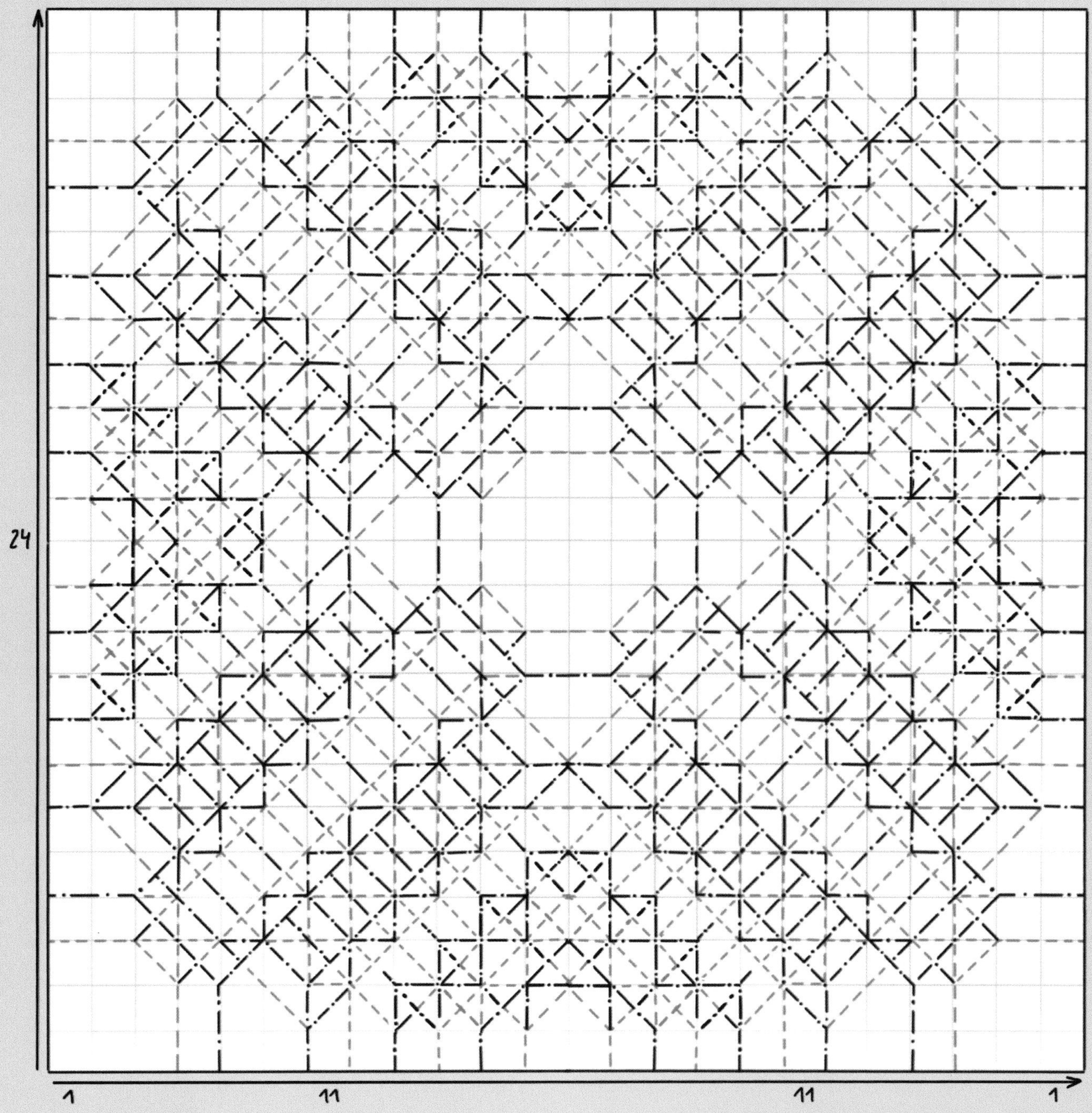

Follow the same process as with the X-shaped project: fold the long rectangles first, then the shorter ones, and then the U-shaped folds.

Printed in Great Britain
by Amazon

46781386R00093